Thomas Muir: 'Lad o' Pairts'

Fig 1 Frontispiece: Sir Thomas Muir Kt., C.M.G., LL.D., F.R.S.. Collection of Peter Elliott.

Cover: Dr. T. Muir, Boonzaier 1901 p. 28. Collection of Peter Elliott

ALSO BY PETER ELLIOTT

Eight Months in the Veneto. A story of the endurance and courage of British Liaison Officers with the partisans in the mountains of the Veneto, Italy. 1944–1945

'*The author's researches in this little history are astonishing. He has told the story with warmth, but also with accuracy and the result is a wonderful read*': SK, reviewer on Amazon, February 2015

First published in 2015. Second edition on Amazon in 2018; ISBN 9781723903069

The Spilhaus Family. Five hundred years of history (1450–1950)

'*A hugely interesting account of how a German family settled and prospered in South Africa's Cape*': Suko, reviewer on Amazon, October 2020

First published in 2015. Second edition on Amazon in 2019; ISBN 978-1-710873-48-1

Nita Spilhaus (1878–1967) and her artist friends in the Cape during the early twentieth century

'*The book is the first major study of the life and work of Nita Spilhaus. It is an accomplished and meticulous study of Nita's life, artist friends at the Cape and her work. The book is superbly illustrated with colour plates showing Nita's broad range of works...The study has the great advantage of placing Spilhaus in the context of her era and relates her work to that of her contemporaries*': SA Art Times, October 2015

First published in 2015. Second edition on Amazon in 2020; ISBN 978-1-658983-27-3

Constance: One Road to Take. The Life and Photography of Constance Stuart Larrabee (1914–2000)

'Constance: One Road to Take *excels in two important areas. First, the book provides a visually stunning overview of her tribal photos ... Second, the volume is especially good in tracing the emergence of urban black life as an important subject for Larrabee in the 1940s*' ...'Constance: One Road to Take *is the only full-length treatment of Larrabee's life and art, and this alone marks Elliott's achievement as an important one*': African Studies Review, June 2020

Published in 2018 ISBN 978-1-720258-06-3

Each book is available on Amazon as a paperback and ebook

Thomas Muir: 'Lad o' Pairts'
The Life and Work of Sir Thomas Muir (1844–1934)
Mathematician and Cape Colonial Educationist

Peter Elliott

Thomas Muir: 'Lad O' Pairts'
The Life and Work of Sir Thomas Muir (1844–1934),
Mathematician and Cape Colonial Educationist

First published in 2021 by Cantaloup Press,
7 Cantaloup, 11290 Alairac, France

Dépôt légal en France: janvier 2021

The following people worked on the book:

Design, layout and typesetting: David Siddall Multimedia

Copy editor: Glenda Younge

Proofreader: Sandy Shepherd

Cantaloup Press

CONTENTS

FOREWORD

Our family held my maternal great-grandfather, Sir Thomas Muir, in awe. However, for most of my life I had known next to nothing about him. He has been a ghostly presence in and around my desk, a contemplative visage captured in an official photograph, gazing out of a gilt frame. His *magnum opus* on mathematics has occupied some 12 cm of horizontal bookshelf space in my study, unopened until quite recently. What was the significance of this doorstop of a book? What was the nature of the man and what did he accomplish in the Cape? My interest in researching his life was further stimulated by a chance visit to the C.P. Nel Museum in Oudtshoorn in 2018. The building is the former Boys' High School and the foundation stone commemorates Muir's opening of the newly constructed building in 1907.[1] It was time to research and write his story.

Who could imagine that the life of a mathematician turned educationist could be controversial? If Thomas Muir had contented himself to remain with his family in Glasgow, this story would have been easier to write, but duller to read. Instead he uprooted the family, including his daughter Nellie my grandmother, and set out for the Cape Colony in 1892. Since his mandate was to implement the policies of Cecil Rhodes, I have had to

Fig. 2: The 1907 school building of Oudtshoorn Boys' High School (pictured in early 2018), now a museum. Photograph: Peter Elliott.

confront the complicated politics, and race bias, of the Cape Colony in those distant times. Anyone who is aware of the polemic stirred by a 2017 article written by Nigel Biggar, a Theology Professor at Oxford, will know how delicately an author needs to tread in any reassessment of an aspect of colonial history. Biggar questioned whether we should feel guilty about our colonial history, and this provoked an Open Reply signed by just under 60 historians. The historians welcomed open engagement in an ongoing reassessment of the histories of the British Empire and their legacies. While they had never believed it was sufficient to dismiss imperialism as simply 'wicked', it could not and should not be rehabilitated because some of it was 'good'.[2]

I have taken the middle ground in this debate: it matters not what I feel about Muir, his attitudes and his policies. I am neither celebrating what was good, or feeling guilty about what was bad, about the man or his times. I have simply attempted to bring together the facts about his educational system in the Cape, and to recapture the sense of things done by, and to, people in those times.[3] Like most of us, Muir was a moral mixture of good and bad, and I have tried to present him unvarnished. Muir was subject to the malefactions and misconceptions of his time, when the Empire was at its zenith and white supremacy was a core belief. I tell of his strengths and abilities, but also of his flaws, his preconceptions, and the difficult area of his relationships with others. In this way we get closer to an understanding of this elusive man.

As I am not a mathematician, I have not sought to evaluate Muir's research and work in his specialist field myself, but merely present a reassessment of this, by bringing together systematically the commentaries of other mathematicians. It is for the experts to evaluate his contribution.

Muir came from a humble, rural Lanarkshire background. Early on at school, it was evident he was bright and knew how to work hard. He advanced fast and it became clear that this was no ordinary man. Yet during his lifetime, Muir defended his privacy by not letting people in, and articles written about him repeated the same brief biography, representing him in the Victorian way he no doubt wished to be seen publicly: he was portrayed as the very role model of the dutiful public servant and academic.

Visually, I am only able to show the reader the series of half-profile, formal, photographs taken of Muir during his lifetime. Although he enjoyed making speeches (and was always most conscious of recording that they had been well-received), he professed to have disliked being photographed. This explains the dearth of informal family photographs. The half-profile formal portrait is a metaphor for the public representation of himself, which Muir nurtured. Overwhelmingly, those who sit for portraits show the left side of their face, which artists believe is more expressive, and Muir's portraits all follow this tradition. Perhaps we can treat this half-profile portrait as representative of the eulogistic commentaries written about him after his retirement and death. My aim is to show the complete profile of this brilliant but complex person, in many ways a typical colonial administrator, a captive of his times.

I have tried to break through Muir's protective shell, mainly through a forensic examination of his *Diaries*: these six journals covered his tours of duty into the interior of the Cape between 1909 and 1912. Unabbreviated, but edited, the *Diaries* form Part II of this book; in his life story (Part I) I frequently quote from the *Diaries* to build his character biography. My hope, however, is that the reader will reach for his original journals in Part II, rather than simply relying on my selective quotation. There is something particularly seductive about hearing first-hand a person's own reflections on the situations he encountered. His journals were not written for public consumption; he wrote with great frankness, humour and keen observation. He told of the people he met, and the places he visited; he revealed his attitudes, his intellectual interests, his capacity for friendship and enmity, his warmth towards those of whom he approved, and his froideur towards those of whom he did not. There is a warmth in Muir that emerges from the Diaries, which the reader will feel. These 120 frenetic days, which he chose to document meticulously, provide a lens through which we can view Muir and become closely acquainted with the man.

ACKNOWLEDGEMENTS

As always, this project has required the help of a range of people. Although the initial research, which launched the concept of the book, was carried out in Cape Town some years ago, most of the work has been carried out remotely; much of the final effort, and writing, has been done in pandemic times. With libraries, archives and museums closed for months I have had to rely on goodwill and co-operation from a range of persons, who have shown their interest in the project.

First, I want to thank my distant Muir cousin in Australia, Anne Andrews. She gave me the initial impetus to embark on this project in 2005, by sharing generously the benefit of her extensive work on the genealogy of the Muir family. More recently, as I got deeper into the background, Anne has always been able to respond with relevant information, which has helped me to complete the jigsaw.

Linda Howe-Ely helped me to access source materials in South Africa, just as she helped me with my research on my earlier book projects; this time round, faced with the COVID-19 restrictions, it has been particularly valuable to have had a supporter in Cape Town.

Special thanks are due to the National Library of South Africa, in Cape Town, who have curated the *Muir Manuscript Collection* and provided a home for the *Muir Mathematical Collection* of books and journals for over 85 years. Melanie Geustyn, Senior Librarian, Special Collections, has gone out of her way to assist me during these difficult times. Also, during lockdown, Najwa Hendrickse, Manager, Information Access Programme, took the trouble to confirm the Library's permission for me to publish the *Diaries* (the originals of which form part of their collection) as part of this book.

Otherwise I wish to single out those who have provided vital help and advice. There were two essential strands to my research for the book: education in the Cape and mathematics, and I was an expert in neither, although I was marginally more comfortable researching the history of education than mathematics (being a Humanities man). I found help and encouragement in both these areas. Peter Kallaway, Emeritus Professor, University of the Western Cape, and Research Associate, School of Education, University of Cape Town, provided insight and thoughtful comment. Tony Crilly is an educator and writer, with a primary interest in the history of mathematics; he is also author of Muir's entry in the *Dictionary of National Biography*. He steered me through the confusing corridors of mathematics, and helped me to develop an approach to understand Muir's research work. Both read a late version of my manuscript and provided valuable feedback.

There developed two sub-sets of research into Cape education, areas into which I needed to delve: Muir's school building scheme, and his travels into the interior on the Cape railway network.

As regards 'Muir's Palaces', the legacy of school buildings created under the scheme he operated, I found vital assistance at the Centre for Conservation Education and Education Museum in Wynberg, where Linda Howe-Ely was able to carry out some initial research for me. The Principal, Sigi Howes, separated from her museum during lockdown, then went out of her way to provide me with images of relevant school buildings and background information on them. These provide a rich record of the building scheme and illustrate both the *Diaries* and the relevant sections of the book. Similarly, to restore to life the places in the interior of the Cape that Muir visited, along the railway, Yolanda Meyer provided me with images from the *Transnet Heritage Library photo collection*, and Johannes Haarhoff provided help and encouragement.

There are, however, a myriad of additional people who have taken time to provide information on, or fill gaps in, my understanding of aspects of the lives of Muir, his family and coterie. I acknowledge the help of such persons by way of a citation in relation to relevant information in the book.

Finally, as always with my book projects, I thank my wife Maddy for her continuing patience and support. It is always a relief to finish a project so that I can, for a time, turn my back on the guilt of toiling in my study, and resume full enjoyment, with her, of the outdoors and the pleasures of the Languedoc.

A NOTE ON TERMINOLOGY

Terminology is a minefield in South Africa. I have followed the approach offered by historian Professor Vivian Bickford-Smith.[4]

I have used terms such as black, white and coloured merely as racialised categories. Where terms are used that are now offensive to South Africans today, such as 'kafir' or 'native', these are only employed because the original referenced texts used the terms. Otherwise I have sought to use the synonym 'African'. I have used 'black' as a synonym for people described by whites as 'other than white' in contemporary censuses. Black is a 'collective noun for the range of people who thought of themselves, for instance and at times, as coloured, African, Malay or Indian'.

Peter Elliott
Carcassonne, October 2020

LIST OF ILLUSTRATIONS

Part I: Thomas Muir: Lad o'Pairts

Part II: The S.G.E.'s Diaries of his Tours (1909–1912)

Part I: Biography

lad o' pairts (pronounced *lad–a–**payrts***):

A **lad o' pairts** is a youth, particularly one from a humble background, who is considered talented or promising.

This country prides itself on giving the lad o' pairts opportunities for advancement.

Britannia Scots Dictionary

THE MUIR FAMILY: SCOTLAND AND THENCE TO THE CAPE

Thomas Muir (1844–1934) grew up in straitened circumstances in Lanarkshire, Scotland, but pulled himself up by his bootstraps to become a renowned mathematician and colonial educationist. He was truly a Scottish 'lad o' pairts'.[5]

The early story of the Muirs of Annieston and Biggar and the birthplace of Thomas Muir (1844)

Thomas Muir was born on 25 August 1844, near the village of Nemphlar.[6] His father George's house, known as Linnhead, was on an 80-acre farm called Midtown, bounded on the south by the River Clyde. The family's farm dwelling was just above the Stonebyres Falls, near Lanark. The Scottish word 'linn' denotes a waterfall, and this is one of the three Falls of Clyde, and the lowest of them. Thomas Croal, writing about Scottish loch scenery, said of the Falls: 'Earth hath not anything to show more fair.' The 90-foot descent to the Falls was a journey made in several distinct leaps:

'It is difficult of access, for the visitor must either content himself with a distant view, or take his heart in his hand and descend a precipitous and dangerous path, where at times to hang on by the eyelids may seem the only resource.'[7]

Muir's father George had moved to Nemphlar from the not far distant town of Biggar. Muir seems to have retained a romantic attachment to the Falls, with which his life was only fleetingly connected: although he dutifully entered his birthplace as 'Nemphlar' on official forms, later he encouraged the romantic idea that he was born at 'Stonebyres'.[8] Perhaps this piece of romance served to distance him from his humble upbringing in his later upwardly mobile life.

George was an agricultural labourer on the farm, and the house was provided to him as a labourer's cottage during the 1830s and early 1840s. Thomas's half-brother, George (of his father's first marriage), had also been born at Linnhead a few years earlier. When George married his second wife, Mary Brown, in 1843, the family continued to dwell there for a brief period. The site of the house is still easy to locate on old maps, but the building no longer exists, and the site is now simply a farm field. One can readily see where the track might have led into the village and beyond.

Fig. 3: Falls of Clyde, Stonebyres, c. 1860. Photographer: George Washington Wilson 1823–93; RCIN 2320179 Royal Collection Trust.

Fig. 4: Linnhead, Nemphlar, the house in which Muir was born. The original photograph bears the inscription: 'this is the house where I was born, George J. Muir', inscribed by Muir's elder half-brother. Collection: Anne Andrews.

Muir conjured up a rather romantic history of his antecedents: perhaps this was a conscious effort to redress his humble origins, or simply represented nostalgia for an idealised homeland. He was clearly the source of an elaborate tale relating to the Muir family dating back to the Jacobite rising of 1745, published in *Musical Times 1906*. In a public lecture in 1945, Alexander Aitken, a friend of Muir and an eminent mathematician who became Professor of Mathematics at the University of Edinburgh, declared the legend Muir had promoted earlier to be historical fact:

> The family originally came from Biggar, and the family name, the Muirs of Anneston, is found in old records going back to 1493. But it seems that in 1745, that critical year of two centuries ago, the last Muir of Anneston left his lands and settled quietly in the adjoining town of Biggar. It is interesting to note that the ancestors of the great Prime Minister, William Ewart Gladstone, were also from Biggar; and that William Muir, the son of the last laird of Anneston and grandfather of Thomas Muir, was associated with the uncle of Gladstone in promoting a secession from the Parish Kirk of Biggar and in founding a Secession Kirk in the town.[9]

The story centres on the ancient town of Biggar, between the Clyde and Tweed rivers, the High Street of which still follows the line of the ancient Roman road. In the town there remains an ancient motte, part of a castle created by the Fleming family in the 12th century. The town has retained its medieval layout of a wide road running through the centre to allow markets and fairs to be held, with closes running to parallel back streets and buildings with long gardens. It is a worthy location for a family legend.

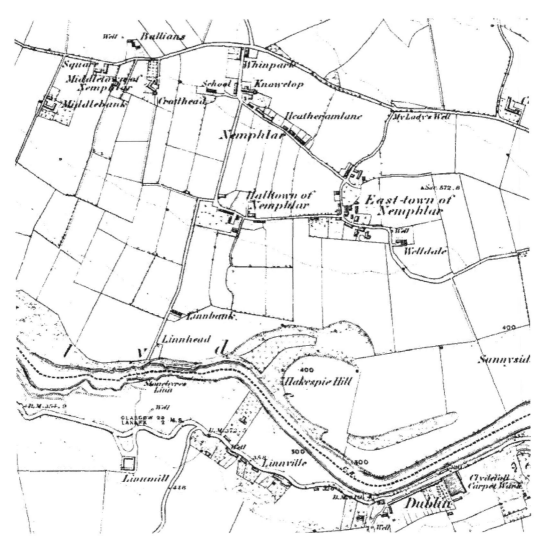

*Fig. 5: Location of Linnhead, in relation to Nemphlar and Stonebyres Linn (or Falls).
Ordnance Survey Lanarkshire, Sheet XXV 1864, National Library of Scotland.*

Muir himself made notes about the story of William Muir and recorded that his grandfather's gravestone was a small square stone in Biggar churchyard, inscribed 'Wm Muir 1829'. This memorial and a Gladstone gravestone are both still to be found there.[10] The two men could conceivably have been late 18th-century contemporaries and have been involved in internal strife within the Biggar Kirk. William Gladstone's is an impressive upright headstone, with a crafted curved-rimmed head, befitting the importance of his family, who were certainly descended from a laird. In contrast, Muir's is a scruffy 'thruch-stane' about the length and breadth of a human boot, lying horizontal and surrounded by lawn. A passer-by might stumble momentarily over William Muir's stone, but his passage would be arrested by the more impressive memorial to William Gladstone. The ironic punch line of the 1906 story is quite appealing: the idea that the co-secessionists, Gladstone and Muir, 'sleep in the churchyard close to the church which in life they deserted'.[11]

Fig. 6: Inscription on gravestone in Biggar churchyard: 'Wm Muir 1829', the church secessionist in Muir's legend. Photograph: Helen Barrington.

Sadly, research reveals that there is no historical evidence to support Muir's romantic story. The Gladstone buried in the Biggar churchyard was a peaceful excise officer, who led a life devoted to the collection of taxes rather than religious upheaval, and there is no record of a Muir involved in church secession at all.[12] The punch line of Muir's original story, therefore, is entirely lost. Moreover, John Gladstone, the secessionist, was a great-uncle of the Prime Minister, and not an uncle. Perhaps the difference in the characters' life dates might have suggested to two mathematicians that they had skipped a generation and were presenting a flawed history.[13]

As regards the more ancient history of the Muir (or 'Mure') family, again the starting point for this is Muir's original story in the *Musical Times 1906*. There were, indeed, Muirs who were lairds of 'Annieston' in the first half of the 17th century.[14] However, the last laird of Annieston, who was a Muir, ceased to be owner of the lands there by the close of that same century, at least two generations before the time of Muir's grandfather, William.[15] The *Musical Times 1906* story, that the Muirs lost their estate as a result of the 'evil times' that came with the 1745 Jacobite Rising, is therefore a fanciful legend, as most of this land was transferred fully half a century earlier.

Until recent times the ruins of the ancient tower of Annieston Castle used to lie not far from the village of Symington, but no vestige of it now remains.[16] As far back as the deeds can be traced (to 1776), there is no evidence whatsoever of Muir family ownership of any part of this estate in the time of William Muir's father, i.e. the mid-18th century.[17] The search for respectable Muir family lineage is at an end!

School and university years in Scotland (1850–1867)

In 1846, to enable the children to receive a better education, the Muir family moved eight miles down the Clyde to the village of Overtown, 1.5 miles south-east of Wishaw.[18] There was an abundance of coal in the parish of Cambusnethan, and the opening of the railway in the 1840s had allowed the expansion of mining in the area. By 1861 the new settlement of Overtown had grown to have a population of just over 300 people; in contrast, the neighbouring police burgh of Wishaw had a population of over 3,000, and enjoyed all the facilities of a larger town, including the school and a public library. Muir's younger brother, Andrew, was born in Overtown in 1846, and his sister, Margaret, some years later.

Muir's father first tried his hand at a modest agricultural enterprise, but this was not a success; so he took a job on the Caledonian Railways. He always struggled to earn enough to maintain the children in school and the youngsters were required to help out at home by working in the garden: since Muir had to walk to school and back, he had precious little time for games or other outdoor pursuits. Although the family was poor, there was always food on the table, and there were books at home: his father was a literate man and enjoyed reading. Muir was particularly close to his mother, Mary, a strong and resourceful woman, and the three children grew up in a caring family home. Some additional responsibility must have fallen on Muir as the eldest of the three children.

Muir first attended the Primary School in Overtown, but then he went on to the Public School in Wishaw. The daily walk to this school from the family house in Overtown might have taken Muir half an hour had he not dilly-dallied. While he could have followed the principal roads into town, one can speculate that he might have chosen to dawdle along the cross-country paths. This would have enabled him to satisfy his enquiring mind, learning about the plants and insects encountered along the way. It is evident from his later *Diaries* that he had this curiosity and wonder, and he closely observed even the minutest detail of the natural world. Through working in the family garden, he also developed into a natural gardener, an activity he enjoyed throughout his life. Home and the school gave him access to books, and he became the omnivoracious reader we encounter later on in his life, quite happy to pick up and read any good book, whether prose or verse, and enjoy it for what it was worth. He must also have experienced a wealth of song and music, both at home and school; later in life it is evident that he boasted a fund of songs, particularly Scottish folk songs. His inquiring mind, and aptitudes, developed during his first 17 years in rural Wishaw within his close family circle.

The Public School of Wishaw was a large school, expressly built for the populous mining district and serving mainly the children of the local mine-workers. Here the young boy soon came to the fore in all the core school subjects, excelling in English, Latin, Greek and mathematics, with the result that he attracted the attention of Lady Belhaven, the wife of Lord Belhaven of Wishaw House. At the age of 14, he was sufficiently promising to become a 'pupil teacher' at the school.[19] With the help of his patron, he was urged to pursue his studies at Glasgow University in 1863. His teachers at the university included William Thomson (later Lord Kelvin), who taught him physics, and Hugh Blackburn, Professor of Mathematics. His ability was recognised, and he headed the class in both Greek and mathematics, but it was Kelvin who persuaded him to pursue mathematics rather than his favourite subject, Greek. Early on, too, he demonstrated a natural ability as an educator, and he spent his summer vacations teaching. Also, to earn money, he broke his studies for 18 months to teach at the Hamilton Academy.

Fig. 7: James Muir, b. 1835 (Muir's half-brother), with Muir's father, George Muir, c. 1860.

At some point during the 1860s Muir demonstrated his flair for music, studying harmony and composition in the Andersonian University, Glasgow, under Professor Kalley Miller, 'the brilliant senior wrangler of 1867'.[20] The long marriage of music and mathematics is reflected in the quotation attributed, probably apocryphally, to Pythagoras: 'There is geometry in the humming of the strings, there is music in the spacing of the spheres.' The notations of composers and the sounds made by musicians are connected to mathematics, and the relationship between the two lies in the 'counting, rhythm, scales, intervals, patterns, symbols, harmonies, time signatures, overtones, tone [and] pitch' in music.[21]

Whilst Muir was an undergraduate, disaster struck the family. His father, a wagon greaser on the railways, suffered a fatal accident in early August 1866: at the Pather sidings on the Caledonian Railway, Cambusnethan (not far from where the family lived), George Muir was killed instantly when caught between the buffers of two wagons of a mineral train. While Thomas and Andrew were well on their way towards earning a living, being 22 and 20 years old respectively, their sister was only 14 and Mary had lived at home as a housewife. The young Muir brothers took on the burden of supporting the family, and they managed to get through this stressful time. Muir again interrupted his studies but was able to resume at the end of the year, although the family must have had to scrimp and save until Muir's teaching earnings became regular.

In the last year of his university course, Muir temporarily occupied the vacant post of assistant professor of mathematics, and although lecturing students of about his own age, he was able to maintain order in the class and he showed a natural ability to impart knowledge. He obtained his M.A. degree at the university in 1868 – a long haul because of the breaks in his studies he was forced to take for financial and family reasons.

Teaching years in Scotland (1868–1892)

On leaving the university in 1868, he became a tutor of mathematics and sub-warden at St. Leonard's Hall, St. Andrews University until 1871; inevitably, there he learned to play golf (which remained his hobby when he later went out to the Cape). The College Hall, for the sons of gentlemen, had only been opened a few years earlier to restore the old college system, akin to that in place at Oxford and Cambridge, and to provide 'domestic comfort and superintendence with moral and religious training' for its elite young students, thereby preserving the 'habits of family life'.[22] It was a difficult environment for Muir as many of his upper-class charges (whose ages ranged between 16 and 19 years) were attending the university not so much because their future depended on it, but because it was a fashionable place to be. Two College Hall photographs show Thomas with these young students

W.H.COOK W.P.BRODIE A.F.MURRAY MR HASLAM MR MUIR A.R.GUERARD
J.S.OGILVIE
                                                                  C.ROCHEID
N.MACLEOD H.HILL C.W.BAXTER J.R.BROWN F.J.W.CRITCHLEY F.ANDERSON R.S.MONCRIEFF J.RAMSAY A.SCOTT
        G.SMITH   C.H.GOSSET   C.ANDERSON   J.M.GRANT   A.OGILVIE
1870–1871

Fig. 8: Residents of St. Leonard's Hall, 1870–1871. Photographer: Thomas Rodger. Thomas Muir, sub-warden of the Hall, pictured front row, second from right. Collection: University of St Andrews Library, image reference number ALB-59-10.

in his care. He is depicted in confident style, top hat in hand and staring challengingly at the camera, very much replicating the pose and fashion of the students of this expensive boarding establishment.[23] Who would have recognised the son of the railway worker from Overtown, who had walked to school in Wishaw only a decade earlier?

Despite the genteel surroundings of the university, and the lack of serious academic intent of his upper-class pupils, it was nevertheless a hard-working time for Muir: in parallel he was studying privately for his M.A. Honours in mathematics, and the pressure was so intense that his health suffered. During the long university vacation, he obtained the position of private tutor to the son of the Duke of Argyll, and as a result enjoyed a more restful time in a beautiful part of Scotland.[24] Restored to health, he sat his examinations in November 1870 and passed with first-class honours. Professor J.C. Shairp, the principal of his college at St. Andrews, said of Muir he had 'seldom met a young teacher who threw such energy into his work and who so communicated that energy to others'.[25]

Following his time at St. Andrews, he travelled in continental Europe, meeting many leading mathematicians. He was in Berlin when the German soldiers returned from the Franco-Prussian War, and later in 1882, he studied in Göttingen, a renowned centre of mathematics that housed many of the greatest experts of the time. Both experiences enabled him to gain a realisation that Continental mathematics had made striking advances, essentially unknown in his own country. He started collecting books and this became a passion. He also concentrated on learning modern languages, and in Germany developed a taste for chamber and orchestral music. He had a relentless determination to broaden both his academic and practical capabilities, and to master the languages he needed to understand arcane mathematical theory; even a non-mathematician, who pages through his later history of the *Theory of Determinants,* must be impressed by his ability to access works in German, French and Italian. At the end of 1871, he was appointed assistant to Professor Blackburn, the Professor of Mathematics in Glasgow, and remained there for three years, further establishing his reputation as a teacher of mathematics.

In 1874 he obtained the coveted post of mathematical and science master of the High School of Glasgow, the oldest school in Scotland, notable for having produced two British prime ministers, Sir Henry Campbell-Bannerman and Mr. Bonar Law. Early in his teaching career, he found the time both to publish a *Text-Book of Arithmetic*[26] for schools and to contribute to an edited update of a history of the High School. His *Sketch of the History* takes the story from 1825; it was shortly after this date that the school broadened beyond its strict grammar school origins of classics teaching, to become the Town School of 1877. By the end of the period covered by his *Sketch,* the curriculum encompassed French, German, mathematics, arithmetic, drawing, writing and natural science, as well as Classics. In his essay on the school, he does not disclose the brilliance that marked him out for a top colonial administrative office only 15 years later. Instead, this publication is a worthy, but parochial, account of a fine school. Muir ends with a flourish, defining the features of the school that he found pleasing to contemplate: its 'high standard of education';

Fig. 9: The High School of Glasgow building in Elmbank Street, sold by the Glasgow Academy Directors to the Town Council in 1878. Collection: The High School of Glasgow.

'being the City school, it was prevented from becoming the school of a particular social class'; and the 'pupil of talent' was always most welcome.[27]

For 18 years he devoted his 'vigour and ability ... to rearing young mathematicians and in developing the science side of the school'.[28] He had a real talent for teaching his subject, and his leadership of the mathematics department ensured that by the mid-1880s, the High School and Glasgow Academy 'stood alone' in the quality of their mathematical work in Scotland.[29] He kindled an intellectual interest in mathematics in his pupils; 'he encouraged individual initiative, not instructing a class until all the pupils had exhausted their own resources'.[30]

Professor John Mackenzie (1860–1935), the son of a Glasgow cloth-worker, attended the School between 1870 and 1876.[31] He was inspired by Muir and later said of him:

> I was undoubtedly more stimulated by the teaching of Dr. Thomas Muir than by that of anyone else. He was a born teacher, and it was a real inspiration to work under him. Just at first he struck one as rather too hard and cold. He had not much geniality of manner, and he did not bear fools gladly; but one soon got to know that he took a very deep interest in his pupils and that he thoroughly understood the art of teaching them.[32]

While Muir's central focus remained on the teaching of mathematics and science, during his time at the High School he became convinced of the importance of the teaching of vocal music in schools and of the place music deserved in the school curriculum.

The nature of a Scottish Burgh School may well explain how it was that this teaching post provided a platform for Muir's leap into high colonial office. To be the master of mathematics and science at this school during the period was not merely to be a school-master in a modern sense; he was instead the principal of a major teaching department and this was a relatively entrepreneurial role. Even though the post of Rector of the School was reinstated after it moved to new premises in Elmbank Street, the five autonomous teaching departments were allowed to continue without undue interference. Thus, Muir remained effectively in charge of his own subject school. In 1877 he failed to secure the professorship of mathematics at St. Andrews, but when the post became vacant again two years later, he decided not to apply for it because the salary offered had been reduced due to financial austerity at the university.[33] Thus, it seems he was being adequately rewarded for running the most successful department of the High School. It was an activity that gave him the autonomy he cherished and enabled him to continue his own mathematics research at a high level.

These were no ordinary times in Scottish education. The Argyll Commission had been set up in 1864 to examine the state of school provision in Scotland. The Commission published its reports between 1865 and 1868 and reported on the wide variety and uneven quality of schooling in Scotland. This contributed to the introduction of the Education (Scotland) Act 1872, which had a profound influence on Scottish school education. One of the main aims of the Act was to produce a state system of elementary or primary education. Schooling became compulsory for children aged 5 to 13 years. The school system was to be organised by a Board of Education for Scotland and the individual schools were to be administered by local school boards. It is evident that these reforms provided the very foundations of Muir's educational thinking, as later he transported the idea of local school boards and compulsory schooling to the Cape (his policies reflecting those implemented as a result of the reforms introduced into Scotland following the 1872 Act).

The new school boards tended not to intervene very closely with their 'higher class' schools like the High School of Glasgow. The new School Board of Glasgow 'took vigorous action to re-organise the internal administration of the High School to its great benefit', but apart from this, it was too busy with elementary education to pay secondary work much attention.[34]

Muir himself set high standards for the role of the teacher: in an address to the Edinburgh Mathematical Society in early 1884, he stated that the highest kind of teaching is that which kindled in the student 'a spark of enthusiasm' for the subject, and awakened a 'longing to know more and to explore for himself'.[35] During the same address, however, he let slip a remark that suggested that he was less than wholly enamoured with schoolmastering. School life, he said, was one of 'compulsory grind, over-examination and education subordinated to mechanical instruction': it was a 'life of uncommonly little sunshine'.[36]

In parallel to his teaching work, Muir continued to further his research work in mathematics. The value of this was duly recognised: in 1881 the Royal Society of Edinburgh awarded him the Keith Medal for his research into the theory of determinants and continued fractions and in 1882, Glasgow University conferred on him the honorary degree of LL.D. Not content with devoting time to his own specialism, he also promoted the study of geography. He was one of the founders of the Edinburgh Mathematical Society and was a Fellow of the Royal Society of Edinburgh. In this respect, he was a wholly unusual schoolmaster, one who continued to engage in the higher lines of mathematical research, as well as in other academic endeavours, and one who maintained a close connection with his universities and with the 'the work that was going on in [his] old haunts', as he indeed urged other schoolmasters to do.[37]

Although his teaching and academic society work absorbed nearly all Muir's time, in 1876 he did court and marry a Dumbartonshire lass, Margaret ('Maggie') Bell. There is a curious entry in the marriage register: the occupation of Muir's father, George, is recorded as that of 'railway superintendent' rather than 'wagon greaser', a significant boost for him into the managerial classes of the railways some 10 years after his death. Perhaps this posthumous promotion was a piece of gentle family lineage improvement by a son, already firmly part of the Glasgow middle classes.

The couple's first home was a flat in Partick, within easy reach of the High School, and Muir called it Beechcroft.[38] He later gave the same name to the subsequent two houses in which the family lived.[39] The Burgh of Partick had experienced rapid industrial expansion, and extensive housing had been built for workers in the nearby factories and shipyards. The couple's elder son George and elder daughter Nellie were both born in Partick, and the flat must have been rather cramped for a family of four. It must have been a relief for the family to move, in 1880, to Beechcroft near Bishopton, a country suburb of Glasgow. This house was detached, had a long wall with rails in front of it, behind which there was a substantial garden.[40] It was in Bishopton that the two younger children, Lillie Cameron ('Cam') and Thomas were born; by 1885 the Muirs were a substantial family, with four siblings. From the age of eight, Muir's daughter Nellie was able to take the train from Bishopton to her school in Paisley, and perhaps George went to the same school.

After her husband's fatal accident, Muir's mother, Mary, continued to live in Cambusnethan with her daughter, Margaret, a trainee teacher. Andrew, the younger of the two brothers, became a teacher, and when he moved into a flat in a tenement building on the Kent Road in the southern portion of Sandyford, Glasgow, their ageing mother moved in with him. Although the city was economically buoyant and was growing, it was intensely overcrowded; even for the middle classes there was little privacy in tenement dwellings and space was at a premium. Mary lived there until she died in 1883.

In 1886 Thomas completed his relentless real estate drive upwards through the middle classes of Glasgow. The family moved to Bothwell, a village near the right bank of the Clyde, close to Hamilton and not far from Glasgow. It had a railway station on the branch of the Caledonian and North British railways, which had opened less than a decade earlier. This country suburb of Glasgow was 'a pleasant, healthy place, commanding charming vistas of Strathclyde': it mainly consisted of plain red sandstone houses, studded with villas and rustic cottages, 'the summer resorts of Glasgow citizens'.[41] In other words, the suburb possessed all the conveniences necessary for a comfortable Glaswegian academic family life. The two elder children, George and Nellie, were able to take the train to Hamilton Academy, a fee-paying co-educational school one stop away; this establishment was then in its premises on the town's Hope Street, and was regarded as one of the finest schools in Scotland. Nellie felt aggrieved that girls only had the choice of needlework, whereas the boys were able to take Latin, but she was able to start French at the age of eight and German when she was 12 years old. George started studies at his father's school, the High School of Glasgow; however, knowing George's strengths lay in Humanities, he probably avoided the eagle eye of Muir while he was briefly at that school.

The family's large detached stone house in Bothwell was again named Beechcroft.[42] In both the previous house in Bishopton, and this one in Bothwell, the family had a young lady domestic servant living in the house, and thus Maggie was relieved of some of the domestic burden. They had a family pet whom Nellie remembered: a large black and tan sheepdog named Kerry. She also recalled the gooseberry and redcurrant bushes in the garden, nurtured by her green-fingered father. There was also a conservatory attached to the house, in which the children were photographed among the more exotic plants

Fig. 10: Beechcroft, Bothwell, the family house between 1886 and 1892.
Collection: Anne Andrews.

13

Fig. 11(a) to (f): The family pictured at Beechcroft, Bothwell, c. 1892, before the Muirs' departure for the Cape. Collection: Anne Andrews.

(a) George Muir and his mother Maggie Muir.

(b) Muir and his younger son, Thomas.

(c) George Muir with his younger brother Thomas, in the conservatory.

(d) The two sisters, Cam and Nellie.

(e) Cam and her mother, Maggie Muir.   *(f) Nellie in the conservatory.*

growing in the warm interior. Nellie also had memories of having to while away her time in the Art Gallery while her father attended his interminable meetings at his two Edinburgh-based academic societies.

Appointment as Superintendent-General of Education; settling in Cape Town

By 1892 Maggie Muir was in poor health. She suffered from asthma and had been advised to live in a warmer climate. The family were already contemplating a move away from Glasgow, where air quality was bad due to coal fires and industrial pollution. A vacancy had arisen in the Cape Colony where Sir Langham Dale was retiring as Superintendent-General of Education (S.G.E.) after a period of over 20 years in that office. Dale had introduced reforms, including state-aided schools, and had reorganised teaching in the Cape. Nevertheless, at the end of his tenure, the education system was open to much criticism and a new impetus was needed.

Rhodes, the Prime Minister of the Cape Colony, visited England at precisely the time at which Muir was deciding whether to accept an offer of the Chair of Mathematics at Stanford University in California. Rhodes did not want to entrust the job in the Cape to a colonial South African but was seeking 'fresh educational blood from Europe';[43] Muir was persuaded to apply for the vacant job in the Cape. Thomas Fuller (who later wrote the *Life of Cecil Rhodes*), a close confidant of Rhodes and a member of the Cape Legislative Assembly, interviewed Muir, and he made a strong impression on both Fuller and Rhodes. When

Fig. 12: Thomas E. Fuller, Boonzaier 1901, p. 27. Agent-General for Cape Colony, who identified Muir as candidate S.G.E. Collection: Peter Elliott.

Fig. 13: Thomas Muir, 'Bailie's Man you know', The Bailie 1892. Collection: Peter Elliott.

an official of the Agent-General's office wanted to scrutinise Muir's testimonials, Rhodes exclaimed at the meeting of the board of election: 'Damn the testimonials! I have seen the man', and Rhodes cabled his cabinet to make the appointment.[44] Muir himself said that he would never have gone to South Africa had it not been for Rhodes: he 'fell under the glamour of his wonderful personality'.[45] Muir's two predecessors, James Rose-Innes and Langham Dale, had both had extensive South African experience, and both had held full professorships at the South African College in Cape Town. However, what Rhodes wanted was this schoolmaster fresh from Scotland, with clear organisational skills and brimful of ideas of a national education system based on that in place in Scotland.

Days before the family left for South Africa, the Glasgow weekly, *The Bailie*, featured Muir as 'Bailie's Man you know', a regular feature of the journal, which discussed prominent Scottish figures. The column was accompanied by a black and white drawing of Muir. In its character sketch, the article described Muir as: one who 'has never hunted after cheap popularity'; his 'relaxation … takes the form of new intellectual pursuits'; throughout all stages of his career he had been 'characterised by the same steady, incessant activity'. It was then this restless man with whom 'no energy goes to waste', who was uprooting the entire family to take them off to the distant shores of the Cape.[46] A grand farewell dinner was held in Glasgow to wish Muir well on his way out to the Colony. As a parting gift, his former pupils presented him with several volumes of *The Collected Mathematical Papers of Arthur Cayley*; this was no doubt apt as Muir was a great admirer of Cayley, although we know from his taste in reading material that he might equally have welcomed something rather lighter. The Rev. Clark spoke of the 'quiet enthusiasm which [Muir] managed to instil even into those who were not born mathematicians'.[47] In his response, Muir chose to focus on a particular educational concern of his, namely the necessity of offering an 'inducement' to enable scientific and engineering students to proceed to university, as bursaries were not then offered other than for those who wanted to pursue a professional career.[48]

After securing the job, Muir, his son George, his daughters, Nellie and Cam, and a maid, left Southampton on 30 April 1892 on the ship the *Spartan*. They disembarked at Cape Town on Friday 20 May (a 20-day voyage) and 'without delay he began work in the Education Office in Adderley Street on the Monday morning'.[49] Maggie, and their younger son Thomas, followed on the *Tartar* a few weeks later. The family moved into a great barracks of a house, Mowbray Hall, Rosebank, suited to the public nature of his office. The family lived there throughout the period that Muir held the educational office.

Fig. 14: Dr. Muir, Cape Town 1892.
Collection: Peter Elliott.

Muir combined a rarified intellectual sharpness with 'a down-to-earth Scots blunt will and bonhomie' and Mowbray Hall became 'a centre of wide-ranging debate in which the leading politicians and non-politicians of the day joined together, particularly on Saturday nights, over a legendary "bottle of chianti"'.[50] Muir liked nothing better than a lively debate in stimulating company, accompanied with liberal quantities of wine. He also enjoyed impromptu readings of narrative poems and comical stories, and a Cape Town advocate, Stapleton, recalled an evening on which Muir read Rudyard Kipling's poem 'Gunga Din' to Sir David Gill, the Cape Astronomer, in the drawing-room at Mowbray.[51]

One would like to know more of his wife, Maggie, whom Muir called 'Mam' in the Scottish tradition, and who must have provided an important influence on his life and work. She was a retiring woman, who may have enjoyed rather less than Muir his evenings spent entertaining the local worthies of Cape Town. Maggie's medical problems went beyond the asthma which drove the family to leave Glasgow: she suffered chronic anxiety and, towards the end of her life, spent a good deal of time in her bedroom being treated with laudanum, an alcoholic tincture of opium used by the Victorians as a sedative.[52] Muir's *Diaries* record his concern about his wife during his absences from home, and he kept in touch with home by telegram, where a combination of two women (Marion and Rita) cared for Maggie. On one of his tours, he noted that he had received news by telegram that 'Mam's trouble had come back on her, and she was in bed'.[53] In 1911 Muir intimated that, because of her condition, he could not continue as S.G.E. indefinitely: 'every year Mrs. Muir had become weaker and required more attention'.[54] Thus, he took into account Maggie's disposition in planning his life and career. However, there is a curious lack of warmth in his references to her in the *Diaries*: a week before Maggie's 66th birthday, he notes that one of his final directions

Fig. 15: Maggie Muir, Cape Town, 1892.
Collection: Peter Elliott.

to his subordinate, Freeman (forever at his beck and call), was 'an order to look after Mam's birthday and a present for Rita by taking out to them himself six Waterman pens to choose from': no doubt these were attractive and relatively novel fountain pens, but one cannot imagine that Maggie would have been overjoyed to receive a similar gift from her absent husband on her birthday to the one given to her carer.[55]

Nellie, their elder daughter, was a serious-minded young girl who went to Wynberg School, where she was a star pupil, matriculating first in all South Africa. She graduated from the South African College (later the University of Cape Town) with high honours and great potential in mathematics.[56] After Nellie had finished her degree, her father did not allow her to follow a career: instead she remained at home 'dabbling in drawing, painting and cooking' until she married.[57] Muir was a strait-laced father, and Nellie did not remember him as being affectionate.

Fig. 16: Nellie Muir and her sister Cam, in their days at Mowbray Hall.
Collection: Peter Elliott.

For Nellie, marriage must have offered a welcome escape from the domesticity to which she was confined under the stern gaze of her father.

Nellie's brother George attended Diocesan College ('Bishops') until 1895. There he proved to be an outstanding pupil: he gained the leading prize for mathematics in December 1894; was an active member of the Literary and Debating Society; was stage manager of the school play and co-editor of the magazine. He was awarded a university exhibition in Arts in 1894 and is recorded as having gained honours in mathematics and natural sciences in the 'university' exams in September 1895 (at that time, an 'intermediate' was still taught at the school but sat university exams).[58] One would have expected his ambitious father to have been bursting with pride, but it is evident that, probably even at this early stage, all was not entirely well with George, and the father/son relationship would in due course be stretched beyond endurance.

Cam, the younger of the two daughters, was not as academic as Nellie, but

Fig. 17: Cam Muir, debutante of Cape Town society. Collection: Peter Elliott.

was musically gifted and vivacious. In her youth Cam played second violin in the first Cape Town Orchestra and sang and played piano concertos in the City Hall. She loved sport, and played in tennis championships, and engaged in mountain climbing. Most particularly, she enjoyed taking part in all the distinguished gatherings that took place at 'the Hall', as their home was known by the family. Cam later reminisced about all the 'famous names' who were close friends of the Muir family and their visitors: Cecil Rhodes, Dr. Jameson, Alfred Milner, W.P. Schreiner, John X. Merriman, J.W. Sauer, Louis Botha, Jan Smuts, Rudyard Kipling and John Buchan.[59] At the time Cam became engaged to be married, her future sister-in-law described her as 'tall and graceful … with very pretty colouring and clever and bright and very well brought up'.[60]

Of Thomas, the younger of the two Muir sons, there is no record whatsoever of his early days in Cape Town.

EDUCATIONIST IN THE CAPE

Cape Town and the Cape Colony: late 19th century

It is a South African myth that Cape Town had its own tradition of multiracialism and that it was the Afrikaner nationalists who imposed racial segregation on Cape Town. Vivian Bickford-Smith dispelled this in his magisterial work on the historiography of the city.[61] The reality was that, between 1875 and 1902, there was already a considerable measure of *de facto* racial segregation in many amenities and institutions within the city and Colony. Indeed, Muir played a central role in delivering *de jure* educational segregation to the Cape, through a piece of legislation with which he was closely associated: the School Board Act of 1905. Racism informed virtually all aspects of cultural life in the Cape at the time.

When the Muir family arrived in the Colony, Cape Town was a city of some 80,000 people, and Cape Town was the pre-eminent commercial centre of the Colony. The agricultural output of the interior, particularly wool, enabled the colonial economy to grow, and the diamond discoveries in Kimberley in 1870 further stimulated this growth. This enabled the railway network to be built, which contributed to the commercial prosperity of the Colony.

The years 1890 to 1902 were a period of great prosperity for Cape Town's merchants, and by 1904 the population of greater Cape Town had grown to 170,000, and there was a similar growth in the suburban population. There was already a chain of elegant suburbs, stretching from Sea Point in the west to Wynberg in the east, effectively the preserve of the largely white, English-speaking social elite of Cape Town. In these leafy suburbs, this privileged community were separated and insulated from the poorer and more densely inhabited parts of the city; residential segregation had been 'purchased' in these suburbs rather than imposed by regulation.[62] As a leading civil servant, with a substantial mansion in Rosebank, which came with the job, Muir and his family had immediate entry into this society. On the voyage from Southampton, they had travelled with their Scottish maid, and it was only later that they employed a local coloured servant in the house. Thus, their contact with members of the local community of colour was extremely limited. In practice, coloured people were also excluded from many areas, including first-class hotels and railway carriages, and this would have further insulated the Muir family from the local community (largely of mixed race). Having little or no contact with the city's coloured population, they – like the other members of the Cape Town elite – picked up the habitual negative stereotypes which reinforced racial prejudice among the white community.

It can, of course, be argued that Muir's *Diaries* only document 120 days of his working life, and that the pattern of his activity back in his Cape Town office might have been rather different to that on tour. Nevertheless, his record is sufficiently detailed and frank that it is fair to reach an educated view of his attitudes based on these accounts. Not once in the *Diaries* does Muir record a formal meeting with a member of the black community concerning black schools. The account covers numerous mission school visits he made: his habit was to engage in direct discussion with the white missionary personnel who administered and taught in those institutions, and he rather ignored the black teaching staff and missionaries. On a single occasion on which a black member of the mission staff was present as well, Muir named each of the white missionaries in his diary, but simply identified the additional black person by his function – the 'house father' at the boarding establishment.[63] On a visit to the Gillespie Mission Station in the Transkei, run by a Scotsman, the Rev. Hunter, he referred to the place as 'a kindly spot, a bright bit of Scotland set in Kafirland, and a bit of pure heathendom when the Hunters arrived a quarter of a century before':[64] this is a quaint concept of the barbarism that retreated before civilisation. On the occasion of another train journey, he remarked that there 'was a nice evening breeze, the pleasure of which was tempered by a band of howling Kafirs in a distant hut'.[65] While it can be argued that use of the k-word was non-derogatory at the time, nevertheless, Muir was a man who liked to choose his epithets, characteristic of a person or people, and he deployed these carefully.[66] In this instance, he added the word 'howling', typically only associated with wolves or a human mob. This underlines Muir's sentiment and turns the reference into a casual slur and stereotype. For Muir, these were a people who barely impinged on his daily existence. He ignored their humanity and individuality. The black community inhabited only the very periphery of his vision; if they were noisy, he noticed their presence, but they were simply an annoyance.

In the lower-class areas of Cape Town, such as Woodstock and districts One and Six, intermingling of whites and blacks continued in the 1890s, and working-class children intermingled in the mission schools that catered for the poor. It is unlikely that Muir ventured into these areas, but, as we will see, he disapproved of mixed-race schooling.

English was the language of commerce and public life in Cape Town, and whilst Muir, in his public life, came across Dutch Afrikaners, in the main they were of a class who spoke good English, and it appears that he never saw any reason to learn Dutch or Afrikaans. There was a *de facto* division of labour in a number of sectors, with whites in skilled, supervisory or management positions and blacks providing the unskilled labour. This division of labour was very largely reflected in the mission schools: the principals and head teachers, with whom Muir engaged, were white, even though their pupils (and supporting teachers) were drawn from the black community.

The state of education in the Cape Colony on Muir's arrival in 1892

When Muir arrived in the Cape to take up his post in 1892, much needed to be accomplished to develop and consolidate the educational system.[67] Rose-Innes, the first S.G.E., had instituted a system of non-denominational public schools, all of which taught a curriculum approved by the Education Department, and these schools were, theoretically, open to any child, regardless of race or gender. Elementary education was free or inexpensive, while secondary education charged higher fees. The number of children attending school and the numbers of schools themselves did certainly increase from the middle of the 19th century onwards, but those who attended school regularly were still a fraction of the total number of children of school-going age in the Cape (between seven and 14 years). There was also an enormous disparity between the number of children enrolled in schools and those who actually attended; in 1891 only around 40 per cent of white children of school-going age were enrolled in government and private schools. Similar statistics were not kept for black children.

In 1865 a three-tier system of public schools was created: first-class schools (A1) provided elementary and secondary education, with matriculation classes; second-class schools (A2) covered the elementary level with some secondary schooling (up to Standard VI, ending with the School Higher Examination); third-class schools (A3) covered an elementary education only, up to Standard IV or V, ending with the Elementary Examination, and these schools only aimed to teach religion and a little reading and writing. The system was paid for on the '£-for-£' principle, namely, schools had 50 per cent of their costs reimbursed by the Education Department; rural third-class schools received extra funding and did not charge parents fees. The Department also provided some funding to mission schools (the so-called B schools), mostly in the Eastern Cape, which provided a basic schooling and some vocational training for black children, although only for a small proportion of those of school-going age; the mission schools also educated impoverished white children. Only a few of the mission schools, such as Lovedale, received substantial aid from missionary societies and churches, and provided an education equal to that available to white middle-class children; the rest of these schools merely provided an education intended for those destined to be servants.

The Education Department disapproved of racially mixed schools, and employers were also antipathetic to the education of black children, believing that book-learning made the pupils unwilling to work. There was a developing political concern about the poverty of the Colony's white rural population in the interior: better education of poor white, and predominantly Dutch Afrikaner, children was seen as the best way of lifting this community out of a backward way of life. To provide for these impoverished white children, the Department had introduced farm schools in 1882. All that was required for these private schools to be formed, and to receive state aid to cover one teacher, was a minimum of five pupils. However, there was no adequate pool of teachers to staff these farm schools and they tended to close at the whim of those who had sponsored their opening. In any event, poorer rural parents were reluctant to release their children from the tasks they had to perform on the farm, in favour of the doubtful benefits of book-learning in school. The sheer distance between farm and school also presented problems for parents, both of transport and boarding costs.

Even during the early years of Muir's tenure, there was a huge disparity in the funding of white and black schools. Between 1893 and 1894, the number of 'European' schools of all classes doubled, with the government spending, on average, more than five times as much on white children as it did on black ones.[68] Thus, the bias against the expansion of black education was already firmly entrenched when Muir took up office, and he did nothing to reverse this.

Muir's impact on education in the Cape

The background

There is one surviving record of Muir, the teacher, dating back to the period only a matter of months after he took up the reins of his high office in the Cape Colony. We can gain some impression of his qualities as a teacher from this account of his visit to the Convent in King William's Town, Eastern Cape, on 8 November 1892.[69]

Muir met with the Mother Prioress, and she accompanied him from one class to the other. In the different classrooms he posed problems suited to the age group of the children. He asked the younger primary pupils to work out sums, written on the blackboard. He posed simple questions of arithmetic and gave some practical examples to others: 'how often can ten oranges be given away from sixty-four?' In the geography Standard III class, Muir 'examined the children on Africa, asking them for Zanzibar and Socotra, Arabia and the Suez Canal, etc., showing them that the practical use of studying geography is travelling in the mind'.[70] He put more stretching questions to the slightly older geography

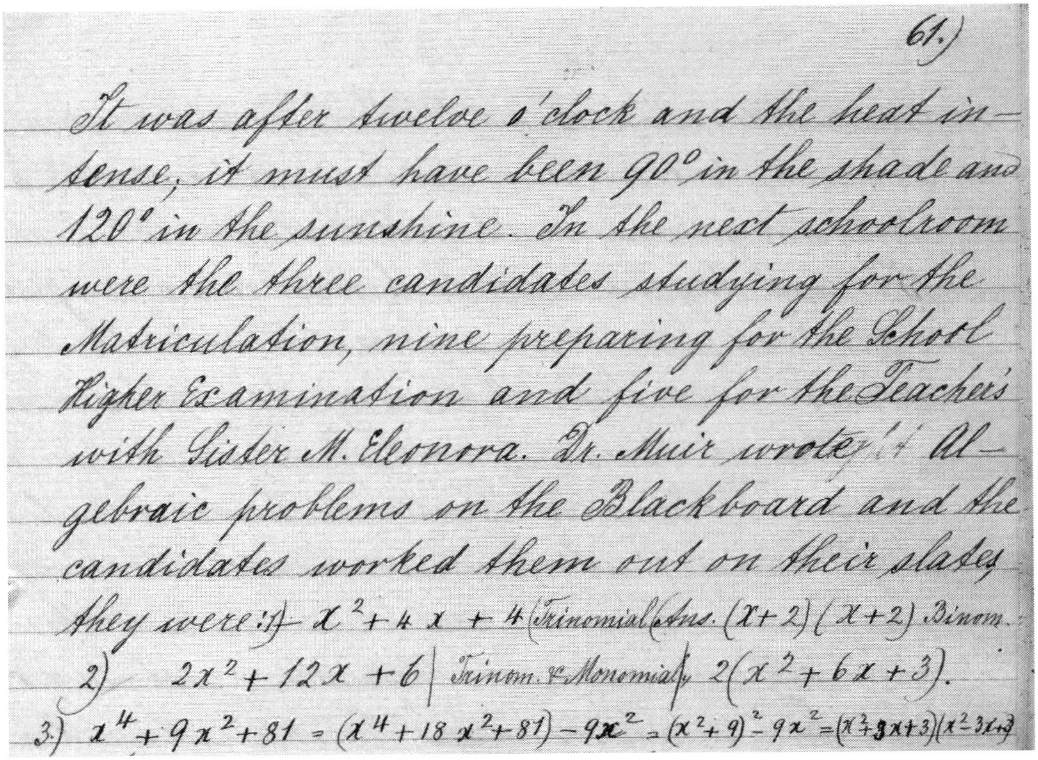

*It was after twelve o'clock and the heat in—
tense; it must have been 90° in the shade and
120° in the sunshine. In the next schoolroom
were the three candidates studying for the
Matriculation, nine preparing for the School
Higher Examination and five for the Teachers
with Sister M. Eleonora. Dr. Muir wrote 4 Al—
gebraic problems on the Blackboard and the
candidates worked them out on their slates
they were:*

1) $x^2 + 4x + 4$ (Trinomial) Ans. $(x + 2)(x + 2)$ Binom.

2) $2x^2 + 12x + 6$ | Trinom. & Monomial) $2(x^2 + 6x + 3)$.

3) $x^4 + 9x^2 + 81 = (x^4 + 18x^2 + 81) - 9x^2 = (x^2 + 9)^2 - 9x^2 = (x^2 + 3x + 3)(x^2 - 3x + 3)$

Fig. 18: Dr. Muir's visit to King William's Town Convent, November 1892. The algebraic problems. Dominican Sisters 1892.

pupils: 'What is climate?' 'Prove that there is moisture in the atmosphere; how to know the degree of temperature? Fahrenheit's thermometer: 32° and 212°; the degree of today, etc.' The questions were, indeed, pertinent on that stiflingly hot day of his visit to the Eastern Cape. Muir then moved to the older classes, some candidates studying for Matriculation, others preparing for the School Higher Examination or the Teacher's Examination.[71] Muir wrote algebraic problems on the blackboard and the candidates worked them on their slates (see Fig. 18).[72]

The visiting party then went to St. Joseph's School, where the little girls and boys assembled in two separate groups and Muir listened to their musical drills. He then moved on to the boys in the fourth and fifth standards, and he gave them problems in mental arithmetic: 'A yard costs 4½ d; find the price of 4 yds. A railway ticket costs 15 s 6 d; I buy two tickets; how much change do I get back from two sovereigns?' Finally, Muir visited the school for the deaf; there the pupils had to read, answer questions, and show their exercise and drawing books. 'Dr. Muir showed much sympathy with them.'

On this visit, Muir remains the quintessential schoolmaster, perfectly able to adapt to the different classes and age levels. He enjoys engaging with pupils pursuing his two favourite subjects: mathematics and geography. At this early stage in the Cape, we observe a senior official, still able to gauge the educational level of each class and to sympathise with those who were disadvantaged. However, during this first year, he must have found it a daunting task to transition from the Glasgow schoolmaster, responsible only for a relatively small

THE ONLY RHODE'S.

Fig. 19: Cecil Rhodes, Boonzaier 1901, p. 7.
Collection: Peter Elliott.

number of privileged pupils in a highly academic school, to a role in which he had control of a system of some 4,500 schools, with an enrolment of more than 250,000 pupils.[73]

It is unlikely, however, that Muir was selected for this post for his abilities in the classroom. Rather, it is likely that Rhodes made sure he had selected a candidate who would implement his policies whole-heartedly and without reserve. The political context of Rhodes and his strategies sets the backdrop for the bias of Muir's own policies throughout his tenure.

Rhodes had become the Colony's Prime Minister in 1890, and he had appointed both Afrikaner Bond and Cape liberal Members of Parliament to his cabinet. Rhodes had plans to conquer and exploit lands north of the Limpopo River. He needed the support of the Bond to get parliamentary support for these expansionist plans. In turn, Bond leaders saw the alliance as a way in which to deliver on their own party strategies, including ensuring that more money would be spent on Afrikaner education and less on black education. At the same time Rhodes gave liberals, such as J.X. Merriman, J. Rose-Innes and J.W Sauer, ministerial positions to defuse their potential opposition to his plans. These, however, were 'liberals' who actively promoted separationist policies. Rhodes's alliance with the Bond helped to promote white ethnicity above Afrikaner or English: 'Solving what was known as the "Poor White question", primarily by greater government expenditure on White education, became Rhodes' *quid pro quo* for Bond support for his imperialist ambitions.'[74] As one by-product of this policy, Muir created the so-called 'poor schools': these were made available specifically for children of the poor white community, attracting more than twice the subsidy of mission schools per pupil.[75] By 1911 there were 270 such schools. Another poor white initiative, the farm schools (in practice for white children), also rose in number from 222, at the outset of Muir's time, to 845 by 1911.[76] The progress towards segregation in Cape schools proved slow after Rhodes split with the Bond in 1895 following his involvement in the ill-fated Jameson Raid. However, the policy was eventually brought to fruition in 1905.

Muir's reforms of the white educational system, 1892–1905

Consistent with Rhodes's strategy, Muir's focus was on white education from the outset. He defined government education policy quite unambiguously: it was aimed at fitting whites and blacks for their 'future positions' in Cape society.[77] This meant restricting black education to the reading, writing and arithmetic lessons they would get in the mission schools, where pupils were not allowed to go beyond Standard IV. Thus, educational progress during Muir's era was almost entirely restricted to white education.

Within this context, Muir did attack the weaknesses of the Cape educational system with vigour as soon as he took office as S.G.E.[78] Muir set out his great watchword in his first Report (1892), namely, that to achieve progress in the educational system 'organisation ought to keep pace with growth'.[79] For this reason he focused first on equipping and reinforcing the departmental machinery, enlarging and improving both the department and the schools inspectorate, to enable the system to grow and benefit from the further reforms he had in mind (the establishment of school boards and the institution of compulsory education, both of which followed later).[80]

The education statute provided for a 'one-man executive' in the person of the S.G.E. Although vaguely responsible to the Colonial Secretary, the S.G.E. 'was left much to his own devices and was practically supreme in his own domain'.[81] He was 'one of the most powerful civil servants in the colony in terms of the influence he wielded over the Cape government and the resources he commanded'.[82] In the implementation of his reform programme, the great advantage of the power he exercised was that Muir was able to take prompt and effective action without the encumbrance of official machinery. However, E.G. Malherbe, a great South African educationist, criticised the rigidity with which Muir managed the system: 'in his great desire for efficiency and organization [he] turned the educational administration into a precise and inelastic machine'.[83] We will see evidence of this rigidity as we consider Muir's programme.

At the very outset of his term, Muir made it clear that he did not wish his decision-making to be second-guessed by a 'second-in command'. When he arrived, there was already in place an Assistant S.G.E., J.H. Brady, whom his predecessor felt would be indispensable to Muir. Within a year of arriving in the Cape, Muir had dispensed with Brady's services as Assistant S.G.E., transferring him sideways to an inspectorate position.[84] Muir's management style was autocratic: while he had officials who were in charge of their own specialist divisions, their role was simply to provide him with any information he might require. There was only one decision-maker and that was the 'Chief'. C. Hofmeyr, a former school inspector who had worked with Muir for many years, wrote of a visit to his office: 'if you wanted to make any impression, you needed to set out your proposal succinctly, but completely. His answer would be immediate: "yes" or "no", "good morning". The meeting was at an end and you knew precisely where you were.'[85] This may be a somewhat one-sided impression of Muir, as Hofmeyr, an Afrikaner, was a critic of his language policies. In the *Diaries*, there is considerable evidence of warmer relationships with other inspectors who would not have been given such short shrift.

In a colony with a predominantly conservative rural population, Muir had to pursue a policy of evolution rather than revolution. The first step he took was to institute a survey of the state of Cape education, and this gave valuable results, especially in the educationally backward rural areas. He widened the primary school curriculum beyond a teaching of the three Rs, adding needlework (for girls), woodwork (for boys), drawing and nature study. To assist teachers to cope with the additions to the curriculum, he appointed itinerant field staff in these subjects and in domestic science. He also developed secondary education. Successful schools were graded as 'High Schools' and these were given a more generous staffing quota to increase the number of matriculants.

At the outset of his term, he was surprised to find that little was being done to develop what he felt was the innate talent for music of the people in the Cape. He commissioned a report on the state of vocal music in schools and the inspector found that it was 'deplorable'.[86] Muir had a music syllabus drawn up by two experts, who toured schools, instructing teachers on how to use this to the best advantage. This resulted in singing being given a proper place, as an extra subject, in Cape schools.

Similarly, Muir remarked that he saw 'little or no evidence of any science teaching in any schools'.[87] Laboratories for physics and chemistry did not exist. He encouraged the teaching of science and experimental work by making money available for laboratories and equipment.

In 1901, he instituted the *Education Gazette* to disseminate information throughout the Colony, to serve as an educational guide and to provide a medium for advertising for teachers without charge. He also established a central lending library of educational books and promoted the spread of school libraries throughout the Cape. This was a progressive policy, but its success was tainted by his distinctly pro-English attitude and his lack of sensitivity regarding the language question (expanded on later). While Muir believed that children should acquire 'a taste for wholesome and useful reading', what he had in mind was access to books predominantly in English and reflecting British cultural life.[88] The list of books for Cape public schools listed in his department's 1903 pamphlet on school libraries focused on British cultural and historic topics, and there was almost nothing on South Africa or by South African authors.

Prior to Muir's time in the Cape, a high proportion of teachers had little or no academic qualifications, and only a minority had received a professional training at one or other of the only two training colleges (one in Cape Town and the other in Wellington). For the most part, the only training for teachers was as pupil teachers in the public schools. Muir increased the qualification requirement, and raised training standards for these pupil teachers. He also established additional Normal Colleges to train high school graduates to be teachers, and there were 12 such colleges by the time he retired. This system, coupled with private education and departmental examination, resulted in a much higher percentage of certificated teachers. His emphasis on teacher training was often questioned in the statement that 'teachers are born and not made', but he replied that the natural birth rate was too low to meet the demand; hence there was a need for improved teacher training.[89] He not only increased the pool of teachers through improved training, but also introduced many new teachers from Britain, including more graduates from Scotland.

From the outset he was critical of the unduly academic Elementary Examination in the schools, which had become the benchmark by which parents measured the educational attainment of their children. Muir said of these examinations: 'They did not test the real knowledge of the child; they did not train it to think, they generated cram and they were a worry and bother to young lives.'[90] It took Muir 10 years to achieve the abolition of these examinations, which he had regarded as detrimental to true educational attainment.

Farm schools in country districts formed one component of the push to expand education for poor white, and predominantly Afrikaner, children in rural areas. Muir's grandson, Claude Cornish-Bowden, believed that these schools were Muir's most meaningful contribution to educational progress since they were 'designed to afford maximum educational advantage to everyone, however remote their home': Afrikaners had told Claude, 'with some emotion, of their gratitude to him and the system he created by which they were given their chance in life'.[91] However, in fact, the farm school scheme ante-dated Muir's time by some 10 years, although, as we have seen, Muir did expand the number of these schools. These schools were notoriously short-lived, and opened and closed with rapidity; arguably, they were a waste of educational effort.

Possibly the most enduring of Muir's reforms was the school building programme he instituted, which enabled schools to raise capital by redeemable loan.[92] Cuthbert, one of his departmental officials, said of the school buildings of 1891, that 'they represented a condition of things in the face of which the school teacher of today would stand aghast' and described the 'objectionable features' the building programme sought to remove.[93]

Fig. 20: Erica Primary School, Port Elizabeth, 1902. Designed by William White-Cooper. Collection: Sigi Howes.

The school building scheme went a long way towards remedying this state of affairs. The substantial new building projects tended to focus on schools already in existence, with a known and established enrolment based on growth already achieved, thus justifying the capital expenditure on new construction.

Even in this first half of his period of office, however, Muir's systems were not universally admired, even among the highest echelons of the white community. Advocate (later General) J.C. Smuts criticised Muir for the bureaucratic procedures on which he insisted; he felt Muir's 'centralised system' took little account of the regions and was alien to the character of the peoples: 'What was formerly done, and often done well, by local school management, now has to be referred immediately to the Education Department. The hallmark of the Department's administration is now its application of hidebound "red tape".'[94]

One issue, which resulted in regular conflict with the teachers' associations, was Muir's insistence on individual (as opposed to class) inspection within schools. He remained firmly wedded to the system of individual inspection, under which pupils were required to sit an individual examination conducted by an inspector, who adjudicated the merits of the child. Those who favoured reform argued that individual inspection encouraged mechanical drill and over-pressure. The inspection process was unnecessarily hurried because of the sheer number of schools involved, and the examination was therefore short and superficial. However, Muir remained opposed to class examination, namely examination of the organisation of the school and its methods of instruction.

There were undoubtedly limitations to Muir's achievements. He was working within a rather impecunious colony in difficult times and his conception of secondary schooling remained narrowly academic. His period of office also spanned the turbulence of the Anglo-Boer War in which Britain sought to defend its empire in southern Africa and the

Afrikaners their autonomy. The war caused enormous suffering and split the entire population of South Africa in two: even within the same family, rifts developed between those on opposing sides of this conflict. There is of course no doubt where Muir's allegiances lay; nevertheless, his prospective son-in-law (who had many friends sympathetic to the Afrikaner cause) said of him: 'In the Muir family, the greatest calm prevailed; there were no heated arguments'.[95] Nevertheless, the war disrupted every sector of life in the Colony. It had a profound adverse effect on schools, particularly in the areas of the Cape Colony affected by the outbreak of hostilities, such as the region adjacent to the western frontier of the Transvaal. School buildings suffered; some were destroyed, others were damaged. A considerable number of schools closed, and attendance fell. In a postscript to his report for 1899, Muir summarised the impact of the war on the schools: 'one clear year's work in the founding of schools [has] been lost' as a result.[96] While the material damage could be repaired easily and within a limited time, it took longer to bring back the prosperity of schools and to found new schools to compensate for those lost.

Years later Muir toured the furthest reaches of the Northern Cape and visited Mafeking. There he was shown the significant battle sites in and around the town, which had been subjected to a 217-day siege during the early stages of the war. Mafeking was eventually relieved by British troops in May 1900, and this was a victory which provided a much-needed morale boost for the British. On the occasion of that much later visit to Mafeking in 1912, Muir referred nostalgically to an ocean voyage he had undertaken a few months before the commencement of hostilities: he remembered 'Baden-Powell, Lord Edward Cecil, Hanbury Tracy and others who had been fellow-passengers with [him] from England in 1899 on their way to Mafeking to be ready for contingencies'.[97] It is possible that Muir also remembered the voyage due to a family problem with which he was wrestling at the time: while the war itself did not provoke heated arguments within the Muir household, in 1899 Muir's relationship with his elder son, George, had become peculiarly problematic (for reasons which will be explained later): George appears to have returned from England with Muir on the same ship, the *Dunnottar Castle*, and this may have also served to embed the voyage in Muir's memory.

The School Board Act of 1905

Muir's work on planning the reform of the school system resulted in a number of Education bills, but none managed to stay the course in the precarious political divide of the Cape legislature. Finally, it was Dr. Jameson, the Cape Premier, who put his foot down and said, in effect, 'we will pass an Education Bill even if we have to have all night sittings for a week'.[98] This effort culminated in the passage of the School Board Act of 1905: 'The Bill was originally drafted by Dr. Muir, and … every amendment to the original clauses … was submitted to Dr. Muir for his consideration before being voted upon in the Legislative Assembly'.[99] The legislation drew substantially on the principles of the Education (Scotland) Act 1872, which had influenced the entirety of Muir's teaching experience in Scotland, and it established in the Cape the long-planned system of school boards. It introduced the system of district school boards, mainly elective, with the power to levy an education rate. Existing school committees were integrated in this system, to ensure that a lively local interest in schools was maintained. The school boards were responsible for the supervision of education locally and had a role in local development and planning.

However, the Act also privileged white interests and diminished the interests of those deemed to be black. The School Board Act of 1905 enabled school boards to enforce compulsory schooling up to Standard IV, but this was limited to white children between the ages of six and 14 years. This blatant act of discrimination was justified on the basis that the cost of the scheme would be borne by taxpayers, very largely white; while this cost

Fig. 21: Postcard of Cradock Girls' High School, 1906. Designed by William White-Cooper. Collection: Sigi Howes.

would be large, to extend the system to the black community as well would have resulted in 'tremendous' cost, unacceptable politically.[100] In his report for 1905, Muir stated: 'the ideal to be aimed at is that all children of European parentage should receive at least a Higher Elementary School education'.[101] The objective was for the white child to 'receive the additional schooling to carry him to the position of skilled workman or foreman'.[102]

The Act had an immediate effect upon white education. Muir was able to report 'the very marked increase in the enrolment of European children for the year ending Dec., 1906' as a result of the actions of the new boards.[103] Thus this reform contributed directly to the pace at which new school buildings were constructed during this latter part of the Muir era; government spending on new building increased so as to enable school boards to opt for compulsory education, and subsequently to enforce it. By 1910 compulsory education was in operation for white children in 91 out of the 119 school board areas.

The fact that there was no parallel provision for black children 'set in motion the legal basis for the institutionalisation of segregation'.[104] The political purpose of the legislation was clear, and separate schooling enabled the government to pursue a strategy of uplifting poor whites through educational preferment.

That Muir was well pleased with the legislative outcome and perfectly comfortable with the government's segregationist approach to education, is evident from his 1909 Report:

> The first noteworthy difference between the school system of 1909 and that of 1891 is the separation of European and Coloured children … The separation between the two races though made in the interests of both was gladly welcomed by the European community, there having been a growing feeling that white children, especially girls, should not be brought daily into contact with Coloured boys of the common street type.[105]

In 1911 the Appellate Division of the Supreme Court held that racially exclusive schools were lawful, as it had been part of the policy of the School Board Act of 1905 to establish separate public schools for different races.[106] Thus the way forward was clear for segregated education in the Colony, which had effectively abandoned its tradition of multiracialism: 'Segregation effectively established the context within which children, differentiated on the basis of race, were provided unequally – in terms of the material environment of their school and different curricula.'[107] Segregated schools were a prelude to the development of disparities in the allocation of funding and resources between white and black schools: 'black educational expansion in the Cape Colony proper was virtually negligible for the decade 1900 to 1910'.[108] This was because there was white opposition to increases in black schooling, as the relatively large white population feared black competition; also there was a political imperative for shifting any expansion of mission education to the Transkeian Territories.[109] White schools received much greater increases in expenditure than black schools, particularly after 1910, and this differential in funding was in fact enabled as a result of segregation.[110] Muir himself was totally unapologetic about favouring white education and made it absolutely clear that white education was the priority; he stated in a public address that: 'the white people of this country should be the best educated'.[111] Muir set out to eliminate mixed-race attendance at schools in the Cape Peninsula, and his reports in the period 1909–1912 demonstrate just how effective he was in achieving this.[112]

The language question ('Die taalvraagstuk')

Muir ignored the linguistic aspirations of the Afrikaners. Throughout the 19th century there had been progressive anglicisation within the Cape schools and by 1900 the government had almost completely succeeded in implementing this policy: 'Cape schools were thoroughly English, and as un-Afrikaans as they could be. The first language in the schools was English; Dutch (and not Afrikaans) was treated virtually as a foreign language; history in school education was overwhelmingly British and no attention was paid to homeland [vaderlandse] history.'[113]

While this process of anglicisation had been driven by successive administrations, and Muir was its administrator rather than its initiator, nevertheless he pursued the policy with particular zeal. Hofmeyr, the same Afrikaner inspector given short shrift by Muir in the office, described Muir's mission 'to strengthen and fortify the English hue of our education system; in short to steer matters in such a direction that the Cape would eventually become monolingual and English'.[114]

As a result of the Anglo-Boer War, the ideological battle between English and Afrikaans intensified and Afrikaans became the focus of Afrikaner nationalism. There were increasingly vocal calls for the language to be raised from the level of a kombuistaal (kitchen language) to a written language. However, in Cape schools there remained only a weak offering of Dutch (not the spoken language of the Afrikaner at home), and the Education Department remained wholly unsympathetic towards Afrikaans. As a result, the Department had to grapple with interminable language infighting, particularly in the rural districts.

The 'Molteno affair' was typical of the ongoing festering language dispute that Muir faced.[115] Molteno, high up in the Stormberg Mountains in the Eastern Cape, was a thriving and growing town by 1903; its growth was based largely on its coal-mining activity and the supply of coal serving the diamond fields in Kimberley. In the area, there was a growing resentment amongst the Afrikaner population of the policy of anglicisation in schools. The Reverend Abraham Pepler, the local Minister of the Dutch Reformed Church, chose to make a stand against the politically biased educational system in the town. The Molteno Public School was run by a committee consisting of Pepler, four Englishmen and another two Afrikaners. Pepler led a campaign to complain of the bad results in the Public School.

He also claimed that when the two principals had been appointed between 1902 and 1906, Scottish candidates had been preferred and alternative good candidates had been ignored. Pepler had complained bitterly to Muir about the lamentable condition of the school, to no effect. He subsequently resigned from the school committee and opened the Afrikaner-oriented Molteno Gymnasium at his own expense, with a boarding house for about 40 pupils, and advertised for staff able to speak Dutch. There was considerable resistance to this initiative from within the English community of Molteno, who insisted it would be better to have one good school rather than two. The controversy gained sufficient attention that Advocate Burton, a member of the Afrikaner Bond and the local constituency member of the Legislative Assembly, pressed Parliament for an investigation into the educational crisis in the town. Dr. Thomas Smartt, an ally of Muir, countered that the government policy was simply to educate the population within the British culture. He argued that there was a 'secretive struggle' among Afrikaners against the English education system, particularly in country towns in the interior. Many school committees, he maintained, were 'steeped in treason'.[116]

Pepler and the simmering 'Molteno affair', were still preoccupying Muir almost a decade later.[117] We do not know the details of all the twists and turns of the 'Molteno case' but in 1911, the Public School and Pepler's Gymnasium finally amalgamated under a single School Board. However, Pepler continued to be a thorn in Muir's side, as the new School Board failed to agree the appointment of a new master to teach science and mathematics, one portion of the Board requiring the man should be Dutch and the other that he should be English. Pepler claimed that the School Board was no longer adequately providing this component of his children's education, and he promptly withdrew them from the school. The School Board, in turn, sued him for unpaid school fees.[118] This was exactly the sort of heated disagreement with which Muir was repeatedly faced on the language question.

Muir fought the language question even at the level of the individual teacher, and he certainly did not countenance opposing views within the schools under his control. Maria Rothmann, the Afrikaans writer/journalist (pen name 'M.E.R.'), had increasingly questioned British loyalism after returning to Swellendam from the Transvaal in 1900. She had a confrontation with Muir after she had been turned down for a job. When she took another job at a nearby private school that received a state subsidy, she had to leave as 'Muir had stopped the state subsidy to the specific school because of her presence there'.[119] Muir had also personally dismissed Rothmann's sister for 'insubordination' when she and a colleague had tried to add a Dutch-language history of South Africa to the school library.[120]

Throughout this period Muir attracted criticism in the Afrikaner press. In a savage character sketch of Muir in 1903, the editor of *Het Zuid-Westen* wrote of him:

> Here he sat for all to see, totally calm, with his firm thin lips, his aspect clearly expressing that he feared no man. His face also displayed a good deal of humour. A strong character is our Superintendent-General of Education, about that there is no doubt. The only question is this: does he not rate himself as too strong? Does he not rely too much on his own judgement? Does he not consider himself too infallible? Does he take enough account of the people of the country, the conditions of the Colony and the opinions of others who also know something about educational matters?[121]

Another fierce critic of Muir was the Cape politician Jan Hendrik Hofmeyr (Onze Jan). Hofmeyr was a newspaper editor and member of the Cape Legislative Assembly for Stellenbosch in the period 1879–1905. Effectively he controlled the Afrikaner Bond and acted as a leader of the Dutch party, but he only briefly held a ministerial office. Merriman nicknamed him the 'mole' as he preferred to work behind the scenes and wielded enough influence to make and unmake the Cape Cabinet. In 1905 he was working towards uniting

Afrikaners and English-speakers behind a single movement to establish Cape leadership in a South Africa rid of British imperialism.

In his position as newspaper editor, Hofmeyr had long been an advocate of the recognition of the Dutch language in public life. He had successfully promoted a language law, that had been adopted in the Cape legislature, to accord equal language rights to English and Dutch in Parliament and in the courts. However, he had become progressively disillusioned at the lack of any practical application of this language equality. In an historic speech in Stellenbosch on 6 March 1905, entitled *Is 't Ons Ernst?* ('Are we in Earnest?'), Hofmeyr appealed to his fellow Afrikaners to be serious in the defence of their oppressed mother tongue:[122] he made a plea for the promotion of the Dutch language in both public and private life, light-heartedly naming Muir, the very 'devil' (*de duivel*), the person whom Afrikaners most liked to blame for the neglect of their language. However, 'Dr. Muir' was a mere scapegoat, covering the Afrikaner people's own failures to promote their language. He urged Dutch-Afrikaners themselves to assert their language rights in the schools they ran and in which they taught. It was too easy for parents simply to turn their back on Dutch because they believed that English was necessary, and therefore sufficient, for their future. Hofmeyr's landmark speech was responsible for initiating a profound national debate about the respective merits of high Dutch, a simplified Dutch and Afrikaans, and about the real value of the mother tongue.[123] His speech did, however, show the extent to which Muir was identified as the bête noire of the Dutch community, in their fight to secure a proper place for their language.

Even after the Union of South Africa came into being in 1910, when Dutch (not Afrikaans) was elevated to the status of an equal official language alongside English, Muir remained indifferent to the language question. He was the Cape delegate at the Imperial Education Conference in 1911, at which a number of British countries were identified as either bilingual or multilingual. The conference was unanimous as to the need to offer education in a child's mother tongue: 'only the delegate of the Cape Province, Dr. Muir, had nothing to say and remained mute on the subject. On his return he spoke not a word about the findings of this Conference.'[124] The Dutch language press criticised his stance on the language question as being not that of an educationist, but the 'work of a politician'.[125]

By 1914, C.J. Langenhoven, a writer and poet who was also one of the foremost promoters of Afrikaans as a language, had taken on the struggle to have Afrikaans officially recognised. The first major success he achieved along this path was to secure the recognition of Afrikaans as a medium of instruction in Cape primary schools up to Standard IV. He was particularly successful in persuading the English Unionist representatives that the unilingual approach isolated them from what he termed 'the most important half of the population of South Africa'.[126] He succeeded in having his motion approved unanimously in the Cape Provincial Council on 23 April 1914. While Muir had not opposed the decision, he did little to ensure that it was implemented in practice.

Battling in a changing political environment (1906–1915)

In the latter part of his period of tenure, the political backdrop against which Muir was working was fast changing. His own thinking was British- and imperialist-oriented, a viewpoint that progressively lost sway as the Cape Colony progressed towards Union with the other South African colonies.

Professor Alex Mouton outlined the English-speakers' opinion at the time as follows:

> Most English-speakers regarded themselves not as South Africans, but as British and expressed their loyalty and patriotism to the King whose authority was symbolised by the Union Jack. They did not see Afrikaners as their

equals, and resented efforts to bring about language equality as they scorned Dutch, and later Afrikaans. English-medium newspapers, which encouraged imperialism and the maintenance of a British identity, reflected the resentment of English-speakers that Afrikaners were able to secure political control only a few years after losing a war that Britain had won at great cost.[127]

The inexorable progress towards bilingualism in schools continued to heap pressure on Muir. J.B.M. Herzog had been Director of Education of the Orange River Colony prior to Union, and was known as a champion of Afrikaner and Dutch language rights. He had successfully entrenched Dutch language equality with English in that colony's schools in 1908. This policy of compulsory bilingualism, dubbed Herzogism by the Unionists, was deeply resented by most English speakers. Herzogism had been one of the main issues of the election, won by the three-party alliance of General Louis Botha in September 1910. After the election, the leading figures of the alliance were Botha, the leader of the South African Party and first post-Union prime minister, Herzog, his powerful Minister of Justice and F.S. Malan, his new Minister of Education. Bilingualism remained a highly contentious issue, and emotions ran high in the newly constituted Union Parliament about a possible compulsion of English-speaking children to receive instruction in Dutch. Botha, with the support of Malan, succeeded in manoeuvring Herzog into withdrawing his plan to compel teaching in both languages. Instead, a Select Committee was appointed to consider the issue. Unusually for Muir, we find him quite flustered about business in Parliament at the outset of one of his journeys, in March 1911: 'Quite fagged out and worried about the Select Committee on Bilingualism when I came home, consequently didn't enjoy my dinner and was forgetful about papers and things to be taken with me.'[128] It was, indeed, a serious matter for Muir not to enjoy his dinner, and for this habitually calm man to lose command of his papers. The Select Committee had recommended that the mother tongue should be used up to the sixth school year, with the second language taught as a subject. After that parents could choose one or both languages as the medium of instruction.

Muir had felt under siege for some time. Following a number of 'unpleasant' incidents, and particularly because he was incensed by the preferential re-ordering of loans to suit political purpose, he had raised the question of his resignation as early as 1907 because he felt the government 'had ceased to have confidence' in him.[129] This situation came to a head in the two years after Union. The Education Commission of 1910 (the Fremantle Commission chaired by Professor Henry Fremantle) was critical of Muir's system: it was concerned about the large number of examinations introduced during Muir's term, criticised his neglect of Dutch, the rigidity of his curricula and his unswerving system of individual inspection of schools, which had 'but one thing, namely absolute uniformity in all schools, in mind'.[130]

A key issue before the 1910 Commission was that of individual inspection: Muir had doggedly pursued this system rather than class inspection in schools. Muir maintained that neither the pupils nor their teachers were sufficiently advanced to undertake the process.[131] His only concession had been to permit class inspection in the two highest standards from 1906 onwards. The Commission came down firmly on the side of reform. When Muir was asked to justify his opinion that the introduction of class inspection would seriously harm education, he ventured no reasons whatsoever but simply replied: 'I know it'.[132] It is difficult to understand his obstinate defence of what had become a discredited system of inspection, other than the fact that this system had remained the most powerful instrument he had been able to deploy to maintain the central control of the Education Department over schools, via its inspectors.[133]

MORE THAN A MERCHANT.

Fig. 22: Mr. J.W. Jagger. Boonzaier 1901, p. 52. Collection: Peter Elliott.

Muir deeply resented the Commission's criticisms of the various aspects of his system, and again he nearly resigned his post. It is a measure of his increasing isolation from the centre of policy and government that he chose to share his frustrations, not with a government minister but with Dr. Thomas Smartt and J.W. Jagger, both Unionists and members of the opposition. Muir complained that the Commission was being used as a political weapon (and the implication is that it was De Waal, the post-Union Administrator of the Cape, who was behind this campaign) and 'as a means of gratifying personal ambitions at the expense of public servants whose lips are closed and whose hands are tied'; he thought better of speaking out, preferring not to 'utter a word in [his] own defence'.[134]

His remaining allies were not particularly influential. It is difficult to imagine what Muir might have discovered in common with J.W. Jagger, described as a 'humourless, dry and lonely man'; Jagger was essentially a businessman turned parliamentarian, and the essence of his career had been 'the making of money, the best ways of saving it, and the best ways of spending it for the good of the nation'.[135] Jagger was 'a man of peculiar contradictions. Although an arrogant and authoritarian martinet, Jagger honestly believed in a non-racial franchise.'[136] The two men, however, shared an enthusiasm for statistics and perhaps this provided some common ground. Most importantly, however, Jagger was a member of the Fremantle Commission, and had the potential to influence the thinking of that body.

It is much easier to pinpoint the community of interest of Muir and Thomas Smartt, who had founded the British Unionist wing, the official opposition in Parliament in 1911. Smartt and Muir were natural political allies and they would both instinctively have shared the view that 'slowly and gradually Dutch traditions, ideals and methods [would] more and more assert themselves, and one fine day the British public [would] wake up to find that South Africa [was] actually Boer'.[137] Both men were deeply opposed to the influence of Herzog within Botha's government. During their long after-dinner meeting on a train journey, Muir and Smartt discussed the two government ministers 'appropriately in the gloom', their mood matching the near darkness of the evening.[138]

After the establishment of the Union, Muir's role continued to be an important one but his executive power was drastically reduced: for the first time, he reported to another, the Administrator of the Cape Province. For Muir it must have proved difficult to find himself working under the oversight of a strong autocratic Administrator, Sir Frederic de Waal. In particular, Muir lost control over financial matters, a function assumed by the Administrator. The role of S.G.E. became more that of an administrator and professional educational official.

Views were evenly divided on Muir's impact on the curriculum in schools. On Muir's retirement the *Christian Express* summed up Muir's approach to education: 'It was the policy which gave the hard and fast curriculum of the "humanities" to the Scots Universities aimed at providing an ideal graded course of mental discipline', regardless of local or individual conditions.[139] On the other hand, Edward Pells, the education historian, took the view that the 'continuous ladder' of education he put in place was one of his greatest achievements: 'Provided the pupil had the necessary ambition and intelligence no barrier exists to impede his passage from primary classes through the secondary and high school to Matriculation and hence entry to a university to train for the profession of his choice.'[140]

Fig. 23: *Sir Thomas Smartt. A partial portrait. Plate 26. Boonzaier 1912. Collection: Peter Elliott.*

Four years prior to the end of Muir's 23-year period of office, J.R. Cuthbert, Railway Education Officer (a delightful fellow, whom we meet in the *Diaries*), published his pamphlet, *Educational Progress of South Africa*; he devoted pride of place to a 13-page review of the record of progress in the Cape, replete with the details of statistical change, dearly beloved of Muir, between 1892 and 1909. It covers sufficient of his period of office to provide a useful record of Muir's positive achievements.[141] However, the pamphlet needs to be read as departmental propaganda, in that Cuthbert was also a loyal departmental subordinate of Muir. A rather more measured analysis of Muir's educational era was provided by the Cape Education Department historian, Martie Borman, almost 80 years later, in his book *The Cape Education Department 1839–1989*; however, he, too, failed to confront Muir's neglect of black education.[142]

According to Daleboudt, the principal early commentator on Muir's education era, Muir 'never commented in any article or speech on the theory or philosophy of education'; although the pages of the annual reports of the S.G.E. were filled with statistical record of developments, year on year, no space was devoted to the theory of education.[143] After his retirement, *De Burger* newspaper noted that he only touched on education matters when he spoke at school openings or at the laying of foundation stones for educational buildings, but 'he did not go out of his way to talk about education'.[144] It may well be that Muir's strength lay in his mastery of statistics and facts and his ability to persuade politicians and public bodies to pursue his objectives. He was then able to develop both the organisation and guide the people to implement his plans. It may be legitimate to question whether he was truly an educationist or an organiser.[145]

The criticism that Muir failed to devote sufficient attention to the lofty objectives of education does, however, ignore the content of some of his public addresses in Cape Town. In 1910, in the context of his presidential address to the South African Association for the Advancement of Science, Muir set out his thinking on the objectives of a science education.[146] At a secondary level, the teacher should foster the natural curiosity of the young, encourage practical experiments and 'hands-on' training, and then only research methods could be gradually introduced into classroom work. At a university level, Muir endorsed the view that scientific teaching could only successfully be carried out by persons themselves engaged in original research. Museums and libraries, he felt, had a vital role to play in education, and more attention needed to be devoted to instruction and research in both types of institutions. He favoured the expansion of state-run scientific departments to do more work to create a comprehensive topographical, geological, botanical and meteorological record. In health sciences, he believed that the state needed to undertake the necessary scientific work that other agencies could not accomplish, but not at the expense of the continuing work of individuals and private corporations. While Muir fully understood that the state was more likely to invest in applied science, in which there was a tangible return for the outlay, nevertheless, he was a great believer, for example, that the pure mathematics of today changes into the applied mathematics of tomorrow. These were all educational objectives and ideals for which Muir strived, through his broad involvement in the scientific associations and institutions of the Cape.

Recalling Muir's watchword laid out by him at the outset of his office, 'organisation ought to keep pace with growth', he certainly succeeded in creating a powerful organisation by the end of his 23-year term in office. By 1915 there were nine sections of the Department comprising a hugely expanded staff. The Education Department had moved three times during his tenure as it required more space; finally, its head office was in a stately building acquired by the Provincial Administration, the Huguenot Memorial Building in Victoria Street. Muir described these moves with his usual dry humour, and particularly the Department's ultimate location, 'a spot sanctified by the church': the head office had 'begun in a garret, they had continued in a Police Court, they had suffered a period of abasement but they were now living in an odour of sanctity'.[147]

Black education

Edward Pells, Professor of Education at the University of Cape Town, summarised Muir's approach to black education as follows:

> Unlike Dr. Dale, Sir Thomas Muir, who succeeded the former in 1892, took no especial interest in the education of the 'Native'. He was absorbed in the task of making the Cape Education Department a powerful organisation. He was content for the most part to leave Native education to the missionaries. What might have been a period of considerable development was one of stagnation. Muir found that 60 per cent of the children attending Native schools were below Standard I. Yet he did nothing to remedy this state-of-affairs. Native education continued to be, from the point of view of secular instruction, completely futile.[148]

Most black scholars in the mission schools were 'destined never to pass beyond Standard IV'.[149] The departmental policy was that African schools would not offer schooling beyond this level and the report of the 1896 Commission on Education endorsed this: 'no public money is given for the instruction of Aboriginal Natives in higher branches of education'; their state-aided education 'should be of a purely elementary character'.[150] Both Muir and one of his school inspectors, Ely, gave evidence before the South African Native Affairs Commission in 1903, restating this stark policy.[151] This neglect of black schooling enabled the Education Department to focus on encouraging more white children to attend school. There was, in any event, a chronic and unremedied shortage of trained teachers for mission schools.[152] There continued to be woeful underfunding of the schools, and average grants per pupil in these schools remained at a level well below that of the white third-class and poor schools.[153] Muir used the metaphor of a social 'staircase' to allude to the gap between the government grant per pupil paid, for example, for first-class public schools and that paid for mission schools: 'Starting in the squalid basement with certain schools paid 15 s per pupil per annum, we gradually find our way to higher mansions where the grant is four times as great. And the moral of the ascent is "To him that hath shall be given".'[154]

John Tengo Jabavu, who later played an important part in the inauguration of the South African Native College (ultimately Fort Hare), felt that Muir had ignored the subject of black education right from the start of his tenure, and was particularly incensed when Muir took the step of 'peremptorily stopping whites from mixing with natives at Lovedale'.[155] Also, Muir had hampered the Lovedale department by withdrawing the grants that had been given by his predecessor, Sir Langham Dale. In consequence of Muir's 'anti-Native policy', Jabavu had sarcastically christened Muir 'u-Duda Mnyule'.[156]

In 1907 Muir had used the pages of the *Education Gazette* to suggest that not a single black candidate had been successful in the Matriculation examination: 'where the students of the Inter-State College are to come from is thus a mystery'.[157] One might observe cynically that this was hardly surprising given the policies pursued by Muir himself. In *Imvo Zabantsundu* ('Black Opinion'), Jabavu wrote shortly afterwards:

> The *Education Gazette* voices the opinions of that bureaucratic institution, the Cape Education Department, and it is an open secret that, under its present head Natives have no greater enemy … Natives are crowed over because they make no appearance at the Matriculation Examination … The Education Department but throws dust into the eyes of the public in writing thus; and that with the sole object of prejudicing the case for the Inter-State College. It knows as well as we do that it has placed all sorts of difficulties in the way of Native Institutions in the direction of taking up University work in any shape or form be it how elementary soever.[158]

Muir took no notice whatsoever of this criticism and continued to argue that the higher department of Lovedale College had more than adequate resources and, therefore, it was 'not want of money that prevents the development of that side of education'.[159] The *Christian Express* countered by pointing out this was entirely at odds with reality. Muir had been loose with the facts in seeking to vindicate his department's failure to assist black secondary education and to justify his contention that it was premature to devote attention to it: 'Lovedale has all along been most seriously hampered by lack of means', not least because of the withdrawal of grants.[160]

Given Muir's interest in musical education, it is worth digressing onto the curious topic of the racialised structure of this part of the educational system in the Cape. Two competing techniques for teaching sight-singing were current in the late 19th century: tonic sol-fa (an easily teachable method which gives a name to every tone according to its relationship with other tones in the key) and the more conventional staff notation (the latticework of music notation on which symbols are placed). By 1892 the sol-fa system was already well embedded in the Cape and certification was administered by the Tonic Sol-Fa College in London. Under Muir, the Education Department became one of the 'more powerful of sol-fa's colonial proselytisers'.[161] The sol-fa system had first been promoted among black pupils and had become associated with the elementary school level, and therefore the white population was prejudiced against the system. In late 1901, the Cape Department of Education stated that it was 'desirable that pupils in Standard V, and upwards should be taught to apply their knowledge to Staff Notation'.[162] Given that Standard V typically represented the end of the school journey for the black pupil, this meant that the sol-fa system became associated with the elementary level and music education in black schools. This boundary between the two systems was, therefore, part of the discourse on race in the colonial Cape. One of the school inspectors we encounter in the *Diaries*, Inspector Farrington, the first instructor in vocal music for the eastern circuit of the Colony, traversed the Transkei on horseback or in horse and cart, promoting sol-fa choralism. This gained acceptance in black schools but not to the same extent in white schools. Thus, a structural boundary was created within South African music education that has endured into modern times; even in post-apartheid South Africa, 'black choirs still ... only sing from sol-fa; white choirs cannot sing from sol-fa'.[163]

Reverting to Muir's policies on black education, it may be argued that he was simply carrying out the diktat of the government. Sadly, it is evident that these policies were entirely in line with his own prejudices. During his extensive examination by the 1908 Select Committee on 'Native' Education (and this committee's brief extended to the education of both the African and coloured populations), Muir stated unequivocally his belief that the mental growth of the 'native' did not progress at the same rate as his white counterpart after puberty: he explained this as a matter of 'physiology'.[164] This statement does seem extraordinary for a man described in the 21st century as 'universally educated' and an 'outstanding scholar and teacher'.[165] Could such a man honestly have held this pseudoscientific belief, based on an unfounded theory peddled at the time and designed to support or justify racism? It is more plausible to conclude that it was simply politically convenient for Muir to promote this facile theory, justifying, as it did, his policy which denied secondary education to black pupils.

The Rev. James Henderson, Principal of the Lovedale Institution, a leading missionary educationist thinker in the Cape and opponent of Muir's policies in mission schools, gave evidence to the same Select Committee and firmly dismissed the theory of arrested mental growth as 'cant': experienced men did 'not recognise that there is this break in development at puberty'.[166] The Select Committee itself rejected the theory, stating that it was 'not supported by facts' and it was a 'deduction from insufficient evidence'.[167]

Whether Muir was simply posturing in his support of this absurd theory in 1908, or whether he had genuinely changed his mind by 1910, in his presidential address to the South African Association for the Advancement of Science he spoke in very different terms about the need to educate all people of all races. He spoke of the keenness of international competition, and the consequent search for intellect by statesmen and leaders of people, to remain competitive:

> If it should be that there are varieties of race and colour in the population, they must have thought out plans not only for preventing loss of power through internal friction, but for obtaining the close co-operation of all the races in the general national interest. In the future, it is only in a relative sense that there will continue to be 'hewers of wood and drawers of water': the State that aims at being in the forefront will have to see that even its wood-hewing and its water-drawing are done intelligently and to the best advantage. Further the exploitation of any race in the interest of a higher race will be fatal folly when the need exists for exploiting all races in the interests of the State.[168]

The continuing battle between Muir and the Rev. James Henderson of Lovedale

Muir 'took a dim view of mission-run schools; in his opinion they undermined the government's efficient administration of education. He expected his department's supremacy in curricular and policy matters to be unchallenged by aboriginal schools such as Lovedale'.[169] It is, therefore, not at all surprising that he had continuing clashes with one of the leading advocates of reform, the Rev. James Henderson. Muir's expeditions of inspection took him into parts of the British territories, not part of the Cape Colony proper, but nevertheless part of his educational bailiwick. He made visits to the mission stations when he toured to Butterworth; from there he was able to travel to outlying schools, and ultimately to Mafeking and back.

In the mid-19th century the British had annexed Kaffraria, an area directly west of the Great Kei, and later attached it to the Cape Colony. Between 1879 and 1894, the other Transkeian geographic regions – Griqualand East, Pondoland and Tembuland – were incorporated into the Cape Colony. The Glen Grey Act of 1894 saw the establishment of District Councils under the leadership of chiefs, the first use of the idea of using chiefs as proxy rulers. By the beginning of the 20th century, these were grouped under a single General Council for the Transkeian Territories (known as the 'Bunga'). This explains why Umtata (now Mthatha) was one of Muir's destinations.[170] As a result of the Glen Grey Act, in contrast to the nil growth of mission education witnessed in other areas, the Transkeian Territories experienced an expansion of such education: politically the view was that this would enhance African acceptance of the Territories as a separate administrative unit and render the District Councils more credible.

In 1877, the state had annexed Griqualand West and Griqualand East, including the Mount Currie district (Kokstad). This period also saw the emergence of the two Boer republics to the east of the so-called Missionary Road running through Griquatown, a British wedge between German South West Africa to the west and the Transvaal Republic to the east, which had been secured by the annexation of further territories. Cecil Rhodes regarded this wedge as the key avenue of British influence northwards, a 'Suez Canal' from the Cape to Central Africa. The lands known as Bechuanaland (whether as colony or protectorate) were similarly secured by the British. Mafeking (now Mahikeng), although south of the protectorate border, became the protectorate's administrative centre. The trade route was further secured by the completion of the railroad from the diamond mines of Kimberley, via Vryburg and Mafeking, further northwards in the later 1890s. For this reason, Mafeking was a key destination for Muir, as the area fell under his educational jurisdiction.

Lovedale Missionary Institute was undoubtedly the leading mission station and educational institution in the Eastern Cape; its fine buildings lay just over three kilometres from Alice. It was a missionary institute with a strong reputation for educating both sexes and, initially, white as well as black pupils. It became a branch of the United Free Church of Scotland and eventually it included a primary school, high school, technical school and a teacher training college.

As early in his tenure as 1896, Muir had clashed with the principal of Lovedale, when he gave evidence before a Select Committee on Education and referred to Lovedale as a very wealthy institution receiving large sums of money from Europe, which it was expending on the teaching of 'Latin and so on' to its black pupils.[171] Lovedale had recourse to the pages of the *Christian Express* to repudiate this suggestion, making it clear that the funds it received from Europe were spent on buildings, general mission work and on teacher

Fig. 24: Dr. James Henderson of Lovedale. Collection: Rhodes University, Cory Library.

training. In that same year, Lovedale's relationship with Muir and the Education Department was further damaged when a 'mortal blow' was dealt to its non-racial policy: the white pupils included in its teacher training course were barred by a government inspector from sitting the examination at the end of the first year of the Normal course, so ending Lovedale's system of training white and black pupils alongside each other. Thus, there was already a history of clashes between Lovedale and Muir, and from the time at which segregation was thrust upon mission schools, its facilities were devoted to the black community.

The Reverend James Henderson (1867–1930) was the third principal of Lovedale from 1906 to his death. As a member of the United Free Church of Scotland, he combined a missionary zeal for the religious conversion of the African peasant population with a commitment to their economic upliftment and social improvement. He and Muir had a running battle on educational matters.[172]

Henderson was a self-deprecating, introspective man, and a committed Christian (diametrically opposed in character to Muir); for Henderson, the aim of a Lovedale education was 'to turn out trained Christian men and women'.[173] The Lovedale philosophy was that education should be suited to the circumstances and needs of the culture and context from which its students came: this was essentially the philosophy supported by the 1908 Select Committee on Native Education. The aim was, first and foremost, to educate an adequate supply of people to meet the needs of white society; as a progressive educationist, Henderson also sought to create a black professional class, believing that even a small class of educated professionals would have more influence on the entire black community than hundreds of semi-educated individuals.

Henderson was of the view that the education offered to black people was too book-centred and far removed from their real-life situation. He had committed Lovedale to quality secondary education and had also incorporated African languages in lower-level instruction to improve student comprehension. He was a supporter of the Inter-State Native College and wanted to develop Lovedale's higher department to produce more students who could meet the university Matriculation standard.[174] Muir, on the other hand, was only interested in promoting the most basic school education for the black population and questioned whether there were black candidates for higher education. Thus, it is not surprising to discover that their relationship was distinctly frosty.[175] When they met, Henderson took every opportunity to continue to press Muir on the subject of the importance of teaching, and developing a literature, in the vernacular, but Muir continued to fend him off. Henderson felt so rebuffed by Muir on the subject that he chose to absent himself from one of the afternoon sessions of the February 1910 Conference. Clearly Muir was delighted as it meant the agenda could be 'got over in double-quick time'.[176] It was, of course, an unequal contest as Muir held all the levers of power.

Muir also met with Alexander Roberts, principal teacher at the Lovedale Training School, and therefore the adjunct of Henderson. There was something of a rift between Roberts and the rest of the Lovedale staff 'as Roberts had problematically associated himself with Muir'.[177] However, the warmth of this association appears to have been entirely one-sided, as Muir was perfectly aware that Roberts was following the careful path of seeking to offend neither Henderson nor Muir. After a meeting on a train journey to Alice, during which Roberts talked all the way, Muir commented: 'He filled me with wonder at his weak flattering talk, a clear indication that he is one thing today and another thing tomorrow.'[178] Muir certainly had more respect for a full-blooded opponent, such as Henderson, than a man of vacillating opinion, such as Roberts.[179] On a later journey, again we encounter Roberts joining Muir on the train, after a visit by Henderson, to 'counteract the supposed Henderson effect'.[180]

To explore the educational policy differences that divided Muir and Henderson, and to gain insight into Muir the wily administrator, a good starting point is a close examination of the mid-1908 evidence of the two men recorded in the Report of the 1908 Select Committee on Native Education.[181] A very considerable part of the examination of Muir by the Committee was devoted to questioning him on his, and hence the Education Department's, viewpoint on the issues raised by the so-called 'Debe Nek Resolutions'.[182] Only six months prior to the examination, John Tengo Jabavu, a fierce critic of Muir and his policies, had convened a 'Native' Electoral Convention near King William's Town. The five 'Debe Nek Resolutions' on education were passed at this convention, and the questioning of the two educationists by the Committee turned on these five topics.[183] Muir and his inspectors attributed the origin of the radical resolutions to the journal *Christian Express,* 'the centre from which they emanated and thereby hangs a tale'.[184] Rather than attributing the proposed reforms to Henderson personally, Muir preferred to lay them at the door of the journal, sponsored by Lovedale Press and which promoted the views of Lovedale; the 'tale' that hung thereby was that of the running battle between the two men.

Taking the outline of the five Debe Nek Resolutions, quoted in the 1908 evidence of the two opposing men, we can contrast their thinking:

First, with regard to the syllabus, Muir and Henderson were not entirely at odds on the subject. As far as Muir was concerned, the 'same subjects should be taught in the same way' in all schools; the curriculum, the textbooks and the syllabus should remain identical for white and black pupils.[185] He conceded, however, that there should be 'less book learning and more manual training' within the elementary course in black schools.[186] Henderson agreed that, within the black community, there was no desire for an independent educational development; 'there should be only one educational goal for races living in juxtaposition, as the white and black races are living in South Africa'.[187] However, he argued that different 'methods' should be applied in schools to take proper account of the fact that the black pupils were disadvantaged, both because their out-of-school environment was less conducive to book learning and because of the language difficulty. With reformed methods, Henderson believed schooling could then pursue the same goal.[188]

Second, with regard to school boards, the logic was that the local community should have some say in the management of their schools, as they provided some of the funding; Henderson argued for the creation of local boards to assist in the management of mission schools, to provide a measure of local control.[189] In contrast, Muir held a completely elitist view on this subject: he favoured the missionary taking into consideration only 'the wishes of shrewd and fairly educated parents' who might 'have some knowledge of school management'.[190]

Third, Henderson argued that larger discretionary powers should be given to teachers in respect of the advancement in their classes of pupils from stage to stage.[191] Henderson had already had a major confrontation with Muir on this subject: a schools inspector had reversed the allegedly incompetent decision of one of Henderson's teachers to promote pupils in a particular class. Henderson had tried to unseat the inspector, but Muir had doggedly defended him, claiming that 'the class had been exceedingly badly taught'.[192] Apparently relying on this single contretemps for which he regarded Henderson to blame, Muir stated bluntly during his examination: 'To put in the hands of teachers, all and sundry, the power of promoting their pupils would simply bring the whole of elementary education into chaos.'[193] A few months later, the *Christian Express* attacked Muir's evidence: the journal felt that Muir had deflected attention by seeking to discredit Henderson personally rather than defending his case on the issue itself. The newspaper urged Muir to 'shake himself clear from some of his prepossessions against the capacity of the Natives for genuine education' and urged him to 'ascertain and build upon the actualities'.[194]

Fourth is the issue of use of the vernacular in schools, the largest issue that separated the two men.[195] Henderson favoured the extensive use of the vernacular in schools: 'Every institution should be required to teach a child in his own language, so that he could read and write and speak it with ease.'[196] He argued that in the early standards, mental growth was facilitated by 'using the language with which the pupils are most familiar'. Moreover, in the case of subjects such as history and geography, 'knowledge should be more easily acquired in their own language'.[197] In contrast, Muir's view was that 'the vernacular should be the medium of instruction in the lower standards … At the same time, from the lowest standard they should begin to get a useful knowledge of English' (spoken before reading).[198] Thereafter, teaching in the vernacular became progressively less practical, because of the absence of textbooks dealing with technical subjects.[199] Effectively the Education Department only encouraged teaching children in the vernacular up to Standard II.[200] No different from his positioning on the Dutch language, Muir had a peculiarly monolingual view on language in education, which is curious given his own personal facility with European languages for his mathematical research.

Fifth, there was the issue of higher education. During his examination by the Select Committee, Henderson was questioned about the demand for higher education among the black population. In an impassioned statement, he proclaimed: 'If education is sound education, no human being can have too much of it. Let men, if they can obtain it, have as much as they can take in, because such education leaves them saner, more peaceable and more humble men.'[201] In contrast, Muir's Department gave no grants for secondary education – indeed, any education beyond Standard VI – except to the teacher training schools. Muir repeatedly used the metaphor of good building practice in defence of his policy of resisting the promotion of higher education for black students: he 'would not keep any form of education from the native, provided he showed a desire for it, and was able to pay for it'. However, it would be a 'waste of money to begin with higher education before you had laid the foundation of elementary and secondary education. You do not want to put on the highest storey of the house before you have laid the foundation.'[202]

An issue also raised during the examination of Muir by the Select Committee was the desirability of introducing agricultural training in mission schools to provide the pupils with practical skills they might then apply in their everyday lives. Muir was not opposed to this form of training by any means, but he argued that there were practical obstacles: most importantly, there was rarely suitable agricultural land proximate to schools, sited with other priorities in mind. The reality was, however, that Muir was content to adhere to an academic curriculum.

During the same committee proceedings, Muir laid out his stall on the matter of funding for black schooling. He considered it a key principle that local people should 'contribute for education according to their means'; he favoured extending the system under which 'the Council taxes the native and gets money into its coffers, and pays out a fixed sum to the teacher from that', this being added to the government portion.[203] The typical funding concept applied to white schools was the '£1-to-£1' system, with community contribution required to match that of the government. As regards mission schools in the Cape Colony, a £1-to-10s system was applied instead, but with the intention of working towards parity.[204] Henderson did not appear to raise any objection to this approach to funding, notwithstanding that the impact on poorer communities must have been extremely harsh.

As a result of the preferential funding of white education, and the progressive extension of the compulsory education of white children (and not black children) after 1905, Muir was increasingly busy opening new buildings, mainly for white schools. It must have been dispiriting for the black communities to witness a school building programme tilted towards white pupils, knowing that the education of their children was not being advanced beyond the primary level at all. In 1913, for example, Muir ventured to Knysna and visited Wittedrift School. After a ceremony, 'Dr. Muir received a deputation from the coloured people asking for school facilities for children of the coloured classes, outside in the district'. Muir's response was categoric: 'The position was explained to them that they must provide a building, rent free, pay half cost of school furniture and equipment and one-third of teacher's salary but absolutely free provision of education could not be done. The part required from the people is surely small in all reason.'[205] Contrary to Muir's appeal for 'reason', these funding hurdles must have appeared nigh impossible.

Before the same Select Committee in 1908, Henderson took the opportunity to deliver a lengthy, and carefully crafted, statement about the dissatisfaction prevailing with regard to the entire educational system in the Cape Colony.[206] The system, he said, concerned itself only with the average pupil; 'it did not concern itself sufficiently with the individual'.[207] The black pupil was disadvantaged within a system framed entirely for white pupils, in which the graded steps to be achieved by the average pupil in the course of the year reckoned upon the pupil receiving a great measure of education outside of the school. 'Out of school the native child, in most cases, plunges into life and thought centuries behind that with which he is concerned in school'; as a result the black pupil felt harassed and was forced to cram, and each step taken by the pupil 'is vastly more difficult and demands far more time for its mastery than each step taken by Europeans'.[208]

Henderson also argued, generally, against book-learning objectives. He felt that the teaching and the course-work books were designed only to satisfy the inspector on the examination day. Instead, he urged that the system should aim at 'the education of mind and character – a fitness for life and its duties'.[209] A method should be devised that would 'concern itself not merely with results that can be tabulated, not with results for the pigeon holes of the statistician'; rather it should gauge mental development, broaden outlook and the growth of moral character.[210] In referring to 'the statistician' Henderson was, undoubtedly, taking a direct swipe at Muir, the mathematician.

Muir was examined again by the Select Committee only 10 days after Henderson had launched this broad attack on his educational system. One would have thought he might have taken the opportunity to respond, at least, on the issue of the disadvantages suffered by black pupils within the system. He provided no response whatsoever.

Higher education

The turmoil and political intrigue that surrounded the development of higher education in South Africa cannot be readily accommodated within this account of Muir's educational era, and in any event, only part of this story belongs to his time. However, it would be remiss to ignore altogether his impact on this sector.

Muir did succeed in giving 'proper shape to higher education'.[211] The University of the Cape of Good Hope had existed as an examining university since 1873, but other colleges provided the tuition. Both the Diocesan College and the South African College, Cape Town, and St. Andrew's College, Grahamstown, were leading schools providing post-Matriculation classes that prepared students for the examinations of the university. Muir reorganised this form of university study: in 1900 he was instrumental in separating these classes from the schools and consolidating the teaching into three higher education institutions: the South African College, Cape Town; the Victoria College, Stellenbosch; and Rhodes University College, Grahamstown. Thus, during Muir's era, the Cape had these three university colleges and an examining university at a time when there were no other higher education institutions in South Africa.

As a result of the Act of Union in 1910, the new national government wrested control over higher education from the provincial governments. Muir played no further part in the later developments creating the autonomous universities.

The *Diaries*

There is a curious quirk of the statutory responsibilities of the S.G.E. to which E.G. Malherbe draws attention:

> The superintendent's position was by no means an easy one. According to law he was obliged to visit all schools in the Colony. This was a practical impossibility when added to his duties as responsible head of department.[212]

To overcome this 'impossibility', Muir instituted a programme of visits to the rural areas of the Cape. It is apparent from his *Diaries* that Muir had made such annual journeys from the inception of his time as S.G.E., as he recalls earlier tours that he had made in the company of his daughter Cam and previous encounters he had enjoyed with some of the characters he met along the way. However, only six journeys, between mid-1909 and 1912, are recorded in his *Diaries*. Perhaps he kept a diary only during this period, or other such journals did not survive. However, they do provide a prism through which we can view the man and his times.

The Superintendent-General of Education's 'progress' through the Cape

Muir's tours may be likened to the 16th-century English royal progress of the king, accompanied by his retinue and entourage. He travelled in style and dealt with the problems of his 'realm' along the way. At each halt, homage was paid to the S.G.E. by his 'loyal subjects'. He interspersed official business with convivial meals with his inner circle; these provided a welcome distraction from his school-related business meetings.

The joy of his *Diaries* is that they bring to life the 'flesh-and-blood' man. Muir describes the landscape through which he travels, and his encounters; he reveals his likes, dislikes and his prejudices. We experience the voracious reader, who snatches time with a book whenever he can. We discover that his reading taste is catholic: he does not confine his reading to the refined poetry and literature that some of the formal accounts of his life suggest.[213] He works from dawn until dusk, but also chooses to relax with a chosen selection of his friends, and he can laugh uproariously at a good (or even indifferent) joke. We see him taking every opportunity to turn to his mathematics. On one occasion, he takes the opportunity of a rest on a cart journey, to walk ahead on the road; there he works 'a little mathematics on a bleached ox-bone for want of a note-book'.[214]

These tours lasted between 11 and 35 days and involved extensive journeys by train on the Cape Railways network. On each occasion, he set out from Cape Town railway station, and his special carriage was taken by a convenient goods or passenger train to the next scheduled destination. There the coach was left in a quiet siding where he could conduct his meetings. After Muir had finished his business at, or within reach of, each stop, his carriage was then transported on to the next stopping point. Muir also needed to reach more remote destinations for school visits and inspections, and to check on building plans in progress. These trips involved drives over hills and across drifts, either by horse and cart or by car. On these more distant visits, he either had to drive all day to reach the remote destination, or would stay overnight, either in a hotel or in the home of a local personage involved in his school business. The descriptions of these trips constitute the highlight of the *Diaries*. One such journey took a full day, from Fraserburg Road Station to Fraserburg, to enable Muir to spend a single day at his destination, to attend the opening of the Public School and the festivities there. He then had to return, making the same stops for victuals, recounting his experiences with the farming folk at the four farms along the way.[215]

It was his faithful subordinate, Cuthbert, Railway Education Officer (never addressed other than by his surname), who orchestrated all Muir's appointments on his travels. Cuthbert established the contacts along the way and made all the advance arrangements. 'C.', as he was sometimes called, had a particular talent for foraging for provisions and beer at their regular halts, and it was often the party's local hosts who made generous contributions to their 'commissariat': to describe their provisions Muir used this expression, signifying the army department charged with food and forage.

To reach a destination distant from their railway coach, they needed to set out early by horse and cart. Breakfast was the highlight of the journey: they would outspan on the veld, and enjoyed cooked chops, accompanied by hard-boiled eggs and polony, washed down by beer. On one trip from Fraserburg to Graaff-Reinet, their friends had handed them two baskets on parting and Muir commented: 'One contained 13 Namaqua "partridges" and a chunk of bread: the other contained two small bottles of champagne. A better breakfast I have seldom had.'[216]

Muir and Cuthbert got on famously; Muir enjoyed Cuthbert's stories, and found useful his sociable way of searching out his old drinking companions, termed his cronies, at every destination. Muir tolerated the fact that Cuthbert was forever allaying his thirst and would return late to the carriage after long evening drinking sessions, during which Cuthbert gathered intelligence, useful for Muir's education business. Muir described his own sleeping quarters on the carriage as rough and ready, and Cuthbert had a bunk which was not sufficiently distant to enable the 'Chief' to escape his snoring late at night, after C.'s return.

Muir's means of conveyance was the same as that developed for the circuit judge, who needed to complete his circuit in the remote interior. He, too, had a special luxury railway carriage made available to him and his entourage on circuit, and this included a chef for the preparation of meals in the special kitchen in the carriage. The corporate social life, and 'jovial conviviality' of the travelling circuit judge was similarly enjoyed by the itinerant

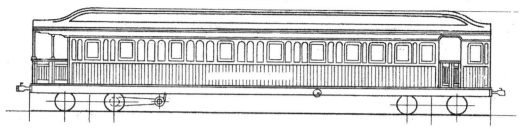

Fig. 25: Side elevation of the reserved saloon of Dr. Muir, 'Old Coach 362', Cape Railways: adaptation from Original Diagram, courtesy Peter Stow.

S.G.E.[217] On the occasion of one of the tours, in addition to the chef and Cuthbert, Muir also had in tow a clerk and a messenger boy from the Office. Muir's centre of operations in the carriage was the saloon, where he was able to take stock of his succession of meetings, and to dictate his memoranda. There was a bathroom on board, and he enjoyed every comfort, including good wines.

Muir referred affectionately to the coach he used consistently between 1904 (when it was built) and 1911 as 'old coach 362'. South African railway historian, Peter Stow, explains: 'Cape Government Railways (CGR) coach 362 … was called a 'Reserved Saloon' which meant that it was used by prominent officials in the railways and government … This bogie vehicle was luxurious and not your typical 4- or 6-wheeler that lesser mortals had to contend with.'[218]

The pattern of Muir's day during these journeys was to wake and take coffee before sunrise and work some mathematics in bed. Then the relentless daily routine of meetings would commence, sometimes on the train and otherwise in nearby rooms. At each stop, local worthies called on him to pay their respects. Muir would then meet with mayors, school inspectors, principals, teachers, secretaries of school boards, and attend school and municipal board meetings along the way. He used meetings to urge compulsory education, discuss board elections and building affairs, and to resolve specific problems. Following each meeting, Muir dictated memoranda and telegrams to all and sundry within his Department to ensure that his agenda was fully implemented.

Formal meetings were interspersed with smaller and more convivial gatherings, whisky-and-soda before lunch, and the occasional rollicking evening with the few whose company he relished. Muir enjoyed reading aloud poetry or humorous prose, often an epic poem of Alfred Noyes (the author of *The Highwayman*), or a sketch from *Mad Shepherds and Other Human Studies* (a book of semi-philosophical parables) by L.P. Jacks. Of an evening, he would read to the small captive audience he gathered around himself, usually including Cuthbert, apparently to their immense pleasure. We forget now how important reading aloud after dinner was for the Victorians. It was part of the day's routine, associated with the drawing room. Muir was a cultured man, and this reflected in the modulation of his voice, and his self-possessed presence. We no longer appreciate the music of words, their rhythm and their shading, to quite the same extent as the Victorians for whom words remained a principal entertainment. For the Victorian: 'Reading aloud holds the listener up, restrains him, cultivates his zest and then rewards his restraint and anticipation in full measure.'[219]

Muir took some exercise on his journeys by walking along the railway line, or he sat out in the evening light on the stoep of his coach.[220] He kept in touch with the outside world by picking up the English mail and the week's papers at each of the major stations. During his trips he communicated with home, Mowbray Hall, by the occasional telegram, and in this way he ensured that his wife, Maggie, was being cared for at home.

It is through the *Diaries* that we become progressively aware of the role that Alice Cogan, a member of his Department, played in his life and we shall talk more of her later.

Visits to the mission stations

We observe in the *Diaries* some of Muir's direct interactions with the mission schools. Quite apart from his visits to the large Lovedale Institution at Alicedale, he also made a foray to Tiger Kloof up near Mafeking. However, as the purpose of that visit was, first and foremost, to open a new school building, we shall pass to that story when we examine Muir's school building scheme later. In addition, however, the S.G.E. visited four other major mission stations:

He visited Clarkebury, a leading Wesleyan missionary institution in Tembuland.[221] There he encountered the principal, the Rev. Arthur Lennard, who exerted a strong influence over the ethos of the school, and Lennard accompanied Muir for a portion of his tour. Alfred Xuma, later a President of the African National Congress, was a young pupil at Clarkebury. The school authorities had already recognised his potential and had invested him with extra responsibilities.[222] Xuma had been admitted to the teacher training course at the institution in 1909, therefore it is likely that he was there when Muir visited. Nelson Mandela also attended Clarkebury Mission School, but much later, during the period 1934–1937. Thus, it remains a school that has a special place in South Africa's history.

Muir also visited Buntingville, a Wesleyan Mission in West Pondoland.[223] There he met with the Rev. J.S. Morris, who had a long association with the mission, and who was finally back there after the institution had faced many years of difficulty as a result of education policy reversal. Muir touches on the story of Buntingville in his diary but does not explain its history in any detail, and it is one that demonstrates the challenges faced by the mission schools. When Morris was first appointed there in 1878, the local people had raised the funding to build the massive stone structure of the institution. This expenditure would never have been incurred had it not been for a government promise of a very substantial annual grant. A political reversal subsequently ruined the scheme: when the Afrikaners gained the ascendancy in Parliament, they cut the grant savagely as they were opposed to expenditure on black education. Morris tried valiantly to keep the institution open without the proper level of funding, but finally had to close it: 'The massive buildings stood for years empty and useless. Mr. Morris's health completely broke down, and he left Buntingville in 1887, after twelve years of labour, very much like a dying man.'[224] As we have noted, after 1894 there was a further change of political direction, and against the background of the Glen Grey Act, the institution was re-opened in 1901, but on a smaller scale and without its industrial department. The *Wesleyan Methodist Church History*, which tells the story of Buntingville, cannot resist a passing swipe at Muir's 1906 policies on the curriculum for mission schools: 'Dr. Muir seems to centre his attention on the training of natives as teachers, whereas God has not fitted every boy and girl for that particular calling. Besides it is an open question whether the making of a door or window has not a higher educational value to natives, in their present state of development, than learning the date of the Norman Conquest, or working a sum in compound proportion.'[225] When Muir visited Buntingville, Morris was restored to good health and was back in his post at the mission station.

The third major institution Muir visited was Emgwali. The United Presbyterian Church's Teacher Training School for Girls was located near the river now known as the

Mgwali, near Dohne in Stutterheim district, Eastern Cape. In 1910, when Muir visited, Miss Dunsmore was at Emgwali, and Muir was thoroughly impressed by her enthusiasm for her school. Resolved to help her more in her endeavours, he inadvertently revealed in his diary his true views on the role of the teacher in mission schools: he found it curious that 'the strong, capable, motherly Miss Dunmore had missed or abjured marriage, and was spending her all on an alien race' at the institution.[226] Thus, we gather his twofold viewpoint that the priority for a woman was marriage, and that teaching in a mission school was a role with a bleak outlook.

Perhaps it was a feature of his busy schedule in his last years as S.G.E., but Muir's visits and inspections of the mission schools, recorded in the *Diaries*, do seem superficial. A cynical observer might suggest that Muir applied the 'God Save the King' test to evaluate the merits of educational progress at these schools:

At two black schools, Roza and Mhlanga, English Church and Wesleyan, Muir found the pupils could not sing 'God Save the King' and when he pressed them to try, the results were disastrous, 'of which Inspector Hobden was kept duly reminded afterwards'.[227]

In contrast, Muir's visit to the Osborn Mission station at Mount Frere proved rather more satisfactory, both chorally and educationally:[228] when Muir arrived at the school, close on 400 children were drawn up in astonishingly long lines, 'a very pretty sight', and 'the assembled pupils sang "God Save the King" well and with good volume'. On this occasion Muir did at least have a discussion on native education, but this was with the magistrate (presumably white). The classes were all inspected from Standard VI downwards, and Muir remarked that the teachers were in the main 'capable and verbose natives'. There followed a general assembly in the church, attended by all the pupils, the delegates of the local Teachers' Association, the chiefs of the valley and the visitors – 'a great gathering'. There followed more songs in English and the vernacular, and 'all were well rendered, the kindergarten rendering of "Shoo fly! Shoo fly! We feel, we feel like the morning star" [was] especially dramatic and entertaining'. As always, Muir was well satisfied by a song well rendered in English, and no doubt the mission station laid the entertainment on precisely for this purpose.

Muir's inner circle

Via the *Diaries*, the reader can establish an emotional connection with Muir, through his friendships with his close circle. The two key characters portrayed in their pages are his assistant, James Cuthbert, and his protégée, Alice Cogan.

James Cuthbert

James Cuthbert (always simply addressed as 'Cuthbert' by Muir) was a fellow Scot; he was a 51-year-old Railway Education Officer, when we first encounter him in the *Diaries* in July 1909, but he had evidently been responsible for Muir's railway journeys in the interior for many years. The Railway Station Schools had been started along the lines of the railway in 1890, primarily to educate children of railway employees, and Cuthbert was responsible for these schools. Prior to this appointment, Cuthbert had been principal of the Public School at Burghersdorp. For the purposes of his railway schools job, 'a railway carriage, in which he virtually lived for years, was put at his disposal',[229] hence the ease with which he directed Muir's itinerant affairs. Cuthbert and his wife, Judith, lived in Stellenbosch, and at the beginning and end of the trips covered by the *Diaries*, we meet him coming from, and returning to, his hometown. The couple had four children, including a daughter, Marjorie.

Cuthbert was the classic sidekick, vital for any important man with volumes of business to which to attend. Cuthbert knew Muir better than anyone else, and he had all the practical skills and capabilities that Muir lacked. For Cuthbert, no practical problem was beyond solution: at the outset of one tour the party discovered that their substitute railway coach was without electric lighting, and it was Cuthbert who could be relied on to 'commandeer a lamp or two before another evening came'.[230]

Cuthbert attended to all Muir's practical meeting arrangements. He always made sure he was able to track down a working telephone near a station, so that he could call ahead to make plans for the next destination. He had a particular mastery of telegraphy. On one occasion when Cuthbert disappeared off to send telegraphs before breakfast, Muir remarked: 'one feels that if he were completely debarred from "wiring" he would pine and die'.[231] It was Cuthbert who invariably took Muir's dictation. On one journey, during which Muir dictated his endless memoranda 'almost every inch of the way', Cuthbert remarked that 'he thought he could manage to draft one of them himself'; Muir 'told him that this raised him in [his] estimation as a secretary, which was something better than a cross between a Cook's conductor and a boy-typist'.[232]

Food and drink were vital to Cuthbert's well-being: his constant quest was for 'suitable company and for a train with a kitchen and bar'.[233] Quite apart from being in charge of the 'commissariat', Cuthbert also prided himself on his cooking skills, and was able to fill in as a chef when required.

He had inexhaustible social stamina and added to the joviality of every occasion. When Muir tired of a formal evening, he was able to depart in the knowledge that Cuthbert would continue where he left off. Thus, after lunch following the opening of the new building at Tiger Kloof, Muir took his leave: 'C. notwithstanding the absence of proper liquid nourishment, was in his element during lunch and after. He gossiped and joked with the women, and laid down the law to the men: when I left to return to the coach, he had just got his pipe lit and was simply warming to his subject.'[234]

Cuthbert was often too talkative, noisy at dinner, and was inclined to drink far too much. After a gathering in Aberdeen, Muir remarked: 'Cuthbert had imbibed much too freely and fell asleep in the most ungraceful and dangerous positions.'[235] On this occasion Muir indicated his displeasure purely through silence, but Cuthbert's positive qualities vastly outweighed his shortcomings.

Like all the valiant, Cuthbert tended to stray into areas in which his expertise was questionable. On one occasion he ventured into battle against a plague of mosquitos:

> The mosquitoes that at dinner seemed to be in millions slackened off with the approaching coolth of the evening. Nevertheless C, knowing an infallible cure was determined on action. He accordingly made for the light of the booking-office, and attained from the Station Master a tin of the specific, Keating's insect powder.[236] With this he besprinkled my pillow, bed-cover and anything else that came in his way. Finished up with a flourish of his tin as if he had already slain thousands. When I went to bed, I couldn't help feeling uncleanly, but then I also hoped for the martyr's crown. By one o'clock I had lost any vestige of faith I had ever possessed. Keating's powder may ordinarily be effective, but the Vryburg Station Master's tin was a failure. Or feasibly, like whisky, the powder may affect different individuals in different ways, stupefying some and in others raising the very devil. The latter was the case with those mosquitoes that spent the night with me, or by nature they must have been 'desperately wicked'.[237]

Alice Cogan

On his travels into the interior in 1909, Muir met Alice Cogan, a vivacious young lady half his age; in the *Diaries* Muir consistently refers to her simply as Miss Cogan.[238] This acquaintance developed into something of a romantic friendship within the 'Office' during the years of the *Diaries*.

At the time, Muir's wife, Maggie, was chronically unwell at Mowbray Hall, and during his travels Muir kept in touch with her at home by telegram, obviously concerned to ensure she was being looked after by the people deputed to this task. We do not know how Muir's relationship with Maggie fared during the difficult last 10 years of her life, but he remained solicitous as to her welfare. Why did Muir choose to keep the *Diaries* covering these journeys, and no others, during his long period as S.G.E.? Is it a mere coincidence that the period covered coincides precisely with the first two and a half years of his friendship with Miss Cogan? One can speculate that the *Diaries,* recording their early encounters, may have amused Miss Cogan, and been retained for this express purpose.[239] While there is no suggestion of physical infidelity on Muir's part, the tenor of the friendship, sustained over the 10-year period before his wife died in 1919, is strong enough to suggest an emotional infidelity.

Muir first met 'Miss Alice' during his 1909 Transkeian tour, made in the company of Cuthbert. She was then living with the Canon of the Cathedral in Umtata (now Mthata). On that first encounter, 'Cuthbert and Miss Alice chummed up at once, the latter having attended Grahamstown Training College with Margory Cuthbert'.[240]

On that same trip, Miss Cogan subsequently joined the S.G.E.'s entourage for a period of four days. On the first evening she joined Muir's supper party, and the next day, interspersing business with pleasure, he broke his board meetings to join her at her lodgings for both morning and afternoon tea, together with her parson host and his wife. The following day Muir's train set off on its journey and he and Cuthbert 'carried off Miss Cogan with [them] amid a rattle of fog signals and hand wavings'; they continued all the way to Elliot Station, and onwards to Cala, where they had a 'jolly' little hotel dinner and Muir attended his evening school board meeting.[241] Miss Cogan had been happy to occupy herself while Muir conducted his business, which suited Muir entirely. She was part of the small group in attendance on 25 August, Muir's 65th birthday. Prompted as to the date by the ever-conspiratorial Cuthbert, Miss Cogan presented Muir with a 'pretty bunch of violets'.[242] Again, Muir performed his official duties and school visits throughout a busy day; however, the mere fact of Miss Cogan's presence produced a remarkable uplift in his spirits. This did not go unnoticed by the rest of the small party: 'the dinner for an improvised birthday function was quite merry: even speeches were not wanting. Wheeldon [one of Muir's guests] said goodbye, having confided to Cuthbert how he had enjoyed the trip, and how especially this last day he had been sore with laughing inwardly at the fun Miss Cogan and I had had'; the school board meeting which followed was a 'tiresome interruption' in the fun. At the end of that day, Muir confessed that he 'parted from Ms. Cogan with regret'.[243]

During his 1910 tour to Butterworth, and ultimately to Mossel Bay, Miss Cogan continued to loom large in the story. She joined the entourage at Butterworth and remained for at least four days. On the first day, a school inspector pre-empted her and swept Muir off on a drive to the Bawa Falls. When Muir returned, he found Miss Cogan had left 'a bowlful of fresh roses' for him.[244] The following day she determined it was her turn to secure Muir for a drive. She claimed his admiration by rescuing him in a 'daring way' from a tiresome meeting with three school missionaries and they set out together on their expedition: 'The air was beautifully fresh; and though the sunset showed little colour, the views of the rolling green hills as we ascended and of the extensive lowlands as we came back were most pleasing. Altogether the outing was enjoyable.'[245] The two of them then spent a 'very happy evening' in the company of Cuthbert, who joined Muir in a bout of teasing at Miss Cogan's expense. The evening closed with Muir reaching for two poems by Alfred Noyes and he 'read aloud for her pleasure on the coach stoep'.[246] On the following days Miss Cogan remained a preferred guest at the lunches and dinners he convened of his inner circle. On the final day, there was a visit to the Bunga Model Farm; one of the visiting party, Mr. Carmichael of the Tsolo School of Agriculture (whom Muir refers to as the 'schemer'), issued a lunch invitation pointedly omitting Miss Cogan from the guest list. The ever-vigilant Cuthbert took the necessary defensive action without having to consult Muir. He declined the lunch invitation altogether, thus ensuring Miss Cogan 'should have the outing which the schemer would have denied her'.[247] Cuthbert then arranged for Miss Cogan to drive Muir to the Model Farm and back; this enabled Muir to avoid talking shop with the schemer during the entire long cart journey. Instead, he and Miss Cogan were able to banter and gossip together on the way and have fun teasing (or as Muir said 'chaffing') each other at the lunch, rather than having to engage in vapid conversation with Carmichael.

Both of Muir's next trips into the interior were made in early 1911 and were of short duration, interspersed with a month back in his office. Miss Cogan made a short stage entry into the second trip, arriving, apparently unannounced, and travelling with the party from Colesberg to De Aar, much to Muir's enjoyment. The mission stations, Lovedale and Blythswood, engaged their conversation and the two exchanged 'relevant and irrelevant gossip'. Muir ended by reading her a couple of poems and then saying a hurried goodbye to her at De Aar, leaving her to the tender mercy of her landlady in the town.[248]

In October of that same year, Miss Cogan made a further brief appearance during Muir's tour to Butterworth:[249] Evidently, by then Miss Cogan's job within the Education Department had progressed to a higher level, under Muir's sponsorship. She was discovered to be 'in town examining the mission schools'; one of the party went to fetch her and brought her to the station, where she and Muir had tea on the stoep of the coach 'while the others waited'. It seemed everyone accepted that Miss Cogan took precedence over their school business. Muir and Miss Cogan gossiped of Lovedale together, and there was 'mutual regret at having to depart without more gossip'.

The personality of Muir that emerges from the Diaries

Even at the age of just over 65, Muir was still an energetic man with an enormous zest for life and an interest in people. In 1905 he was described as follows: 'standing about five feet nine inches, he weighs between eleven and twelve stone. Broad-shouldered and deep-chested, he is all wire and whipcord; he would give one the impression of a man of no more than fifty were it not that his hair is white.'[250] The *Diaries* reveal Muir as sociable, but also jealous of the time he needed to spend on his own pursuits, such as his reading and mathematics. He restricted close friendship to a small circle of intimates. These included his wife, Maggie, his daughters Cam and Nellie, Cuthbert, his loyal assistant, and Alice Cogan.

As to the next outward layer of his acquaintance, he also had a relaxed relationship with a number of the school inspectors whose circuits fell within his travel route, but he remained slightly aloof, their 'Chief' within the Office and also in the social gatherings that followed work. After a hard day's conference, Muir would think nothing of potentially offending some of his official visitors, by confining his evening dinner invitation to his favoured personal coterie; after two full days spent in discussion with three missionaries, including his mission school foe Henderson, he rather pointedly spent his evening in the company of Inspectors Bennie and Hobden and Miss Cogan.[251]

Inspector Grant (whose circuit included De Aar) was one of Muir's stalwarts, who knew and understood him and was inventive to boot. Whenever Muir was in the area, Grant would join the entourage and was quick to spot when Muir was eager to shake off a persistent education business visitor. On one occasion, Grant had witnessed the Rev. Venter subjecting Muir to a long exposition of his 'educational theories'. When Venter arrived 'refreshed' the following day, ready to re-enter the fray, Grant came to the rescue: he invited Muir to 'glance at certain statistics' in his hotel, whereupon the parson immediately declared that he would not be interested in the figures and headed off. Grant's cunning plan mercifully left Muir, Cuthbert and Grant to retreat into the cool interior of the hotel to enjoy ice-cold beer: 'We saw no statistics, and we have since been in the habit of asking for "figures" when something less dry was really meant.'[252]

Another of Muir's favourites was Inspector Anderson, whose circuit included Sterkstroom and Molteno.[253] Anderson was an intellectual, and this endeared him to Muir: he was a man whose 'sound taste for really good literature' was manifest, and he kept in the background 'his assumed love for anything – good, bad or indifferent – that bore a Greek or Latin dress'.[254] Despite his infatuation for Greek epigrams, Anderson was clearly a man who could also enjoy a raucous evening with Muir and Cuthbert, 'noisome with the fumes of tobacco and whisky'.[255]

Not so favoured was Inspector Morrison, whose circuit included Alicedale and hence Lovedale, a troublesome one for Muir. On one occasion Morrison joined Muir's coach, and we sense Muir's irritation: 'full of his work as usual he fastened on me like a leech. I think I dree'd my weird without wincing, but I nonetheless suffered from internal combustion.'[256]

However busy his working schedule, on countless occasions in the *Diaries* we find Muir pausing and engaging in conversation with a pretty, and usually younger, lady who happens to be passing. Invariably he comments on their looks. A striking example is the tea party he attends with 30 women in a tearoom in Aberdeen, at which he is allotted three 'intelligent and agreeable' ladies, all English and good looking. He remarks particularly on Mrs. Le Roux who 'had real beauty of the plump pink-and-white type'.[257] His observations cannot be dismissed as a mere interest in youth or vitality; he rarely comments on the outward appearance of the men who encircle him, unless they are strikingly ugly. He has a marked penchant for woman who will engage with him in wordy fun. For example, in Matjiesfontein he encounters Miss Grant, who reminds him 'with a demure smile' that she knew him although he had forgotten her; he then recalls their previous encounter and remarks with pleasure that she 'had developed into a quietly charming young lady with a lot of latent fun'.[258] Age was no barrier as long as the woman in question proved vivacious and interesting. In Kimberley Muir encounters again Mrs. Haarhoff. He drives off with her in her car, which she 'silently left [him] to admire … a dream of comfort and elegance'; the two were 'soon engaged in wordy contests'.[259] There is no photographic record of his friend Alice Cogan, but she was half his age, and one can be sure she was pretty. It was, however, her mischievous wit that captured Muir's attention.

To see Muir at his human best, we need simply to enjoy his racing account of his adventurous journey from Oudtshoorn to Mossel Bay, in the company of Dr. George Russell, District Surgeon for Oudtshoorn, motor engineer and chauffeur extraordinary.[260] Muir likened his host to *Tartarin of Tarascon*, the plump, middle-aged, but prodigiously brave, eponymous hero of Alphone Daudet's novel. Russell had three motor cars, and each bore a silver plate with a girl's name engraved on it. Muir's entourage travelled in the Siddeley named 'Alice', and their luggage was borne in a separate cart. Due to the recent heavy rains, the party had to contend with fast-flowing rivers and drifts; they had to dig the car's wheels out of the sand and mud, and 'Alice' was hauled by mules through the river. Russell performed miraculous roadside repairs to correct an electrical fault. The 68-mile journey took six hours 'notwithstanding all our mishaps'.[261]

On occasions Muir was evidently prepared to go out of his way to intervene personally to help and protect a teacher, or a member of his Department, in trouble. An example of this was the case of Ida Wesner, a young teacher who had 'misconducted herself in the Zambesi Express' and had been summoned to appear in court:[262] although Muir was on his travels in the middle of nowhere, he leapt into action setting 'the wires amoving in the hopes of arresting trouble'. He defended the girl, arguing that the Railway people had 'behaved discreditably on the train and had exaggerated the story afterwards'. He followed this up by meeting with an Inspector of the Railway Detective Department, who undertook to do his utmost to have the scandal case withdrawn. A telegram was handed to Muir a few days later, which reported that the case would proceed, but would 'be withheld from the newspapers'. We see Muir rushing to the aid of a young teacher in distress, and at least he succeeded in preserving her reputation from adverse publicity.

Yet, on at least two other occasions, Muir appears to have been utterly indifferent to the situation of similarly distressed teachers. On visiting Cookhouse, Muir told the story of the unfortunate teacher, Miss Twycross, who had attempted suicide, following a romantic entanglement:

> Reached Cookhouse late and didn't get to bed till one o'clock, the excitement of the place being Miss Twycross' attempted suicide consequent on the breaking-off of her most recent engagement at East London. One of her least alarming attempts was made with a combined draught of chlorodyne, tatcho and red ink; doubtless the result would have been more effectual if she had been more cleanly in her instincts, and left some of the ingredients out. She had just been sent off to Grahamstown in charge of an able-bodied nurse.[263]

While the story is told with humour, it is a somewhat hollow and unfeeling tale.

There is a similar instance of Muir's indifference to the personal woes created in his Department as a direct result of the whirlwind of his policies. This tale related to an unnamed teacher who had lost his employment following Muir's introduction of higher qualification standards for teachers. While the reform was ultimately beneficial, in that it raised the quality of teaching in schools, the immediate and unfortunate consequence was that an unqualified teacher could no longer hold, or secure, employment in his schools. Muir told the story of a 'begging call' he received from an 'old reprobate', whom he was able to identify, but who did not know Muir; this was a somewhat unequal encounter, but apparently 'not free from humour' as far as Muir was concerned. The out-of-work teacher recognised in Muir the possible 'sympathy of an old teacher, one whom fortune had favoured'. Muir made a donation to the unfortunate man, 'ostensibly because of the said sympathy, but really as an inadequate solatium to a good man for having ruined him'.[264] Muir's companion, School Inspector Milne (one of his favourites), laughed unrestrainedly when the 'old sweep' departed.

In the spectrum of Muir's response to individual plight within his Department, ranging from concern and positive action to callous indifference, the story of Inspector Satchel lay somewhat between these two extremes. Satchel was a subordinate he liked and valued, and whom he had apparently assisted in the past. On one tour, however, Muir caught Satchel at a low ebb:

Had a prompt call from Inspector Satchel, who to my surprise had the air of an intending suicide. He reported himself as being disappointed and depressed beyond measure because of the changes in his circuit. I was forced soon to pull him up, and even to remind him of the depth of woe in which I had first found him, after the war. Then I lectured him and then I asked him to stay to supper much to C.'s discomfort.[265]

Cuthbert, evidently, did not have the same tolerance of Satchel as did Muir; however, the latter's 'pull yourself together' lecture was hardly the sort of medicine that would have helped to restore Satchel's equilibrium.

Muir was quick to root out from the schools under his control, any opinions of which he disapproved. At a point during his 1910 tour, he discovered that one of the teaching sisters of the Grahamstown Training College was promoting Dutch. He made several successful manoeuvres to thwart her efforts: after dinner one evening, a small caucus held a long chat about the school and this teacher's 'new fad-Dutch'.[266] Instead of tackling the teacher directly on the subject, he has 'a long and rather serious talk ' with the Mother Superior at the college about this particular teacher's *Schwärmerei* (fanaticism); the result was that the Mother Superior agreed to 'take action quietly but firmly'.[267] Muir termed this isolated act of rebellion on the part of a lone nun in the Training College 'Fenianism', and immediately crushed it.

He cultivated friendships and alliances among those Cape politicians and public figures who were like-minded, and who could help to ease through and promote his policies. One such figure was Thomas Smartt, a leading post-1910 Unionist politician. Following a meeting the two held on the train, and long discussions they had had about all the developments that were troubling them, Muir remarked, 'it was pleasing to find how well [Smartt] and I agreed in our judgements'; both men readily reached a shared view on those with whom they had dealings, classifying them either as 'straight' or a 'scoundrel', with little gradation between the two, save that the worst category of all was that of the 'sanctimonious scoundrel'.[268] Muir limited his time and attention to those who, in his view, qualified as 'straight' (and that meant intelligent and agreeable; and whose views did not clash with his own). He applied this judgement to all and sundry: eminent politicians, school inspectors, missionaries, clergymen and the prominent people he met in the areas he visited.

However, Muir was no respecter of rank and was happy to seek out the most unlikely of company. He continued to be drawn to honest, hardworking country people, who had come from nothing as he had. Thus, when he visited the Stutterheim area, he renewed an old acquaintance with Farmer Coutts of Horseshoe Farm, a man who had manfully stood by Muir's Department in local school affairs:[269] 'Outwardly Coutts was a picture. His clothes were the colour of the soil, the lower half of his vest had no buttons, and his hat was only fit for a scarecrow. Yet ... what a splendid intellectual head he showed when his hat came off!' Muir went out of his way to call on Coutts and his sister at their farm cottage near Dohne. It was a spartan two-roomed dwelling in stark contrast to the handsome new shearing house and dairy the farmer had built alongside: 'Money apparently was available for anything and everything save the personal comfort of the possessors: it may be however that what the rest of the world called comforts may have proved the opposite to these old Scottish peasants.' Despite his modest dwelling, Coutts had recently bought an additional farm for £5,000, and had leased part of it to a member of the same Aberdeenshire family on whose estate he had been brought up as a herd-boy, and the reversal of fortunes would have amused Muir.

Muir had a dislike of organised religion, and he steered a wide berth round the rural parsons and their kinfolk, largely Dutch Reformed, that he encountered on his tours. He received a particularly large dose of ministers of religion on his tour centred on Graaff-Reinet in March 1911. Ever the master of the striking epithet, he described the parson's wife in Fraserburg as the 'hard and rather virile Mrs Daneel who had "Calvinist" written on her countenance'; similarly, the parson of Aberdeen, Cilliers, was dubbed 'wily and sanctimonious and heartily tyrannical as ever'.[270] On the same trip and on a return journey, they revisited Oudekloof Farm, oblivious of the fact that it was a Sunday morning and a social visit was unlikely to be welcome. Put off by the less than cheery welcome they received from the farmer, Sieberhagen, Muir and Cuthbert decided to stretch their legs and call later. They were thankful they did so when they heard the family worship in progress. When 'all was quiet' they returned to the door to pay their call, but 'abruptly stopped on the lowest step when a hoarse voice struck up another psalm tune. After a second, long wait … we observed a lanky youth proceed from the house, leaving the door open, and make for the stables. We now felt safe enough and with a reconnoitring once, we entered.'[271] The danger of entrapment in the worship was narrowly avoided and they were able to proceed with a sociable visit to the farmer.

Muir was quite used to receiving a rather muted reception on the part of the local community when he ventured into school areas in which Dutch/Afrikaans speakers were dominant, but in which the position of their language remained precarious. However, he records two occasions on which he was relieved to receive a positive welcome. He visited Prieska in the Northern Cape to lay the foundation stone for the new building for the Public School in the town. Muir arrived to find the structure adorned with strings of flags, and a large crowd of people 'roasted in the open Prieska sun'. There followed a dinner in the evening, with numerous speeches, alternately in English and Dutch. Muir was struck by the 'strikingly friendly' address of the principal speaker, whose statement that Muir 'should find a hearty welcome in every Dutch household in the district' was 'loudly cheered'.[272] A similar occasion was Muir's visit to Fraserburg to open the new Public School: when Muir gave his speech in English to a predominantly Dutch/Afrikaans-speaking crowd, the local parson thoughtfully providing a translation. Muir remarked that this was 'a trifle unnecessary'. 'Strangest of all, the anti-Englander Louw led with three cheers at the close.'[273] His view that there was no need for translation rather underlines his assumption that his audience really ought to have been able to understand his language, rather than his having to communicate in theirs.

Muir's ability to manage a meeting and steer a decision

Muir was able to take command of a meeting and turn discussion to his advantage. In Barkly West, a local school headmaster, 'Captain' Tuckey, began the meeting before Muir arrived and was already 'in full blast with the delegates in a horseshoe in front of him'; Muir 'bore with the rigmarole' for a little longer than he ought, but then 'brought the speaker up with a round turn and a broad hint that [he] had come to do business'.[274] Having interrupted Tuckey's 'harangue', Muir conducted affairs himself, taking the various delegates in their turn but leaving Tuckey's school to the last, putting 'the redoubtable in his proper place' and winding up the meeting in decent form.[275]

His meeting tactic was to allow his opponents to talk themselves out and thereby eventually to achieve the outcome he desired. One such lively and lengthy discussion was held in a smoking room closely adjoining the hotel bar in Cedarville, in the Transkei. The meeting was attended by the 'table-thumping Dr. Pope', 'the rampageous and perfervid leader of the Cedarville opposition "Wha-What" Smith', and five other local worthies; Muir remarked: 'My patience was equal to the emergency, and at the breakup the temperature was normal'.[276]

Muir's negotiating skills were not confined to schools business; even on the matter of the tariff to be charged for the four-day return journey overland from Prieska to Kenhardt by horse and cart, Muir weighed in to put pressure on the contractor, Messler, to reduce his charge: 'Had him in and in the presence of the others talked to him in business fashion; when he left he was subdued and moderate.'[277]

This long journey to Kenhardt, and back, involved changes of horsemen and fresh horses along the way. It was a particularly arduous trip to undertake. His objective was to resolve school trouble by holding a single, plain-spoken meeting with the school board. As soon as he arrived at his destination, the board members gathered at the local hotel. Muir quickly identified the member of the school board at the bottom of the trouble: 'The time occupied was 2 ½ hours and the conclusion arrived at was what I sought, viz., resume office and trust to me to do what I had originally intended. How much better the outcome would have been had they not listened to the excitable Irishman! and the said man almost owned as much'.[278] For Muir, the effort of four days on the road had been entirely worthwhile, as he had successfully imposed his viewpoint on this local School Board.

Even on a full day's railway journey, Muir was able totally to absorb himself in his work, but then relax in the evening. On one such day he commented:[279] 'I at once settled down to a long day of reading and work, scarcely ever looking up at the surrounding country as it sizzled in the blue'; however, the evening found the party out on the stoep of the coach 'with the books laid away'.

The school building programme in the Cape: 'Dr. Muir's Palaces'

The scheme

The school building scheme was one of Muir's key educational reforms, enabling schools to raise capital by redeemable loan. When Mr. Merriman, the Cape Colony's prime minister, visited Victoria West in April 1910, to lay the foundation stone of the new Public School, he emphasised the advances that had been made in education: despite two years of depression, money had continued to be spent in erecting school buildings, and the Colony was 'pretty nearly in the position that America was in when it was said that when one went into any village the best and handsomest building that one saw was the village school'.[280] In Muir's scrapbook of newspaper cuttings, the report of this speech is carefully headed in his own handwriting: 'one of Dr. Muir's Palaces'; evidently, he considered that Merriman's praise was a just riposte to the journalist who had coined this mocking phrase, criticising the level of spending on first-class school buildings in the Cape.

The scheme certainly improved the number, and standard, of school buildings erected across the Cape Colony; it enabled the system to cope with the increasing numbers of enrolled pupils following the introduction of compulsory schooling post-1905. However, the scheme could also be seen as 'elitist': it was characterised by bureaucratic obstacle, and this red tape disadvantaged the poorer and less educated communities, while those that were educated and had money could erect substantial school buildings. Those that did not (such as those along the West Coast), had to make do with portable wood-and-iron shacks.[281] Many of the buildings that resulted were 'the splendid series of High School and First-Class Public School buildings', the 'impressive memorial of Muir's tenure of office'.[282] Of the 120 new schools, or buildings, opened in the period 1900 to mid-1915, the vast majority were schools serving better-off white pupils, and this account reflects this bias.[283]

Fig. 26: Crowd gathered outside Mowbray Public School at the opening by Dr. Thomas Muir in 1906 (Muir is centre front, hat in hand). Western Cape Archives, AG 15400.

In September 1902, the *Education Gazette* announced that the S.G.E. felt that 'it would be well if school managers and teachers throughout the Colony were made aware of the excellence of some of the new school buildings which are being erected'; a photograph of any new school building would be a frequent feature in the *Gazette*, with the object of bestirring other districts to 'secure in the near future buildings of a more creditable description' to replace the historic low quality of those that existed.[284] It is this record, advertising Muir's school building programme over the period to his retirement in mid-1915, which provides a window into this, his most enduring educational legacy. Ninety of the new schools or buildings listed in the pages of the *Education Gazette* up to Muir's retirement in 1915, were opened, or had foundation stones laid, by Muir himself. In 1942 Daleboudt commented: 'The great majority of school buildings to be seen throughout the Cape Colony date from this period.'[285]

Quite apart from all his other duties, Muir had a busy time attending openings or laying foundation stones for new school buildings. The task of laying foundation stones was one often commandeered by senior politicians who were keen to ride on the coattails of the successful S.G.E.. Muir did lay some foundation stones, but generally he preferred to turn out for the official opening.[286] These events provided him with an opportunity to make a stirring speech to the assembled populace and to drum up support for his educational objectives and policies. His grandson, Claude Cornish-Bowden, remembered 'as a youngster all the glass cabinets in his living rooms in which were displayed ceremonial silver trowels, keys and mallets commemorating the opening of so many schools throughout the country'.[287] Muir himself reminisced fondly in his retirement of this 'collection of gold and silver keys'.[288]

Fig. 27: Muir High School, Uitenhage, 1904. Collection: Sigi Howes

Celebrated school building architects

William White-Cooper

First, we turn to Muir's namesake school in Uitenhage, Muir College, one of the oldest English-speaking high schools in South Africa, tracing its origins back to 1822.[289] Muir opened the new school building in Park Avenue on 12 April 1904.[290] It was designed and built in warm red Grahamstown brick by architect William White-Cooper (1882–1935) of Grahamstown.

White-Cooper had made his name as a church architect, but subsequently also specialised in school architecture. His stock in trade was Flemish Renaissance-influenced detail and the use of 'red brick relieved at intervals by white bands of brickwork'.[291] Another distinctive feature of these school buildings was White-Cooper's extensive use of gables to articulate their architecture.[292]

Parker and Forsyth

Another architectural practice active in school building design in the Cape was Parker and Forsyth.[293] This firm covered all manner of architectural projects, commercial and residential, but was also responsible for the design of a number of Cape Town schools, including the West End Public School (1910), Prestwich Street, Green Point and the East End Public School (1912), Chapel Street.[294] Sigi Howes describes the common features of the design of the two buildings:

> English-style red brickwork, with white cement bands, Victorian central teak ventilating turret and air vents, pressed lead ceilings, glazed brick stairwells, separate entrances and playgrounds for boys and girls, separate staffrooms for male and female and kindergarten section of four rooms. Instead of a hall, the kindergarten classrooms had wooden folding partitions with glass panes between every two rooms that allowed their conversion to two larger assembly venues.[295]

Fig. 28: Prestwich Street Primary School, 2011 (original building of West End Public School, Prestwich Street, 1911). Photograph: Sigi Howes.

Muir's own account of some school openings

Muir wrote his own diarised account of a few opening ceremonies between 1909 and 1911. These diary entries conjure up the atmosphere of a scattering of different occasions in disparate parts of the country.

Mossel Bay Boys' High School, 1910

During his tour of the Eastern Cape interior in early 1910, one of Muir's commitments was to open the new school building of Mossel Bay Boys' High School. Both the Boys' and Girls' Schools in the town were paying schools, so that less privileged children were sent to the mission schools. As the town grew, so did the schools, and in 1909 a new building was constructed at The Point for the Boys' Public School; it was this building that Muir opened on 15 February 1910.

Muir's visit to Mossel Bay was the culmination of his adventurous cross-country motoring tour from Oudtshoorn with the indomitable Dr. Russell as his chauffeur. The motoring party arrived in the town on the evening before the ceremony, when Muir met those who were to be involved in the morrow's school opening: Mr. Vintcent, Chairman of the Municipal School Board; Mr. Moodie, Chairman of the Divisional Board; and Mr. McGaffin, the headmaster of the Boys' School. The next morning, the day of the opening, Muir continued the story:[296]

> Rose at seven to find the bay half obscured by a bank of sea mist. Spent a little time jotting down on an envelope a few hints of matters, to speak at the day's ceremony. At eleven o'clock the school processions started from the old building, and at 11.15 Mr. Vintcent called to drive me to the new [school]. On arriving there, we found a large concourse of people, more than had been hoped for considering the state of the drifts. After introductions on the stoep, and the

Fig. 29: Mossel Bay Boys' Public School, 1910. Collection: Sigi Howes.

formal opening of the door, the whole gathering passed through to the back quadrangle and assembled for the speech-making. Meanwhile I had examined all the rooms, and found everything satisfactory, not to say beautiful. Mr. Vintcent's remarks were quite nice and not unfluently made and Mr. Moodie's, though halting, were still more gratifying. My own talk lasted half an hour, and I was fortunate in being able to say one or two things that may sting the people who talk about economy and 'Dr. Muir's expensive palaces'. The Rev. Murray and Mr. McGaffin followed in eulogistic style, and the pleasant gathering broke up.

Muir had become so practised at the art of making the principal speech at school openings that he only needed to jot down a few hints for his address beforehand. From the pages of the *Education Gazette*, one can glean Muir's themes, only marginally altered to suit the town and the setting: congratulations on the fine school buildings secured for the community; tributes to the energy of all those involved; encouragement of higher school attendance; and the desirability of adopting compulsory schooling.[297]

Butterworth and Komgha Public Schools, 1911

During his tour to Butterworth in the east and Kenhardt in the north-west in late 1911, Muir opened buildings at both Butterworth and Komgha Public Schools.

Muir told of his journey by train to Butterworth in anticipation of his rendezvous to open the new school building there on Monday 9 October 1911:[298] On reaching Butterworth Station, Muir was met by local worthies, including Mr. Blanck, the mayor and Mr. Gerrie, the headmaster. He had a moment to make 'a few notes as heads of [his] proposed speech'; then he was escorted to the school where the 'function was quite successful, including the distribution of sports prizes and the trial of being photographed'. Much more importantly, he enjoyed a pleasant dinner with the circuit judge that evening as the circuit court was then in session in the town.

Fig. 30: Komgha Public School, 1911. Architectural drawing, Herbert J.C. Cordeaux F.R.I.B.A. Collection: Sigi Howes.

The following day he attended a School Board meeting in Komgha (now known as Komga):[299] The new school building had been designed by East London architect, Herbert Cordeaux (1866–1923).[300]

The school building opening was a relatively subdued occasion.[301] Mr. Swan, Chairman of the School Board, and Mr. Williamson, the headmaster, led Muir on a conducted tour of the new building. That evening Muir dined with members of the School Board at the local hotel and remarked: 'dinner dragged along until my reply-speech, when the ice thawed'. Muir, never modest, had an infinite belief in the positive effect of his own speech-making. When Muir proposed the health of the Chairman, he again noted that he enlivened the proceedings by 'working in some fun about the auditors'. This provoked two replies, and a speech of thanks by Mr. Campbell (Secretary of the Board), whose Scottish reminiscences proved 'uproariously amusing'; 'by the time it was over we were a roomful of brothers. "God save the King" was sung heartily, and "Auld Lang Syne" with clasped hands!'

Worcester Girls' High School 1912

Muir opened Worcester Girls' High School on 6 March 1912; he woke early that day in his railway carriage to find that there was promise of a delightful day. Members of the School Board arrived and all the while he was feeling that he ought to be thinking of his opening speech:[302]

> When 11 o'clock struck a procession was formed headed by the Predikant De Villiers and the S.G.E., *arcades ambo*, and uncoiled itself in the direction of the new building.[303] There we found the adult public of the town already assembled, and they and we were rewarded for braving the open sun by seeing the school girls approach in two bands from different directions and take up their prearranged positions with just enough military precision to enhance the charm of their white dresses and bright faces. Their numbers were surprising for a town of the size, and it was indeed a charming sight. When all was in place the Predikant 'took speech in hand': Dutch speech followed by English; his processional partner formally declared the building open; and the large crowd rolled in.

Fig. 31: Worcester Girls' High School, 1912. Collection: Sigi Howes.

Tiger Kloof Educational Institution, 1912

A contrasting occasion was Muir's visit to the Tiger Kloof Educational Institution on 11 and 12 March 1912, to open the new industrial building.

The Tiger Kloof Institution had been founded in March 1904 'on a piece of bare veld' just south of Vryburg, when the Rev. W.C. Willoughby unpacked a borrowed wagon and started to build a school.[304] The main railway line to Mafeking and beyond (termed the Cape to Cairo line) passed the very door of the institution, and a railway siding had been provided at the gate of the site. From its inception, the institution had committed itself to both academic and technical training. Since Tiger Kloof taught all the disciplines of building work, its own apprentices had been able to accomplish the entire construction of the new school block.[305] By 1912 the Rev. W.R. McGee was the headmaster, and he was assisted by other missionaries, including the Rev. G.C.H. Reed, and these were two of Muir's hosts during his visit.

Muir recounts his arrival by train on the afternoon before the day of the ceremony:[306]

> On approaching Tigerkloof we saw all the students and their teachers drawn up in front of the railway shelter, and when the coach was left behind in the siding, three parsons advanced towards it. These turned out to be the Rev. Reed, the Rev. Cullen, and the more or less reverend McGee. With them we walked back towards the Halt, and were introduced to the various white teachers and trade instructors severally, and to the native teachers collectively. Then the students, having given a military salute and been marched off to their quarters, we and the other Europeans walked leisurely towards the Institution.

The Rev. Reed then led the visiting party on a stroll around the place to get an idea of what it was composed. Reed showed them 'the school proper, the dining hall, the workshops,

Fig. 32: Tiger Kloof Industrial Mission School, The New Block, 1912. Collection: Sigi Howes.

the teachers' quarters, the row of Bible readers' houses, the garden, the quarries, the rock water-tanks' and finally the party emerged out of the grounds not far from Muir's railway coach. In the evening Muir's party had supper with the missionaries, during which Muir found one of their number, Rev. Reed, the most interesting as he 'knew Edinburgh well': he was a 'sturdy old Scotsman in black clothes and heavy ploughman's boots'. A shared Scottish background always offered Muir the possibility of creating a bond.

As was his custom, the next morning Muir awoke early and read for a while in bed:[307] 'A little before 7 there came from the direction of the Institution the sound of hymn-singing and we were reminded of our surroundings. Set off at 10.30 to see all the Institution's classes at work with their teachers.' There followed lunch with all the students and staff:

> In the body of the large hall the students were arranged across the breadth as if at church service, while on a raised platform at the end was the table for Europeans. The meal was obviously a light one for the students, as it did not last as long as ours. Our waiters were the native teachers in training, the office being considered an honour.

A little later in the afternoon, the train arrived from Vryburg 'as visitors were expected thence to grace the function':[308]

> A bugle soon sounded to show that all was ready, and the chosen there assembled, marched in pairs to seats opposite the main entrance of the school, having in their front the students, 160 in number, in uniform; on their right and left the teachers and friends of the Institution: and more trying than all, at their backs the burning sun. A hymn was first sung, with the bugle to lead. The principal then welcomed the S.G.E. and spoke of the history of the place. The S.G.E. on being thus introduced gave the history from his point of view, and thereafter improved the occasion, and finally declared the building open.

The close was marked by the bugle leading off with 'God Save the King', which was robustly sung.

Muir captures the hierarchical nature of this occasion, and the racial divisions in the dining room. Muir's view of mission education was jaundiced, and it is not surprising to read that the 'history of the place', from his point of view, was different from that of the Rev. McGee. We can expect that the Principal would have talked of the lofty ideals of the school's founder, the Rev. Willoughby, only recently retired. We can conjecture he would have given a stirring account of the 'eight years of strenuous labour' since the school's foundation, during which they had built a multi-department school on a site that had simply been 'unfenced wilderness', a miracle of sorts.[309] We cannot conjure up the content of Muir's delicate riposte as readily, as he was no enthusiast of missionary education at all.

Muir-era school buildings today

Many of the school buildings opened during Muir's time remain in use as schools.[310] One of the best known is the building built for Rondebosch Boys' High School and opened in 1905. The building was originally a single storey, but had an additional storey added at a later stage, featuring the distinctive central bay window, topped with a clock. The building has become the Preparatory School and is one of 27 school buildings in greater Cape Town holding a blue heritage plaque.

Mossel Bay Boys' High School (opened by Muir in 1910) is now a primary school, the high school having moved to another site.[311] Butterworth Public School and Komgha Public School (opened by Muir on consecutive days in October 1911) both continue as schools, the former as the high school and the latter as the junior school.[312] Some schools were caught up in the maelstrom of apartheid. Both the West End Public School (1910) and East End Public School (1912) were originally white schools but the West End Public School became a coloured school in 1935 and changed its name to Prestwich Street Primary. Likewise,

Fig. 33: Rondebosch Boys' High School, 1905 (now Rondebosch Preparatory School). Collection: Sigi Howes.

in 1938 the school in Chapel Street (known for a while as East Park Public School) was declared a coloured school, reflecting the demographics of that part of Woodstock, and changed its name to Chapel Street Primary.

Several of the buildings constructed under the Muir-era building scheme have now been converted to alternative educational uses.[313] The Muir College building (opened by Muir in 1904) is now part of the East Cape Midlands College (Park Avenue Campus) and Muir College itself has moved to a new modern site. Other buildings have transitioned to alternative public uses.[314] Worcester Girls' High School (opened by Muir in 1912) has since been converted into a double-storey building, and is now the Hugo Naudé Art Centre, teaching all manner of the arts.

Other Muir-era buildings have disappeared completely, destroyed by fire or demolished to make way for new contemporary buildings.[315] Fine new buildings (designed by Parker and Forsyth) were constructed for both East London Girls' and East London Boys' Public Schools in 1903 and 1906, respectively, and a new Assembly Hall for both in 1908. The schools themselves are now the separate institutions, Clarendon Girls' High School and Selborne College. The original buildings have since been demolished, and the Laerskool Grens is now on the site of the old buildings; the address of the school, Muir Street, Arcadia, retains the only vestige of the connection.

One school constructed during the Muir era, that has now disappeared entirely, deserves a special mention, as it forms part of the story of apartheid within Cape Town itself. Protea Village School, Claremont, was one of the very few mission schools constructed within the building scheme during Muir's era. It was an Anglican mission school, and the new building was opened by the Archbishop of Cape Town in 1911. However, the school's origins went back to the time of an earlier archbishop, Robert Gray, whose wife, Sophie, had established a night school on the estate of the episcopal residence at Protea (Boschheuvel). In the early 1950s, the Group Areas Act restricted the freedom of the different races to

Fig. 34: Pupil in front of Protea Village School, 1930s. Collection: Martin Plaut.

live together and one of the early casualties in Cape Town was the community of Protea Village, predominantly coloured. In January 1952, the school building was demolished, just before the community was forcibly removed to townships on the Cape Flats.[316]

In contrast, Tiger Kloof, where Muir opened the new school block in 1912, has risen like a phoenix from the ashes of apartheid. The post-Union history of the school is a microcosm of those segregationist and turbulent times. In 1914, the institution expanded to become a centre for elementary, higher and specialised education, with a teachers' training college, a Bible school for the training of ministers, and an industrial school. Thus, Tiger Kloof was one of the few black educational institutions that managed to make real headway in secondary education during Muir's time. It continued in operation during the first half of the 20th century, and, indeed, was known as the school at which the first two presidents, and other senior leaders, of Botswana were educated.

Early in 1956 the London Missionary Society withdrew from Tiger Kloof, in protest against the Bantu Education legislation of the apartheid era. While the school continued to function under the auspices of the South African government, resistance increased at the school; several of its buildings were burnt down. The school was eventually closed in 1963, when the area was declared a 'black spot' under the Group Areas Act and was demarcated for white occupation. After South Africa's democratic elections in 1994, the school's supporters took steps to reopen Tiger Kloof. Part of the property was reacquired, the buildings were renovated, and the institution was reopened in 1995. The school recovered the remainder of the Tiger Kloof property through the land restitution process in 2004. The institution has continued to restore the buildings and the school now forms part of the Historic Schools Restoration project. Today there are 800 scholars in both the primary and secondary schools.[317]

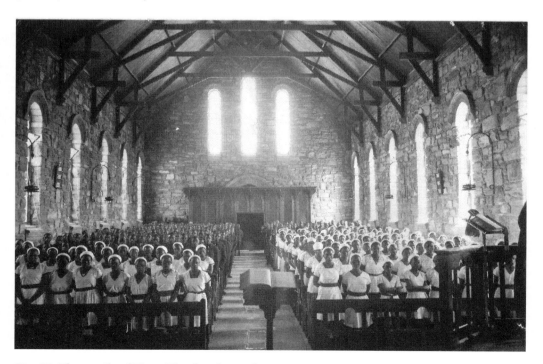

Fig. 35: The pupils of Tiger Kloof in the Arthington Memorial Church. Collection: Tiger Kloof Educational Institution.

RESEARCH AND MATHEMATICS

Any fervent mathematician who reads the *Muir Tour Diaries* may recognise a kindred spirit in Muir: this was a man who woke early and would reach from his bed for the mathematics volume on which he was currently absorbed, as a preparation for the hectic activities of his day. He would also do this during any break in the tempo of his daily schedule, or last thing at night. For Muir, mathematics was not only a research obsession, it also was a diversion from the stresses of his duties. He indulged in his mathematics and used it to refresh his mind.

Muir carried out some of his mathematics work under the most extraordinary conditions during his tours of the arid Cape interior. On one unpleasantly hot afternoon, he returned to his railway coach after lunch and felt that a siesta was then excusable:

> By 3 o'clock the thermometer had risen to 104°, and sleep became impossible, I consequently got up and went into the writing-room, and, in order to divert my attention from the heat, doggedly sat down to copy out the mathematical article on which I had been spending odd moments since leaving home. By 6 o'clock the task was finished, a properly sized envelope made to hold it, and the address written. I question whether Metcalfe and Co. of Cambridge have had many manuscripts copied under such circumstances.[318]

This is not the place to evaluate Muir's contribution to mathematics. Pieter Maritz has already described Muir's mathematics work admirably, listing all of his 321 mathematical papers.[319] However, as mathematics was central to Muir's life, and he continues to be recognised for his monumental work, an attempt will be made to provide a layperson's commentary on his mathematics (based on the observations of other mathematicians, who had, or have, the expertise to provide insight).

The *Dictionary of National Biography, Thomas Muir 2004* summarises Muir's contribution as follows:

> Muir's mathematical reputation rests on his work on determinants (a numerical value obtained from an array of numbers). Between 1875 and 1880 he conceived the ambitious project of writing a history of determinants. His first bibliography (forty pages) of writings on determinants appeared in *Quarterly Mathematical Journal* of 1881, and a second in 1886. He published his first book, *Treatise on the Theory of Determinants,* in 1882, and his second in 1890. During the Second South African War (1899–1902) he found determinants offered a welcome distraction from the worries of war and he temporarily revived his previous studies. The 1890 book was the precursor for the volumes which will always be associated with his name, the monumental *History of the Theory of Determinants* in five volumes, published in 1906–29 (the final volume when he was eighty-six). A projected sixth volume was never finished. The complete work encompasses a catalogue with commentaries of all the known papers on determinants from Leibniz's work in the seventeenth century until 1920. Muir's commentaries varied in length from eighty-four pages devoted to Cauchy's classic paper of 1812 to a few lines for slight contributions. The subject material emphasizes the importance of determinants in nineteenth-century mathematics in contrast to the more

fundamental subject of matrices, which only developed from a halting start in the 1850s. Muir's work was of great assistance to those who wished to consult the papers of important mathematicians of the eighteenth and nineteenth centuries.

This commentary touches briefly on the distinction between Muir's subject, the determinant, and that of the matrix, a convenient book-keeping device; the matrix was formalised prior to Muir's work but only brought to prominence a little later. Matrices did not replace determinants, but they provided a more concise way to express the ideas in Muir's volumes.

The material Muir had to describe and assess for the early volumes was particularly onerous as, pre-1841, writers indulged their own notational idiosyncrasies. His labour was described by a fellow mathematician as 'almost intolerably tedious' and he brought to the task 'a dour Scottish thoroughness and a determination to see justice done'; he took 'unbounded pains' to classify and analyse each paper on determinants in a balanced manner.[320] Over a period of 42 years, Muir laboured at this monumental task, combining it with his education work until his retirement in 1915, and thereafter he devoted the entirety of his time to his research and writing. By any standards it was a colossal piece of intellectual work. A.C. Aitken could not resist measuring the 3,160 volumes of mathematical memoirs (some short, others long) Muir had to analyse to complete his five volumes. He called this the 'curve of growth' of Muir's labours, and remarked on the 'mounting growth of the task undertaken, and the strength of will that could carry it through to a conclusion'.[321]

Muir's work was interrupted for some years when he first went out to the Cape, a period during which his new undertaking was so absorbing that for a time his 'research work had to go to the wall'.[322] However, he resumed his research when the official worries of war time (the Anglo-Boer War, 1899–1902) made such mental-relief work a necessity. Muir observed, however, that progress was very slow, 'reference libraries, for one thing, being 6,000 miles away'.[323] His work continued in the face of all obstacles, not least of which was the dislocation caused by the First World War. He remedied the handicap of remoteness from adequate libraries of reference by building up his own remarkable library of mathematical books and periodicals. In a letter he wrote in 1921 to his mathematical protégé, Professor Lawrence Crawford (a fellow-Glaswegian whom Muir had taught at the University of Glasgow), he commented: 'The collection of books and papers on Determinants will be the most complete in the world, and the collection of serials the largest south of the equator.'[324]

Until the end of his life, he continued to pursue his work as if he fully expected to enjoy immortality. He published *Contributions to the History of Determinants* in 1930, at the age of 86, and would have needed to live to over 100 years to have completed the final sixth volume of his grand treatise.

Professor H.W. Turnbull, Regius Professor of Mathematics at the University of St. Andrews, who also wrote on the theory of determinants, set the tone of adulation in an article he published in 1935 (and many of the contemporary accounts of Muir's life drew on his account). He said of Muir's work:

> For prolonged singleness of purpose amid official duties Muir's five-volume *History of Determinants* is a monument unparalleled in the scientific world. It is a classic: if there exists anywhere a more detailed and comprehensive history of any branch of theoretical knowledge one would be interested to hear of it.[325]

The Royal Society of Edinburgh, on awarding Muir the Keith Medal for the second time in 1899, similarly referred to his monograph as a 'monument of learning and mathematical acumen': 'it cannot fail to remain a permanent chapter in the history of mathematics'.[326]

However, a reviewer of the first two volumes of his *Theory of Determinants* (Muir 1906–23) was more measured in his response, although welcoming them as important additions to the literature on the subject.[327]

As early as 1931, there are hints that the theory of determinants might already have been overtaken by advances in mathematical thinking. E.T. Bell was a Scottish-born mathematician who wrote much later an anecdotal history of mathematics, *Men of Mathematics*. He produced a lively review of Muir's *Contributions to the History of Determinants* (Muir 1930) and ventured that the abstract part of the theory could 'be stated in a couple of pages; the rest is mere repetition and variation, endlessly, on a theme which is neither intricate nor subtle'.[328] Bell's view was that the theory had been 'buried' and had 'petered out': 'determinants are a comparatively trivial incident in the vaster and simpler theory of tensor algebra'.[329] Bell, nevertheless, praised the human touch which 'heightened' Muir's writing, a 'dry joke' or a 'warm appreciation', and described Muir's notation of determinants as a 'thing of beauty to those who can appreciate that sort of beauty'.[330] Mathematicians did write effusively on the subject of determinants: in a review of *Muir 1890*, the reviewer, almost certainly P.A. MacMahon who used determinants extensively in combinatorics, wrote that the theory of determinants was 'one of the most artistic subdivisions of mathematical science, and accordingly has never wanted enthusiastic admirers'.[331]

The more sober judgement of E.T. Bell may be nearer the mark as to the legacy of Muir's work; his viewpoint, whilst by no means the last word on the subject, is echoed in a much more recent work on *Linear Algebra*. David Poole, a mathematics teacher at Trent University, refers to Muir's monumental five-volume work on determinants:

> While their history is fascinating, today determinants are of theoretical more than practical interest. Cramer's Rule is a hopelessly inefficient method for solving a system of linear equations, and numerical methods have replaced any use of determinants in the computation of eigenvalues. Determinants are used, however, to give students an initial understanding of the characteristic polynomial.[332]

A.J. Crilly, the historian of mathematics who wrote the biography entry on Muir quoted at the outset, regards Poole's statement as a 'balanced viewpoint'. According to Crilly, determinants provided an elegant solution of linear equations; however, 'the number of calculations required for a large determinant makes it a very inefficient way of getting solutions', and this is the reason why, by the 1930s, pure mathematics had moved on and those who wished to solve equations had other methods.[333]

Since Muir's time there has been a relative dearth of literature on determinants. However, there are two articles by different authors, written on either side of the 2000 millennium, which reconsider the role of determinants in linear algebra from contrasting viewpoints. Sheldon Axler, currently Professor of Mathematics at San Francisco State University, wrote in 1995 in favour of banishing determinants 'from much of the theoretical part of linear algebra'. 'Determinants are needed in one place in the undergraduate's mathematics curriculum: the change of variables formula for multi-variable integrals.'[334]

Garry Tee, now an honorary academic at the University of Auckland, countered Axler's view somewhat, but relegated the theory to 'high-school' and 'undergraduate mathematics'; nevertheless, it needed to be 'kept as a small part of linear algebra'.[335] Darij Grinberg, an assistant professor at Drexel University, takes a moderating view:

> Determinants used to be treated as a panacea, for lack of other tools of comparable strength; but now that the rest of linear algebra has caught up, they have retreated to the grounds where they belong, which is still a wide swath of

the mathematical landscape (many parts of abstract algebra and algebraic combinatorics have determinants written into their DNA, rather than using them as a tool; they are not very likely to shed them off).[336]

Peter Gibbard, a great-great grandson of Muir and a lecturer in Behavioural Economics at the University of Otago, adds the following thoughts:

> The determinant is still a key concept in linear algebra, and is actively used in high school and in undergraduate mathematics courses. At high school, determinants are primarily used to solve systems of linear equations; high school students are taught the Cramer rule to calculate a solution. For an undergraduate, however, in a first course in linear algebra, perhaps the most important use of the determinant is to calculate eigenvalues and eigenvectors, as well as to obtain areas and volumes. At this level, the 'Cramer rule' is generally not emphasized, as there are more straightforward and efficient methods for solving systems of linear equations.[337]

Jennifer Morse, a great-great-granddaughter of Muir and Professor of Mathematics at the University of Virginia, also adds:

> It is difficult to emphasize properly to the non-expert just how important and beautiful determinants are in contemporary areas of mathematics and physics, in which the determinant is widely used. It is used as the very definition of fundamental objects in research, and the properties of determinants, collected in Muir's volumes, provide essential tools for extracting key information about them.[338]

Matrices were formalised by Arthur Cayley (1821–1895) but remained little known until Werner Heisenberg (1901–1976) 'reinvented' matrices in 1925 for quantum physics: 'Most of the work on determinants which was surveyed by Muir makes more sense in terms of matrices than in terms of determinants.'[339] In 1931, a friend of Muir's in Scotland brought to his notice certain results on the theory of matrices: Muir wrote that he 'welcomed the light matrix proofs in contrast to the heavy-footed method of 35 years ago'.[340] Turnbull saw this as indicative of Muir's extraordinary flexibility of mind, but equally it could have evidenced a resigned recognition on Muir's part that determinants were being side-lined in favour of matrices. Perhaps, had he not been working so far from the epicentre of discourse on algebra, he might have come to this realisation earlier.

Evidently, concepts have changed over time, and contemporary mathematicians are no longer particularly interested in determinants and certainly would no longer contemplate doing research on them. Given the obvious change that has occurred in mathematical concepts, how then do we view the intellectual work of Muir, pursued over half his lifetime? Muir's books were neither textbooks nor were they works of original research. He wrote a history of a concept of mathematics, the work of a historian of science rather than a mathematician. Why did he choose to devote himself single-mindedly to this particular concept? 'Perhaps he saw the determinant as the key tool for most/all problems of linear algebra, rather than, as it has turned out, just one chapter in a linear algebra textbook.'[341] His work was hugely respected and honoured in his time and he derived enormous personal pleasure from it. Who would deny a hard-pressed education administrator the welcome diversion into mathematics, which relieved him of the strain of his official tasks? One can conclude that for Muir, as for his 1892 reviewer, MacMahon, the 'trick' of this great analytical implement continued to excite his imagination; he was continually enchanted by the 'power and beauty of the notation', an exquisite example of 'constructive art', which he chose to unfold to 'his intellectual eye' over such a considerable part of his life.[342]

LEISURE AND PHILANTHROPY

In Cape Town, Muir was actively engaged in the musical world. He was Chairman of the Chamber Music Union of Cape Town and Vice-President of the Cape Town Musical Society and he devoted himself energetically to their interests. Under his leadership of the Cape Town Musical Society, it assembled an orchestra for a 'Grand Choral Festival' both in 1907 and 1908, and these events were a great success and drew capacity audiences. Looking at the programmes of both festivals, one can detect Muir's influence. Included were ballad concerts consisting of opera arias and songs by different composers, his favourite musical genre; it was also Muir who was responsible for calling the special meeting in 1912 which gave birth to the Municipal Orchestra in Cape Town.[343]

Quite apart from his public activity furthering the performance of music in Cape Town, Muir also delighted in informal musical evenings. The *Diaries* recount tales of such occasions, often in humble surroundings and company, in which music and song combined. In Oudtshoorn, he spent an evening with Mrs. Reed, the teacher at the station school who provided a good musical entertainment: 'a railway official hailing from Lincoln, where he had been a choir boy, supplied music-hall songs with wasted ability when he could sing 'The Holy City' like a full grown cherub.'[344] In George, quite unannounced one evening, he tracked down Mrs. Meyer of the Girls' School, to 'run the chances of hearing some music':[345] Miss Hamilton, one of the local teachers, and Ida, the niece of Mrs. Meyer, performed an impromptu concert in the latter's private drawing room; Muir was delighted with the pieces for violin and piano they played, and by the way they exchanged instruments with such ease. Then Muir (having received a hint of Ida's talent) asked her for her songs, and Ida rendered a favourite 'with a yearning feeling not to be expected in a person of twice her years'.[346]

Muir's obliging hosts on his travels into the Cape interior, predominantly Afrikaners, obviously knew that his favourite evening entertainment was music. Often, they went to extraordinary lengths to provide the musical fare that would appeal to this eccentric Scotsman who administered their educational system. On one occasion, after the opening of the Fraserburg Public School, the community put on a musical evening, including a cockney song sung in Dutch and a performance on the bagpipes by the local agent of the Standard Bank (to amuse a party of whom only very few were from 'the old country', Scotland). As usual Muir could rely on his faithful assistant to rise to the occasion, and when the bagpiper played a stirring march on the stoep, this caused Cuthbert to 'start from his seat and follow the pipes with a martial strut that set the company into shouts every time the performers passed the open door'.[347]

Muir was also an enthusiastic singer himself, combining song with liberal quantities of alcohol. Dr. Young of Steynsburg recalled a jovial night Muir had spent in his house, when Muir and Mrs. Young had sung 'O wert thou in the cauld blast' 'with great applause and much whisky-drinking'.[348] On a visit to Cradock, Muir told of the wood fire being kindled in the parlour after dinner, the party assembled round the piano singing 'songs jovially until bedtime'.[349] However his participation went considerably beyond recreational singing: his personal scrapbook records his favourite poetry, 'Scots and other Verses, from a S.A. scrapbook, 1892–1933', filled with poems in his own beautiful handwriting.[350] In view of his interest in music, it was natural Muir would have been keen to write lyrics;

Fig. 36: 'A Highland Idyll', words by Sir Thomas Muir, music by James Rodger, sheet music (page 1). Muir and Rodger, Musical Score: National Library of South Africa.

he had the requisite knowledge of the theory of music and song structure. One piece of sheet music survives, 'A Highland Idyll', for which Muir wrote the words and James Rodger the music. The composer, James Rodger, had his roots in the Department of Education, and had made a contribution to elementary music education by writing and arranging two series of collections of songs and exercises for schools, namely the *South African Songster* (1905–1907) and the *Native Songster* (1907). Even books of songs for schools catered for a segregated music student base.[351] Muir wrote the lyrics in the Scottish dialect and his words may be more descriptive than narrative. Jennifer Statham, a violinist and soprano, comments that 'the music [feels] slightly more emotionally charged than the lyrics'; nevertheless, the combination presents a 'lovely melody and song'.[352]

Muir gave one further account of a memorable evening centred on music in Kimberley. It was a supper at the home of the local Member of the Legislative Assembly, Haarhoff.[353] During 'the after-supper smoke, a wondrous gramophone was turned on, and [they] listened with delight and amazement to Caruso, Melba, Clara Butt, Tettrazinni and others'.[354] Listening to recorded music on a superior gramophone was still a novel experience, and Muir confessed that he would be 'compelled to buy one of the originally hated instruments'.[355]

Muir had broad literary interests, and sprinkled his diaries with literary allusion, not always accurate, but mostly amusing. His love of books developed at an early age, and he amassed a large library until the more general literature had to give way to his mathematical collection, for reasons of lack of space, particularly in his Rondebosch home. Herbert Turnbull, both mathematician and friend, spoke of Muir's 'refined appreciation of poetry', and singled out his apparent love of the writings of Pauline Smith, the novelist who wrote about the Little Karoo but spent most of her life in England.[356] This rather depicted Muir as the academic, only interested in high literature. It may be that he was drawn to the writings of this author as she did record her impressions of the countryside and people of the Cape interior, which Muir knew well from his travels. However, Turnbull's comment ignores Muir's catholic taste in prose and verse (evidenced in the *Diaries*). Quite apart from his enjoyment of after-dinner poetry and prose readings, Muir also enjoyed the socio-comical essays of Oliver Wendell Holmes. He was a voracious reader and could become readily absorbed in any book that came to hand, be it a biography, a scientific tome or a novel, recent or classic. When he ran out of his own literature, brought with him for the train journey, he was just as happy to pick up a Walter Scott or a Charlotte Brontë novel. For his choices of books, he drew on fortnightly literary reviews and the *Times Literary Supplement*, and ordered a wide range of recently published books direct from England. He would read the scientific journal *Nature* and the weekly London *Times* in bed before going to sleep.[357]

In his Glasgow days, when the Muirs first acquired the house in Erskine, and also in Bothwell, Muir ensured the family enjoyed a large garden. He maintained this passion for gardening in the Cape, and the house which he built in Rondebosch after his retirement not only had a magnificent garden, but also a tree plantation. He was not simply a leisure gardener but was also a close observer of nature. He had a broad knowledge of plants and trees, and enjoyed identifying those he encountered in the Karoo be they verbena, mimosa, thorn trees, pepper trees or other. There are several instances of his fascination with the natural world in the *Diaries*. He observed the swallows nesting; he took pleasure in the abundance of flowers in the Karoo, and the wattle trees when they were in blossom. Occasionally, he would come to a halt on one of his solitary walks and observe nature at work. At Naauwpoort he remarked: 'Took a short walk up the hill behind the workmen's cottages, and

Fig. 37: Dr Muir: Gives practical encouragement to a famous movement. Boonzaier 1912, p. 44. Collection: Peter Elliott.

was lucky enough to discover a curious larva that encloses itself in a collection of spikes like a hedgehog. This I managed to convey to the coach in a paper bag, where we fed it with a bit of potato and caged it in a match box.'[358] Who else, other than Muir, would have diverted attention, on a visit to the experimental plots at Lovedale, to have the pods on one soybean bush counted; there were 'close … on 300'![359]

On another occasion he took an early morning walk along the railway from Naauwpoort towards Norval's Pont, and watched dung beetles hard at work:

> In one case the spouse was crunched on the ball and was being trundled along by the vigorous head of the household. She received many bad bumps, but never budged. If a more than common accident happened, the worker hurried up to her to ascertain if all were right, and then took to work again with renewed vigour. In another case there were two fighting for the crown. At the close of the second round, the defeated beetle first thought of trying a third, but changing his mind took to the air with a revengeful hum, trying to make believe that he would live to fight another day.[360]

One of Muir's philanthropic interests reveals an additional side to his beliefs. D.C. Boonzaier, a well-known and talented Cape cartoonist, depicted Muir in a caricature in 1913. He showed Muir in the uniform of a youth movement leader, dressed in short trousers, neck scarf and long socks, stave in hand and ready for the outdoors. At first glance one might assume that this was a Scout movement reference, but not so. The Boy Scout movement was a relative newcomer to Cape Town in that year; it was the Boys' Brigade, which was already well established in the city. This was a movement with which Muir would have been familiar before his arrival in the Cape, as it had been founded in the West End of Glasgow in 1883. It, too, promoted scouting activities and, indeed, Baden-Powell, whom Muir knew personally, first promoted the idea of scouting and outdoor activities within the Boys' Brigade and later formed the Scouts. During the period 1894–1904, Muir became a member or patron of the Boys' Brigade; he was an early Brigade Battalion Office bearer and its Vice-President.[361] The Brigade's objective, formulated by its Scottish founder, was the cultivation of 'respectability', emphasising the 'habit of Obedience, Reverence, Discipline, Self-Respect and all that tends towards a true Christian Manliness'.[362] Members of the administrative elite of Cape Town, such as Muir, saw the Brigade as a useful philanthropic cause to promote religious and moral values within the poorer communities, and the movement bore a strong Scottish evangelical flavour. Muir would have been rather less interested in the religious fervour of the organisation, and rather more enthusiastic about the ethical and disciplinary training.

THOMAS MUIR'S CHILDREN

To complete a history of Muir's life, we need to cover the story of his children. As someone who enjoyed overall responsibility for the education of a vast population of children in the Cape, Muir only had partial success in the upbringing of his own children. The two girls, Nellie and Cam, were compliant and followed the paths that their strict father would have wished, but both George and his brother, Thomas, rebelled in different ways, and pursued their own paths in life. Both appear to have rejected the Boys' Brigade ideals of 'obedience, reverence [and] discipline' that their father would have sought to instil in them: so much so that they were both virtually blotted out of the history of the family in the Cape. Thomas, who emigrated to Australia, maintained a closer relationship with his family than did George, and certainly visited his parents after leaving South Africa. George, however, separated from the family rather more radically.

What went wrong in these relationships with his sons, we shall never fully know or understand. There is every indication that Muir considered himself a family man, even though he may have been rather distant and remote because of the sheer amount of time he dedicated to his work, both to his formal education tasks and his mathematics research and academic associations.

In the *Diaries*, there are numerous instances of Muir's empathy with children. For instance, on a visit to Kokstad, he remarked on his early morning rude awakening in the house of his host Mr. Elliot: 'Awake early after a fairly good sleep, but not earlier than Mr. Elliot's two little sons.'[363] It amused, rather than annoyed him, that the young pair woke early and were noisy, and this was surely the reaction of a family man. He was, at least, tolerant of children.

On a visit to De Aar, Muir took delight in the visit of the 'station master Wilson and all his pretty family, the desire of the little folks being to see the wonders of the coach. Along with them also came the little son of the postmaster, who twice a day had been sent with a present of milk for "Dr. Muir's coffee": he now introduced his small sister "Maggie", who with her fine black eyes was a striking contrast to the station children. It was a pretty sight to see the six little ones piloted through our quarters.'[364] This is a busy man, who nevertheless took pleasure in allowing the children of the station master to look round his coach, a sight which must have intrigued them.

At Tiger Kloof, an unusual child caught the attention of Muir, rather than irritated him. As he and the visiting party walked towards the institution, he was met by a young white-haired girl, who introduced herself to Muir as 'Nellie McGee': 'And taking my hand [she] toddled along and chattered as if I had known her from her birth.'[365] The next day at the formal lunch, he was also amused to observe Nellie's baby sibling: 'there was deposited on the platform between two cushions the four-months baby with "Nellie McGee" ostensibly in charge, but with the mother visibly in charge of both.' ... 'I observed that after lunch baby McGee was much in demand, the men taking her little hand or chin, and the women borrowing her to hold. The explanation given of this was that she was the first and only child born in the Institution.'[366] Again, this was a man who understood the family relationships and observed closely their interactions.

Muir was more successful in his relationship with his daughters. After one of his school functions, he referred to the 'trial of being photographed', and this may explain why there is a dearth of family photographs.[367] Yet, towards the end of his life, he was visibly proud

Fig. 38: Sir Thomas Muir (centre) is pictured in mid-1933. With him are his daughter, Nellie, his elder married granddaughter, his two married Spilhaus grandsons, and three of his young great-grandchildren. Collection: Peter Elliott.

to be in the centre of a four-generation family group, including Nellie, his elder daughter, and her extended family.[368]

Nellie had married Karl ('Carlos') Spilhaus, a member of an established Cape family of German origin, who himself was a successful businessman and became South African Commissioner of Commerce in Europe, and subsequently Managing Director of Imperial Cold Storage in Cape Town during the 1920s. The story of Carlos and Nellie and their family has already been fully told.[369] Nellie herself inherited Muir's passion for education: she was a family woman but also devoted her life to education, and from 1927 to 1954 she represented Convocation on the Council of the University of Cape Town. For a quarter of a century she served on the Cape School Board and devoted much of her own time to the interests of underprivileged coloured children. She was the first woman to serve on the Cape Provincial Council and was an active member of the National Council of Women of South Africa and of the South African Institute of Race Relations: 'In all these activities she remained the educator, teaching less gifted people about things that needed reform. Indeed, to her tireless and enlightened advocacy is due much of the advance which has been made in overcoming the disabilities of women in South Africa.'[370]

Her sister Cam married Athelstan Cornish-Bowden, a government land surveyor, who became Surveyor-General of the Cape Colony in 1906. During the Second World War, Cam set up the Soldiers' Club: there she provided 'hospitality for troops of passing convoys. She turned the old post office in Adderley Street in Cape Town into a hostel, providing 600 beds and meals for the soldiers.'[371] Cam revitalised the Girl Guide movement in the Cape and became a militant and staunch champion of the coloured people in the Cape. She was an active member of the Torch Commando, the first real anti-apartheid protest movement formed to defend the Constitution and the voting rights of the coloured community. Cam was one of the chief torchbearers during the Torch Commando march to the Grand Parade in Cape Town in May 1951; she was also one of the prime instigators in the Cape of the Black Sash movement, a liberal white women's resistance organisation founded in 1955.[372]

The fate of Muir's elder son, George, remains shrouded in mystery. We know the origins of his estrangement from his father: he forged and uttered a cheque, a fraudulent misdeed for which it appears Muir never entirely forgave him.[373] This may not, however, have been an isolated incident as later he was economical with the truth of his academic record.

One crucial document provides important clues as to how George spent the years after his time at the Diocesan College. He had been awarded a University Exhibition in 1894 and, thus, he appears to have embarked propitiously on his university education. He completed his first year of university courses at the Diocesan College in 1895 and might have

Fig. 39: Nellie Spilhaus, née Muir, 1934, Independent Candidate for Rondebosch in the Cape Provincial Council elections (and victorious over the S.A. Party candidate). Collection: Peter Elliott.

been expected to have graduated in 1897. However, around this time it happened that the British Secretary of the Board of Education decided to prepare a series of reports on colonial education, including that of the Cape Colony. George, miraculously, appears in the eventual Report as a graduate, an employee of his father's Education Department and author of a substantial part of the section on the history of education of the Cape Colony.[374] George made a trip to Britain in 1897, returning to the Cape in that year, and this visit may have related to his work on the education report. The section he wrote is elegant and interesting (fully bearing out what we know of his academic potential). Enigmatically, the distinguished editor of the series records at the mid-point of the published Report that, 'Mr. Muir found himself compelled … to break off the composition of his report'. The remaining sections on the Cape had to be prepared from official materials supplied by the Colony, and they do provide thin reading compared to George's scholarly history.

By whom was George compelled to break off the composition of his report? As to the caption on his authorship, there is no evidence that he graduated with a B.A. degree from the university and this adds to the mystery surrounding George, and the impression that he lived in a fantasy world of his own.[375] It is a fair assumption that Muir, his father and 'Chief' of the Department, terminated his work following the incident of the fraudulent cheque or other misdemeanours. If so, this must have resulted in humiliation for George, as the affair must have become a matter of public knowledge, at least within the Education Department. Did a father sacrifice his errant son on the altar of principle? It seems a perfectly plausible theory, based on the man we know, and, if so, one can imagine it was a sanction quite sufficient to have destroyed George's confidence and driven him to leave the Cape. He departed for England in January 1899. This same promising young man, with the ability to have written a credible history of education in the Cape, albeit based on inaccurate academic credentials, had ceased his promising and gainful employment. George and his father may have explained his absence from the Cape as that of the 'traveller' student, but the abruptness of the cessation of his work and departure does look more akin to a banishment.

The pattern of George's life between early 1899 and 1906 is unclear. It seems that Muir 'recovered' young George from his travels after only a few months: the errant son appears to have returned with his father to the Cape in mid-1899 on the *Dunnottar Castle*, the same ship on which Muir travelled from England with Baden-Powell and his staff.[376] If George did return for a brief period to the Cape, it is unclear how he occupied himself, and it appears in any event he returned to England in mid-1903.[377] We will never know what happened during this period, but we can assume that the attempt to re-establish comity at home failed.

Whatever his movements during this period of seven years, one cannot but feel they were unhappy years in which George was seeking to regain some sense of direction. It seems probable that George crumbled under the pressures of an existence under the roof of an ambitious and driven father, who put principle before family and whose expectations may well have weighed on him too heavily at a young age. George was not a robust person, and perhaps he was also emotionally fragile, like his mother Maggie. In the *Diaries* we catch the occasional glimpse of Muir as a man who had wielded unrestrained power within his educational fiefdom for too long, and who, at times, displayed an evident lack of empathy for members of his own Department who had fallen by the wayside; perhaps this unfeeling side of Muir extended even to his own troubled son.

In England, sometime before the end of 1906, George met Ethel Devereux, a young actress on the London stage. There is a record of Ethel taking a minor role in a 'melo-farce', *The Flood Tide*, at Drury Lane in 1903 but apart from this fleeting stage presence, there is no imprint remaining of her theatrical career.[378]

George and Ethel married in early 1907 at which time he was working as a clerk. When they were wed Ethel had no occupation.[379] Four years later, he and Ethel, still unemployed, were living in Brighton. George worked for Macmillan & Co., the publishers, for seven years prior to World War I, and although described as a 'confidential clerk', his own declaration made during the war, when he applied to become an Officer Cadet, would lead us to believe this had been a responsible job. His account of his work experience is plausible, given that it was the head of that same publishing company, Sir Frederick Macmillan, who provided his 'moral character' reference on his Officer Cadet application: Sir Frederick confirmed he had known George for 10 years. Perhaps George's father helped him obtain this job, as Muir had a good relationship with the publishing company himself: it was the house that published all his major works on determinants.

It was in late 1915 that George responded to Kitchener's call for a new army, then describing his trade mysteriously as 'independent'. He served in the Army Service Corps (ASC) from November 1915 to September 1919. The ASC was responsible for keeping the army supplied from Britain, hence George spent most of the war as part of the Home Service, a much less dangerous military occupation than being in the thick of the fighting in France. The activity of the ASC was, of course, vital to the war effort but it was largely peopled by men who were not fully fit for service on the front line. If we knew why George was assigned to this service we might understand the course of his later life rather better.

At the outset George was a N.C.O. but it was in the second half of 1916 that he made his Officer Cadet application. He was released for officer training in early 1917 and his commanding officer described him as 'a man of untiring energy, possessing excellent powers of organisation. Tactful and reliable in every respect'.[380] Based on this glowing testimonial and despite his chequered past, by 1917 George appears to have developed into a son whom Muir could have embraced. However this positive impression of the man into whom George had developed is marred by a further embellished, and unsubstantiated, statement within his Officer Cadet application (written in his own hand) of his educational background.[381] It seems he gained his commission as a Lieutenant in early 1917 in part on false pretences.

George remained together with Ethel until the mid-1920s. The same one-bedroom flat in London S.W.1 is consistently recorded for one or other of them for a 24-year period between 1918 and 1942, but after 1923, it is only Ethel's address and not that of George. This long period of property stability would suggest that George owned the flat, and the only possible source of capital could have been George's father. Thus, perhaps he was at least generous financially to his outcast son.[382] The war seems to have operated as a watershed for George, and we know nothing of his experience or whether he suffered trauma or injury; however, there is little further sign of the energy and organisational skill, which had been identified by his wartime commanding officer.

A curious quirk of circumstance lifted George and Ethel momentarily out of obscurity and into the harsh light of public attention. It would appear that by 1924, George had time on his hands and was helping a friend to let a bungalow known as 'Officer's House' in Eastbourne. He managed to let the bungalow to one Patrick Mahon, who took the place under an assumed name, and produced a false reference, neither of which the Muirs detected. Regrettably, the consequence of the two-month let was disastrous: Mahon killed his pregnant lover at the bungalow, and George was required to give evidence at his trial.[383] Whether they were still living together or not, George and Ethel both cooperated to complete the letting, taking the reference and drawing up a cutlery list (including a carving knife, which proved material to the trial). One hopes that this was their last foray into the letting business for which they were ill equipped, and following this event, the pair lapsed once again back into the anonymity of their uneventful lives.

In 1925 Muir, sitting in Cape Town, altered his will to the distinct disadvantage of his elder son: he provided that George and his wife would only receive the interest, and not the capital, of his eventual inheritance.[384] The couple may well have been living on the margins until Muir died in 1934. Then, however, the other three children received an equal capital sum of approximately £2,850, but George and Ethel received only the interest on his share until George's death. The individual one-quarter share legacy of the four children represented a tidy inheritance in those days for each one, each portion being worth more than the value of the house and garden, Elmcote, in Portland Road, Rondebosch.[385] No doubt the income from 1934 onwards transformed George and Ethel's life in England, as there is no evidence that they ever worked again.

Clearly, by 1927 George was separated from his wife and living on his own in a rural cottage in Hertfordshire.[386] Just after the outbreak of the Second World War, he was still living on his own in a residential hotel in Shrewsbury, and Ethel was living separately in Dorking, both of 'private means' (and not working), possibly deriving an income from the London flat. Ethel died in 1942, leaving little or no money of her own.[387] George then remarried an interesting and discerning Yorkshire-born woman, Christine, one of three Roberts sisters, all of whom were without a man in their lives. Christine was the 'brainy' sister, and the relationship between George and Christine may well have been founded on common intellectual interests. It was her sister, Elsie, who lived in the same Yorkshire village, who added fun to their lives in High Fremington. George died only four years later at the age of 70, but in a rare photograph, Christine and George seem to have found a brief domestic happiness together (see Fig. 40).[388] George is remarkably unchanged compared to the winsome Scots youth aged 14 years, captured in the photographs made of him over 50 years earlier in the conservatory of the family home in Bothwell; the only element of formal day attire that George appears to have discarded, to meet the lesser needs of rural life in Yorkshire, is his waistcoat.

We do not know the extent to which George's family members in the Cape (or indeed Australia) kept in touch with him during his life in England. It is probable that he will have seen something of his father and mother, when Muir visited England on his education business.[389] It also seems that, throughout her life, his sister Nellie quietly maintained the contact, even though she never mentioned George.[390] One would like to think so.

Passing on to George's brother, Thomas, it seems that before he left the Cape he completed a degree at the South African College; he was a mediocre student but one who stayed the course.[391] Thomas's story is then is taken up by his granddaughter.[392] He was 'banished' from South Africa by his father, following a relationship across the forbidden colour line, possibly with a member of staff at 'the Hall'. Muir's grandson, Athelstan, said of his grandfather: he 'was rigid about many facets of life, particularly about the philandering of his youngest son, Thomas'.[393] Thomas did not only 'philander' in Cape Town. Following a brief and unsuccessful first match he demonstrated an insouciant disregard for the institution of marriage until much later in life. Thomas arrived in Australia some time between 1904 and 1908 and must have started work as an itinerant sheep shearer, but he was swift to become a station overseer on Wellshot Outstation, a sheep farm in the district of Ilfracombe, Queensland. For many years Wellshot was Australia's largest sheep station, measured by the number of sheep on the property; in 1898 there were almost 380,000 sheep on the farm. Between 1898 and 1901, there was a dramatic reduction in the flock number due to severe drought; nevertheless, by 1904 Wellshot had recovered

Fig. 40: Christine and George Muir in the garden, probably at Hobsons, High Fremington, Richmond, Yorkshire, at some time during the period 1943–1947. Left to right: Christine Muir, George Muir (with dog) and a friend, Elsie Roberts. Collection: Mrs. Roger Gifford/ Roger Martineau Walker LVO.

relatively well and shore 180,000 sheep, by far the largest tally in Queensland, as a consequence of the arid and difficult conditions.[394] Thomas was still the overseer at Wellshot in September 1911, but by July 1916 he had made an abrupt move away from Queensland and accepted a more junior position, that of boundary rider at a smaller station, Yabtree, in Tumblong, New South Wales. This was a solitary job touring the boundary to check the fences and collect escaped stock; however, within a year he had bounced back and was again the overseer at his new station and he remained at Yabtree until he enlisted in 1918.[395] He did not return to Yabtree at the end of the hostilities.

To understand Thomas's subsequent lifestyle in Australia and his outlook, we need to enter the unique male domain of the shearing shed: the 'harshness of the outback and the "nomadic" work patterns drew men together into a culture of mutual sharing'.[396] Sheep shearers harvested the wool on the huge stations; during the peak season, the permanent hands could not cope with the shearing and additional itinerant shearers were employed as contract workers. It was a task that demanded skill, endurance and strength; although the work was arduous and repetitive, it avoided all the tedium of factory work. At times the heat and dust must have been unbearable and the accommodation lonely, but it was a life relished by those who worked in it, unrestrained by normal conventions (including the 'civilising' influence of women). It was also a lifestyle that fostered individualism and an irreverence to authority, and these were traits Thomas displayed.

Thomas became an overseer, a 'boss', but the 'mateship' of shearing meant the boss really did not need to cajole or bully the shearers. They were eager to maximise their tallies and the grazier maintained the regular flow of sheep up to the shearers. Rather, it was for the overseer to ensure that all involved struck the right balance: 'chasing big tallies compromised the quality of the shearing'; 'the overseer was required to be a diplomat. More often he wanted to slow shearers down to ensure a neat job.'[397] As shearers got older, they got slower, and learning to live with that decline was difficult for someone who had worked in this tough environment. This may explain Thomas's restlessness throughout his life, and the difficulty he had in coping with domesticity. It certainly explains the individualism that marked his character throughout. He did commit the indiscretion of marrying in 1908, but this early legal union did not endure. His wife Bessie went on to have several children in a separate *de facto* relationship, but the pair never divorced or remarried.

By September 1911, when he was still at Wellshot in the Longreach area of Queensland, Thomas had struck up a relationship with a married woman, Amy O'Farrell, whose husband posted advertisements seeking his whereabouts. It may well be that Thomas and Amy had eloped with Amy's two children. The scandal caused by this elopement may explain Thomas's abrupt move away from Queensland to New South Wales in 1916, and the fact that effectively he accepted a demotion at his new station, Yabtree, at least for a year. Thomas and Amy continued their lives together, having six children between 1912 and 1920. Because of the nature of Thomas's sheep station existence, family life was itinerant. Their twin children, George and Nellie, were born in a New South Wales hotel in June 1917, and the boy's second name, Carmody, was derived from the hotel owner, a witness to the birth.[398]

At first Thomas tried to become a family man but his domesticity did not endure. He continued to flaunt convention and disregard the values instilled in him by his Victorian father. By 1926, he had abandoned Amy and thrown off his family responsibilities entirely, and was living with a married woman, Lily Newman by name. Lily's husband divorced her on the grounds of her 'misconduct' with Thomas, who was cited as co-respondent in the divorce that was decreed.[399] In the mid-1920s, Nellie and Margaret, Thomas's daughters of his relationship with Amy, went to live in a convent, as did Annie (Daly), another of Amy's own children; their mother, Amy, could not cope on her own after Thomas had left home. Later, Nellie said that she felt that her father had neglected her, recalling that he visited her only once and never returned. By 1934 Thomas had left Lily and moved on once more, true to the pattern of his restless life.

In 1934 he moved in with Edith (Edie) Elizabeth Brest, at first living in her house in Newtown, Sydney. He then benefited from the windfall of Muir's legacy, and bought a house in Melbourne, to which the couple moved in 1935. With the benefit of the cushion of this generous bequest, Thomas's itinerant existence came to an end, and he settled in one place and with one companion. However, this voluntary interstate move, from New South Wales to Melbourne, Victoria, a city 550 miles away from where his family was growing up in Sydney, effectively cut him off from his children. His son George Bell Carmody Muir was then still only a lad of 17, and the two younger girls and his youngest son could certainly have benefited from more regular contact with their father. Thomas's children, and he, made sporadic attempts to see one another, but the distance that separated the family meant that these reunions were rare.

In late 1938 Thomas and Edie married. He and his sister, Nellie, in distant Cape Town, maintained contact with one another. When one of Nellie's grandchildren emigrated to Australia, Nellie gave her Thomas's address and asked her to visit him in Melbourne. She did this and found Thomas and Edie to be a cultivated couple living in their older-style

Nov. 1931

Fig. 41: Carmody's Royal Hotel, Wagga Wagga, Nov. 1931. The 'scion' of the Australian Muir family, George Bell Carmody Muir, was born in the hotel in 1917 and named after Mrs. Carmody, the hotel owner. Collection: Noel Butlin Archives Centre, Australian National University.

and comfortable Melbourne cottage; Thomas reminisced about district Six in Cape Town, and his early days working as a boss of a sheep-shearing gang in Australia.[400] The couple continued to live together in the same house until Thomas died in 1969.[401]

Thomas was an easy-going lone wolf of a man who chose his own path and paid scant regard to his immediate family relationships. On the analogy of the wolf, excluded from the pack, perhaps one can defend him by saying he had been somewhat arbitrarily separated from his own erstwhile family in the Cape. This experience, as well as his subsequent nomadic life on remote sheep stations, may well have altered his whole perception of his place in society. Nevertheless, he remained a sociable man and interested in his Cape family connections.

The only sense in which Thomas inherited his father's ideal of 'discipline' was that he was a non-commissioned military man during both world wars. Both he and his two sons, Thomas (b. 1912) and George (b. 1917) were depicted in photographs alone, or together, in their military uniforms, and a grandson also continued the military tradition.[402]

Thomas's Australian brood were not entirely forgotten by his family in the Cape. Thomas's youngest son later visited South Africa and the visit of 'cousin Henry' is still remembered by at least one of Nellie's grandchildren in the Cape: he was 'made very welcome by the entire family'.[403] However, after Thomas's sister Nellie died at the end of 1972, interest in the Australian branch of the family waned and contacts lapsed.[404]

Also, because the succeeding generations of the Muir family in New South Wales saw almost nothing of their father Thomas during his lifetime, they did not learn of their unusually dislocated family history. During the lifetime of George Bell Carmody Muir, the siblings kept in touch with one another. Then, it appears, the families simply

*Fig. 42: Thomas P.B. Muir, Muir's son,
pictured in military uniform.*

moved on. One of Thomas's children died young, but there must be numerous Muir descendants of the other five siblings who now have no contact with one another. Thomas bestowed on his Australian family the gift of dislocation.

Muir's attitude to his two sons was marked by his overriding philosophy of 'duty'. A journalist, interviewing him at the age of 84, asked him to express a 'maxim for youth'. After some thought, he quoted a couplet book of his own verse: 'if duty calls thee, haste to go; if mere desire, be slow and sure'.[405] He added that the tendency of the modern age was that 'people followed desire too easily'.[406] Muir's sons were the casualties of his relentless pursuit of duty.

RETIREMENT (1915–1934)

During the 23 years Muir held the office of S.G.E. in the Cape, he received recognition and many awards: he was elected a Fellow of the Royal Society in 1900; he held the post of Vice-Chancellor of the University of the Cape of Good Hope during the period 1897–1901 and served as a member of the Council for much longer; he was also President of the South African Association for the Advancement of Science in 1910.[407]

In 1912, Muir had written that he 'had a desire to devote some time of [his] leisure towards [his] purely scientific work, which unfortunately had suffered immensely by [his] coming to the Cape'.[408] South Africa came under financial pressure as a result of the First World War and the Union Government requested the Provincial Administration, as an economy measure, to place on pension all senior officials who had already reached pensionable age. Finally, it was time for this still energetic 70-year-old to retire, and in 1915 he was knighted for his services to science. His grandson, Claude Cornish-Bowden, relates: 'He had no wish to be known as anyone other than Dr. Muir F.R.S., but ... accepted

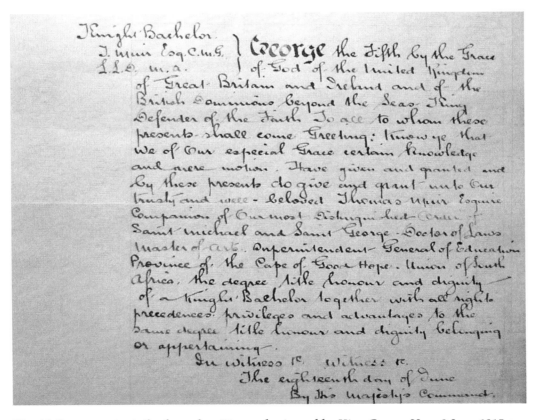

Fig. 43: Letters patent, the formal written order issued by King George V on 8 June 1915, conferring on Thomas Muir the title of Knight Bachelor. The U.K. National Archives: TNA1582444519Y25.

a knighthood on the condition that it was unconnected with an Order of Chivalry, which would take precedence over his Fellowship of the Royal Society.[409] Hence, he was made a Knight Bachelor.

Muir's farewell to education

Two rather different gatherings were held in Cape Town to mark Muir's retirement. The first was an assembly of Education Department staff at the Royal Hotel on 25 June 1915. The song for which he wrote the lyrics, 'A Highland Idyll', was performed to the assembled guests: 104 inspectors, instructors and members of his office staff signed a presentation address drawn up in the form of an illuminated manuscript, a eulogy to their 'Chief'. They praised the way he had shaped the 'school system during a period marked by social change and economic growth, by political unrest, and by the calamity of war'; they declared that he had discharged his duty 'faithfully and successfully, uninfluenced by any purely political or sectional interests ... by the exercise of wide knowledge, unswerving impartiality, clear judgement, thoughtful prevision, unflinching determination and unabating personal energy'.[410]

Even Muir must have blushed to hear this idealised portrait of himself, but one cannot deny his knowledge, his determination and energy.

A second, and even more splendid, farewell evening was held by the Mayor of Cape Town at the Mount Nelson Hotel on 9 July 1915. Invitees were asked to subscribe for the sumptuous dinner at one guinea a head, and the banquet was attended by all the luminaries of the Cape, 'one of the most brilliant gatherings' that Cape Town had known. Mr J.X. Merriman, who had remained a Member of Parliament after Union, was the main speaker at the dinner. He said that no better day's work had ever been done than when they secured Sir Thomas for South Africa. 'For nearly a generation,' he said, 'no man has led a more strenuous life in the public service than Sir Thomas Muir. Whatever little village you go to, you find that there is no better building than the school. And, I make bold to say, these schools you owe to the labours and energies and persistency of Sir Thomas Muir. Future generations will remark these things and will be proud of them. We owe them to Sir Thomas Muir. The next generation, I feel sure, will regard this as one of the finest acts of a life spent in the service of this country.'

This was a tribute by a politician with whom Muir may not necessarily always have seen eye to eye. Merriman had been regarded as anti-imperialist during the Anglo-Boer War and sat in opposition to Jameson's government until 1908. He served as the last prime minister of the Cape Colony until Union in 1910. In terms of Cape politics, he was a liberal and a supporter of the multiracial franchise, but, nevertheless, he believed firmly in white dominance; thus, his beliefs were a curious mix of the progressive and reactionary. He declined to accept a post in Botha's first Union Cabinet but remained a government supporter in Parliament. Post-Union, however, Muir's sympathies were with those in opposition to Botha (and Herzogism).

It fell to the writer and politician C.J. Langenhoven to counter the praise bestowed on Muir, immediately after he had received his knighthood:[411] Langenhoven conceded that Muir had been 'a faithful servant, dedicated to carry out the mission for which he was appointed'. As far as Langenhoven was concerned, however, Muir had not acted in the interests of South Africa, but had served British interests, and this was what the terms of his mandate had required of him: 'Muir was sent here to denationalise the Afrikaner youth, and he carried out this objective to the very best of his ability.' His knighthood, in Langenhoven's view, was a well-deserved honour conferred on him precisely by the British interests he served. Not content with that back-handed eulogy, Langenhoven added a thrust in Muir's direction about his failure to grapple with the Dutch language: 'Every learned Afrikaner is bilingual,' he wrote. 'Every learned Brit is monolingual, or he must be somehow flawed in a way that disqualifies him for high office. Sir Muir was free from any such flaw. I wonder how many Dutch words he takes back to Scotland together with the other curios and kudos and memos of his long-standing management of the education of a Dutch-speaking nation?' Of course, Langenhoven was mistaken in his belief that Muir would return with his 'curios' to Scotland post-retirement; however, his judgement concerning Muir's failure to embrace any elements of the Dutch language was entirely well founded. To the extent that Muir peppered his *Diaries* with the odd Dutch word, to add local flavour, it was hit-and-miss as to whether he plumped for the correct word.

At the end of his period of office, the *Cape Argus* recognised Muir's skills as an 'organiser' as opposed to an educationist: 'The most conspicuous service of all consists in the fact that he has provided the machinery which was required to render possible an immensely greater advance in the near future if the work which has been done so well is permitted to proceed unchecked.'[412]

Life in retirement in Rondebosch

After his retirement, Muir gave up Mowbray Hall and a large part of his library, for lack of room to contain it in the house to which he planned to move.

Fig. 44: Mr. Merriman, Boonzaier 1912, Plate 1. Collection: Peter Elliott.

He bought a tract of land fronting on Portland Road, Rondebosch, halfway between the homes of his two daughters. There he built a substantial house, Elmcote. Maggie did not survive long enough to spend any appreciable time in the new family home, as she died there in early 1919. Muir, however, spent an extended retirement there, resuming his research work in earnest. The house had a front and side stoep, a large formal garden, and unrivalled views of 'the buttresses of Table Mountain behind, and the great sentinel hills, Lion's Peak and Devil's Peak'.[413] Beyond the garden stretched a substantial pine plantation – an integral part of the property.

Fig. 45: Sir Thomas Muir's residence, Elmcote, Portland Road, Rondebosch. Collection: Peter Elliott.

James Cuthbert remained on the staff of the Cape Education Department and became a school inspector. However, regrettably, he paid the price for all the years he spent gathering gossip for Muir on the local educational scene. Those long evenings in the company of his cronies, at every railway station, 'allaying his thirst and in hearing the grievances', finally caught up with him.[414] During what must have been either a visit back to Scotland to see his sister or to seek medical attention, he died in Edinburgh of cirrhosis of the liver in March 1918 at the early age of 59.[415] He died only a year before his second daughter, Marjorie, married Wouter de Vos Malan, a young man who was only a year away from completing his doctorate in Education at Columbia University in New York; thus the educationist tradition of the Cuthbert family continued. Muir must also have enjoyed the fact that young Malan, husband of the daughter of his trusty subordinate, became Superintendent-General of Education of the Cape Province in 1929 at the relatively young age of 36. It was, however, no longer the powerful role that Muir had occupied. Malan was criticised for his stance on not promoting teachers who opposed the racist policies of the state; he remained in office until 1953, just exceeding the length (but not the impact) of Muir's term.[416]

Alice Cogan, who had so quickly become a valued member of his personal coterie, continued to make swift progress under Muir's tutelage, to become a teacher and then a school inspector within the Cape Department of Education. After 1912 (the year of the last of the *Diaries*, which records her presence) she may well have acted as a personal assistant within Muir's office, and we can assume she continued as a departmental employee at least until his retirement.[417]

After Maggie's death in April 1919, there is no doubt that Alice Cogan became the most important person in Muir's day-to-day life. By 1920, when she was only 41, she described herself as having no occupation.[418] Alice Cogan and Muir travelled on the same ship, outward and return, in that same year; thus the implication is that they holidayed in

Britain together for five months and were already companions at this early stage. She had given up her job to devote herself to looking after Muir and, even if she was doing the work of a housekeeper, she was not being remunerated for it. Later records list her as a former school inspector and a pensioner of the Department of Education. Yet Muir's grandson, Athelstan (known as 'Athel'), referred to Miss Cogan as the 'sleep-in housekeeper'; it is as 'housekeeper' that the family appears to remember her, not a particularly apt description of her role. Athel's further observation was that his grandfather 'was so tough on his son, but in his life he found it necessary to have a companion'.[419] He implied that Muir, in taking a companion as a lonely widower, had allowed himself moral leeway in his own home, but had laid down a strict and unachievable code for his son, young Thomas. However, Alexander Aitken, the renowned New Zealand-born mathematician, who wrote two essays on Muir after he died, saw matters entirely differently and painted a rather more positive picture of Alice's role in Muir's life. Miss Cogan, he wrote, was Muir's secretary, displaying 'unobtrusive devotion': it was she who 'copied in full all the manuscripts of his later years'.[420] We can assume that Alice Cogan may have been sorely disappointed that Muir never married her, as this would have been a perfectly reasonable expectation, given that she had sacrificed everything for the old man. In 1925, when he wrote the second codicil to his will, Muir named her a co-executor of his will (in addition to his two sons-in-law). It is a mystery what he hoped to achieve through this change, as he left her no specific legacy. It was an appointment that conferred burden and responsibility but no reward. The testamentary freedom of the times entitled the testator to act capriciously and in a manner that might now appear unfair.

Muir remained physically active throughout his retirement but slowed down to some extent, and took more gentle exercise, after a severe illness suffered in 1925: 'He presented a figure of admiration and curiosity to his neighbours, who watched a gentleman from the Victorian age diligently pursuing mathematics, sitting upright at his desk in winged collar and bow tie, preparing his work.' In a whimsical *Cape Times* sketch of Muir at the age of 84, he is represented in the illustrative photographs in winged collar, bow tie, formal dark jacket and waistcoat, floral buttonhole and striped trousers. In this somewhat elaborate garb, he is depicted reading, writing and even pruning the roses in his garden and sawing wood in his plantation. The piece observes that at this 'advanced' age, 'he is still actively exercising brilliant intellectual powers which might well be the envy of most men in their prime'.[421] One can only hope that he was able to wear something a trifle more comfortable when the interviewer and photographer were no longer present.

By a deed of gift, drawn up in 1920, Muir bequeathed his mathematical serials and books to the South African Public Library.[422] He was a huge enthusiast of mathematical journals, which he felt encouraged and promoted original investigation. He said that they 'keep alive a young student's mathematical life'; he advocated that there should be full sets of mathematical journals in every university town.[423] It was this that, no doubt, motivated him to make his gift to the library. The collection is still shelved and kept together as the Muir Mathematical Collection in the National Library of South Africa in Cape Town. New periodicals are still added to the collection, and it is accessible to researchers as a special collection.[424] An endowment for maintaining the collection accompanied the bequest with the positive result that periodicals continue to be added to the collection (thus maintaining its unique strengths, the long runs of mathematical serials).[425] In this way, Muir sought to preserve the legacy of his library.

Despite his noble concept, the continuing usefulness of the library collection is open to question. Current journals, of course, are now available online and the lifeblood of the physical collection, and library, is now of reduced importance. The collection is no longer a

Fig. 46: Bust of Sir Thomas Muir, pictured in the NLSA Reading Room, January/ February 2020. Photograph: Linda Howe-Ely.

practical working mathematical resource: few researchers now consult it and then the items of interest may be the smaller curiosities. Prof. John Webb, Professor of Mathematics at the University of Cape Town, commented that he 'explored it out of general interest, and found some unusual items, such as the *Gentleman's Mathematical Companion*, little leather-bound volumes dating from the early 19th century, in which readers posted challenge problems for others to solve'.[426] A collection, which Muir had hoped would 'keep alive' the mathematical life of students, has now lost its power to instil life. The unfortunate George Muir, the great man's son, might understandably turn in his grave to think of the cause to which the quarter share of his father's entire capital, which Christine, his second wife might reasonably otherwise have inherited, was diverted.

Muir also meticulously maintained over the years a neat handwritten list of 'Letters from Mathematicians and a few others'.[427] However, on a single day in an otherwise ordinary Cape winter, he casually recorded, at the foot of that same list, that he had destroyed this historical treasure trove: 'all burned 17/7/1932'. No one can doubt that the correspondence was his to destroy, but it does seem to have been an inexplicable act of archival vandalism.[428]

In the National Library of South Africa Reading Room in Cape Town, the bronze bust of Muir was recently on display. It is a work of a relatively unknown Eastern Cape artist, W.G. Bevington (1881–1953).

Muir became one of the first honorary graduates of the University of Cape Town, receiving an honorary D.Sc. degree in 1921.[429] He continued to carry out his research, and to write and published his last great mathematical tome (*Muir 1930*) at the end of that same decade. He died at Rondebosch on 21 March 1934. His funeral was an entirely private one, attended only by 11 members of the Spilhaus and Cornish-Bowden families (his two daughters' families) and, of course, Alice Cogan.[430] Muir was buried in the Maitland Cemetery not far from his home. Muir's eldest granddaughter recalls the family receiving a very cold reception from Alice Cogan at Elmcote after Muir's death.[431] In the administration of his estate, only his two sons-in-law were appointed testamentary executors and his four children inherited equally (subject to George's anomalous position of being denied access to a capital sum). We can surmise there may well have been a private settlement with Alice Cogan, as she did not formally intervene in the estate as an executor (but we have no way of knowing the outcome of this strange saga).

We need to spare a thought for Alice Cogan: her 25 years of devotion to the old man went entirely unrecognised. She lost the shared home in which she had lived with Muir for more almost 15 years. Fortunately, she had her Department of Education pension to fall back on, until her own death in April 1947.[432] The value of her total estate was less than the residual amount received, under Muir's will, by the Public Library for the maintenance of his collection of books and periodicals, after the capital amount earmarked to provide an income for his son reverted to the Library following George's death, in that same year. It does not appear that any member of the family ever saw Alice Cogan again after the sale of Elmcote.

EPILOGUE

How then does one view Muir's life and his achievements?

Muir's rise from rural Scottish boy in Lanarkshire to world-renowned mathematician and powerful educational administrator in the Cape was an impressive one. His 'success' was not entirely attributable to intelligence. It was in large measure due to his phenomenal appetite for hard work, and his formidable concentration and determination.

He was a man who turned his back on his humble origins, and was readily absorbed into middle-class Glasgow and later into elite Cape Town. Muir was an 'Aladdin' of his times, the story of his life's progress being entirely in keeping with that popular literary theme, to which his copious reading would have introduced him at an early age: that of the person born outside his natural rank or class, who eventually finds his rightful place in life through his own traits and aptitudes. Despite spending just under half his life over 10,000 kilometres from Scotland, he remained attached to his Scottish roots and always warmed to a Scots accent and song.

Some of Muir's family relationships were disastrous: his single-minded devotion to his work, rather than family, created its own casualties within his family circle. In contrast, Muir was fully capable of creating warmer relationships outside his family and one sees the best of Muir in his enjoyment of the company of his personal coterie, his absorption in music and song, and his passion for literature of all sorts.

His dogged pursuit of his mathematical research, and his devotion of such a vast proportion of his life to a meticulous record of one mathematical concept, resulted in his history of the *Theory of Determinants*. This 'monument' has proved less than immortal and is now something of a work of curiosity, a legacy of his prodigious output and of his ability for organisation. Perhaps it was Muir's trait of obsession, rather than his brilliance, that propelled him forward. A person of equal talent might have fallen by the wayside, whereas he was able to set himself to the arduous combination of stressful administrative office and painstaking and complex research. Nevertheless, for Muir his mathematics was also a diversion, something into which he could retreat, away from his working schedule.

Educational historian Peter Kallaway observed: 'Muir is one of a new breed in his time – perhaps ahead of his time – the educational planner/bureaucrat (scientist vs missionary)!'[433]

In centralising education, Muir wrenched schools from their community. His system was characterised by a central form of governance and administrative structures that relied on science and professional expertise. His organisation, and the infrastructure resulting from his school building programme, enabled the Cape school system to cope with the large numbers of additional white pupils enrolled in schools following the introduction of compulsory education. It offered these pupils an array of innovative educational services. However, this created the 'one best system' that ill served the pluralistic character of Cape society and left out of its ambit a vast proportion of the population.

During his time in the Cape, Muir did not express a 'philosophy' concerning education, but his actions, to some extent, spoke to his beliefs. In the educational arena, his priority was the efficiency of his system and as much control over schools as possible. He was interested in a system designed for the 'average' child; he did not concern himself with the needs of the individual. These special needs, whether due to language or social disadvantage, simply got in the way of the overall efficiency of his system.

Muir was perfectly content to serve the purpose of his political masters, and this meant advancing white education, particularly uplifting the poor white child, and neglecting the needs of the black child. The mission schools, and missionary influence, simply got in the way of his department's direct and invasive administration of the governance of the individual school. Although Muir was a supremely intelligent man, he shared the prevailing racist and white supremacist views of the elite of Victorian Cape Town, and casual racism abounds in his *Diaries*.

He remained a cultural imperialist throughout his time in the Cape, in the sense that he believed that his education system (including its focus on English language tuition) brought the benefits of British civilisation to the Cape. His closest political friends were like-minded thinkers. His position became more acute towards the end of his time as he was marginalised due to the inexorable march of the Cape towards Union. Although he had respect for the individual Dutch Afrikaner, and warmed particularly to the hard-working rural type, in general he was disparaging about the Calvinism he saw as inherent in the people he encountered, and had no sympathy for their national and language aspirations.

Nevertheless, Muir achieved a great deal within the context of his times. It must have required deft footwork for him to have been able to balance all the competing interest groups of the Cape: the Afrikaner Bond/South African Party, the Progressives/Unionists, the missionary lobby and the teaching associations. It is remarkable that he managed to stay out of trouble and remained in office for 23 years during such turbulent times. It remains to develop a full understanding of how Muir was truly perceived by all these very disparate factions.[434]

What is there that remains of the Muir legacy? A quiet debate continues about his contribution to mathematics; the Thomas Muir Chair of Mathematics at the University of Glasgow was founded in 1966 and named for him; there are his mathematical papers, the tomes he wrote on the *Theory of Determinants* and his specialist collection of mathematical books; as regards education, there remain elements of his system that have survived for over 100 years since he retired; there are the physical school buildings in the Cape that resulted from his school building programme; there is Muir College in Uitenhage, the school that bears his name. His daughter, Dr. Nellie Spilhaus, eminent in her own right, maintained the Muir connection with this school by opening its Memorial Gates on 12 October 1966, a continuing educational imprint of the Muir name.

It is a difficult time at which to evaluate any colonial life. Fortunately, in Muir's case there is no statue, representative of his legacy, that must either stand or fall. We can be content, therefore, merely to examine the ingredients of his life, the good and the bad, and learn something about humanity and its condition.

Fig. 47: Muir's daughter, Dr. N.B. Spilhaus, opening the Memorial Gates at Muir College, Uitenhage, on 12 October 1966. Collection: Peter Elliott.

FAMILY TREE

Four generations of the family from about 1750 to 1975, in Scotland, the Cape and Australia (the principal characters in Muir's story are highlighted in bold).

1	**William Muir** Resident in Biggar, Lanarkshire d. 1829 Biggar	m.	Margaret Donaldson

2	**George Muir** b. about 1804, Biggar, Lanarkshire d. 4 August 1866, Wishaw, Lanarkshire	m1.	Elizabeth Robb, 16 December 1827, Lanark d. between 1839 and 1843

Issue:

3.1 William, b. 1830, d. 1912
3.2 John, b. 1832
3.3 James, b. 1835, d. 1915
3.4 George J., b. 1836 Nemphlar,
Lanarkshire, d. 1923
3.5 Peter b. 1839

Issue:

3.6 **Thomas** (see generation 3)	m2.	**Mary Brown**, 19 November 1843, Lanark
3.7 Andrew, b. 17 August 1846, Overtown, Cambusnethan, Lanarkshire d. 1901		b. 19 July 1804, Lanark; on birth and baptismal record registered as 'Marion' but afterwards always as 'Mary' (Parents: James Brown, b. 1779, Lanark, and Rachel Paterson, b. 1783,
3.8 Margaret, b. 17 April 1852, Overtown d. 1912		Lanark. Marriage: 22 January 1804, Lanark) d. 5 May 1883, 79 Kent Rd., Glasgow

3	**Thomas Muir** b. 25 August 1844, Nemphlar, Lanarkshire d. 21 March 1934, Rondebosch, Cape	m.	**Margaret Bell ('Maggie')**, 12 October 1876, Nigg Rossshire b. 10 October 1845, Bonhill, Dumbarton (Parents: Dugald Bell and Isabella Young)

Issue:

d. 2 April 1919, Rondebosch, Cape

4.1	**George Bell** b. 6 May 1877, Partick, Lanarkshire d. 11 December 1947, High Fremington, Richmond, Yorkshire *No issue*	m1.	**Ethel Jane Devereux** (birth surname: Pember) 12 January 1907, St. Luke's, Chelsea, London d. 22 March 1942, Notting Hill, London
		m2.	**Ida Christine Roberts ('Christine')**, October 1943, Leominister d. 3 May 1984, York

4.2 **Nellie Brown**
b. 8 July 1878, Partick, Lanarkshire
d. 16 December 1972, Cape Town

m.   Karl Antonio Spilhaus, 19 November 1903, Cape Town

Issue:

Karl William ('Karl')
Thomas Muir ('Muir')
Margaret Virginia ('Peggie') m Barry
Mary Antonia ('Mollie') m Elliott
Athelstan Friedrich ('Athel')

4.3 **Lillie Cameron ('Cam')**
b. 13 November 1882, Erskine, Renfrewshire
d. 25 February 1977, Johannesburg, South Africa

m.   Athelstan Hall Cornish-Bowden, 30 October 1908, Mowbray Presbyterian Church, Cape Town

Issue:

Athelstan Claude Muir ('Claude')

4.4 **Thomas Paterson Brown**
b. 7 April 1885, Erskine, Renfrewshire
d. 5 November 1966, East Melbourne, Australia

m1   Bessie Ball, 1908, Sydney

[m]2 *de facto* relationship with Amy O'Farrell (who had been married previously) in Longreach, Queensland from about November 1908:
b. 1888 Queensland
(Parents: James O'Farrell and Anne Elizabeth Stanton)

Issue:

Thomas Paterson
Lily Cameron
George Bell Carmody
Nellie Brown
Margaret Bell (registered Maggie Bell at birth)
Henry Robert

No issue

m[3] Edith ('Edie') Elizabeth Brest, 20 December 1938, Melbourne

BIBLIOGRAPHY

For ease of citation an abbreviated reference heads each bibliographical item, and items are set out in alphabetical order. It is these abbreviated citations that are used in the Endnotes.

Adonis 1995
Adonis, D.S. (1995). 'Today's Boys, Tomorrow's Men': A short history of the Boys' Brigade of Britain, with further reference to the Boys' Brigade in South Africa (c. 1880s–1980s), M.A. thesis, University of Cape Town. [online] Available at: https://open.uct.ac.za/bitstream/handle/11427/8490/thesis_hum_1995_adonis_df.pdf?sequence=1 [Accessed 14 January 2020].

Aitken 1936
Aitken, A.C. (1936). Sir Thomas Muir, C.M.G., LL.D., F.R.S. *Proceedings of the Edinburgh Mathematical Society*, 4 (4), pp. 263–267. [online] Available at: http://mathshistory.st–andrews.ac.uk/Obits2/Muir_obituary.html [Accessed 28 January 2020].

Aitken 1950
Aitken, A.C. (1950). Thomas Muir. *The Journal of the Glasgow Mathematical Association*, I (3), pp. 65–76.

Alkema 2012
Alkema, S. (2012). Conductors of Cape Town Musical Society: A historical perspective. PhD. thesis, S.A. College of Music, University of Cape Town.

AMS Mathematics and Music 2010
American Mathematical Society. (2010). *Mathematics and Music*. [online] Available at: http://www.ams.org/publicoutreach/math-and-music [Accessed 25 July 2020].

Anderson 1985
Anderson, R. (1985). Secondary Schools and Scottish Society in the nineteenth century. Past & Present, 109, pp. 176–203. [online] Available at: JSTOR: www.jstor.org/stable/650614 [Accessed 28 January 2020].

ArteFacts SA
www.artefacts.co.za. (n.d.). *Artefacts, South African Built Environment*. [online] Available at: https://www.artefacts.co.za/. [Search People/Firm/Structure.]

Axler 1995
Axler, S. (1995). Down with Determinants. *The American Mathematical Monthly*, 102 (2), pp. 139–154. [online] Available at: https://www.maa.org/sites/default/files/pdf/awards/Axler-Ford-1996.pdf [Accessed 15 February 2020].

Bailie 1892
Men You Know. (1892). *The Bailie*, XL (1017), pp. 1–2.

Bell Review 1931
Bell E.T. (1931). Review: *Contributions to the History of Determinants 1900–1920* by Thomas Muir. *The American Mathematical Monthly*, 38 (3), pp. 161–164.

Beyers 1935
Beyers, M. (1935). Onderwys in die Kaap kolonie gedurende die eerste sewe jaar van die bestuur van Dr. Thomas Muir as Superintendent-Generaal van Onderwys, 1892–1899. M.Ed. thesis, University of Stellenbosch. [online] Available at: https://scholar.sun.ac.za/handle/10019.1/50774 [Accessed 5 February 2020].

Bickford-Smith 1995
Bickford-Smith, V. (1995). *Ethnic pride and racial prejudice in Victorian Cape Town: group identity and social practice, 1875–1902*. Cambridge ; New York: Cambridge University Press.

Biggar 2017
Biggar, N. (2017). Don't feel guilty about our colonial history. *The Times*, 29 November. [online] Available at: http://www.web.pdx.edu/~gilleyb/NigelBiggar_Don'tFeelGuiltyAboutOurColonialHistory.pdf [Accessed 10 June 2020].

Biggar, House of Fleming 1867
Hunter, W. (1867). *Histories of Scottish families: Biggar and the House of Fleming (1867)*, National Library of Scotland. [online] Available at: https://digital.nls.uk/histories-of-scottish-families/archive/94839290 [Accessed 21 March 2020].

Biographical Sketch Muir 1905
Biographical Sketch Muir. (1905). How a Wishaw Public School boy got on in the world. Career of Dr Thomas Muir, M.A., LL.D., F.R.S., C.M.G. *South Africa*, 19 August. Muir Manuscript Collection, NLSA, MSB 691.2 (1) newspaper cutting.

Bissett 1973
Bisset, J. (1973). John William Jagger and the South African Railways, 1921–1924. Extended Essay B.A. (Hons) degree, University of Cape Town.

Boonzaier 1901
Boonzaier, D.C. (1901). *Owlographs. A collection of South African celebrities in caricature.* Cape Town: Cape Times.

Boonzaier 1912
Boonzaier, D.C. (1912). *My Caricatures.* Cape Town: D.C. Boonzaier.

Borman 1989
Borman, M. (1989). *The Cape Education Department 1839–1989.* Cape Town: The Cape Education Department.

Cape of Good Hope Native Education Report 1908
Cape of Good Hope Parliament. (1908). *Report of the Select Committee on Native Education* (Fremantle, H.E.S). Cape Town, Cape Times Limited, Government Printers. [online] Available at: https://archive.org/details/reportofselectc00cape/page/n8/mode/2up [Accessed 27 February 2020].

Cape Times 1928
Impressions of Sir Thomas Muir. (1928). *Cape Times*, 22 September.

Cape Times 1934
Editorial, Sir Thomas Muir, p. 8; and 'Sir Thomas Muir Dead', p. 9. (1934). *Cape Times*, 22 August.

Chisholm 2019
Chisholm, L. (2019). *Teacher Preparation in South Africa: History, policy and future directions.* Bingley, UK: Emerald Group Publishing.

Christian Express 1908
(1908). Prepossessions and Facts. Dr. Muir's Evidence before the Select Committee on Native Education. The *Christian Express*, 1 December, pp. 190–192.

Citation Hon. LL.D. 1955
Nellie Brown Spilhaus: Citation for Honorary Degree of Doctor of Laws, University of Cape Town. (1955).

Cleophas 2009
Cleophas, F.J. (2009). Physical education and physical culture in the coloured community of the Western Cape, 1837–1966. Ph.D. thesis, University of Stellenbosch. [online] Available at: https://scholar.sun.ac.za/handle/10019.1/1227 [Accessed 30 July 2020].

Coetzee 1951
Coetzee, J.C. (1951). *Die Onderwys en Opvoeding van die Afrikaner in die Twintigste Eeu.* [online] Available at: https://www.koersjournal.org.za/index.php/koers/article/download/1744/1839 [Accessed 30 July 2020].

Cogan Records
Cogan. A.M.M (1946). Last Will and Testament, 27 September 1946.

(1947). Form of Information on Death, Cogan A.M.C. Entry 464, 5 Apr. 1947, East London, Eastern Cape.

Death Notice relating to death, 3 April 1947. Cape Province, South Africa, 2353/47, Cogan A.M.C, 9 April 1947.

(1948). First and Final Liquidation and Distribution Account, Estate Cogan, A.M.M., 19 May ('Cogan Record: Estate Administration').

Cornish-Bowden Memoirs
Cornish-Bowden, A.C.M. (n.d.). Build or bust in our Africa. Unpublished.

Crawford 1934
Crawford, Lawrence. (1934) Sir Thomas

Muir, MA., LL.D., D.Sc., F.R.S., C.M.G. *Transactions of the Royal Society of South Africa*, 22 (1), pp. 101–102.

Creese 2010
Creese, M.R.S. and Creese, T.M. (2010). *Ladies in the Laboratory III. South African, Australian, New Zealand, and Canadian Women in Science: Nineteenth and early twentieth centuries: A survey of their contributions*. Lanham, MD: Scarecrow Press.

Croal 1882
Gutenberg.org. (2012 [1882]). *The Project Gutenberg eBook of Scottish Loch Scenery*, by Thomas A. Croal. [online] Available at: https://www.gutenberg. org/files/39892/39892–h/39892–h. htm#STONEBYRES_FALL [Accessed 28 January 2020].

Crilly 2020
Crilly, A. (2020). Notes on Thomas Muir. [Email to Peter Elliott, 10 February.]

Cuthbert 1911
Cuthbert, J.R. (1911). *Educational Progress of South Africa. A record and review.* Cape Town: Cape Times Limited. Available at: Africa Studies Library Pamphlet Collection (BAP 370.968 CUTH).

Cuthbert 1950
Cuthbert, P. (1950). *The Administration of Dr. Jameson as Prime Minister of the Cape Colony 1904–08.* [online] Available at: https://open.uct.ac.za/ bitstream/handle/11427/15432/ thesis_hum_1950_cuthbert_patricia. pdf?sequence=1&isAllowed=y [Accessed 29 April 2020].

Cuthbert Records
James Robertson Cuthbert: Death Notice, 4 March 1918 (South Africa).

Statutory Death 685/02 0076 (Scotland), district of Saint Andrew, Edinburgh.

Marjorie Anna Cuthbert (daughter of James Robertson Cuthbert): Marriage Register, No. 195, 15 July 1920, marriage at home in Stellenbosch to Wouter de Vos Malan (signed by the D.R.C. Predikant).

Daleboudt 1942
Daleboudt, H.M. (1942). Sir Thomas Muir en die onderwys in Kaapland tydens sy bestuur as superintendent–generaal van onderwys, 1892–1915. D.Ed. thesis, University of Stellenbosch. [online] Available at: https://scholar.sun.ac.za/ handle/10019.1/63758 [Accessed 5 February 2020].

Diary or **Diaries**
In the **Muir Manuscript Collection, NLSA**: *Diary 1*: Transkeian Territories, 29 July to 2 September 1909, MSB 691.1 (2); *Diary 2*: Emgwali, Komgha, Butterworth. Grahamstown, Port Elizabeth, Oudtshoorn, Mossel Bay, 27 January to 19 February 1910, MSB 691.1 (3); *Diary 3*: Prieska and Barkly West, 21 January to 2 February 1911, MSB 691.1 (4); *Diary 4*: Fraserburg and Graaff-Reinet, 1 to 18 March 1911, MSB 691.1 (5); *Diary 5*: Butterworth and Kenhardt, 3 to 23 October 1911, MSB 691.1 (6); *Diary 6*: Mafeking, 5 to 16 March 1912, MSB 691.1 (7).

Dick 2004
Dick, A.L. (2004). Building a nation of readers? Women's organizations and the politics of reading in South Africa, 1900–1914. [online] Available at: https:// ojs.tetherprop.co.za/index.php/historia/ article/download/4221/8393 [Accessed 5 February 2020].

Dictionary of National Biography, Thomas Muir 2004
Crilly, A.J. (2004). *Sir Thomas Muir: Oxford Dictionary of National Biography.* Available at 'Other web sites' link 1, provided at the end of the biography: http://mathshistory. st–andrews.ac.uk/Biographies/Muir.html [Accessed 3 January 2020].

Dominican Sisters 1892
'King' Dominican Sisters, King William's Town (1892). *Dr. Muir's Visit to the Convent School*, XXIV, pp. 59–62.

Duff 2015
Duff, S.E. (2015). *Changing Childhoods in the Cape Colony.* London: Palgrave Macmillan UK. [E-Book: Play Books.]

Duncan 2000
Duncan, G.A. (2000). 'Coercive agency': James Henderson's Lovedale, 1906–1930. Th.D. thesis, University of South Africa. [online] Available at: https://core.ac.uk/download/pdf/43175944.pdf [Accessed 11 April 2020].

Du Toit and Nell 1976
Du Toit, P.S. and Nell, W.L. (1976). *Onderwys in Kaapland 1652–1980: 'n historiese oorsig*, Second edition. Pretoria: J.L. Van Schaik.

Education Report 1912
Cape of Good Hope. (1912). Education Commission Report. [online] Available at: https://ia601601.us.archive.org/17/items/mainreportminori00cape/mainreportminori00cape.pdf [Accessed 18 June 2020].

EG
The *Education Gazette*, Department of Public Education, Cape Town.

Elliott 2019
Elliott, P. (2019). *The Spilhaus Family. Five hundred years of history (1450–1950).* Reprinted 2019. Alairac, France: Cantaloup Press.

Elliot & Walker
www.ellwalk.co.za. (n.d.). *Elliot & Walker Attorneys.* [online] Available at: http://www.ellwalk.co.za/history-and-heritage-elliot-and-walker.php [Accessed 9 March 2020].

Erasmus 2013
Erasmus, H.J. (2013). Circuit courts in the Cape Colony during the nineteenth century: Hazards and achievements. *Fundamina*, [online] 19 (2), pp. 266–299. Available at: http://www.scielo.org.za/scielo.php?script=sci_arttext&pid=S1021-545X2013000200005 [Accessed 3 March 2020].

Ferguson Paper
Ferguson, W.T. (n.d.). Sir Thomas Muir: Educationist and mathematician. Unpublished article.

Fox
Fox, H. (n.d.). The Cornish-Bowdens of Newton Abbot. Family Letters.

Gibbs 2014
Gibbs, P. (2014). *Coal capital: The shaping of social relations in the Stormberg, 1880–1910.* [online] Available at: http://wiredspace.wits.ac.za/handle/10539/15790 [Accessed 2 May 2020].

Gilliland Husband 1909
Gilliland Husband, M. (1909). Women as citizens. *International Journal of Ethics*, [online] 19 (4), pp. 466–476. [online] Available at: https://www.jstor.org/stable/2377016 [Accessed 13 May 2020].

Harris 1921
Harris, M. (1921). On reading aloud. *The North American Review*, 214 (790), pp. 345–351. [online] Available at: https://www.jstor.org/stable/25120825?seq=7#metadata_info_tab_contents [Accessed 6 June 2020].

Hodgson 2001
Hodgson, B (2001). *In the Arms of Morpheus: The tragic history of laudanum, morphine and patent medicines.* [online] Available at: https://dokumen.pub/in-the-arms-of-morpheus-the-tragic-history-of-laudanum-morphine-and-patent-medicines-1nbsped-1550548697-9781550548693.html [Accessed 31 July 2020].

Hofmeyr 1913
Hofmeyr, J.H. (1913). *The Life of Jan Hendrik Hofmeyr (Onze Jan).* Cape Town: Van de Sandt de Villiers Print Company.

Hofmeyr 1935
Hofmeyr, C. (1935). 'n Oud Inspekteur kyk terug. *Die Huisgenoot*, 8 March.

Howe-Ely 2020
Howe-Ely, L. (2020). List of new schools/buildings referenced in *Education Gazette* 1902 to mid-1915. Unpublished.

Howes 2011
Howes, S. (2011). Are these the finest school buildings in Cape Town? *WCED News* (Western Cape Education Department), 08, pp. 10–11. [online]. Available at: https://issuu.com/wcednews/docs/wcednews_feb2011_08 [Accessed 5 February 2020].

ILAS 2002
Farebrother R.W. and others (2002). Sir Thomas Muir and nineteenth-century books on Determinants. *IMAGE, Bulletin of the International Linear Algebra Society*, 28, pp. 6–15. [online] Available at: https://www.ilasic.org/IMAGE/IMAGES/28.pdf [Accessed 5 February 2020].

Irving and Murray 1864
Irving, G.V. and Murray, A. (1864). Google Books. (2018). The Upper Ward of Lanarkshire Described and Delineated, Volume 2. [online] Available at: https://books.google.fr/upper+ward+of+lanarkshire+volume+2 [Accessed 21 December 2019].

Jabavu 1922
Jabavu, D.D.T. (1922). *The life of John Tengo Jabavu*. [online] Available at: https://ia801600.us.archive.org/20/items/lifeofjohntengoj00jaba/lifeofjohntengoj00jaba.pdf [Accessed 26 March 2020].

Kannemeyer 1996
Kannemeyer, J.C. (1996). *Langenhoven. 'n Lewe*. Cape Town: Tafelberg. [online] DBNL. Available at: https://www.dbnl.org/tekst/kann003lang01_01/ [Accessed 17 March 2020].

Kantor 2001
Kantor, H. (2001). In retrospect: David Tyack's 'The One Best System'. *Reviews in American History*, 29 (2), pp. 319–327. [online] Available at: http://www.jstor.com/stable/30031234 [Accessed 24 June 2020].

Kapp 2005
Kapp, P. (2005). Is't ons ernst? Na 100 jaar. [online] Available at: http://hetjanmarais.co.za/wp-content/uploads/2018/01/HJMNF_Kapp_toespraak-1512975470955-1.pdf [Accessed 24 March 2020].

Kidd 1908
Kidd, D. (1908). *Kafir Socialism and the Dawn of Individualism: An introduction to the study of the native problem*. [online] Available at: https://ia801607.us.archive.org/14/items/kafirsocialismda00kidd/kafirsocialismda00kidd.pdf [Accessed 1 April 2020].

Kies 1939
Kies, B.M. (1939). The policy of educational segregation and some of its effects upon the coloured people of the Cape. B.Ed. thesis, University of Cape Town.

Kyte 2013
Kyte, T. (2013). *Your hand and mine*. England: Tiki Kyte.

Le Roux 1998
Le Roux, C.S. (1998). A historical-educational appraisal of parental responsibilities and rights in formal education in South Africa [1652–1910]. D.Ed. thesis, University of South Africa. [online] uir.unisa.ac.za. Available at: http://uir.unisa.ac.za/handle/10500/17183 [Accessed 27 March 2020].

Le Roux 2016
Le Roux, C.S. (2016). Creating a British World: British colonial teachers and the Anglicising of Afrikaner children. *Yesterday and Today*, 15. [online] Available at: http://dx.doi.org/10.17159/2223-0386/2016/n15a1 [Accessed 27 March 2020].

Linear Algebra, Muir Legacy 2005
www.sciencedirect.com. (2005). *Linear Algebra and its Applications, Special Issue on Determinants and the Legacy of Sir Thomas Muir, ScienceDirect.com*. [online] Available at: https://www.sciencedirect.com/journal/linear-algebra-and-its-applications/vol/411 [Accessed 26 February 2020].

Lockhart 2010
Lockhart, B.R.W. (2010). *The Town School: A History of The High School of Glasgow*. Edinburgh: Donald.

Loram 1916
Loram, C.T. (1916) The retirement of Sir Thomas Muir. *The American Mathematical Monthly*, 23 (3), pp. 74–75.

Loram 1917
Loram, C.T. (1917). *The Education of the South African Native*. London: Longmans, Green and Co. [online]. Available at: https://archive.org/details/educationofsouth00lora/page/n6/mode/2up [Accessed 5 April 2020].

Mahon Trial 1928
Dilnot, G. (ed.). (1928). *The Trial of Patrick Herbert Mahon*. Famous Trials Series. London: Geoffrey Bles. Held by Bodleian Library, University of Oxford. [online] Available at: http://dbooks.bodleian.ox.ac.uk/books/PDFs/N11052034.pdf [Accessed 15 August 2020].

Malherbe 1925
Malherbe, E.G (1925). *Education in South Africa (1652–1922)*. [online] Available at: https://archive.org/details/educationinsouth00egma [Accessed 8 Jan. 2020].

Maritz 2005
Maritz, P. (2005). Sir Thomas Muir, 1844–1934. *Linear Algebra and its Applications*, 411, pp. 3–67. [online] Available at: https://www.sciencedirect.com/science/article/pii/S002437950500011X [Accessed 16 January 2020]. [This paper is an integral part of *Linear Algebra, Muir Legacy 2005*, but is listed separately, because of its significance.]

Maritz Unpublished Paper
Maritz, P. (n.d.). Thomas Muir, Retiree Part V: 1915–1934. Unpublished article.

Mathematics Stack Exchange 2016
Mathematics Stack Exchange. (2016). Linear algebra: Why does Friedberg say that the role of the determinant is less central than in former times? [online] Available at: https://math.stackexchange.com/questions/1999693/why-does-friedberg-say-that-the-role-of-the-determinant-is-less-central-than-in/1999821 [Accessed 23 March 2020].

McDougall and Others 2017
O'Halloran, E., Hussein, A., McDougall, J. and Hill, P. (2017). Ethics and empire: An open letter from Oxford scholars. *The Conversation*. [online] Available at: https://theconversation.com/ethics-and-empire-an-open-letter-from-oxford-scholars-89333 [Accessed 10 June 2020].

McDougall 2018
McDougall, J. (2018). The history of empire isn't about pride – or guilt. *The Guardian*, Opinion, 3 January.

Memorial Address Cam 1977
Anon. (1977). Memorial Address: Lillie Cameron Cornish-Bowden ('Cam'), Somerset West, Cape.

Miller Review 1907
Miller, G.A. (1907). Book review: *The Theory of Determinants in the Historical Order of Development. Bulletin of the American Mathematical Society*, 13 (5), pp. 244–247.

Miller Review 1912
Miller, G.A. (1912). Review: Thomas Muir, *The Theory of Determinants in the Historical Order of Development*, Volume II: The period 1841 to 1860. *Bulletin of the American Mathematical Society*, 18 (10), pp. 512–513. [online] Available at: https://projecteuclid.org/euclid.bams/1183421828 [Accessed 1 Feb. 2020].

Moen 2015
Moen, S.M. and Minnesota Sea Grant (2015). *With Tomorrow in Mind: How Athelstan Spilhaus turned America toward the future*. Duluth, Minnesota: University of Minnesota, Sea Grant Program.

Mouton 2011
Mouton, F.A. (2011). 'Great and lasting service to this country': Sir Leander Starr Jameson, conciliation and the Unionist Party, 1910–1912. *The Journal for Transdisciplinary Research in Southern Africa*, 7 (2), pp. 167–184. [online] Available at: http://dspace.nwu.ac.za/bitstream/handle/10394/5266/TD_7(2)_2011_167-184.pdf.txt [Accessed 9 May 2020].

Mossel Bay Schools History Materials
Dias Museum Mossel Bay [Marx, E.] (2020). Mossel Bay Schools History. [Email 25 February.]: (1) History of Mossel Bay Schools; (2) A Catalogue of Buildings of Architectural, Historical or Contextual Importance in the Central Area of Mossel Bay; (3) Extract from NG Kerk Mossel Baai Gedenk Boek, Opvoeding en Onderwys in die Gemeente, pp. 64–73. Dias Museum, Mossel Bay.

Muir 1878 (1)
Muir, Thomas. (1878) A sketch of the

history from 1825 to 1877. In Burns, J.C. (ed.) *The History of The High School of Glasgow*. Glasgow: David Boyce & Son.

Muir 1878 (2)
Muir, T. (1878). *A Text-Book of Arithmetic for Use in Higher Class Schools*. London: Daldry Isbister & Co.

Muir 1884
Muir, T. (1884). The promotion of research; with special reference to the present state of the Scottish universities and secondary schools, *Proceedings of the Edinburgh Mathematical Society, Nature*, 31, (148) 1884. (An address delivered before the Edinburgh Mathematical Society, 8 February, 1884.) London: Alexander Gardner, Paisley. [online] Available at: https://doi.org/10.1038/031148b0 [Accessed 15 May 2020].

Muir 1890
Muir, T. (1890). *The Theory of Determinants in the Historical Order of its Development*. London and New York: Macmillan.

Muir 1906–1923
Muir, T. (1960 Revised Edition). *The Theory of Determinants in the Historical Order of Development*. New York: Dover Publications Inc. [Volumes I to IV bound in two volumes.]
Note: Garry Tee has informed the author that this 1960 edition, expanded and enlarged by Metzler, contains a substantial number of misprints. Tee, G. (2020). Sir Thomas Muir. [Email 26 February] For convenience, this compendium is cited rather than the four individually published volumes: however, each original volume is available online at: archive.org.

Muir 1930
Muir, T. (1930). *Contributions to the History of Determinants 1900–1920*. London and Glasgow: Blackie & Son. [The supplementary fifth volume to *Muir 1906–1923*.]

Muir and Rodger, Musical Score
Rodger, James (music) and Muir, Sir Thomas (words) (n.d.). A Highland Idyll, sheet music. Available at: National Library of South Africa, Cape Town Campus, Special Collections.

Muir and Rodger, Highland Idyll Recording
Rodger, James (music) and Muir, Sir Thomas (words) (n.d.). A Highland Idyll, recording: [online] Available at: https://www.youtube.com/watch?v=07cOe-Lz6Ug [Accessed 1 November 2020]

Muir Estate File
Estate File of Thomas Muir d. 1934. Cape (KAB) Estate File, Thos. Muir, MOOC 6–9–4410 Ref 41039

Muir, George, Military Record
National Archives. (2020). *Lieutenant George Bell Muir, Royal Army Service Corps*. [Military Record] Ref. WO 339/77983.

Muir Manuscript Collection, NLSA
Sir Thomas Muir Manuscript Collection (bequeathed 1934). National Library of South Africa (NSLA), Cape Town. Reference MSB.691, including:
– *Diaries* when on tour as S.G.E. (1909–1912), ref. MSB 691.1; and
– Three volumes of newspaper cuttings, letters, programmes, etc., concerning his life and work ('Cuttings etc.').

Muir Mathematics Papers
National Library of Scotland (n.d.). *Papers of Sir Thomas Muir on Mathematics*. Archives and Manuscripts Collections, Acc. 10068.

Muir Memorandum 1912
Muir, T. (1912). Typed memorandum re. 'Fremantle Commission': *Muir Manuscript Collection, NLSA*, MSB 691.1 (8).

Muir, Published Address(es)
Muir (n.d.). Available at National Library of South Africa, Cape Town Campus, General Collection:
President's address, Cape Town 1910, South African Association for the Advancement of Science. OCLC No: 1017434631. Ref. 605.d.109(9);
Presidential address: Education and Science, South African Association for the Advancement of Science. OCLC No: 1017272109. Ref. 605.d.99(4);
A Word on Training, University of Cape of Good Hope, Degree Day, 10 August 1900. OCLC No. 814227774.

Musical Times 1906
Musical Times. (1906). Dr. Thomas Muir, C.M.G., F.R.S. Superintendent-General of Education in Cape Colony. *Musical Times*, 47 (756), 1 February, pp. 87–91. [online] Available at: https://www.jstor.org/stable/902739 [Accessed 28 November 2019].

Nellie, Biographical Letter c. 1948
Spilhaus, Nellie. (*c.* 1948). Biographical letter written to her daughter Peggie Barry.

Neville 1934
Neville, E.H. (1934). Sir Thomas Muir. *The Mathematical Gazette*, 18 (230), p. 257.

O'Dowd 1972
O'Dowd, M.C. (1972). Education, John Adamson. In: De Villiers, R.M. (ed.) (1972). *Better Than They Knew*, pp. 162–185. Cape Town: Purnell.

Olwage 2003
Olwage, G. (2003). Music and (post) colonialism: The dialectics of choral culture on a South African frontier. Ph.D. thesis, Rhodes University. [online] Available at: https://core.ac.uk/download/pdf/145055315.pdf [Accessed 10 August 2020].

O'Malley 2009
O'Malley, T.R. (2009). Mateship and money-making: Shearing in twentieth-century Australia. Ph.D. thesis, University of Sydney. [online] Available at: http://citeseerx.ist.psu.edu/viewdoc/download?doi=10.1.1.899.1014&rep=rep1&type=pdf [Accessed 12 August 2020].

Oxford History of South Africa 1971
Wilson, M. and Thompson, L. (1971). *The Oxford History of South Africa*. London: Oxford University Press.

P.A.M. 1892
P.A.M. (1892). The History of Determinants. *Nature*, 45, pp. 481–482.

Paterson 1992
Paterson, A.N.M. (1992). Contest and co-option: The struggle for schooling in the African Independent Churches of the Cape Colony, *c.* 1895–1920. Ph. D. Thesis University of Cape Town. [online]

Available at: https://open.uct.ac.za/bitstream/item/8617/thesis_hum_1992_paterson_anm.pdf?sequence=1 [Accessed 25 Feb. 2020].

Paterson 2005
Paterson, A. (2005). "The Gospel of Work Does Not Save Souls": Conceptions of Industrial and Agricultural Education for Africans in the Cape Colony, 1890-1930. *History of Education Quarterly*, [online] 45(3), pp.377–404. Available at: https://www.jstor.org/stable/20461986?seq=1 [Accessed 12 February 2020].

Pells 1954
Pells, E.G. (1970). *300 Years of Education in South Africa*. Westport, CT: Greenwood Press. Revised edition of Pells, E.G. (1954). *Three Hundred Years of Education in South Africa*. Cape Town: Juta.

Poole 2010
Poole, D.C. (2010). *Linear Algebra: A modern introduction*. Stamford, CT: Cengage Learning.

Popular Educator 1871
Cassell, Petter and Galp. (1871). *The Popular Educator: A complete encyclopaedia of elementary, advanced and technical education*, pp. 124–125. London: Cassell. [online] Available at: https://play.google.com/books/reader?id=7DECAAAAQAAJ&printsec=frontcover&pg=GBS.PA124) [Accessed 13 January 2020].

Report on Educational System of the Cape Colony 1901
(1901). *Special Reports on Educational Subjects, Volume 5. Educational Systems of the Chief Colonies of the British Empire, including the Cape Colony*, pp. 1–196. London: Board of Education. [online] Internet Archive. Available at: https://archive.org/details/specialreportso23educgoog/page/n12/mode/2up [Accessed 22 July 2020].

Ritchie 1918
Ritchie, W. (1918). *The History of the South African College*. Cape Town: Maskew Miller.

Royal Society Obituary 1934
H.W.T. (1934). *Sir Thomas Muir, 1844–1934.*

Obituary Notices of Fellows of the Royal Society, 1 (3), pp. 179–184. [online] Available at: *JSTOR:* www.jstor.org/stable/768819 [Accessed 28 January 2020].

Roxburgh 1971
Roxburgh, James, Maclean. (1971). *The School Board of Glasgow, 1873–1919.* London: University of London Press.

Sasine 1776
Sasine 1776. James Muir. Registered in *National Records of Scotland*, Volume ref RS42/20, folio 354.

Schoeman 2014
Schoeman, C. (2014). *The Historical Karoo: Traces of the past in South Africa's arid interior.* Cape Town: Random House Struik.

Scholtz 2018
Scholtz, M. (2018). The Bay View Hotel was a grand dame. *The Village News.* [online] Available at: https://thevillagenews.co.za/the-bay-view-hotel-was-a-grand-dame/ [Accessed 26 April 2020].

Scotlands Places, Lanarkshire
scotlandsplaces.gov.uk. (n.d.). *Lanarkshire, Volume 57 | ScotlandsPlaces.* [online] Available at: https://scotlandsplaces.gov.uk/digital-volumes/ordnance-survey-name-books/lanarkshire-os-name-books-1858-1861/lanarkshire-volume-57 [Accessed 21 March 2020].

Scottish Places 2019
Scottish-places.info. (2019). *Bothwell from The Gazetteer for Scotland.* [online] Available at: https://www.scottish-places.info/towns/townhistory4703.html [Accessed 21 March 2020].

Shepherd 1940
Shepherd, R. (1940). *Lovedale, South Africa: The story of a century, 1841–1941.* Lovedale, C.P.: The Lovedale Press.

Short Obituary 1947
(1947). Obituary Mr E.H.W. Short. *South African Railways and Harbours Magazine*, November, pp. 965–966.

Slater's Directory 1878
(1878). *Slater's Royal national commercial directory and topography of Scotland.*

[online] Available at: https://deriv.nls.uk/dcn23/9022/90220973.23.pdf [Accessed 21 March 2020].

Snedegar 2015
Snedegar, K. (2015). *Mission, Science, and Race in South Africa: A.W. Roberts of Lovedale, 1883–1938.* Lanham, MD: Lexington Books.

Soudien 2018
Soudien, C. (2018). Institutionalising racial segregation in the South African school: The School Board Act, 1905. *Paedagogica Historica*, 55 (1), pp. 21–37.

S.A. Biography Muir
Rautenbach, C.H. (1968). Muir, Sir Thomas. In: *Dictionary of South African Biography*, Cape Town: South African Library.

South African Science Biographical Database
Plug, C. Prof. (n.d.). Sir Thomas Muir (Mathematics) SS2A3 *Biographical Database of Southern African Science.* [online] Available at: https://www.s2a3.org.za/bio/Biograph_final.php?serial=1982 [Accessed 19 February 2020].

South Magazine 2011
South Magazine (2011). The ostrich kings. 1 September. [online] Available at: https://southmagazine.co.za/2011/09/01/the-ostrich-kings/ [Accessed 10 May 2020].

Spilhaus 1960
Spilhaus, K. (1960). *Memoirs of Karl Spilhaus.* Cape Town: Self-published.

St. Andrews University Photographs
Thomas, Rodger. (n.d.). *University of St. Andrews, Collection of Photographs of the residents in St. Leonard's Hall 1861–1873*, General Album 59. [online] Available at: https://collections.st-andrews.ac.uk/photographs/album-book-portfolio/university-of-st-andrews-collection-of-photographs-of-the-residents-in-st-leonards-hall-1861-1873/355571 [Accessed 13 August 2020].

St. Mary's Churchyard, Biggar
Survey of St. Mary's Churchyard, Biggar. [online] Available at:

http://biggararchaeology.org.uk/
survey–of–st–marys–churchyard–biggar/
[Accessed 13 August 2020].

Tee 2003
Tee, G.J. (2003). Up with determinants!
*IMAGE, Bulletin of the International
Linear Algebra Society*, 30, pp. 7–11.
[online] Available at: https://www.ilasic.
org/IMAGE/IMAGES/30.pdf [Accessed 13
August 2020].

Tiger Kloof
www.historicschools.org.za. (n.d.).
*Historic Schools Restoration Project:
Tiger Kloof*. [online] Available at: http://
www.historicschools.org.za/view.
asp?pg=Schools&subm=Pilot%20
Schools&school=tiger [Accessed 17 April
2020].

Times Obituary 1934
Times. (1934). Sir Thomas Muir:
Mathematician and educationist, *The
Times*, 22 March.

Turnbull 1935
Turnbull, H.W. (1935). Thomas Muir.
*The Journal of The London Mathematical
Society*, 10, pp. 76–80.

Wearing 2013
Wearing, J.P. (2013). *The London Stage,
1900–1909: A Calendar of Productions,
Performers, and Personnel*. London:
Scarecrow Press.

Whiteside 1906
Whiteside, J. (1906). *History of the
Wesleyan Methodist Church of South
Africa*. Internet Archive. London:
Elliot Stock; Cape Town: Juta & Co.;
Methodist Book Room. [online]
Available at: https://archive.org/details/
historyofwesleya00whitrich/page/n8/
mode/2up [Accessed 9 March 2020].

Willoughby 1912
Willoughby, W.C. (1912). *Tiger Kloof:
The London Missionary Society's native
institution in South Africa*. London:
London Missionary Society. Internet
Archive. Available at: https://archive.org/
details/tigerklooflondon00will/page/n8/
mode/2up [Accessed 17 April 2020].

Xuma History
www.sahistory.org.za. (n.d.). Dr Alfred
Xuma. *South African History Online*.
[online] Available at: https://www.
sahistory.org.za/people/dr-alfred-xuma
[Accessed 9 March 2020].

ENDNOTES

1   Throughout I refer to my great-grandfather as 'Muir' (a name I also bear, as my second name). I refer to other members of the family, either by their first name (with or without surname, e.g. his wife 'Maggie Muir'). This seems fitting as I now understand the formality of the man, and he would not have invited his great-grandson to call him 'Thomas'.

2   *Biggar 2017* and *McDougall and Others 2017*.

3   This is the path suggested by *McDougall 2018*.

4   *Bickford-Smith 1995*, p. xxi.

5   A reading of *Anderson 1985*, p. 194, describing the opportunities which a Scottish academic education offered a young 'lad', suggested to me the sub-title for this biography as Muir was truly a Scottish 'Lad O' Pairts'.

6   In the *Muir Manuscript Collection, NLSA*, Muir records the location of the baptismal record of his birth in Nemphlar: Hope St. Free Church Lanark, 1 Sept. 1844. The records of this church have not survived.

7   *Croal 1882*.

8   His birthplace is recorded as 'close to the Stonebyres Falls' in *Musical Times 1906* and this gloss on his birthplace was later followed in other formal records: *Times Obituary 1934; Royal Society Obituary 1934; Aitken 1936*. This romantic sleight of hand caused the author a futile search on the ground for the non-existent village of Stonebyres in Lanarkshire!

9   *Aitken 1950*, p. 65.

10 Muir's notes on the family history in Biggar are in *Muir Manuscript Collection, NLSA*, newspaper cuttings, etc. In the churchyard inventory, *St. Mary's Churchyard, Biggar*, W. Muir is recorded on page 21 and Wm Gladstone is listed on page 12: Map sector E, Grave No. 251, Wm Muir 1829; Map sector C, Grave No. 134, Mr Wm Gladstone of Excise d 17.2.1816 in 87th year. The secessionist churches did ultimately reunite with St. Mary's and the church is now known as Biggar Kirk.

11 *Musical Times 1906*, p. 87. The subject of the article was Muir and his interest in music.

12 *Biggar, House of Fleming 1867*, pp. 143–144. John Gladstone (1726–1800) was 'the chief leader of the Secession from the parish church in 1780': he was a cousin of William Gladstone, excise officer (1730–1816), the one buried in the churchyard. The record of the second secession (correct in terms of the chronology of the pair), makes no reference to the names of either William Muir or John Gladstone: Christie, R.C. (2020). Secession from the Parish Church of Biggar. Report of a search of the Records of the Relief Church in Biggar, 1788–1906 (NRS ref. CH3/1249/1). [Email 21 Mar.]; Vieth, H. (2020). Records, Relief Church of Biggar. Report, Search Room Archivist, National Records of Scotland. [Email 24 Mar].

13 The dates of Prime Minister W.E. Gladstone were 1809–1898.

14 There is only one reference to two generations of Muirs: *Biggar and the House of Fleming 1867*, p. 191–192. The then Lairds of Annieston (John Muir and his son) both broke the law in 1625 and 1646, by giving a kirk burial to their fathers (a practice that then smacked of popery).

15 In 1646 'John Muir of Aniston' owned the substantial Symington estate (and held the Barony of Symington), but in 1667 transferred most of this to the Lockharts of Lee, retaining only the Annieston estate. It remained a substantial estate, with a handsome mansion: *Irving and Murray 1864*, pp. 184–185, 191–193 and 199. In 1689 and 1690, however, it was a 'James Lockhart of Anniston' (and not a Muir at all) who was appointed

a Commissioner of Supply of the county: *Ibid.*, p. 193. The estate is described with various different spellings: Annieston/Anniston/Annistown/Anandstone.

16   The archaeological survey identifying the ruin was carried out in 2005: canmore.org. uk. (n.d.). Annieston Tower | Canmore. [online] Available at: https://canmore.org.uk/ site/47464/annieston-tower. [Accessed 29 February 2020]. The tower and underground chamber, therefore, must have been demolished in the last 15 years. The stones were apparently used to build nearby properties: Barrington, H. (2020). Ruins of Annieston Castle. [Email 30 May.]

17   In about 1860, the Dickson family owned the entire estate and earlier transfers show their proprietorship went back to the 1790s. In 1860, Annieston farmstead was still in good repair, although even then the castle was a ruin: *Scotlands Places, Lanarkshire*, p. OSI/21/57 pp. 5–6. There is evidence that a James Muir transferred land near Biggar to the Dickson family in 1776: Sasine 1776. The rubric of this Sasine notes 'sasine- James Muir', 'mason, Newbigging, formerly apprentice to George Veitch, mason, Sunnyside'. However, there is nothing to connect James Muir to William Muir, and there is no reference to the land transferred having any connection with the Annieston estate.

18   The author has drawn extensively from the biographical elements of *Daleboudt 1942*, Chapter Two, Thomas Muir: Early Life, pp. 39–45; The University Period, pp. 45–49; The pre-South African Period, pp. 49–53. Although focusing mainly on education in the Cape, Daleboudt provides useful additional insights into Muir's upbringing and early life. Researching and writing in 1942, he enjoyed the distinct advantage of being able to obtain his information direct from members of the family, and in particular, he had the benefit of access to Muir's daughter, Nellie: at that stage, she had retained some materials relevant to Muir's early life, which regrettably are no longer known to exist. One document, his diary of 1865, is a particular loss to the record of his life.

19   His brother Andrew, similarly, was a pupil teacher by the age of 14: 1851 Census, Overtown, Cambusnethan.

20   *Musical Times 1906*, p. 88.

21   *AMS Mathematics and Music 2010.*

22   *Popular Educator 1871*, p. 124.

23   There are two College photographs of Thomas's time at St. Leonard's Hall, the ninth and tenth photographs in the collection: *St. Andrews University Photographs.*

24   The son of the 8th Duke of Argyll, tutored by Muir, was undoubtedly Lord Colin Campbell, the Duke's youngest son. He was a student in College Hall and is pictured in a group photograph, including Muir, in 1869–1870: *St. Andrews University Photographs,* Residents of St. Leonard's Hall, 1869–1870.

25   *Daleboudt 1942*, p. 48.

26   *Muir 1878 (2).*

27   *Muir 1878 (1)*, pp. 75–76.

28   *Musical Times 1906*, p. 88, column 1.

29   Fifteenth Annual Report of University Examiners, p.25, quoted in *Lockhart 2010*, p. 147.

30   *Lockhart 2010*, p. 148, partly quoting *Bailie 1892.*

31   Prof. Mackenzie went on '…to a brilliant career first at Glasgow and Edinburgh Universities, then Cambridge, where he was elected to a Fellowship at Trinity. In 1895 he was appointed Professor of Logic and Philosophy at University College, Cardiff. He was elected a Fellow, British Academy in 1934. He is held to be a representative of the later phase of the neo-Hegelian school of British Idealistic philosophy' (*Lockhart 2010*, p. 159).

32   Quoted from a cutting in the Muir Manuscript Collection in *Daleboudt 1942*, p. 51. His mentors had always spoken highly of his skill as a teacher and *Daleboudt 1942*, p. 45, also

quotes two glowing testimonials to this effect: first, the headmaster of Wishaw School spoke of his 'peculiar power of interesting and swaying the minds of his pupils' (dated 11 November 1863, and then in the possession of Nellie Spilhaus); secondly, in June 1874, Professor H. Blackburn of the University of Glasgow praised him as 'the most skilful teacher of elementary mathematics with whom he had had to do' (dated 13 June 1874, and in the Muir Manuscript Collection).

33 *Daleboudt 1942*, p. 53.

34 *Roxburgh 1971*, quoted in Anderson, R. (2020). Roxburgh. [Email 21 Jan.]

35 *Muir 1884*, p. 8.

36 *Ibid*, p. 26.

37 *Ibid*, p. 27.

38 It was a three-bedroom flat in Crow Road, with a small garden. It formed part of a recently built villa next door to the Jordanhill Free Church manse.

39 It is a mystery why he should have chosen to call all three homes Beechcroft. Perhaps it is more than a coincidence that a directory of a century earlier lists, among gentry, Mr. Thomas Muir, Beechcroft, Bishopton [Slater's Royal National Commercial Directory of Scotland 1785, Houston Renfrewshire, Nobility Gentry + Clergy]. Was this earlier Muir part of the unsolved genealogical legend?

40 The house, still called Beechcroft, remains recognisable compared with the family photographs, and is now 23 Paisley Rd, Renfrew, Renfrewshire. The long garden has disappeared, and it must have been sub-divided a long time ago. The 1881 census listed Muir's house as being in the hamlet of Rossland, parish of Erskine, but the Post Office Annual Glasgow Directory 1884–85 clearly lists the house and address in Bishopton (p. 461). The birth records of both Cam and Thomas record their place of birth as Erskine, but later (in recording his details for military enlistment and in all other official registers in Australia), Thomas entered Paisley as his place of birth; this may indicate that he regarded that town as the centre of the family's activities.

41 *Scottish Places 2019*. Nellie's reminiscences of Bothwell are from a hand-written note drawn up by the author's mother before Nellie's death.

42 The house, now 8 St Andrews Avenue, Bothwell, is still readily recognisable from Muir's own photograph of it. It still bears the same house name on the gate.

43 *Daleboudt 1942*, p. 38.

44 *Cape Times 1934*, is quoted as source of this story in the *Dictionary of National Biography, Thomas Muir 2004*. The same account is given in the *Times Obituary 1934* and in *Aitken 1936*, p. 264. *Daleboudt 1942*, pp. 37–38, quotes Fuller: C.J. Rhodes, p. 167 *et seq.* and says the story originated in Anders, 'Muir at 89', *Cape Times*, 24 August 1933.

45 *Biographical Sketch Muir 1905*.

46 *Bailie 1892*.

47 Dinner to Dr. Muir. (1892). *Glasgow Herald*, 13 April 1892.

48 *Ibid*.

49 *Aitken 1950*, p. 68.
In 1892 the head office of the Education Department was on the 'top floor of the rebuilt verger's house next to the Dutch Reformed Church in Adderley Street, the D.R.C. Chambers': *Borman 1989*, p. 126. This small office housed the entire staff of eight persons, including Muir.

50 *Cornish-Bowden Memoirs*, pp. 1 and 2.

51 *Diary 5*, Monday 9/10/11: Sir David Gill was a fellow Scot, who was H.M.'s Astronomer of the Cape Colony (1879–1906).

52 Laudanum 'reigned almighty in the pantheon of opium drugs': *Hodgson 2001*, p. 45. It was a potent mixture of wine, opium, saffron and cinnamon, and was widely used to alleviate pain, both of body and mind.

53 *Diary 5*, 20/10/11 Friday.

54 *Muir Memorandum 1912*.

55 The quotation is from *Diary 5*, 3/10/11, seven days before Maggie's birthday on 10 October. The Waterman was a popular fountain pen, marketed after 1908, that had solved the perennial problem of leakage.

56 Nellie was at the South African College, 1893–1898. *Ritchie 1918* records her outstanding record: University Exhibition at Intermediate Examination and Class I in that Examination, 1896 (pp. 809 and 822); Honours in Mathematical and Natural Sciences, 1898 (p. 813); B.A. Science prize, 1898 (p. 810). Although Nellie did not go on to do scientific work, she is nevertheless included as one of South Africa's Women in Science: *Creese 2010*, p. 26.

57 *Nellie, Biographical Letter c. 1948*, p.1.

58 Information from extracts from the Diocesan College magazines, 1894 and 1895: Murray, P. (2019). Bishops Archives. [Emails 2 December].

59 *Memorial Address Cam 1977*.

60 *Fox*, p. 83. Letter dated 12 August 1908, Maude Cornish-Bowden to her sister May.

61 This section draws substantially on this work: *Bickford-Smith 1995*.

62 *Bickford-Smith 1995*, p. 76.

63 *Muir Diary 2*, 5/2/10 Saturday.

64 *Muir Diary 1*, 17/8/09 Tuesday.

65 *Muir Diary 2*, 17/2/10 Thursday. This is not simply an isolated reference: see also Muir Diary 2, 7/2/10 Monday. He makes similar remarks in his diary the following year, using the epithet 'noisy', which is a similar stereotype: *Diary 5*, Sunday 8/10/11 and Monday 9/10/11.

66 The k-word is now regarded as offensive, a racist slur. However, it only became a pejorative term in the mid-20th century. It is clear from pre-1915 Parliamentary reports that the word was still being used widely at that time, even in official circles. Usage was non-derogatory in literature: e.g. in John Buchan's Prester John in 1910.

67 The material for this introduction to Muir's tenure in the Cape is drawn principally from *Duff 2015*, 100–107 and 215.

68 Cape Parliamentary Papers, G3–1894, cited in Bickford-Smith 1995, pp. 142, note 53.

69 *Dominican Sisters 1892*. All quotations, relating to this visit, are from this source.

70 'Socotra': this is an island in the Arabian Sea, not far from the eastern entrance to the Gulf of Aden. The island is part of Yemen: it seems a rather tough question for a Victorian primary school pupil in the distant Cape Colony.

71 These classes are the equivalent of a contemporary set of mathematics students, G.C.S.E. and above.

72 A contemporary G.C.S.E. mathematics pupil would manage to solve the first two of these algebraic problems. The third, however, would be unfamiliar: 'It's a straightforward enough algebraic transformation but not something you would expect to see in a modern textbook'; the problem is 'a bit convoluted – this is an algebraic trick to factorise a quartic expression by using the difference of 2 squares': Haigh, D. (2020) and Pink, J. (2020), Emails, Victorian mathematicians, respectively dated 21 and 20 May.
The nun made an error in transcription of the answer of the final problem. The answer should be: $(x^2 + 3x + 9)(x^2 - 3x + 9)$. The problems were put to three mathematicians, all of whom spotted the mistake: Damian Haigh, Jonathan Pink and Peter Gibbard. Thus, it could not have been the mistake of a mathematician of the calibre of Muir.

73 Statistics from *Loram 1916*, p. 74.

74 *Bickford-Smith 1995*, p. 139, and he explains the background on pp. 138–139.

75 *Bickford-Smith 1995*, pp. 142. For detailed comparisons of the average grant per pupil in the mission schools and in the poor schools, in 1893 and 1894, see *Kies 1939*, p. 39. This disparity in funding continued throughout the period to 1905 and was further accentuated when the War Economy was introduced in 1899, at which point the mission schools were worst hit: *Kies 1939*, p. 40.

76 *Cuthbert 1911*, p. 7.

77 Cape Parliamentary Papers, G39–1893, evidence of Thomas Muir, quoted in Bickford-Smith 1995, p. 142.

78 Muir's positive achievements during his term of office are set out in *Cuthbert 1911*, pp. 7–13. This pamphlet contains no critique, whatsoever, of Muir's policies, hardly surprising as the author, Cuthbert, was a subordinate within his department: he was 'Railway Education Officer' for the Cape, a role developed to provide schools at suitable locations along the railroad (see p. 6 of the pamphlet).

79 *Malherbe 1925*, p. 140; Malherbe included Muir's watchword as one of his key educational system truths in the foreword to his book (p. xii).

80 A good summary of the way he reorganised the Department of Education into nine divisions, and equally strengthened the Schools Inspectorate, is provided by *Du Toit and Nell 1976*, pp. 83–85.

81 *Malherbe 1925*, p. 113.

82 *Duff 2015*, pp. 97–98 and 215.

83 *Malherbe 1925*, p. 113.

84 Cape Archives Correspondence C.O. 4364, referenced by *Daleboudt 1942*, p. 76.

85 Approximate translation from *Hofmeyr 1935*, p. 57 [also quoted by *Daleboudt 1942*, p. 75].

86 *Musical Times 1906*, p. 89.

87 *Turnbull 1935*, p. 77.

88 *Dick 2004*, p. 29.

89 *Malherbe 1925*, p. 172.

90 *Daleboudt 1942*, p. 243: he quotes from a report of Muir's talk on National Education at Graaff-Reinet, Cape Argus, 1 December 1892.

91 *Cornish-Bowden Memoirs*, p.1.

92 Fully described in *Daleboudt 1942*, in the section of his thesis entitled Meubelering van Skole en Skoolgeboue, pp. 226–235.

93 *Cuthbert 1911*, p. 11.

94 Leading article in Ons Land, 22 October 1895, approximate translation of quote by *Daleboudt 1942*, p. 96.

95 *Spilhaus 1960*, pp. 14–15.

96 *Report on Educational System of the Cape Colony 1901*, p. 194. As to the effect of the war on the schools of in the Cape Colony, see generally pp. 192–194 of this Report.

97 *Diary 6* 13/3/12 Wednesday; in the original diary entry Muir simply refers to Baden-Powell as 'B-P', the latter's nickname.
Colonel Baden-Powell (1857–1941) commanded the garrison of Mafeking and led the defence of the siege. Commentators record that B-P sailed to Cape Town on R.M.S. Dunnottar Castle in July 1899. He took with him Lord Edward Cecil (1867–1918) as his Chief Staff Officer. B-P's Intelligence Officer was Hon. Algernon Hanbury-Tracy (1857–1941).
Lord and Lady Cecil are both listed as cabin passengers on the same voyage, travelling with a valet and maid. There is no listing of either B-P or Hanbury-Tracy; however, this may be

explained by the fact that the transportation of military personnel, travelling as such, was not listed. Both men were then still unmarried and presumably travelled on military business; Lord Cecil was a married man, travelling privately with his wife and retinue. Also listed as a passenger is Dr. Thomas Muir, incorrectly listed as a 'doctor' and with the wrong recorded age. It is a reasonable supposition, despite inaccuracies of the record, that this was the voyage on which Muir got to know Baden-Powell and his senior staff members. ancestry.co.uk (n.d.). Passenger Lists Dunnottar Castle, Southampton to Cape Town, departing 8 July 1899.

98   *Biographical Sketch Muir 1905.*

99   *Ibid.*

100 Merriman Papers: Lord De Villiers to John X. Merriman, 22 Oct. 1904 (288/04), cited in *Cuthbert 1950*, p. 45.

101 Report of the Superintendent-General for Education for 1905, p. 14, quoted in *Kies 1939*, p. 44.

102 *Ibid.*

103 Report of the Superintendent-General for Education for 1906, p. 2, quoted in *Kies 1939*, p. 45, together with Muir's supporting statistical detail of the increase.

104 *Soudien 2018*, p. 11.

105 Report of the Superintendent-General for Education for 1909, p. 6. Quoted by *Kies 1939*, p. 46. Muir made a similar statement in Report of the Superintendent-General for Education for 1910, pp. 3–4, quoted in *Olwage 2003*, p. 71.

106 Moller v. Keimoes School Committee (1911), A.D. 644.

107 *Paterson 2005*, p. 383.

108 *Paterson 1992*, p. 70, and Paterson explains the strategies in the following pages.

109 For background on the status of the Transkei, and this 'political imperative', see the separate section below: *The continuing battle between Muir and the Rev. James Henderson of Lovedale.*

110 *Paterson 1992* sets out the statistics on the differential expenditure on pp. 72–73.

111 Muir speaking at the formal opening of Alice Public School; Alice Times, 22 Nov. 1906, quoted by *Paterson 1992*, p. 74.

112 *Paterson 1992*, p. 76, quotes the reports which set out the statistical reduction in mixed school attendance: Cape Education Dept., Annual Report of the S.G.E. 1909, p. 3; Cape of Good Hope Education Commission Report, 1912, p. 7.

113 *Coetzee 1951*, p. 201 (approximate translation).

114 *Hofmeyr 1935*, p. 57.

115 The background on the crisis is drawn from *Gibbs 2014*, pp. 197–199.

116 See the references to the press reports in The Albert Times and Molteno News between April 1902 and December 1903, cited in *Gibbs 2014*, p. 198.

117 *Diary 2*, 31/1/10 Monday and 18/2/10 Friday.

118 Pepler v Molteno School Board 1912 CPD 519 [case report courtesy Professor Marita Carnelley, Faculty of Law, North-West University].

119 *Dick 2004*, p. 28.

120 *Ibid.*

121 Approximate translation from leading article in the Oudtshoorn journal, Het Zuid-Westen, 31 March 1903; quoted in *Daleboudt 1942*, pp. 439–440 (who sets out the entirety of the 'character sketch', which he opined was 'not an unfair summary of Muir both as a man and S.G.E.').

122 The part of his address, relating to the language question and referring to Muir, is set out in *Hofmeyr 1913*, pp. 598–600. Quotations are from this source. Both *Daleboudt 1942*, pp. 325–326, and *Maritz 2005*, p. 28, quote a long extract from Hofmeyr's address (respectively in the original Dutch and in a translation).

123 See *Kapp 2005*, pp. 10–11, for a discussion of the impact of Hofmeyr's speech.

124 'Muir en de Taalordonnansie', Skoolmeester, quoted by *Daleboudt 1942*, p. 322.

125 Report of a speech of Ds. J.R. Albertyn at the Synod, De Burger, 22 November 1915, quoted in *Daleboudt* 1942, pp. 322–323.

126 *Kannemeyer 1996*, p. 293; inevitably in making this argument, Langenhoven concerned himself only with the white population of South Africa, and their need for mother-tongue instruction; he totally ignored the parallel argument that should have been made for teaching in the vernacular as well.

127 *Mouton 2011*. [No page reference online.]

128 *Diary 4*, Wednesday 1/3/11.

129 Letter written from De Aar, 30 March 1907, *Muir Manuscript Collection*, NLSA, MSB 691.1.8.

130 For a summary of the Commission's stance, see *Maritz 2005*, pp. 26–27.

131 The merits of the alternative approaches to school inspection were exhaustively examined and reported on by the Education Commission 1910 and reported on in *Education Report 1912*, pp. 100–119. The issues with regard to the two competing systems are summarised earlier in the section *Muir's reforms of the white educational system, 1892–1905*.

132 Muir, evidence before the Education Commission 1910, Question 1133, quoted in *Daleboudt 1942*, p. 136.

133 *Daleboudt 1942*, p. 138. Also referred to in *Education Report 1912*, p. 112.

134 Letter to Mr. Jagger, 8 December 1911, *Muir Manuscript Collection*, NLSA, MSB 691.1.8. See also, in the same collection, 1912 Memorandum re. The Fremantle Commission, recording Muir's meeting with both Smartt and Jagger, and his Confidential Memorandum, 21 May 1912, to Sir Thomas Smartt; after publication of the Commission report Muir felt he had his 'back firm against the wall'.

135 *Bissett 1973*, preface. There is a dearth of material on J.W. Jagger (1859–1930), but this essay provides a brief biography of him, with biographical notes, entitled 'the skull beneath the skin', pp. 99–103. Jagger was a major benefactor of the University of Cape Town and its Library (now the Reading Room) is named after him.

136 *Ibid*, p. 101.

137 This was the view expressed by prominent Unionist politician, Drummond Chaplin: referenced at note 54 in *Mouton 2011*. The background set out in the following paragraph, concerning the progress towards bilingualism, is similarly drawn from *Mouton 2011*.

138 *Diary 5*, Sunday 15/10/11.

139 Leading article, *Christian Express*, June 1915, quoted in *Daleboudt 1942*, p. 432.

140 *Pells 1954*, p. 45.

141 *Cuthbert 1911*, pp. 7–13.

142 *Borman 1989*, pp. 124–194.

143 *Daleboudt 1942*, p. 427. Maritz 2005, p. 26, simply endorses Daleboudt's view on Muir's lack of interest in the theory of education.

144 (1915). De Schoolmeester, De Burger, 23 Sept., referenced in *Daleboudt 1942*, p. 427.

145 Daleboudt devoted the final chapter of his thesis to just this question: *Daleboudt 1942*, pp. 427–445.

146 The following part of this paragraph is drawn from the content of *Muir Published Address 1*, pp. 5–11. *Muir Published Address 2* expands on his views on the importance of the teacher

doing practical research; also, he sets out his endorsement of the importance of fields of research that did not necessarily require originality of mind: work on bibliography, the history of science, and work on textbooks.

147 *Borman 1989*, p. 136. The previous office locations, to which Muir alludes, are referenced on p. 127.

148 *Pells 1954*, p. 134. *Du Toit and Nell 1976*, p. 90, effectively endorses this view that Muir neglected black education altogether.

149 *Paterson 1992*, p. 87.

150 Select Committee on Education, 1896, p. v, cited in *Duff 2015*, p. 136–137 and 215.

151 Their evidence is quoted in *Paterson 1992*, pp. 86–87.

152 Paterson explains the factors that contributed to this shortage of teachers throughout Muir's tenure: *Paterson 1992*, pp. 88–92.

153 See the comparisons covering the period ushered in by the School Board Act of 1905, up to 1909 in *Kies 1939*, p. 47.

154 Report of the Superintendent-General for Education for 1895: xxvi–vii, quoted in *Olwage 2003*, p. 71.

155 *Jabavu 1922*, p. 105.

156 *Ibid*. Jabavu excelled in the invention of 'apt sobriquets for illustrious public men': *Jabavu 1922*, p. 129. This playful sobriquet has proved impossible to translate meaningfully, and it may simply sound like 'Muir' rather than having any deeper significance: this is the view of Tessa Dowling, Professor of African Languages at the University of Cape Town, quoted by Hudson, K. (2020). Xhosa Phrase. [Email 6 April.]

157 *EG (1907)*. VI (19), 31 January, General Notes. Muir repeated the argument the following year: *Cape of Good Hope Native Education Report 1908*, p. 618, para. 4063.

158 Imvo 12 February 1907, quoted in *Jabavu 1922*, p. 85.

159 *Cape of Good Hope Native Education Report 1908*, p. 606, para. 3991.

160 *Christian Express 1908*, p. 190.

161 *Olwage 2003*, p. 69. Olwage deals with the topic in detail, pp. 68–71, and much of this paragraph is drawn from this source.
Muir collaborated energetically with a few talented individuals, including his Education Department colleague James Rodger, to promote vocal music throughout Cape schools. Central to their strategy was use of the tonic sol-fa notation system; this is an entire story in itself and the author has prepared a separate article to cover it: 'Thomas Muir (1844–1934) and James Rodger (1871–1952): Pioneers of Music Education in the Cape Colony' (currently unpublished).

162 *EG* 25 October 1901: 43, quoted in *Olwage 2003*, p. 76.

163 *Olwage 2003*, p. 71.

164 Muir's statements are set out in *Cape of Good Hope Native Education Report 1908*, pp. 43–44, paras. 246 to 250, and pp. 46–47, paras. 267–272; see also *Christian Express 1908*, p. 190.

165 *Linear Algebra, Muir Legacy 2005*, preface p. 1.

166 *Cape of Good Hope Native Education Report 1908*, p. 375 para. 2339: The then-current book that promoted the theory was *Kidd 1908*, pp. 238–242. Henderson dismissed Kidd's argument as based on methods which were 'totally unscientific' (*Ibid.*) This was evidently a theory that held sway for a considerable period of time. It was a prevalent notion held by 19th-century anthropologists, and as late as 1917, the inspector of schools in Natal devoted a 15-page section of his book to an evaluation of this 'generally accepted' theory: *Loram 1917*, p. 209. To Loram's credit, he concluded that the so-called arrested mental development at puberty was 'not a racial characteristic' but was due to a deficiency of teaching methods, which failed to engage the continuing efforts of pupils beyond a certain age.

167 The Select Committee's categoric rejection of Muir's stated belief (they do not specifically refer to his evidence) is at p. vi, para. 5, *Cape of Good Hope Native Education Report 1908*.

168 *Muir Published Address 1*, p. 5.

169 *Snedegar 2015*, p. 60

170 *Diary 1*, 10/8/09 Tuesday: Muir's visit included the Bunga Parliament.

171 The background of the early deteriorating relationship between Lovedale and Muir is covered in *Shepherd 1940*, pp. 243–244.

172 See *Christian Express 1908*.

173 *Duncan 2000*, p. 201. The background on the approach to education at Lovedale is drawn from this same source, pp. 201–224.

174 *Snedegar 2015*, p. 59. The campaign to establish such a college resulted in the foundation in 1916 of the South African Native College, later the University of Fort Hare.

175 Muir visited Alice and the Lovedale Institution in late July 1909: *Diary 1*, 27/7/09 Friday. He again met with Henderson on his visit to Butterworth in February 1910: *Diary 2*, 2/2/10 Wednesday to 4/2/10 Friday. Muir recorded the pair's cold parting, Henderson shaking hands 'dutifully and without a smile': *Diary 2*, 2/2/10 Wednesday.

176 Muir drew on the language of jousting to describe the aftermath of the tough morning session, which resulted in Henderson absenting himself: rather like a battered and bruised knight, the disappointed Henderson 'retired into his tent': *Diary 2*, 4/2/10 Friday.

177 This is according to Roberts' biographer, *Snedegar 2015*, p. 60.

178 *Diary 2*, 8/2/10. Muir was also scathing about Roberts' susceptibility to providing the answers his questioners on the Locations Commission had wanted to hear, rather than sticking to his principles: *Diary 2*, 8/2/10 Tuesday.

179 Muir made a full day's visit to Lovedale in March 1911, but was surprisingly tight-lipped about his impressions of the institution. However, he was pleased to take the opportunity to goad Dr. Roberts about the Inter-State Native College Scheme, which had just suffered the set-back of negative comment from members of the visiting United Free Church Commission: *Diary 4*, 12 /3/11 Sunday, and 13/3/11 Monday.

180 *Diary 5*, 12/10/11 Thursday.

181 *Cape of Good Hope Native Education Report 1908*.

182 *Ibid.*, p. 38, para. 229.

183 The Convention was held on 17–18 January 1908, and it was attended by a range of persons who were representative of African opinion. There is no formal record of the detail of the 'Resolutions' on black education and, therefore, this discussion follows the topics of the resolutions, as summarised in the evidence Muir gave to the Committee: *Cape of Good Hope Native Education Report 1908*, p. 38, paras. 228–229.

184 *Ibid.*, p. 38, para. 229.

185 *Cape of Good Hope Native Education Report 1908*, p. 63, para. 357.

186 *Ibid.*, p. 41, para. 237.

187 *Ibid.*, p. 339.

188 *Ibid.*, pp. 357, para. 2261.

189 *Ibid.*, p. 370, para. 2323.

190 *Ibid.*, pp. 51–52, paras. 298–300. He took the same view on the question of the appointment of teachers: rather than parents having any say in this, it should in the hands of 'people who know about the management of teachers': *Ibid.*, p. 48, para. 275.

191 *Ibid.*, p. 359, para. 2269.

192 *Ibid.*, p. 594, paras. 3934–3935.

193 *Ibid.*, p. 597, para. 3941.

194 *Christian Express 1908*, p. 192.

195 *Ibid.*, p. 365, para. 2300: Henderson defines 'vernacular' (be it Sesotho, isiXhosa or any other language) as: 'the language of the parents of the child coming to [the] school, and the language in which the child has spoken during its years of infancy up to the time when it joins [the] school.'.

196 *Ibid.*, p. 369, para. 2320.

197 *Ibid.*, p. 335, para. 2224 and p. 347.

198 *Ibid.*, p. 600, para. 3964.

199 *Ibid.*, p. 600, para. 3966.

200 *Ibid.*, p. 34, para.211.

201 *Ibid.*, p. 364, paras. 2297 and 2298.

202 *Ibid.*, pp. 48–49, para. 282. In relation to secondary education, see also Muir's statements at p. 65, paras. 371 and 375. He developed the 'building' analogy again in his later examination: p. 618, para. 4058.

203 *Ibid.*, p. 626, para. 4102.

204 *Ibid.*, p. 627, paras. 4108–4109.

205 (1913). Knysna Notes. George and Knysna Herald, 16 July.

206 *Ibid.*, pp. 337–351, para. 2235.

207 *Ibid.*, pp. 338–339.

208 *Ibid.*, p. 341. He makes the same points at p. 342.

209 *Ibid.*, p. 344.

210 *Ibid.*, p. 344.

211 See *O'Dowd 1972*, p. 168. For the most part, O'Dowd's essay deals with the later Transvaal educationist, John Adamson (1857–1947). A future researcher might well compare the detail of the Cape and Transvaal systems, influenced by these two different educationists, Muir and Adamson. The latter was able to draw lessons from the Anglo-Boer War and, through his collaboration with Smuts, managed to achieve a fairer system in Transvaal schools to address the 'language question'. He also achieved more for black education in that province than did Muir in the Cape.

212 *Malherbe 1925*, p. 133.
The travel requirement imposed on the S.G.E. was more moderately expressed in the Memorandum of Instructions for the Guidance of the Superintendent-General of Education, drawn up for Muir by his predecessor Dale; according to this memorandum, the S.G.E. had to 'see that all schools were inspected by inspectors and occasionally undertake journeys himself to keep up-to-date. These journeys should not result in long absences from his office': quoted by *Borman 1989*, p. 126.

213 For example, Prof. Turnbull attributes to him a 'refined judgement in poetry' and notes that at one time he had a 'fine library of English literature': *Royal Society Obituary 1934*, p. 182.

214 *Diary 1*, 4/8/09 Wednesday.

215 *Diary 4*, 3/3/11 Friday to 5/3/11 Sunday.

216 *Diary 4*, 5/3/11 Sunday.

217 For a description of the entourage of the early circuit judge, see *Erasmus 2013*.

218 Stow, P. (2020). Special Railway Coach of the Cape S.G.E. [Email 8 March.] The illustration of 'Old Coach 362' gives some idea of the look of the side elevation of the original coach. It has been adapted from a 1918 diagram, made after the renumbered coach 32 was modified and lengthened post-Union.

219 *Harris 1921*, p. 350.

220 A stoep is a veranda (originally Afrikaans). From the 1918 diagram of the coach, it is apparent that this stoep of the railway carriage was a roofed porch area at the rear, partly enclosed by a railing on all three open sides: it was sufficient to accommodate a Madeira chair to seat the 'Chief' comfortably.

221 *Diary 1*, 4/8 Wednesday.

222 *Xuma History.*

223 *Diary 1*, 9/8 Monday.

224 *Whiteside 1906*, p. 301.

225 *Whiteside 1906*, p. 302.

226 *Diary 2*, 31/1/10 Monday.

227 *Diary 1*, 11/8/09 Wednesday.

228 Quotations from *Diary 1*, 14/8/09 Saturday.

229 *Borman 1989*, p. 148.

230 *Diary 5*, 3/10/11 Tuesday.

231 *Diary 6*, 15/3/12 Friday.

232 *Ibid.*

233 *Diary 4*, 2/3/11 Thursday.

234 *Diary 6*, 12/3/12 Tuesday.

235 *Diary 4*. 9/3/11 Thursday.

236 Keating's Powder was an insecticide containing pyrethrum, found in the chrysanthemum flower. The advertisements for the powder advised that it be sprinkled on the pillow before bedtime. Enthusiastically, Cuthbert applied this product as advertised.

237 *Diary 6*, 10/3/12 Sunday.

238 Miss Cogan, the eldest of 10 siblings, was born in 1876 in Grahamstown: *Cogan Records.* Therefore, she was 33 years old when she first met Muir, then aged 65.

239 Of the six records, only *Diaries 2* and *5* are typed, and this must have been the handiwork of Miss Cogan.

240 *Diary 1*, 5/8/09 Thursday.

241 *Diary 1*, 24/8/09 Tuesday.

242 *Diary 1*, 25/8/09 Wednesday.

243 *Ibid.*

244 *Diary 2*, 2/2/10 Wednesday.

245 *Diary 2*, 3/2/10 Thursday.

246 *Ibid.*

247 *Diary 2*, 6/2/10 Sunday

248 *Diary 4*, 17/3/11 Friday.

249 All quotations in this paragraph are from: *Diary 5*, 7/10/11 Saturday.

250 *Biographical Sketch 1905.*

251 *Diary 2*, 4/2/10 Friday and 5/2/10 Saturday. Inspector Bennie makes a number of appearances in the *Diaries*. William Govan Bennie (1868–1941) was a grandson of J. Bennie, one of the original founders in 1824 of the Lovedale Mission Station. He was the son of J.A. Bennie, who also taught at the Lovedale Institution (founded in1841 on the same site as the Mission Station). Bennie was schooled at the Lovedale Institution and was Inspector of Schools in the Transkei from 1894 and in the Albany Circuit, 1902–1920. In the 1920s he became Chief Inspector of Native Education (from which post he retired in 1929). Source: Bennie, D. (2020). Biography W.G. Bennie. [Email 5 September]

252 *Diary 3*, 24/1/11 Tuesday.

253 H.J. Anderson appears in the *Diaries* on a number of occasions; he was recruited from overseas in about 1906 to be a Special Inspector of teachers' training institutions, and his work contributed to the raising of the standard of training: *Borman 1989*, p. 187 (who provides a photographic portrait of Anderson).

254 *Diary 5*, 21/10/11 Saturday.

255 *Diary 5*, 22/10/11 Sunday.

256 'dree one's weird' (Scots): submit to one's fate. *Diary 2*, 18/2/10 Friday.

257 *Diary 4*, 9/3/11 Thursday.

258 *Diary 3*, 22/1/11 Sunday.

259 *Diary 3*, 29/1/11 Sunday.

260 The trip, and all its mishaps, is recounted in *Diary 2*, 12/2/10 Saturday to 14/2/10 Monday. His driving host, Dr. Russell, was the same man who drove first over the Swartberg Pass in 1904: *Schoeman 2014*, p. 75. The Swartberg Pass, a Thomas Bain road project, was opened in 1904 and one can imagine that Dr. Russell would have made sure he initiated his local pass in one of his gleaming motor cars.

261 *Diary 2*, 14/2/10 Monday.

262 The entire story is recounted in three entries over a period of days: *Diary 3*, 28/1/11 Saturday; 30/1/11 Monday; 1/2/11 Wednesday.

263 *Diary 2*, 8/2/10 Tuesday.

264 *Diary 2*, 10/2/10 Thursday (all quotes).

265 *Diary 6*, 9/3/12 Saturday.

266 *Diary 2*, 5/2/10 Saturday.

267 *Diary 2*, 9/2/10 Wednesday.

268 *Diary 5*, 21/10/11 Saturday.

269 All quotations from *Diary 2*, 31/1/10 Monday.

270 Fraserburg: *Diary 4*, 3/3/11 Friday; Aberdeen: *Diary 4*, 9/3/11 Thursday.

271 *Diary 4*, 5/3/11 Sunday.

272 *Diary 3*, 25/1/11 Wednesday.

273 *Diary 4*, 4/3/11 Saturday. Louw was the former School Board secretary of Oudtshoorn.

274 *Diary 3*, 30/1/11 Monday.

275 *Ibid*.

276 *Diary 1*, 19/8/09 Thursday.

277 *Diary 5*, 16/10/11 Monday.

278 *Diary 5*, 18/10/11 Wednesday.

279 *Diary 2*, 17/2/10 Thursday.

280 (1910). Education System. Dr. Muir Praised. 15 Apr. *Muir Manuscript Collection, NLSA*, MSB 691.1 (8).

281 Howes, S. (2020). Commentary. [Email 5 February.]

282 *Cuthbert 1911*, p.7.

283 Linda Howe-Ely researched new schools/buildings referenced in the pages of the *EG: Howe-Ely 2020*.

284 (1902). New School Buildings. EG, II (5), p.41. The photographs identified in captions as 'Collection Sigi Howes' are images drawn from the pages of the *EG* between 1902 and 1915.

285 *Daleboudt 1942*, p. 230.

286 There was often a delay of several months between the actual day on which a school opened for pupils and the 'official' opening, the ceremony Muir attended.

287 *Cornish-Bowden Memoir*, p. 1.

288 Cape Times, 22 September 1928, 'Intimate Impressions of Sir Thomas Muir'. *Muir Manuscript Collection, NLSA*, MSB 691.1 newspaper cutting. What happened to this collection is a complete mystery.

289 In the year that Muir arrived in the Cape, 1892, the school adopted the name Muir Academy in his honour. When first opened in 1904, it was known as the Muir High School, but by 1906 it became 'Muir College'.

290 Van Renen, C. (2020). Muir High School. [Email 22 February.]

291 ArteFacts SA: White-Cooper, William.

292 During Muir's era, White-Cooper also carried out the projects at Victoria Girls' High School, Grahamstown (1902), Erica Girls' School, Port Elizabeth (1902) and at Rocklands Girls' School, Cradock (1906).

293 ArteFacts SA: Parker and Forsyth.

294 The full story of the history of both school buildings referenced in this paragraph is told in *Howes 2011*. The West End and East End were simply terms to describe the western and eastern ends of Cape Town. The area within which the East End Public School lay became known later as District Six.

295 *Howes 2011*, p. 11.

296 *Muir Diary 2*, 15/2 Tuesday.

297 See outlines of Muir's speeches: opening of buildings at Graaff-Reinet College, 14 March 1906: (1906) *EG*, V (27), p. 621; (1906) Alice Public School, VI (15), p. 330.

298 *Diary 5*, Monday 9/10/11.

299 *Diary 5*, Tuesday 10/10/11.

300 Both architect and building are listed in ArteFacts SA: Herbert Cordeaux and Komgha Junior School.

301 *Diary 5*, Tuesday 10/10/11 and Wednesday 11/10/11.

302 *Diary 6*, 5/3/12 Tuesday.

303 'arcades ambo' Latin (Virgil): both Arcadians; two people of like occupations.

304 The information in this paragraph is drawn from: *Tiger Kloof History* and *Willoughby 1912*.

305 *Willoughby 1912*, p. 73.

306 *Diary 6*, 11/3/12 Monday.

307 *Diary 6*, 12/3/12 Tuesday.

308 *Ibid.*

309 *Willoughby 1912*, pp. 109 and 99: background on the ideals of Tiger Kloof, pp. 28–31, and on the eight-year record of the school to end 1911, pp. 99–109.

310 They include: Victoria Girls' High School (1902); Graaff-Reinet Girls' High School (1911): a large part of the original building was destroyed by fire in 1949, but much has survived, and is now the Laer Volkskool, Graaff-Reinet; Kimberley Boys' High School (1913), listed in ArteFacts SA: Kimberley Boys' High School; Laingsburg Public School (1914), now the Acacia Primary School.

311 *Mossel Bay Schools History*: The school was renamed Point High School when the two schools in Mossel Bay amalgamated as a mixed school, the Boys' School building housing the senior school. This school moved to a new site in 1976. Since 1993, the old 1910 building has been the premises of Milkwood Primary. The street in front of the school continues to be named Muir Street.

312 Artefacts SA: Butterworth High School and Komga Junior School. Butterworth High School suffered extensive damage by fire in 2016.

313 Examples are: Huguenot Girls' High School, Wellington (1902), now part of the Cape Peninsula University of Technology, Wellington Campus; Rhenish Institute, Stellenbosch (1906), vacated when the school moved to a new building in Krigeville, and now possibly used by the local Education District Office; George Boys' Primary School (1914), now part of South Cape TVET College.

314 Examples are: East End Public School, De Villiers Street (1903), the 1903 predecessor building of the East End Public School (1912), now part of the Cape Peninsula University of Technology (Ophthalmic Sciences Dept); the Swellendam Public School (1904), now occupied by the Traffic Department and the Department of Correctional Services; the Graaff-Reinet Teachers' Training College (1906), now the SA Police Academy; the Elementary School Grahamstown (1905), known for a while as Shaw Hill School, and now the Settlers Day Hospital Clinic.

315 For example, the entire original building of the Girls' High School in King William's Town (1908) was destroyed by fire in 1962; Somerset West Public School (1904) was demolished to make way for a new building in 1973.

316 The Good Shepherd (n.d.), History Protea Church and Village. [online] Available at: http://www.goodshepherd-protea.org.za/history/ [Accessed 17 April 2020].

317 Ferris, L.C. (2020). Tiger Kloof. [Email 6 July]. Tiger Kloof's Arthington Memorial Church, in which the pupils are depicted in the illustration, was built in 1925: Artefacts SA: Arthington Memorial Church, Vryburg.

318 The recipient of the article was W. Metcalfe and Son, a printer and publisher in Cambridge, who published The Messenger of Mathematics. Muir published two articles in this particular journal in 1911 and it would have been one of these on which he was working on that impossibly hot day: *Maritz 2005*, p. 56, Muir's mathematical writings nos. 204 and 207.

319 *Maritz 2005*, pp. 33 – 63.

320 *Aitken 1936*, p. 266.

321 *Aitken 1950*, p. 75.

322 *Ibid*, p. 71.

323 *Muir 1930*, Preface p. v.

324 Muir T. (1921) Letter to Lawrence Crawford, 13 November. (Source unknown.)

325 *Turnbull 1935*, p. 79; see also *Royal Society Obituary 1934*, p. 182, by the same author.

326 Quoted in *Daleboudt 1942*, p. 57.

327 *Miller 1907*, p. 246 and *Miller Review 1912*, p. 513.

328 *Bell Review 1931*, p. 161.

329 *Bell Review 1931*, p. 163.

330 *Bell Review 1931*, p. 162 and pp. 163–164.

331 *P.A.M. 1892*, reviewer identified in *Crilly 2020*.

332 *Poole 2014*, p. 292.
Sheldon Axler, whose article is quoted below, agrees that the author's description of the historical order of development of the theories is correct; however, contemporary mathematicians, not well versed in the history of the subject, may well be surprised that the theory of determinants was developed before the theory of matrices since, as the subject is usually taught today, determinants are based upon matrices: Axler, S. (2020). Determinants. [Email 22 March.]

333 *Crilly 2020*.

334 *Axler 1995*, pp. 140 and 139 respectively.

335 *Tee 2003*, pp. 7 and 11. See also *ILAS 2002*, which identifies research on determinants as a distinctly 19th-century activity.

336 *Mathematics Stack Exchange 2016*, 4 November answer. See also the answer of Prof. Jean-Marie Morvan.

337 Gibbard, P. (2020). The Determinant Concept. [Email 29 March.]

338 Morse, J. (2020). Determinants. [Email 14 May.]

339 *Tee 2003*, p. 7.

340 *Turnbull 1934*, p. 183.

341 Gibbard, P. (2020). The Determinant Concept. [Second email 29 March.]

342 *P.A.M. 1892.*

343 *Alkema 2012*, pp. 9–11, and 14.

344 *Diary 2*, 13/2/10 Sunday.

345 *Diary 2*, 15/2/10 Tuesday.

346 *Ibid.*

347 *Diary 4*, 4/3/11 Saturday. When he visited Aberdeen, Eastern Cape, amidst a similarly Afrikaner gathering, again the choir sang for him a traditional Scottish folk tune with a Jacobite twist: *Diary 4*, 9/3/11 Thursday.

348 *Diary 6*, 5/3/12 Tuesday.

349 *Diary 1*, 20/8/09 Friday.

350 Muir, T. (undated). Scots and other Verses, from a S.A. scrapbook 1892–1933. *Muir Manuscript Collection, NLSA*, MSB 691.3(2), referenced in *Maritz 2005*, p. 30. This anthology comprises 39 poems, mostly in Scots dialect, including two of Muir's own verses.

351 *Olwage 2003*, pp. 76–77 explains the structural educational boundary that had been created in music education in the Cape and which was recognised by these two different series.

352 Statham, J. and D. (2020). A Highland Idyll. [Email 9 August.] There is a music video of this song on YouTube: *Muir and Rodger, Highland Idyll Recording*.

353 Daniel Johannes Haarhoff (1846–1917): apart from being an active politician, Haarhoff was an attorney in Griqualand West.

354 *Diary 3*, 29/1/11 Sunday.

355 *Ibid.*

356 *Royal Society Obituary 1934*, p. 182.

357 *Diary 5*, 20/11/10 Friday. Alternatively, he might take the latest issue of Nature and his notebook with him on a walk, in case he had a moment to sit down, read and reflect: *Diary 5*, 22/10/11 Sunday.

358 *Diary 4* ,17/3/11 Friday.

359 *Diary 4*, 13/3/11 Monday.

360 *Diary 5*, 15/10/11 Sunday.

361 *Adonis 1995*, pp. 82 and 94.

362 *Ibid*, p. 96.

363 *Diary 1*, 18/8/09 Wednesday.

364 *Diary 3*, 26/1/11 Thursday.

365 *Diary 6*, 11/3/12 Monday.

366 *Diary 6*, 12/3/12 Tuesday.

367 *Diary 5*, 9/10/11 Monday.

368 In detail the photograph includes:
Back row: Karl Spilhaus and Muir Spilhaus (holding his son David); Front row: Margaret (Peggie) Barry née Spilhaus (holding her daughter, Margaret [Poelie]); Sir Thomas Muir; Nellie Spilhaus (and seated on her lap, Antonia [Toni], daughter of Karl Spilhaus).

369 *Elliott 2015*, pp. 79–102.

370 *Citation Hon. LL.D. 1955*.

371 *Kyte 2013*, p. 31.

372 *Memorial Address Cam 1977*.

373 The origins of George's 'disgrace' were confirmed by Gilbert, Antonia (Toni) née Spilhaus (2020). [Telephone discussion 30 January. SMS messages 30 July.] Toni was told this story by her own mother, Iris Ruby ('Paddy') Spilhaus, wife of Karl Spilhaus, eldest son of Nellie Spilhaus née Muir.

374 *Report on Educational System of the Cape Colony 1901*. The background to the commissioning of the Report is set out in the Introductory Letter to the Volume, *Report* pp. iii–vi. The author's theory concerning George's activities in Cape Town until 1900 is based on: the listing of 'Mr. G.B. Muir, B.A., of the Department of Public Education, Cape Town' as the author of Part. I., Sections 1–74 of the History and Present State of Education in Cape Colony (Report, p. vii) and on the enigmatic note of the editor, in italics at the end of the last section of the report George completed: 'At this point Mr. Muir found himself compelled, by pressure of other engagements, to break off the composition of his report' (Report, p. 55).

375 Although both his sister Nellie, and his brother Thomas, are recorded in the alphabetical listing of alumni of the South African College (the university educational college as opposed to the examining university), there is no record of their brother George in that list: *Ritchie 1918*, p. 883. Likewise, the university archivist identified the detailed record of both Nellie and Thomas in the university records, but found no trace of George: Ogterop, S. (2020). Report on University of Cape Town Archivist Search, Muir. [Email 26 August 2020].

376 The additional cabin passenger on this voyage is listed as Mr. G.B. Muir, occupation 'traveller' (age recorded inaccurately): ancestry.co.uk (n.d.). Passenger Lists Dunnottar Castle, London and Southampton to Cape Town departed 7/8 July 1899.

377 ancestry.co.uk (n.d.). Passenger Lists Carisbrook Castle, Cape Town to Southampton, arrived 13 June 1903.

378 The skeletal history of the adult lives of George and Ethel Muir is drawn from their marriage and death records, as well as the following: England Census 1901 Ethel Devereux, Westminster London; England Census 1911 George and Ethel Muir, Brighton, Surrey; 1939 England and Wales Register, George Muir (Shrewsbury, Shropshire) and Ethel Muir (Dorking, Surrey). The brief reference to Ethel's stage career is from *Wearing 2013*, Production 03.176.

379 Marriage Register St. Luke Church, Chelsea, London: 12 January 1907, George Bell Muir and Ethel Jane Devereux.

380 *Muir, George, Military Record*, Proceedings on Discharge, 7 January 1917.

381 He wrote of his education: 'University of Cape of Good Hope B.A. Honours, Ll.B (Pt. I) etc. Cambridge Univ.': *Muir, George, Military Record*, Application for Admission to Officer Cadet Unit, 12 September 1916. Not content with again claiming a degree from Cape Town (unsubstantiated), he added that he had started law studies at the University of Cambridge. However, a search of records (1901–1918) reveals no reference to George having been a student at that university: University of Cambridge Archives (Cox, J.) (2020). George Bell Muir. [Email 7 September 2020]

382 Electoral Roll, 55B Greencoat Place, London S.W.1: Ethel and George, 1918–21, and Ethel alone, 1923–26, 1929, 1933, 1938–39; Probate Ethel Muir 1942.

383 *Mahon Trial 1928*, pp. 76–77. There is no doubt that the witness at the trial was George: his full name and the Greencoat Place address are both cited in the record of his evidence. Mahon was convicted and hanged for the murder in September 1924.

384 *Muir Estate File*, second codicil, 19 August 1925.

385 *Muir Estate File*: Muir's substantial house, Elmcote, and four plots, as well as 12 additional sub-divided plots, were sold in 1934 for a total of just over £4,400; the house, and the garden sold with it, represented £2,200 of that value (thus equating to the value of each legacy).

386 Electoral Register 1927, Parish of Kingsland, Leominster: Address, Hazeldene Cottage, Shirlheath, Kingsland.

387 Death Ethel Jane Muir, 22 March 1942, London. Administration to her sister. Effects: £205 15s 6d.

388 Background on Elsie Roberts, Christine Muir née Roberts and High Fremlington: Gifford, S. and Walker, R. (2020). George and Christine Muir. [Emails 28 July–8 August.] Death Certificate George Bell Muir, Richmond, Yorkshire, 11 December 1947.

389 In late 1905 Muir was in London accompanied by his family: (1906) The Musical Herald, Reception of Dr. Muir by Sol-faists. 1 January, (694) p. 23. A few years later Muir was one of the South African representatives who attended the Education Conference in London in April–July 1911: Chronicle (Adelaide, S.A.) (1911). South African Affairs: Dr. Thomas Muir, 22 April, p. 37. He was accompanied by his wife, Maggie; outward from Cape Town, 15 April 1911; return from Southampton, 15 July 1911. In this period of three months, he and Maggie would have had ample opportunity to spend time with George and his relatively new wife.

390 The author was close to his grandmother, Nellie, but he never learned of the existence of George. Perhaps Nellie had become used to keeping his story in the background. However, Nellie appears to have remained in contact with George's widow, Christine; in 1954, at least seven years after George's death, Christine's Natal-based sister-in-law, Betty, and her daughter visited Nellie's home on Rhodes Drive, Cape Town: Gifford, S. (2020). George and Christine Muir. [Emails 28 July–10 August.]

391 *Ritchie 1918*: Along with his brilliant sister, Nellie, Thomas is listed as an alumnus of the South African College, in his case for the years 1902–1904 (p. 883). However, Thomas coasted in as a Class III student in the Intermediate Examination in 1902 (p. 823), which probably did not please his father. Nothing more is known of his studies.

392 The story of Thomas P.B. Muir has been researched by a great-granddaughter of Sir Thomas Muir, Anne Andrews. She is the daughter of George Bell Carmody Muir (1917–1985), whose father was Thomas, Muir's younger son. This account of his life draws on a number of cited sources including Andrews, A. (2020). Thomas P.B. Muir, Australia. [Emails 22 January and 31 July.]

393 Both quotes: *Moen 2015*, p. 12.

394 (n.d.). Wellshot through the years 1846–1948. The Wellshot Centre, Ilfracombe, Longreach Area, Queensland. Brochure.

395 Wolfgarten, F. (2020). Thomas Muir, Yabtree. [Emails 16 and 28 August and Ledger page images 30 August.] Muir was paid 25 shillings per week as a boundary rider, but within a year he was on £3 per week as overseer. In October 1918, the sheering count at Yabtree was just over 16,000 – considerably lower than at Wellshot.

396 *O'Malley 2009*, p. 20.

397 *O'Malley 2009*, pp. 33–34.

398 The twins, George Bell Carmody and Nellie Brown Muir, were born in the Royal Hotel, Wagga Wagga, New South Wales in 1917. It was Mrs. M. Carmody, the hotel owner, who was witness to the birth. The author refers to George Bell Carmody Muir as the 'scion' of the family, notwithstanding that he had an elder brother Thomas Paterson. This is simply because very little is known of the course of the family life of the other descendant members of the family.

399 The Daily Telegraph, Sydney, NSW, Saturday, 14 August 1926, p. 20.

400 Gibbard, R. (2020). Thomas P B Muir, Australia. [Email 11 August.]

401 Andrews, A. (2020). Thomas Muir, Australia. [Email 22 March.] The couple's address during the period 1935–1969 was 43 Wellington Street, East Melbourne.

402 The military career of Thomas himself was wholly unremarkable. He enlisted as a private in 1918 and embarked ship for Europe. However, he was recalled when the Armistice was signed. In 1941 he again enlisted when he was well into his fifties. He continued in service as a corporal until 1943. There is no doubt that his early background in the male domain of the shearing shed would have suited him to the lifestyle of a soldier.

403 Antonia ('Toni') née Spilhaus (2020). [SMS 30 July.]

404 Len Muir, an Australian great-grandson of Muir, took the trouble to track down Nellie's address in Cape Town and reached out to her; but this was after her death. Nellie's daughter replied, merely passing Len's letter on to 91-year-old Cam, and nothing came of the contact: Muir, Len (1974). Muir family. [Letter 14 June]; Barry, Peggie (1974). Muir family. [Letter 15 July].

405 *Cape Times 1928*. The interviewer was compiling the article, 'intimate impressions' of Muir.

406 *Ibid.*

407 *Crawford 1934* provides an exhaustive listing of the academic honours and awards conferred on Muir, and of the offices he held. *Maritz 2005*, p. 16, also adds information on this subject.

408 *Muir Memorandum 1912*.

409 *Cornish-Bowden Memoir*, p. 2.

410 The text of the entire presentation address is set out in *Loram 1916*, pp. 74–75.

411 *Kannemeyer 1996*, pp. 340–341. Langenhoven's piece, in the very first issue of *De Burger*, was entitled 'Sir Muir and after him'.

412 'A Retrospect', Cape Argus, 14 October 1913, quoted in *Daleboudt 1942*, p. 442.

413 *Aitken 1950*, p. 69.

414 The quotation is from one such extended drinking session in Komgha: *Diary 5*, 10/10/11 Tuesday.

415 *Cuthbert Records*.

416 *Cleophas 2009*, p. 74.

417 Essential detail of the life of Alice Mary Maude Cogan (consistently called 'Miss Cogan' in the *Diaries*) is drawn from the *Cogan Records*. In 1926 she is recorded as a 'retired teacher' but on her death in 1947, her sister declared her to be a 'retired school inspectress'; this is consistent with the information on her death certificate, and tallies with what is known of her career progression from the *Diaries*. Freed from the constraints of Muir's *Diaries*, and his rather stiff etiquette on personal names, she is now referred to as 'Alice Cogan'.

418 ancestry.co.uk (n.d.). Passenger Lists Llanstephan Castle, Cogan A.M.M. and Muir, Sir Thomas; Cape Town to Southampton, departed 4 May 1920; Southampton to Cape Town, returned 8 October 1920. On the outward journey, Alice Cogan's occupation was recorded as 'nil'. On the return journey she described herself as an 'instructress'.

419 *Moen 2015*, p. 12.

420 *Aitken 1936*, p. 296.

421 *Cape Times 1928*.

422 In library parlance, 'serials' are periodical publications, including those designated as serials, such as annuals, proceedings, symposia and transactions of societies. Muir's collection consisted of his mathematical series and 2,500 books and pamphlets, and according to the terms of the bequest, the serials had to be kept up to date and suitably bound: *Maritz Unpublished Paper*, p. 3.

423 *Muir 1884*, p. 28.

424 Geustyn, M. (2020). Muir Collection, National Library of South Africa. [Email, 11 February.]

425 Muir enabled this endowment through his testamentary requirement that his son George and his wife should only benefit from the income of 'his' quarter share of the original estate, with the capital reverting to the Public Library on their deaths: *Muir Estate File*, second codicil, 19 August 1925. Between 1934 and 1948 there would have been an inflationary devaluation of the capital, but it still remained a tidy sum to provide a continuing permanent endowment for the collection.

426 Webb, Prof. J. (2020). Muir Mathematical Collection at NLSA [Email 18 March].

427 *Muir Manuscript Collection, NLSA*: 'Letters from Mathematicians and a few others', MSB 691.2.1.

428 Three letters from other mathematicians to Muir, together with his workings on the problems raised by them, do survive among the *Muir Mathematics Papers* in the National Library of Scotland, one from Arthur Cayley and two from F.S. Macaulay. His *Papers*, which also include Muir's notes on his own work and in connection with indexing of his own volumes, and related papers, would all require review by a mathematician rather than the author: Roden, J. (2020). Findings on Muir Mathematics Papers. [Email 30 August].

429 There appear to have been only two earlier recipients of an honorary doctorate: both Sir Otto Beit and Viscount Buxton received an honorary LL.D. in 1920.

430 *Cape Times 1934*, p. 9.

431 Gilbert, Antonia ('Toni') née Spilhaus (2020). [Telephone discussion 30 January.]

432 *Cogan Records*, Estate Administration: Alice Cogan died after a nine-month battle with cancer. In her last months she was cared for by one of her sisters, who lived in East London, not far from the Cogan family roots, and her entire life savings at death amounted to only about £2,200.

433 Kallaway, P. (2020). Sir Thomas Muir, S.G.E. [Email 23 June]. Kallaway introduced the author to the ideas of David Tyack, in 'The One Best System'. Due to a lack of access to libraries in pandemic times, for purposes of this paragraph, the author has drawn on a retrospective assessment of Tyack's contribution: *Kantor 2001*, pp. 319 and 323.

434 The Covid-19 pandemic has resulted in a prolonged period of closed libraries and archives, both in the United Kingdom and South Africa. In more benevolent times it might have been possible to delve further into journals of teachers' associations, missionary publications and government papers, both published and in the archives. Fortunately, previous studies, focusing specifically on Muir, including *Beyers 1935*, *Kies 1939* and *Daleboudt 1942*, and other studies on related educational history topics, have already mined much of this data. On any research project there is always more to be done.

INDEX

The Index covers Part I: Biography. References in the Contents, the List of Illustrations, the Family Tree, and the Bibliography are not indexed as these listings serve as indices in themselves. Page references to Endnotes list the Endnote number (n) followed by the page number.

Part II: The S.G.E.'s Diaries of his Tours (1909–1912)

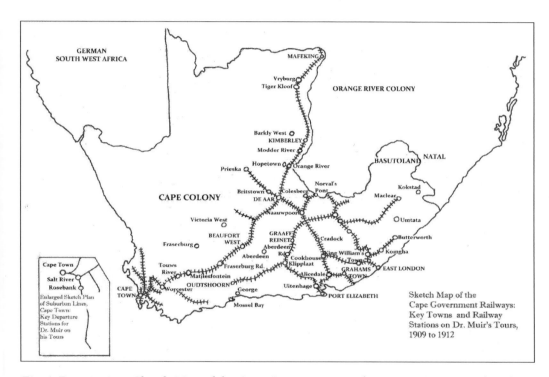

Fig. A Frontispiece: Sketch Map of the Cape Government Railways. Key Towns and Railway Stations on Dr. Muir's Tours, 1909 to 1912. Compiled from data shown on the Map of the Cape Government Railways, the Royal Mail Route to the Orange River Colony, Transvaal, and Rhodesia 1903: Peter and Madeleine Elliott.

INTRODUCTORY NOTE ON THE DIARIES AND THE ILLUSTRATIONS

Presentation of the *Diaries*

The *Diaries* are presented unabridged and edited only to eliminate obvious error. This, it is felt, is the best way for the reader to enjoy the nuances of Muir's flowing style of writing, and to capture the spirit of his travels in the Cape interior. For the same reason, his eccentricity of style has been retained e.g. Muir wrote 'Capetown' instead of 'Cape Town' and treated similar place names in the same way; he used idiom which may sometimes strike the contemporary reader as peculiar (possibly influenced by Scots idiom); his use of numerals and words throughout is haphazard; his spelling of the names of people was erratic (but in this case, where the correct name has been ascertained, the correction has been made). This conservative presentation, therefore, errs on the side of authenticity, and (as explained in the Foreword to Part I), this also means that terms now offensive to South Africans today, such as 'kafir', are retained as integral to Muir's written text.

A sketch map of the Cape Government Railways has been added to help the reader follow the course of Muir's travels on the network. This map does not show all places or railway stations that Muir mentions, merely sufficient to enable the course of his journey to be followed, and the rough location of some of his principal visits away from his railway coach to be traced. Added to the beginning of each daily diary entry, in brackets and italics, is a listing of the principal places he visited that day. Railway stations are shown in bold, other towns merely in italics. Where he visited a farm, institution or other place not having the status of a town, the place is simply listed as 'visited'. Only visits Muir made to schools for an opening ceremony are recorded in the diary entry headings; other visits recounted in each entry should be able to be related to the town via the listing of the place visited.

The illustrations

The illustrations are mainly railway photographs, drawn from the work of the *Digital Rail Images South Africa* (DRISA) project, an ongoing effort to digitise the collection of the Transnet Heritage Library. A good proportion of these photographs were made in 1895–1896 by photographer Edward Henry William Short (1862–1947), but others are drawn more generally from that collection. They are interspersed with some additional pictures of schools relevant to the narrative of the *Diaries*.

The reader may well question the relevance of the slightly earlier railway images to *Diaries* written by Muir in the later period, 1909–1912. However, Short and other photographers depicted in these images the self-same railway stations and surroundings in the Cape interior, in which Muir's coach stationed in sidings, and from which his school business was conducted. Muir travelled these routes on the Cape railway network throughout his period of office as S.G.E. from 1892 onwards; we simply do not have a record of these earlier tours. Thus, he would have been travelling the same tracks, and lingering in the same sidings, during these earlier years when the photographs were taken. Besides which, with an intervening Anglo-Boer War and its negative effect on economic progress, the scenes photographed in those earlier years of Muir's era would not have been materially different from those he saw from the stoep of his comfortable official railway coach.

Short (and his surname was not apt, as the photographer stood well over six feet) devoted the greater part of his working life to bringing the railways, and the Cape Colony, to the notice of the outside world.[1] Having worked first on British railways, Short came out to South Africa and joined the Cape Government Railways (CGR) as a clerk in the general manager's office in Cape Town in late 1891; there his photographic work came to the notice of Sir Charles Elliott, General Manager of the CGR, who encouraged him to undertake photographic projects. Short remained an employee of the CGR until the end of 1915. Thus, like Muir, he was an immigrant to South Africa: they arrived and retired at almost the same time, having put their energies into such very different pursuits. Short, however, taxed the resources of the government superannuation fund for even longer than Muir. It is not inappropriate, therefore, to marry their works to some extent in this account of travels on the CGR rail network, which they both traversed so closely.

DIARY 1

S.G.E.'s Diary of a tour to the Transkeian Territories

29/7/09 to 2/9/09

Fig. B: Cape Town c. 1906. Departure of locomotive with main line passenger train. DRISA 1525. Transnet Heritage Library Photo Collection.

29/7/09 Thursday

(Salt River; Wellington; Hex River)

There having been so many mishaps already as to the date of starting, no intimation was given this time until three hours before leaving, namely, after lunch when I said I was not going back to the office that day and when asked the reason I replied that I had to proceed to the Transkei at 4.45. Caught the saloon at Salt River, and delivered my last messages to Freeman and Duffett.[2] The rain was soon left behind, but the cold increased. At Wellington met Harvie of the Training School by appointment, and soon thereafter turned in for the night. On going up the Hex River, the mountains were found to be clad with snow.

30/7/09 Friday

(Matjiesfontein)

Morning cold and bright. At Matjiesfontein had a little private chat with Logan, who has put the place in spick and span conditions as of old. Cuthbert found on the train a P.W.D. man who had been recently pensioned, Morkel by name, and who had taken to cattle-

---

2   G.H. Freeman (not to be confused with Inspector Freeman, who was a school inspector) was the office help/caretaker in the Cape Education Department's head office at the outset of Muir's term of office: *Borman 1989*, p. 126. It is assumed that Freeman continued to serve in this role throughout Muir's tenure; perhaps Duffett was added to provide additional 'office help' as he appears to have been also very much at the beck and call of Muir.

Fig. C: Matjiesfontein 1895. Station buildings, looking south. E.H. Short. DRISA PB0379. Transnet Heritage Library Photo Collection.

dealing and now had two trucks of cows on board. Had him into the saloon to meals, and was well amused when not bored by him. Arranged that milking time suited our kitchen operations, and profited accordingly.

31/7/09 Saturday
[De Aar; Naauwpoort]

Awoke to find it freezing. As no washing could be done, we went from bad to worse, and had breakfast in bed. Forenoon beautifully bright when we reached De Aar. Met Inspector Grant, the resident engineer, Mitchell the new vice-principal of De Aar, and Thomas the principal of Philipstown – all on school affairs. Left at 12.30 for Naauwpoort, dictating nine memoranda by the way. After lunch finished Oona H. Ball's 'Their Oxford Year' and then dreamt on something mathematical.[3] Reached Naauwpoort at 5.30, and then parted with Morkel and his cows at 6.30, the latter being truly missed. Mr. Lord, the new vice-principal called to 'pay his respects'; also Mr. Smith, the principal. Evening still and lovely, with beautiful Karroo colours in the sky. Instructor Farrington joined us and had to report his engagement to Miss Jennings and promise certain farm produce for our use at Ugie Station on the return journey. He and Cuthbert had engagements to play 'bridge', and I therefore contrived to keep them talking until the engagements were irrevocably broken, and they then settled down to tobacco and sodas and pungent gossip about the Logies and Miss Todd. Farrington left at 1.15 and our train moved off about an hour later. Night bitingly cold and brilliantly clear.

1/8/09 Sunday
(Stormberg; Queenstown; Amabele)

Wakened to find a bright and frosty morning, and worked mathematics in bed, until reaching Stormberg at 8.30. Dictated memoranda after leaving. Frost soon disappeared

3   *Their Oxford Year* (1909) by Oona Ball: scenes and legends of Oxford.

under a warm sun, and we had a nice run to Queenstown, which was reached at 12.30. Met Inspector Logie on business. Chief Constable Nimmo, late of Steynsberg and later still an old pupil at Glasgow, called 'to pay his respects': he has now a valuable post at Queenstown. On [the] way to Cathcart all the fields were brown, but bright with sunshine. Reached Toise River at 5.30, the early evening being still and grey and beautiful. Paddy Ryan, a cousin of Rosebank Paddy, called. He had been staying a fortnight with Fincham at Imvani and reported Fincham to be working like a slave, being the only white man on the farm: kind inquiries from him about Thos.[4] Arrived at Amabele about 6.30, and on sitting down to dinner Inspector Bond arrived, having ridden over from Kingwilliamstown. Chatted on business matters with him until 11. After a stroll in the bright moonlight up and down the station platform, and seeing coach attached to morning train, turned in quite ready for rest.

2/8/09 Monday

(*Amabele; Komgha; Butterworth; visit to Lamplough Institution*)

The train having left Amabele about 6, I awoke just before reaching Komgha at 8.30. Dressed hurriedly and found O'Connell the R.M, and old 'High School' Campbell the secretary of the School Board already in the saloon, also later Williamson the teacher. Campbell was again interesting to meet, with his long words and legal accuracy, his trustworthiness and Scotch kindliness. The cold and clean morning was delightful as we made the long descent through the scrubby hills to the Kei Bridge. Made a long halt at Sihota just after crossing the Kei, and then began the laborious ascent on the Transkei side. Stopped at 11.30 at Eagle and saw the train we had to cross, corkscrewing down the opposite slopes, and saw also groups of blanketed natives – men and women – smoking and taking their ease on the railway bank at the station. What beautiful views we had down the valley as we slowly advanced, clinging to the mountain side! Shortly after reaching the upper level we came to Ndabakazi and found Inspector McLaren waiting for us. Lunch was immediately brought in and occupied us till the terminus (Butterworth) was reached. There we were met by the mayor, the secretary of the School Board, the Reverend Baker, and later by the magistrate (Mr. Warner), and soon had the arrangements for the rest of the day mapped out. First drove with the Inspector to the Lamplough Institution, and inspected the Girls School (Miss Morris), the Industrial School, and the Elementary School, finishing up by discussing with Rev. Baker his troubles connected with them all – troubles arising mainly out of the fact of the survey and the granting of title to the natives.[5] Hurried back to meeting with School Board at 4, a dry and formal affair, the magistrate being chairman. Remained to talk with Mr. Gerrie the teacher, then back to [the] saloon to dictate three memoranda. At 6.15 Inspector McLaren called to take me back to his house to supper, where Stormont of Blythswood was wanting to discuss troubles at Blythswood.[6] After supper met Warner (R.M.), Daly, Martins, Taylor (mayor), and Gerrie. Back to [the] saloon about 11, and dictated memoranda while Inspector McLaren waited. Went to bed with 'The First Violin', Cuthbert being disabled by biliousness and being sound asleep.[7]

---

4   This must be an enquiry about Muir's younger son, Thomas, who by this time had emigrated to Australia. The enquirer's cousin had lived in Rosebank, thus not too far from the Muir home, and may also have known Thomas at school at S.A.C.S.

5   The Lamplough Training Institution for Girls was established in 1890; its aim was 'to prepare the girls to make good housewives and mothers': *Whiteside 1906*, p. 291.

6   Blythswood: a Presbyterian Mission Station.

7   *The First Violin* (1877) by Jessie Fothergill: a Victorian love tale.

3/8/09 Tuesday

(Idutywa)

Woke early to a beautiful cold morning, Cuthbert still gloomy and unfit. Took a good breakfast, and had time for a walk up and down the platform with 'The First Violin' before Inspector McLaren arrived. Petrie, a Scot, is still station master and member of the School Board. Wheeldon with cart and four horses arrived at 9.30, and we had everything ready to start the day by 9.50. Beautiful drive over rolling grassy hills for 11 miles to Wood's, where we had tea, and where Mr. Jelliman of Maclear introduced himself with kindly offers of help. Here Inspector McLaren left us, and we proceeded on our own full responsibility. The next stage was one of 13 miles to Idutywa, where our own first business was to lunch, and where we were to find Inspector Rein and didn't. Cumming the magistrate called, and under his guidance as chairman I visited the little public school and took a stroll through the town, ending up with afternoon tea at his house. Before dinner, Inspector Rein arrived, his garb being modelled on that of a Russian Uhlan, and his air that of a religious monomaniac.[8] Dined altogether and discussed circuit affairs, missionaries and magistrates. In the evening the R.M., having visited the bar with Cuthbert and being thus rid of his diffidence, called with a Mr. Warner and had a jovial chat and smoke.

4/8/09 Wednesday

(Visit to Clarkebury Institution)

Up at 7.30 to find a hot windy morning. Left at 9.15, and left my gloves as well. Drive like yesterday's, up hill and down dale, all alike brown. Wind very trying, one side of face and one nostril being specially annoyed. Outspanned at 11.30, a considerable distance from water for the horses: the water for our whisky we carried with us in a railway bag. On being refreshed I walked on ahead, expecting the cart soon to overtake me; but after a couple of miles I became uneasy at its non-appearance, and kept constantly looking back. In a short while I accidentally saw our four horses scampering on a distant hill with a native boy in chase. Sat down on a stone to wait, and worked a little mathematics on a bleached ox-bone for want of a note-book. At long length the cart arrived, and when Cuthbert began to explain about the catching of the horses, I told him I had seen them looking for me! Reached a trader's place which we thought might be Clarkebury about 1.30, and were there shown the Institution in the distance on the other side of the river (Mgwali?). Rev. Lennard welcomed us warmly, and we were soon sitting at lunch with him and Mrs. Lennard. After lunch there was a great reception, speech-making and photographing, the pupils being drawn up with their teachers in three sides of a square. Mrs. Lennard, placid and motherly, acted as photographer, and Mr. Lennard relieved us all of the trouble of making conversation. Then all the class-rooms were visited in turn, and the pupils seen at work. A standard V class who engaged with their music-teacher, rendered a chorus from Mendelsohn wonderfully well. After supper the teachers (two Underwoods, Beardmore, etc.) and their wives came in for conversation. This was interrupted by a closeting with Mr. Lennard for business purposes, and by the arrival of apprentices who as sea-lawyers wished to utilise the S.G.E.'s visit so as to obtain views from him likely to embarrass their masters. Fortunately, time sped, and bed had to be thought of even by the untirable Mr. Lennard. Tried to soothe my brain after retiring by reading 'The First Violin', having stood my portmanteau on end near my pillow to serve as a stand for a candle.

---

8 'Uhlan': a reference to the uniform of the Polish-Lithuanian light cavalry, which included a double-breasted jacket.

5/8/09 Thursday

(Umtata; Engcobo)

Up at 7:30 and talked business again at breakfast. Old Mr. Barrett (Rev.) of Buntingville, who has definitely retired, called to shake hands. Got off at last at 9.40; had a delightful quiet breeze on starting, and first part of journey was charming. When sandwiching, however, a little after 11 in a drift, a wind like the preceding days arose, and travelling became unpleasant. Inspector Bain met us about 12.30 and escorted us to All Saints. Canon Waters received us most kindly into his humble home, and we all lunched with him and Mrs. Waters and Miss Alice. Surprised to find mission supported from Scotland, which had just sent a valuable 'mission parcel'. Cuthbert and Miss Alice chummed up at once, the latter having attended Grahamstown Training College with Margory Cuthbert, and as a consequence there was played to us a little piece of Beethoven's.[9] I was most taken, however, with the father who on a salary of the poorest had brought up five children and kept them from losing caste. Visited Training School alone, the two European households on the knoll being separated by a gulf of misunderstanding. Sister Hildegarde, who received me and took me round, was not so bright as of old, but was no less determinedly devoted to her work. Devotion alone can on occasion have its pathetic side. The loss of their school building in the fire must have been very trying when their only male help is their young teacher of woodwork, Lavery, from Glasgow. Had a cheery send-off by the Waters, who would have me take a Kafir 'harp' with me. Drove on to Engcobo which was reached about 6 o'clock. Learned that Sihlali had got tired of waiting and gone homeward;[10] but was immediately greeted by the doctor of the village, Dr Weir, a brother of Weir of Kingwilliamstown, and taken off to see his fine garden with its numerous specimens of foreign trees. He had known me well by sight in Glasgow where he had attended the university and the Philosophy Society, and he talked of Glasgow and Edinburgh men without end while we had coffee in his bachelor drawing room. Gave me a Kafir walking-stick on leaving, and a Kafir bead-bag. After dinner he called again at the hotel, and we had evening coffee and more talk. Cuthbert and Bain having found friends about the bar, I went off early to bed with 'The First Violin'.

6/8/09 Friday

(Engcobo; visit to Baziya Mission)

After breakfast Dr Weir, Dr Young (his nephew and son of Rev. Young of Marn) called to accompany me to the Public School, being joined there by the Rev. Jones, late of Mowbray or Woodstock, and a Mr. Daniels. Had an amusing meeting while trying to extract from all of them the boundaries of the school property. After a kindly goodbye the cart journey was resumed, and a last look taken of the pretty village. Outspanned at trader Lang's and merely rested, having lunched on the veld; household apparently Roman Catholic, as the usual convent copies of German chromolithographs were on the walls of the sitting room. In the evening we reached an untidy trader's (Moore's) at Baziya after a windy day's journey. After supper the Moravian missionaries Clements and Hartmann, with their wives, arrived, and were interviewed closely on all sides of native education. This led to the dictating of memoranda to Inspector Bain and Cuthbert until bedtime. Soon asleep with 'The First Violin', but not before Cuthbert was snoring opposite. Accommodation rough and ready.

---

9   This is the first reference in the *Diaries* to Alice Cogan, whom Muir subsequently refers to as Miss Cogan throughout. It is probable that Alice Cogan's contemporary as a student was Cuthbert's daughter, Marjorie Ann Cuthbert (1888–1974), who was 12 years younger than Alice Cogan. This would suggest that Alice did her training later in life than most.

10   The Rev. S.P. Sihlali.

7/8/09 Saturday

(Visit to Tabase Mission; Umtata)

Wind gone and morning beautiful. Clements with his school and teachers arrived about 9.15. Listened to their English and Kafir songs and talked to the teachers and pupils. Left at 9.30, parting with Inspector Bain. Reached trader Vidge's (German) and on learning that Inspector Tooke was at Tabase (Rev. Moths, Moravian) drove thither. There discussed native education, visited church and school, and lunched with Mr. and Mrs. Moths and their small boy who had been kept undefiled by English. Given photographs of mission station on leaving at 2.30. Inspector Tooke's cart followed in charge of his boy, as did Inspector Bain's on two previous days. Arrived at Umtata at 4 o'clock, and found the Imperial Hotel a comfort after a week in the rawer country. Had at once a change of clothing and a thorough freshening up, before being taken to the club by Inspector Tooke. Met there Hill of the Training School (native) who is sort of secretary of the Club, Dunlop of A.B.C. Bank and an old High School pupil, Elliot of Standard Bank and Carmichael of Transkei General Council. Dunlop who was particularly kind, though in his honeymoon, and his bride has been at least twice married before! After supper the three of us worked till 10.45 over the Bunga Report of which Tooke fortunately succeeded in procuring an early copy.

8/8/09 Sunday

(Umtata)

Rose at 7 to find the morning lovely, but apparently with wind and dust in store. After breakfast Dr. Walsh (sister, the principal of K.W.T. Girl's School) and I talked School Board affairs, this being followed by a further compiling of case against the Council secretary as soon as Inspector Tooke arrived. Meanwhile Cuthbert had arranged, notwithstanding the day, that my meeting with the Acting Chief Magistrate and Carmichael should take place at 2.30. And sure enough we met, a room of the hotel being provided, and a load of papers installed by a clerk (Kenyon). What an afternoon! Four steady hours of it! Is the story not told in the office records? After supper Inspector Tooke returned, and we set to work at drawing up a memorandum, which although we kept at it till 10.30 had to be left unfinished.

9/8/09 Monday

(Visit to Buntingville Mission)

Wakened at 3 and didn't get to sleep again. Up at 7 to find morning grey but without dust. Started for Buntingville at 9, leaving Cuthbert but having Inspector Tooke and Rev. Lennard with me. Arrived at 10.15 and were met outside by Rev. Morris, his staff and pupils. After tea visited all the class-rooms and discussed native education. Talked with Morris of the old days of the founding of the institution to which he has returned a worn-out man; also of his more recent time at Beaconsfield, etc. Said goodbye a little after 11 and reached the hotel again about 12.20, just as the wind and dust began to rise. After lunch lay down for an hour or so while the wind was at its height, Cuthbert having arranged a meeting with McFiggins, editor of the 'Territorial News' and late of Uitenhage, who was burning to tell me his experience of the Bunga, Carmichael and 'Stanford and Co'.[11] Found him as described, and had [an] entertaining hour. On him followed Lowry the Mayor who was not less outspoken and instructive. Then long educational interview with Canon Bulwer and Mr. Hill, and finally a visit to the club with the Mayor, being detained there till

---

11   Col. Walter Stanford, a Cape politician focused on the affairs of the African people.

7.15. Dinner had to be scrambled over to enable me to attend School Board meeting at 8. This lasted till 9.30 and was very pleasant: was glad to meet, as new headmaster, Smith late of Butterworth, and Acting Chief Magistrate Brownlee also late of Butterworth, both of whom had called in the forenoon when I was engaged. Went soon to bed, while Cuthbert went to the club with Inspector Tooke and McFiggins and returned late.

10/8/09 Tuesday

(Umtata; Tsolo)

Rose at 7 to find air clear and sharp but morning delightful. Started promptly at 9 to visit schools. First, the Convent with Inspector Tooke, two little Swiss-peasant sisters showing us round with much kindness. Second, the Public School, where we were met by the Mayor, Mr. Klette, Dr. Walsh, etc. Third, the Town Hall, where the town clerk is a Mr. Ramsay of Glasgow. Fourth, the Bunga Parliament House with McFiggans. Fifth, the English Ch. Girls' School under Miss Haig.[12] Sixth, St. John's Training School where we had lunch with Canon and Mrs. Bulwer, the Bishop (Williams) and Mr. Hill, and where I took the arithmetic lesson of the PT1 and PT2 classes, and generally had an instructive time, especially in speaking to the Bishop of the state of affairs at All Saints. Back to hotel with early lunch so as to be ready to start shortly after 1 o'clock. Some time spent in last chats and goodbyes, but got away at 1.30. After two hours outspanned at trader Moldenhauer's and had beer on the untidy stoep, and a talk with an Aberdonian called Dunbar, in a white linen suit and practising as an inoculator of cattle. Just about sundown reached Tsolo, narrowly escaping a bad accident in descending the hill towards the village. Hotel a little uninviting. Dr. Melville, a Scotsman from Barrow-in-Furness, who had been examined by me at George Watson's College, came in after supper and talked Edinburgh University gossip till 11.30. Dictated memo to Inspector Tooke and then he and Cuthbert went to sleep in a Kafir hut, whence however there were sounds of revelry till early morning.

11/8/09 Wednesday

(Visits to Bunga Experimental Farm, Tsolo; and Tsitsa Bridge)

Broken sleep. Coffee came at 6, three-quarters of an hour before the sun began to rise. Copied two pages of mathematical paper in bed. After breakfast visited village school with Dr. Melville and found everything nice, the teacher being Miss Barr from Grahamstown Training School. Left at 9.30 and had pleasant drive to St. Cuthbert's, where an interesting hour was spent with Fathers Puller, Callaway and Wallace. Visited their beautiful church, the weaving school (Miss Wigan and another), the workshop (Old Thwaites), the classrooms, the hospital (Dr. McMurtrie and sisters). On leaving struck across country, and after rough drive and lunch on the veld reached the Bunga Experimental Farm about 2 o'clock. Mr. Hughes, the manager who had called on us in the morning, showed us his stallions, his rams, and his stables, his substantial house, etc.; and then we had tea with Mrs. Hughes, and left for Tsolo with Mr. Hughes, our own cart having gone on before. Having collected all our belongings, we left Tsolo at 4 o'clock, and after a pleasant afternoon drive of two hours arrived at Tsitsa Bridge, the delightful station of Mr. Black. There Inspector Hobden was awaiting us; and Cuthbert, Inspector Tooke and he had a merry meeting. Strolled around the grounds encircled by the river and returned in time for a chat with Captain Ward (late of CMR), an official in the Ch. Magistrate's office at Umtata, before

12 'English Ch. Girls' School': Umtata Christian Girls' School, now co-educational.

dinner was served.[13] Our dinner party included Mr. Black and Captain Ward, and was compact and confidential:

	Cuthbert	Tooke	
Dr Muir			Mr. Black
	Hobden	Ward	

The Bunga was discussed with much laughter; and having all gathered in a sitting room with a wood fire after dinner, we kept the talk and fun going until 11 o'clock .

12/8/09 Thursday

(Visits to Roza and Mhlanga Mission Schools, Shawbury Mission Station and Tsitsa Falls; Qumbu)

Though awake, was yet a little late for breakfast. Had a pleasant walk around another part of Black's grounds. Started at 9 after saying goodbye to Inspector Tooke who was loth 'to part good company'. On the way inspected two Kafir schools, Roza and Mhlanga, English Church and Wesleyan; and having found that they couldn't sing 'God Save the King', we pressed them to try with disastrous results, of which Inspector Hobden was kept duly reminded afterwards. Found the drive to Shawbury distinctly roughish. There the Rev. Lennard was again found, being a visitor to the Rev. Mears. After a cup of tea inspected the Girls' Training School, and the Practising School, the former under Miss Fair and two young lady T3s, the latter under Miss Hoodless(?). After lunch met deputation of the Quaker Teachers' Association, when an interesting address was read and conversation followed. Just on starting Rev. Lennard intimated that he had arranged after all that I should see the Falls of Tsitsa, he guaranteeing that though the main cart went on ahead to Qumbu, he would drive me to within a mile of the Falls, to which I could then walk with Rev. Mears, and yet have me arrive at Qumbu very nearly as soon as the others. He kept his word, and I was delighted with the little outing although it was done in haste, the time taken being exactly an hour till we returned to the Mission Station, where also I was given a photograph of the Falls by Mrs. Mears. The exceedingly difficult hill-road of the morning was no less trying on the way back, but having got to the top we struck away to the right and reached Qumbu in safety in the gloaming. Before dinner the school chairman (Dr. Culligan) and the teacher, Miss Gash of Grahamstown Training School, called. Dinner table of four, the Rev. Lennard being with us. Afterwards returned to a little outside sitting room and discussed education for two hours with Rev. Lennard and Inspector Hobden. Cuthbert had been talkative during dinner, and was more so later, ending up by super-intending affairs in the kitchen, preparatory for a dance [the] next night.

13/8/09 Friday

(Qumbu; Tina Bridge; Mount Frere)

Woke about 3 o'clock, and had difficulty in falling asleep again. At last about 4 o'clock lit acetylene gas, which seemed to set all the cocks of the village crowing, and did some copying of mathematics. Wakened again at 6; there had been a drizzling mist during the night, and on getting up at 7 found it still damp and close – the first morning of the kind since leaving Capetown. Bade goodbye to Rev. Lennard at breakfast. Visited school with Dr. Culligan, and then accompanied him to his house to meet his wife, a Miss Cloete of the Gardens, who had met Cam at the Tom Grahams – a nice household of two with a

---

13   CMR: Cape Mounted Rifles.

pretty cat and a fine garden. The morning soon brightened, and the drive was delightful to Tina Bridge, where we outspanned and had the pleasure of meeting the Pondoland Giant, Mellor, 6 ft 9 ins in height and weighing 368 lbs. Cuthbert foraged at once for sandwiches and beer. The former were excellent: gruyère cheese, brawn and beef. Had quite a pleasant chat with Mellor and one of his sons-in-law, Morant, who showed me the flourishing kitchen garden where all was stony ground three years ago. Found Mellor gentlemanly and his stories not seriously to be questioned, notwithstanding his reputation as a romanticist. After crossing the bridge there was a strong pull and a long pull uphill, and at long last we arrived at Mount Frere where Mrs. Hobden awaited us. Had at once a wash and nice afternoon tea. Then the Rev. Lock of Osborn, and formerly of Mowbray, arrived on horseback, being accompanied by his woodwork instructor, McGillivray, and after discussion it was arranged that I should visit Osborn that day. Nice dinner and long evening chat, Mrs. Hobden being formerly Miss New of Wynberg Girls' School.

14/8/09 Saturday
(Visit to Osborn Mission Station; Mount Frere)

Unusual sounds kept me awake, but was brightened up by the morning sun streaming in about 7. By 9 the household was all ready for the great expedition, except Cuthbert, who was indisposed, and after trying on Hobden's riding breeches decided not to form part of the cavalcade. About 9.30 all had started, Mrs Mackay's party consisting of herself, a daughter, Mrs. Hobden and her son, with Mrs. Mackay's manager (Blackbeard) as driver of the four-in-hand; the magistrate (Mr. Harris) and Inspector Hobden riding; and last myself in Mr. Wheeldon's charge. About two miles out of the village we were met by McGillivray on horseback to show the way. The morning was beautiful and the road though steep was not nearly so bad as painted by the Rev. Lennard. Were received by the boys and girls of the school, drawn up in astonishingly long lines, close on 400 children in all – a very pretty sight. The Rev. Lock introduced his wife and Mrs. McGillivray and the teachers, and the assembled pupils sang 'God Save the King' well and with good volume. We then had tea and a talk on native education with the magistrate, and the pupils marched to their classrooms. Next the classes were all inspected from Standard VI downwards, the teachers being in the main capable and verbose natives. Another general assembly then took place, but now in the church – all the pupils, the delegates of the Mount Frere Teachers' Association, the chief natives of the valley and the visitors – a great gathering. First, we had some songs, English and Kafir, and all were well rendered; the kindergarten rendering of 'Shoo fly! Shoo fly! We feel, we feel like the morning star' being especially dramatic and entertaining.[14] An address from the Teachers' Association was next read and replied to at length, and the 'kirk skailt'.[15] Lunch followed at a long table in Mrs. Mears' house, and there I talked with Mrs. Mackay, an interesting old lady, the last survivor of the founders of Mt. Frere who, she said, arrived 33 years ago after a seventeen days' journey from Kingwilliamstown. Immediately after lunch we had to proceed to the church again to meet the headman and people of the location. Two speeches of welcome were delivered, and these and my reply were translated by McGillivray who spoke in fluent and sonorous Kafir. The fine mission garden with its plentiful oranges and varied vegetables was then hurriedly visited, and we prepared to leave in three detachments as before. On reaching Hobden's, found Inspector Porter had arrived, and all the native education questions had to be talked over with him. Later in the evening we went by invitation to Mrs. Mackay's and talked

---

14 The children's song 'Shoo Fly, Don't Bother Me!' (1869) by T. Brigham Bishop. Today the original lyrics would be regarded as racially offensive.

15 'the kirk skailt': the church ended (Scots).

of the old times with her, and joined in the singing of the young people, and heard Mrs. Hobden recite. After a night-cap at Hobden's, we sat up talking shop till very late.

15/8/09 Sunday
(*Mount Frere*)

High wind all night, and cold. Rose to find snow on the hills, and a biting blast coming off them. No pleasure out of doors. Capt. Lorch of C.M.R. and a Mr. Van der Riet, a surveyor, called; then the R.M. with whom I went over his paper on Native Education; and with them and Inspector Hobden I came to an arrangement to try his scheme in Mount Frere district. In the afternoon the School Committee called (Davies, etc.). Walked to [the] town offices to view [the] sod wall and wattle hedge, meeting on the way the Rev. Yates who had called yesterday. On returning found Mrs. Davies, the teacher of the village school, and her helpless husband. After supper Mr. Garner (local attorney and secretary of Nickel-Copper Co.) and surveyor Van der Riet called and we talked mining affairs, and arranged to pay [a] visit to the Waterfall Mine the next day on our way to Mount Ayliff. Sat late chattering; pleased to find wind fell before we went to bed.

16/8/09 Monday
(*Visits to Rode and Waterfall Mine; Mount Ayliff*)

Rose at 7 and found wind entirely gone, and morning lovely though cold. The cavalcade was ready by 9 o'clock – Inspector Porter and I in his cart accompanied by his boy on horseback, Inspector Hobden and Cuthbert in the main cart-and-four, Inspector Hobden's boy with the luggage in the buggy, and Surveyor Van der Riet on horseback. On [the] way through the village called at [the] little Public School, held in R.C. church. At the Umzimbuba Bridge no halt was made, it being thought better to go on to the Rode (Mr. and Mrs. Jarman) where we had tea before setting off on foot to inspect the Rode School. Affairs at [the] school most disappointing, and I spoke straight to the headman and people after inspection, following this up by dictating two memoranda on returning to the carts. Had a very comfortable lunch and received much kindness, being even presented on leaving with a 'tusk' of kesibe (Pondo) tobacco. Reached a native school on the plain at a point opposite the Waterfall Mine just as the children were being dismissed, and Mr. Van der Riet learned from the teacher the route we should follow. Most of the way there was no road, and it was with difficulty that we reached the huts on the bank of the mountain stream where the footpath began. A stiff climb then followed up the gorge, and we were well blown on coming to be introduced by Van der Riet to Mr. Brooks, the manager, who was also a large shareholder but an amateur at mining. On being provided with lamps, we were conducted into all the openings and drives, one of the latter being 400 ft. long, and the ore was visible everywhere. At the end of each drive, four naked Kafirs were found labouring at shot-holes with the light of only two candle dips.[16] The investigation was most interesting, so that one forgot the hardness of the climbing until it was over. Cuthbert and Hobden were easily satisfied and saw little, returning to the huts and camp where we had left the horses. There Van der Riet and I joined them just as the sun was setting, and there the sandwiches and viands were distributed, although not, we thought, in proportion to the work done. As the inspanning had been done we soon got into the carts, and then the scrambling downhill and through field to the main road began. Meanwhile the wind had

16 'shot-holes': holes bored in the rock to take explosives; 'candle dips': candles formed by repeatedly dipping a weighted wick in melted wax.
Muir closely observes the technical detail of a mining process, and takes the trouble to describe it in detail, using the appropriate terminology.

got bitingly cold, and by the time we reached Mt. Ayliff, we were all chilled to the bone. Inspector Porter fortunately had exaggerated the defects of the hotel. He succeeded in ferreting out some hot water after a little, with which I bathed my feet and so got thawed and felt alive again. Cuthbert became noisy at dinner and after, his ragging of Porter being a little tiresome, although not unkindly meant. The School Committee turned up in the evening (Young R.M., Pearson and Scott), the outcome being not unsatisfactory. Memoranda and telegrams dictated, and then to bed at 11.

17/8/09 Tuesday
(Visits to Gillespie Mission Station and Brook's Nek; Kokstad)

Had a good night's sleep. Up at 7 to a cold, still, sunny morning. Saw Porter go off bravely with his towel towards the river and saw him also change his mind when he had had time to consider. After breakfast, and when inspanning was going on, had a conversation with Campbell, a prospector, about the Insizwa Mines, he having been a resident for three years in the district and knowing similar mines in Canada. Reached Gillespie Mission Station about 11 o'clock, and were received most kindly by the Rev. Hunter, his wife, and three young girls, their three eldest being at the Boroughmuir Higher-Grade School in Edinburgh. A nice family last met in the mail steamer from England about two years ago. Mrs. Hunter comes from Dunfermline and we talked of Dr. Ross, etc. most eagerly as the time of our stay was short. A coloured Miss Saga with a soft Scotch voice was also there, with whom it was pleasant to shake hands. After tea and Scotch gingerbread we visited the school, and the Church, the latter in course of renovation by a white-haired carpenter name Fraser from Inverness, who had fought in all the Kafir wars, having originally come to the country as a solider. Having been told by Mrs. Hunter that Fraser came from Aberdeen, I introduced him jocularly as a fellow townsman to Cuthbert and was delighted with his earnest disclaimer. Although we had stayed a little over an hour, we were sorry to hurry away from such a kindly spot, a bright bit of Scotland set in Kafirland, and a bit of pure heathendom when the Hunters arrived a quarter of a century before. The drive to the hotel at the foot of Brook's Nek was cold and trying, but a nice warming lunch well served soon made us comfortable. There we rested until 2.15, learning in time that the little un-English peculiarities of the lunch were due to the fact that the proprietors, Mr. and Mrs. Aubert, came from the Channel Islands. A long pull and a slip brought us up to Brook's Nek, where we looked down on Kokstad with Mount Currie at its back – a fine view. About 4 o'clock we were met by Mr. Elliot (chairman of [the] School Board and son of Sir Henry Elliot), his partner Mr. Walker, and Mr. Barclay the Mayor.[17] Rearranging ourselves in the carts, we soon reached the town and drove straight to Mr. Elliot's house and had tea. Took a walk with Mr. Elliot back toward the mountain from which the town-water comes, and called, while he waited, on Mrs. Sutton, formerly Mrs. Garner, with whom Cuthbert and Hobden were found to be staying. After supper my hosts talked Capetown gossip, Mrs. Elliot having been born at the Manor House of Mowbray (a Porter perhaps) and Mr. Elliot having been articled with Buissinne.[18] Then Inspector Porter and the School Board secretary came in, and all the applications for the headmastership had to be gone over by a woodfire, which seriously sufficed to keep out the frost.

17 Sir Henry Elliot: Sir Henry Elliot (1826–1912), Chief Magistrate of the Transkeian Territories (1891–1902). Muir's host, Mr. J.F.D. Elliot, was the founder of the local Kokstad firm of attorneys, Elliot & Walker, and three generations of Elliots practised in this firm (still under the same name today).

18 'Messrs Van Zyl & Buissinne': Cape Town attorneys.

18/8/09 Wednesday

(Kokstad)

Awake early after a fairly good sleep, but not earlier than Mr. Elliot's two little sons. After breakfast, Mr. Elliot and the Inspectors accompanying, I visited the public school at drill (Mr. Eason, Mr. du Toit and Miss Potts) and then the R.C. Convent with its numerous sisters and numerous classes. Next met the school board where Mr. Barclay the Mayor spoke at length, and where matters in the end were smooth all round. After business I was interested in the members – King an old High School boy who told me his masters in John Street;[19] Adam, another Scot; Barclay, another Scot (these last two of a less fine clay than King, but equally tough); Elliot, a Colonial Scot, his mother a Drummond; and Nourse and Walker, both English – a good set of men. Went thence to the Griqua School (Rev. Richardson, a Scot and successor of Rev. Dower and probably also of Rev. and revered Murray) and had lengthened meeting with the Griquas, Zietsman, ex M.L.A., being present. After lunch an old pupil Agnew of Standard Bank called, Leary the R.M., and Woolley, a school board member who had arrived in town too late for the meeting. At 3 o'clock met the Town Council, and thereafter visited the Spinning School (Miss Kirk and Miss Usher). Went then to Cuthbert's room in Mrs. Sutton's and dictated memoranda and telegrams. After tea brought in by Mr. Zietsman's little daughter, I walked down with Cuthbert and Hobden towards the club, and meeting Zietsman walked back with him to Mrs. Elliot's, where a second tea was waiting. At tea talked music and read 'A Morning Study' from Tucker's Poems.[20] Dined at Sutton's and had a rollicking evening. There were old Mrs. Sutton, her husband, her daughter Mrs. Zietsman, Mr. Z and family, another son-in-law, Mrs. Potts, etc. Mrs. Z's daughter recited and read some of her own verses. Mrs. Sutton, who was very formal throughout, showed me her pantry storeroom with endless home-made comestibles. Got back to bed about 11, and found Mr. Elliot reading in his dressing-gown.

19/8/09 Thursday

(Cedarville; Matatiele)

Beautiful cold morning. Sorted out yesterday's pile of letters, including those from England, and had everything ready to start by 9. Zietsman and Sutton called to say goodbye. Porter's own cart being first at the gate, he and I after adieus drove off together. At Keal's the main vehicle stopped, but we passed by and outspanned at the side of a clear little stream and waited so as to have 11 o'clock sandwiches all together. At 2 o'clock Cedarville was reached – a rather poor-looking place. There we had lunch, and met Mr. Warren, who has worked for Cedarville school so long, and who gave me some idea of the troubles of the Matatiele Board and of the approaching Board election.[21] About 4.20 pursued our journey, and a little after sunset reached Matatiele. Discussion had arisen as to the best hotel, and Inspector Porter's decision was followed: but the others of course were not long in finding out that we had hit on the wrong one. After some trouble about her bedrooms, the welcome signal for dinner was given. Inspector Morrison joined us, although staying at the other hotel. Meanwhile a meeting with the School Board had been arranged for, and a

---

19 The pre-1878 premises of the High School of Glasgow were at John Street; therefore King, a former pupil of the school was telling Muir of his former teachers at the school (of interest to Muir, who had taught there for so long).

20 *Songs of Love & Nature* (1909) by Herbert Tucker.

21 'Matatiele': Cedarville is in the Matatiele Municipality.

smoking-room closely adjoining the bar secured for the purpose. The sederunt[22] was lively and lengthy, the speakers being the table-thumping Dr. Pope, the Magistrate Hargreaves, Attorney Seymour, the secretary of the Old Committee, the teacher Melville, the local editor, formerly a bank-clerk, and later in the evening the rampageous and perfervid leader of the Cedarville opposition, 'Wha-What' Smith.[23] My patience was equal to the emergency, and at the breakup the temperature was normal. Afterwards Coutts, the manager of the Standard Bank, called and had a night-cap with us.

20/8/09 Friday

(Visits to Isigogo and Kenegha Drift)

Rose early and went out in dressing-gown and slippers and strolled round the untidy hotel-quarters. Sun just peeping over the hills on coming in at 6.45. After breakfast visited one part of school at [the] jail and another in a corrugated-iron hut, and then had another long talk with the Chairman Pope and the young attorney Seymour, the Inspector convicting the former of gross inaccuracy in his previous night's statements. At 11.30 said goodbye to all. Parting from Inspector Porter and Inspector Morrison with regret. The country traversed was now less interesting, the prevailing rocks being sandstone. Lunched in a dried vlei and had tea about 3 o'clock at a Mr. Garner's store at Isigogo. There I was kindly humoured with a short nap on the stoep, and it was almost 4 before we left. Kenegha Drift was reached about 5.30, the evening and the place being beautiful.[24] The drift though bad was crossed with safety, and we were delighted to see a row-boat moored to the bank. Found the inn being renovated, and were given a nice fresh bedroom, the housekeeper having been a teacher with Miss Hockly of Cradock. In the newly furnished parlour, we had a wood fire kindled after dinner, and we strummed the piano and sang songs jovially until bedtime. The cold in my head, which had been developing, became very annoying. Resolved to start early next morning.

21/8/09 Saturday

(Visits to Mount Fletcher Moravian Mission and Katkop)

Rose and begun dressing by candlelight, but the sun came peeping over the mountains by 6.45. Lovely morning but bitterly cold. Everybody ready to start by 7, and start we did. After going a little way, we had to stop and wrap ourselves better, I putting on my motor-coat and a rug for my feet. At 9 we outspanned for breakfast on the veld. The usual veld fire was made, and a grid impressed out of a length of hoop-iron, which had formed part of a structure of a bed. While the chops cooked, we worked at hard-boiled eggs and polony, which in ordinary circumstances would have been enough. The chops however were so sweet that we all ate about twice as much as usual; the drink taken too was out of proportion being not coffee but beer. About noon we reached Mount Fletcher, an uninviting place, where a rest nevertheless was welcome because of the shaking we had got by the way. The Moravian missionaries Steinmann and Marx were met before lunch and the Acting R.M. (Barry from Rosebank) and the Rev. Barrett of English Church after. At 2 o'clock we

22 'sederunt': a formal meeting of an ecclesiastical body (Scottish).

23 'perfervid': ardent or hot-headed, as in 'perfervid Scot'. The epithet used to describe Smith possibly identifies him as a stammerer.

24 'stoep' (Afrikaans): a verandah. In the context of the *Diaries*, however, the word has a special meaning. It was the roofed porch area at the rear of his railway carriage, partly enclosed by a railing on all three open sides; here Muir was able to sit outside either while the carriage was in a siding, or when the train was travelling, to take the air.

left and had a four hours' drive over a bad road to Katkop, a hotel so-called kept by Scotch people from Kingwilliamstown or Grahamstown called McLuckie. Glad to find a telegram awaiting from home, and Cuthbert, having discovered with delight a telephone working in Maclear, called up his clerk Stewart and arranged to have a prodigious lunch ready the next day at 3, by which time it was hoped we would reach rail-head. After dinner strolled out for a walk in the moonlight, the evening being wonderfully fine. Went soon to bed, however, as my cold was still troublesome and my hands and lips chapped.

22/8/09 Sunday

(Maclear)

Sun came streaming in about 6.30: head cold bad and sleep disturbed but was dressed and ready by 7.30. Left about 8.30 and was glad to find that part of [the] drive was through a better country. Although the morning was charming, it was impossible to ignore the bad roads. About 11 we outspanned at a store of McLuckie's on the Tsitsa River and had a sandwich and a drink, sitting by the bank where an overhanging branch sheltered us from the sun. Read 'Guy Mannering' as at odd times during the last few days until time for inspanning.[25] At the Pot River, a drink had to be halted for as the sun was broiling. About 2 we came in sight of Maclear and began the long descent. Drove straight to the saloon where Stewart and the station master were awaiting us, the rest of the village being asleep. Our great lunch at 3 was not quite up to expectations, though good; the short rest after was more enjoyable. About teatime Miss Cogan called, and I had a long talk with her until dusk. She stayed to supper with us, and Mr. Cuthbert and Inspector Hobden went home with her about 9 to Dr. White's. Glad to go to bed.

23/8/09 Monday

(Maclear)

Awoke about 3.30. Put on my overcoat, and went out for a little, everything being dark and still inside the saloon and out. Then back to bed and tried to sleep or doze until about 6.30. Morning chill a little, but bracing and sunny; delighted to hear the doves chirring as I waited for Joe to start work on the kitchen. After breakfast Dr. White and the Rev. Glasson arrived, then a Mr. Sephton, and a Board meeting was arranged for 2.30. At 11 went to tea with Dr. and Mrs. White, and Miss Cogan, and had quite a delightful chat, the Whites being nice and kindly Fifers. Chat broken in upon by arrival of Jelliman and Benson who would talk School Board matters; had to get a laugh against the former in order to bring the talk to an end. Went straight to Board meeting after lunch, and had a full attendance, young Vlock the R.M. being in the chair. Urged compulsory education and, as elsewhere, had friendly converts. Jelliman then drove me to Mrs. White's to afternoon tea and thence to the saloon, when I was glad to have a quiet walk by myself along the railway. To supper, the wife of the station master (Nicol) contributed a plateful of thick oatcakes (bannocks) which we all enjoyed. A Dr. McDonald, a New Zealander, from Indwe supped with us. Afterwards the English mail arrived and we had lots to read. Ian Colvin's 'Romance of S. Africa' came from the Rectory for the 25th, and I read aloud his dainty verses on 'Capetown long ago'.[26] Afraid of change of weather.

---

25   *Guy Mannering* (1815) by Walter Scott: a novel.
26   *South Africa* (Romance of Empire Series) (1910) by Ian Colvin.

24/8/09 Tuesday_

(Ugie; Elliot; Cala)

Awoke about 5.30 and found thunderclouds gone and the morning beautiful. Breakfasted early so as to be able to receive morning visitors. Jelliman came first, and was most kind in his own way, having as I learned afterwards, brought to the kitchen an 18-lb turkey. Called on the station master's wife who had given us a second supply of bannocks. The Whites and Miss Cogan came punctually at 8.55, and Dr. White took a snapshot of five of us on the platform of the saloon. Bade a warm goodbye to Inspector Hobden and carried off Miss Cogan with us amid a rattle of fog signals and hand wavings. At Ugie Station found the Rev. Vlok (of Piketberg fame) ready to talk education, and Messrs. Allan and Farr (sung of in the trout ballad) to 'pay respects'. After leaving Ugie, discovered that Rev. Dewar, the 'Wee Free' representative, was on the train and invited him to a talk.[27] He was delighted to come, and still more delighted to find, as the conversation went on, that I knew all the people connected with the 'African Lakes Co.', and that we had many acquaintances in common.[28] We pressed him to stay to lunch, and though he would not join in a whisky-and-soda, he enjoyed himself like a sandboy. Meanwhile Miss Cogan and Dr. McDonald chatted by themselves in the office-room. At Elliot Station found the R.M. (Verschuur) and the Rev. du Plessis and the whole School Board awaiting me. Had an hour's meeting with them in the station master's dining room, and we parted in wonderful friendliness. The Rev. du Plessis evidently being in fear that I should fall on him for his rudeness recently to Mr. Murray in the office. (Poor man! I learned, after he had left, that my fears for his sanity were too well founded, he having just recently returned to Elliot from the West, where he had left a daughter in Valkenberg.)[29] Meanwhile Mr. Wheeldon had detrained his horses and cart, and after a cup of tea from the station master, we (Miss Cogan, Mr. Cuthbert and myself) started at 4 by cart. It was 6 o'clock before we reached Cala, the long and steep descent on it in the gloaming being very enjoyable. The R.M. (Mr. Bell) met us, and arranged for [a] meeting at 8. Our little hotel dinner was very jolly, a wonderfully good bottle of wine being forthcoming. The School Board meeting (Mr. Fenix, Mr. Hyde, etc.) was a trifle lengthy and depressing, but we afterwards had a whisky-and-soda with the whole of them in the hotel saloon, the Mayor (a Major Strutt) and others joining.

25/8/09 Wednesday

(Cala; Garryowen; Indwe)

Awoke early and found that wind and dust had both risen. At breakfast had a pretty bunch of violets from Miss Cogan, the significance of the date having been known by Cuthbert. Found another bunch in my bedroom afterwards, and later on a beautiful bouquet arrived purporting to be from the ladies of the local Loyal Women's League. With Mr. Fenix, visited the decadent Public School; then with Father Murray, the Convent and Marist Brothers' School; then with the R.M., the Poor School, the R.C. Coloured School and the independent Mission School (Sihlali's).[30] Tea at 11.30 at Mrs. Bell's, where her daughter

---

27 'Wee Free': the epithet used to identify the Free Kirk, the smaller of the two Scottish Presbyterian Churches.

28 'African Lakes Co.': a company set up by Scottish businessmen to cooperate with Presbyterian missions on the lakes and rivers of Central Africa.

29 'Valkenberg': a psychiatric hospital in Cape Town founded in 1891.

30 The reference to Sihlali's Mission School must be a reference to the Rev. S.P. Sihlali of Cala. He was the first African to pass the Cape university matriculation examination in 1880 and was the first President of Imbumba Yamanyama (solid unity), the very first African political organisation in the Eastern Cape.

who served tea told me she had been at Cam's marriage. Was interviewed at the hotel by the Rev. Flowerday and his native missionary, who contrived to keep me an hour late. After friendly goodbyes, however, we continued our journey at 1 o'clock in a storm of wind and dust. Kept a look-out on leaving the town and saw Athel's old house.[31] At 2.30 lunched in the cart in a less exposed hollow, and at 4 outspanned at Garryowen (Anderson's) and had tea. It was 6 o'clock before we reached Indwe, where in the saloon there were a lot of telegrams with birthday wishes. Miss Cogan went to the hotel, and Wheeldon also; the arrangements being that they should come back to dinner in the saloon, and that I should meet the School Board in the station waiting room at 9. Meanwhile, I at once set to and wrote until our two guests arrived. The dinner for an improvised birthday function was quite merry: even speeches were not awanting. Wheeldon said goodbye, having confided to Cuthbert how he had enjoyed the trip, and how especially this last day he had been sore with laughing inwardly at the fun Miss Cogan and I had had. The School Board meeting was very friendly, but was a tiresome interruption nevertheless (Court the R.M., Whittaker, Duncan, Rev. Kruge, Rev. Menton May, etc.). The fact was that the turkey having proved excellent, we had freely dined, and were only ready for a smoke and a talk. Cuthbert's talk had just the proper amount of confused thought about it to make it amusing, and his goodbyes, when the train carried us off at 10.40, had a tendency to be prolonged. Parted from Miss Cogan with regret and being tired soon went to bed.

26/8/09 Thursday

(Sterkstroom Junction; Dohne; Amabele; Blaney Junction)

Wakened early with shunting at Sterkstroom Junction where, after breakfast, Dr. Robertson called. The forenoon was occupied with 'Gazette' proofs.[32] In the afternoon at Dohne, a Mr. Martin, a passenger from Capetown, who knows Miss Fuechsel, and whom I suppose I should have known, called at the saloon and remained until Amabele was reached; his destination being Umtata to consider [a] request for [a] Waterworks loan. On reaching Blaney Junction, where Inspector Smith called, we were fortunate to catch a special train to K.W.T., which was reached about 9 – a secret visit.

27/8/09 Friday

(King William's Town)

Up early, and before breakfast sent a message to Miss von Held that I should visit the new building of the Girls' School after 9. Did this and fully discussed accommodation. On returning to [the] station, found Mr. Whittaker and Mr. Varder and [the] School Board secretary, and talked election matters and compulsory education. Mrs. Bond also called and brought violets and a cake. At Debe Nek met unexpectedly Inspector Anderson and Inspector Ely and took the former on with us to Alice. Here Henderson of Lovedale was waiting, and a long conversation took place on much changed times. The train having suddenly started, I couldn't shake hands with Dr. Roberts, Dr. Kelbe, Mr. Cowan and other members of the Lovedale staff. Dr. Kelbe, in running after [the] saloon, tripped over points and was apparently hurt. At the station Inspector Rein had joined us, and Lovedale and allied affairs were talked over with him until he left at Fort Beaufort. There Mr. Crozier the R.M. called, Mellor the headmaster, and Dr. Miller an old High School boy formerly met there. Reached Adelaide in the dusk, and met Mrs. Peart, the wife of the headmaster, Miss van Vuuren of the Spinning School, and Mr. Gray, the secretary of the Public School

31   'Athel': Athel Cornish-Bowden, Muir's son-in-law.
32   'Gazette': *The Education Gazette*, the journal of the Education Department.

Fig. D: King William's Town Station 1895. E.H. Short. DRISA P0335. Transnet Heritage Library Photo Collection.

Committee. Also took on board Mr. Hockly, ex M.L.A. of Bedford, who talked School Board elections until his own siding was reached. At Bedford, Mr. Ferguson called and brought naartjies.[33] Soon after I went to bed having talked and dictated memoranda the whole day. Learned by telephone before going to bed that Dr. Kelbe had been unhurt. Temperature in the saloon absurdly high: during [the] day it had been 90° plus.

28/8/09 Saturday

(Grahamstown)

Awoke at 6 with the train almost stuck at Atherstone, having slept through the shunting at Cookhouse, the rattling speed of the Johannesburg train, which we had there joined, and the shunting at Alicedale. At Highlands and at West Hill, the morning was perfect. Before dressing found that Inspector Milne had joined us at Alicedale. After breakfast Inspector Bennie called and Inspector Duerden. At 10:15 began day's programme. First met Art School Committee, and examined the school work. Then visited the Public School and the 'Mother Cecile' Memorial Hall, remaining to discuss matters with the Mother Superior until 10 o'clock. Was a little embarrassed by her humble confession in reference to Cooking School affairs. After lunch in saloon drove to Stone's Hill, and Inspector Russell having joined us, we enjoyed the outing notwithstanding the driving mist on the top. Dined five of us with Inspector Bennie in the Railway Hotel, where I spoke to ex-Attorney-General Sampson who was sitting alone at a neighbouring table. Afterwards attended [a] concert in the Memorial Hall – the object of my visit to Grahamstown. Enjoyed the music, especially Mr. Auld's playing and Mr. Streatfields's singing of 'Annabel Lee'.[34] At the conclusion was introduced to Rev. Gray (successor to Mr. Dower) and the new warden. Judge Graham, the chairman, then went with us all to the School House (Mr. Nelson's) for a night-cap and a talk about the Bunga and related things. Sat up late with Mr. Milne and Mr. Cuthbert, while the mist of the afternoon developed into rain.

33 'naartjies' (Afrikaans): small tangerines.
34 'Annabel Lee': a poem of Edgar Allan Poe, set as a ballad for voice and music.

29/8/09 Sunday

(Grahamstown)

Found rain gone and temperature fallen, and by breakfast time, a blue sky with fleecy clouds. Had a quiet forenoon. Groves of the Art School called;[35] Prof. McFadyen, haggard a little, but interestingly oblivious of his altered circumstances; the Warden of St. Peters; and Armstrong of the Art School; went with Inspector Milne at 6 to supper at School House where Prof. Ogg was met, and walked back just in time for [the] train. Inspectors Bennie and Russell came with us as far as Adelaide, and we had much discussion and talk, which finally wearied Inspector Russell out, so that leaving us to our levity, he turning into his own compartment and fell asleep.

30/8/09 Monday

(Port Elizabeth)

Awoke in Port Elizabeth about 6.30, and about 9.30 the School Board secretary arrived to arrange programme. Had meetings with Committees at 10.30, 11, 12.15; and at 1.15 without lunch drove to Walmer to visit new school building. Enjoyed the drive and, having lunched at Bunton's, returned to the saloon and rested and wrote a little. At 4.30 drove to Mr. Mackintosh's to talk business, he being unable to leave his house through an attack of gout. Back to [the] Library at 6 to a meeting with Committee of [the] Art School. Finished this just in time to reach coach and leave with goods train at 7. Took Inspector Milne with us as far as Alicedale, where he caught a return train at midnight and where we went to bed.

31/8/09 Tuesday

(Cradock; Rosmead Junction; Naauwpoort; De Aar; Fraserburg Road)

Rose to find the train in Cradock Station. Not inclined for much work. Dr. Ireland and his small boy joined us and talked to Rosmead Junction. Took a nap after lunch and it developed into a drugged sleep from which I only awoke at 6 o'clock when we were on the way from Naauwpoort to De Aar. At De Aar learned that Rev. Pagan, ill in health, was in the train on the way to Barkly West. Went early to bed, as the temperature had fallen, and I did not feel very fit.

1/9/09 Wednesday

Had a very bad disturbed night, but on rising felt much readier for work than the day before. Dictated long memoranda on Port Elizabeth meetings, and had them all finished before the English mail arrived at Fraserburg Road with the week's papers, which occupied the whole afternoon.

2/9/09 Thursday

(Worcester)

Awoke at Worcester and before breakfast had finished, old Mr. Meiring and the School Board secretary had arrived. Visited the two High Schools and had full and lengthy meeting with the School Board, mainly on building affairs. Left at 2 o'clock, and reached home about 7, where all was well.

---

35   Charles Sidney Groves (1878–1964) went to teach at the Grahamstown School of Art in 1905. He was later a leading figure in the Cape Town art world.

DIARY 2

S.G.E.'s Diary of a tour to Emgwali,
Komgha, Butterworth, Grahamstown,
Port Elizabeth, Oudtshoorn,
Mossel Bay, etc.

27/1/10 to 19/2/10

Fig. E: Old Station at Salt River c. 1912. DRISA N04247. Transnet Heritage Library Photo Collection.

27/1/10 Thursday

(*Rosebank; Mowbray; Salt River*)

Left town by 4.10 train, having to return from Rosebank by 5.38. Found things in readiness and after selecting some books, had a cup of tea, said goodbye to M. and marched off in the rear of Sam to the station. At Mowbray, Mr. Millard joining the train and he and Freeman and Sam saw me off at Salt River.[36] The coach was not quite shipshape, but it was nice to have old associations awakened. At supper I was interested in the new ways of Atkinson, our white chef, a little limp and greasy homelander. Read two of Noyes' poems aloud to Cuthbert before turning in.

28/1/10 Friday

(*De Aar*)

Had a bad night, feeling in the morning as if we had been shunting all night with the brake on. Learned at breakfast that we had been put onto the through passenger train at Worcester – a heavy train with two powerful engines – with the result that we shall be in De Aar twelve hours before we had hoped to be and shall have to wait there. Rev. Pienaar of Uitenhage of the Educatie Commissie was in the train, and came to the front to shake hands and smile benignly. Next to us, in a second-class carriage, was the Rev. Beyers, once

36   Mr. Millard is another official who appears to have performed relatively lowly tasks for Muir (but his appellation 'Mr.' might indicate he was a rung higher in the pecking order than Freeman and Duffett). Sam may well have been more in the nature of a personal chauffeur.

of Willowmore, and still as good as of old. The Karroo was not unpleasantly hot, and save for the dust, the journey would have been very enjoyable. We reached De Aar in the dark, an hour late, and found the platform and trains crowded with teachers and pupils. When all had gone we were shunted unto a quiet corner for sleep. Went to bed late, however, having much talk with Inspector Spurway about the Molteno affair, he having been telegraphed to join us at De Aar. Cuthbert, meanwhile, had been among his old friends gathering news of the School Committee's two meetings with the Colonial Secretary.

29/1/10 Saturday
(*Naauwpoort*)

At breakfast with Inspector Spurway, when Bishop, once of Salt River Technical School, called to lay off all his grievances against Dr. Symington and Symington's majority on the Committee, and to explain why he did not meet the Colonial Secretary with the others. Fortunately, Inspector Grant called, and the conversation became general. Left for Naauwpoort after 10, Inspector Spurway with us. There we had a long wait, but it was tempered in the evening by an excellent gramophone belonging to a dining saloon, which was drawn up opposite us. Dr. Baird also called. The water tanks of the coach gave us trouble and before they were finally mended, I retired to bed.

30/1/10 Sunday
(*Stormberg Junction; Molteno; Sterkstroom; Queenstown*)

Awoke after passing Steynsburg, Inspector Spurway having gone. Morning beautiful. Reached Stormberg Junction more than an hour late to find trains waiting and platforms full. Young, our clerk, had a dramatic meeting with a girl niece and members of her family, whom he had not seen for years. A girl's high-pitched cry of "Oh Arthur!" suddenly woke him and me as the train stopped, and I naturally left the scene to him alone. At Molteno, Cuthbert struck on a Scotsman called Duncan, in white veldschoens, who said that the place was seething with excitement and that the Colonial Secretary had got his head in a proper noose this time. At Sterkstroom, Dr. Robertson called with a glad welcome. All the neighbouring country looks well, indeed particularly so, because of the rain. Found Inspector Logie awaiting me at Queenstown, and talked with him seriously about the Tarkastad trouble, his side-taking, a possible change of circuit, etc. Headmaster Wilkinson also called. Unhooked coach just as train was leaving and sent a note to Miss Webb that I proposed to call at 5. After lunch, a fearful thunderstorm broke over the town. It lulled for a minute till I got to the Girls' School, but while talking with Miss Webb, it burst forth again in greater fury, and in a few minutes the street was a pair of rivers. Learned from her, the story of Mrs. Logie's candidature for the Girls' School Committee, and much other gossip worth knowing. Young came with an umbrella and I reached the coach about 6, the thunder still rolling in the distance. Left about 6.30 and, after supper, sat with Cuthbert on the coach stoep and watched the lightning for hours. Although the sky was bulging with heavy dark clouds and lurid clouds, there was no wind and the air was cool and pleasing. In passing Tylden without stopping, we saw 'the blighted begonia' on the platform, or at least we saw a white figure that waved from under the station lamp.[37]

37 'blighted begonia': This was a nickname that Alice Cogan bestowed on one of the middle-aged ladies involved in school business, and whom Muir and she tended to sight on the platform at Tylden as they passed by train. See also *Diary 5*, 7/10/11 Saturday. This lady was also known to Cuthbert as 'Mother Cameron'; perhaps this was her surname. Since blight or leaf spot is a disease afflicting Begonia plants, the nickname was a trifle unkind, but it clearly amused Muir.

31/1/10 Monday

*(**Dohne**; visits to Emgwali Institution and Horseshoe Farm, Stutterheim)*

Awoke about six and found we were in the old siding at Dohne. Everything was shrouded in mist and not a soul was stirring – a dismal morning. A little before breakfast, Inspector Young turned up, and was a little doleful about the proposed journey. Occasionally the mist would clear somewhat and show a portion of beautifully green field with a large pond in its middle and a strip of plantation on its right; but then again it would begin to drive from the west and develop into a wetting rain. At last about ten I decided to go, rain or no rain; and having sought out waterproofs and rugs, we started in middling comfort but not in high hopes. After half-an-hour things improved, and the remaining two hours were really enjoyable. The mist never wholly cleared away, but it receded, and we had charming views of the rolling country with its occasional strips of wattle plantation. By one o'clock we had reached the top of the last knoll, and there was Emgwali Institution nestling below, the single-storeyed manse being less prominent among the trees, and two or three of the Kafir hamlets being visible on the surrounding slopes. As we neared, we found everything quiet, for the school holidays had not expired. At the entrance to the garden there awaited us, to my great delight, the very man I had purposed calling upon on the way back, farmer Coutts, whom I had met on my first visit to Stutterheim and who had, at the recent School Board election, stood so manfully by the Department. He had heard of my intended visit and had ridden eight miles to renew old acquaintance. Outwardly he was a picture. His clothes were the colour of the soil, the lower half of his vest had no buttons, and his hat was only fit for a scarecrow. Yet what a self-possessed and courteous welcome he gave me; and what a splendid intellectual head he showed when his hat came off! Then Miss Dunsmore appeared, tall and plump and soft complexioned, with grey hairs not a few mingling among the black. After our little introductory chat, as we walked from the gate to the door, we scarcely sat down in the drawing-room, but got ready at once for lunch, which was nicely served at a table for four in the large school dining room. Miss Dunsmore talked quietly about the school's recent success, and was evidently happy; and Coutts was easily induced to be reminiscent, much to my enjoyment. He had come out originally as a mason to Lovedale, had been at the building of Blythswood and Emgwali, and recalled with ease the virtues and weaknesses of his old employers. "Dr. Stewart," for example, "kenned mair aboot squarin' a stane than I did, and sae I sune left him." He is also a great newspaper reader, and when the Molteno affair was mentioned, he readily laid down the essential points of the case, closing drily with the remark, "I built the tronk there, and I've thocht mair than ance that I wad like noo tae gie Pepler and De Waal a cell apiece."[38] After lunch Miss Dunsmore conducted me through all the building, and I soon got to know the secret of her success, and got [a] glimpse of her scheme for the future. Then we talked finance and I secured copies of her accounts for three years in order to bring home to others the fact that such an institution can be made self-supporting. At four we stepped down to the

---

38 The Molteno case was clearly pre-occupying the Department in February 1910, at which time a government application had been made for a court order to amalgamate the separate Dutch- and English-oriented schools in Molteno. Pepler had, for some time, been the leader of the Dutch language education campaign in the town; the reference to De Waal suggests that the Colonial Secretary (later first Administrator of the Cape) may have been sympathetic to his cause (and on the opposing side to Muir on the language issue). For the background to the education crisis in Molteno, see the section of Part I entitled, 'The Language Question'. Farmer Coutts's comment on the case is Scots dialect, but with one Dutch word, *tronk*, thrown in for good measure: "I built the gaol there, and I have thought more than once that I would now like to give Pepler and De Waal each a cell."

manse, and joined Coutts and Young at afternoon tea with the Stewarts – a kindly but uninspiring pair. Found Mrs. Stewart to be one of the Sinclairs of the 'Glasgow Herald' and the sister of four lads who had been under me in the Glasgow High School, and two of whom are now in Chile. She seemed sadly worn and in poor health, with little brightness left. Her husband had more appearance of vigour but would probably have still more in different surroundings: his father had been Librarian to the Merchant's House in Glasgow. We talked of accents – Scotch and Colonial – and got some amusement by comparing pronunciations. We sat in the part of the manse, which had been erected by Tiyo Soga, and we afterwards had pointed out to us the barn-like Scotch kirk, which the same divine had built.[39] In front of the manse is an improved Kafir hut where the few white people meet for Church service, and this we visited. About half past four Mr. Coutts mounted and left for home, explaining that being a heavyweight, he only exacted a walk from his horse and, therefore, had to start early. We ourselves left about five, leaving the lady of the domain once more to the society of her black retainers. As we drove off, one could not but muse on the haphazardness of human arrangements. The anaemic Miss Sinclair had married or been married by Mr. Stewart, and joy had not abounded; nor was their progeny (a single girl) likely to advance the world's work; while, on the other hand, the strong, capable, motherly Miss Dunsmore had missed or abjured marriage, and was spending her all on an alien race. Fortunately, there must be compensations, or the outlook would be poor. Inspector Young hinted at a love story of Miss Dunsmore's – the story of a fine woman attracted by a waster – and it was so far reassuring to know that the outcome might have been infinitely worse than it is. The visit had increased my respect for her and made me wish still more to help her in her work. When about an hour out we saw Mr. Coutts's broad back in the distance, slowly bobbing up and down with his horse's motion, and on coming up with him, he dismounted and explained how he had been making inquiries about his sheep, fine flocks of which, marked C.C. (Charlie Coutts), were visible on both sides of the road. We had also a little additional chat, and he moralized a little, having evidently been thinking of how I had jocularly cautioned him at lunch about becoming cynical as he grew older and keeping his eyes too much on the setting sun. A second time we said 'goodbye' to him and went on ahead. Shortly after, we came to a gate leading off the road downward and to the right, and as Mr. Young knew that it was a short cut to Dohne, which passed Mr. Coutts's farm-house, we resolved to make a change of route. Soon 'Horseshoe' farm steading came in sight, and as Mr. Young was diffident, I jumped out when the cart stopped and opening the tiny garden gate, knocked at the door.[40] The little old woman who came in answer was not in the least like Mr. Coutts, save in the absolute plainness and untidiness of her clothing. She was, however, his sister, and had guessed who I was, and so would have me enter. I then called on Mr. Young to join me. The cottage was a mere but-and-ben, with a bed and other miscellaneous furniture in each apartment and all of the very plainest.[41] A cup of tea for me was hospitably prepared in my presence, and Inspector Young took a couple of tumblers of 'amasi' instead.[42] All the while the old lady talked and questioned in the most quaint manner. Then Mr. Coutts arrived, and we found it hard to get away. At the

39 Tiyo Soga (1829–1871) was a journalist and missionary evangelist. He was the first black South African to be ordained and he also translated the Bible into isiXhosa. Soga and his wife founded the Emgwali Mission in 1857.

40 Horseshoe Farm, near Stutterheim in the Eastern Cape, still exists. It is known for its Horseshoe Tuli stud cattle.

41 'but-and-ben' (Scots): a two-roomed cottage.

42 'amasi' (isiXhosa and isiZulu): a milk drink fermented in a calabash, a traditional means of preserving the milk.

door she plucked a rose for my button-hole from one of the starved-looking bushes in her little square of garden; and while she prattled on, giving me hardly recognizable French names for them, she added a few sprigs of lavender to the posy. Mr. Coutts accompanied us to the tumble-down farmyard gate, where we learned that the handsome new building on the left, which we had thought was the dwelling house, was in reality a shearing house, and that the other on the right was a dairy! Money apparently was available for anything and everything save the personal comfort of the possessors: it may be, however, that what the rest of the world called comforts may have proved the opposite to these old Scottish peasants. As we drove on, Inspector Young told me old Mr. Coutts had recently bought an additional farm for £5,000, and how he had leased part of it to a Captain Gordon, belonging to the Aberdeenshire family on whose estate Coutts had been brought up as a herd-boy.[43] Guiding ourselves by the light of the Dohne railway signal, we at last reached the station in the dark, and eagerly sought the coach for dinner. To our surprise, the table was laid for seven and three ladies had already taken their seats. They were the Emgwali teachers who had arrived by train, and were unable to proceed that night – Miss Douglas M.A., who had originally brought out an introduction from Mrs. Dugald Bell, Miss MacGregor L.L.A., late of Lovedale, and Miss Hannah. What a crowded table it was, and what a merry dinner we had! Atkinsons's flustered countenance was a treat in itself, and his efforts to maintain the dignity of the establishment in the matter of table equipment and food were most amusingly praiseworthy. Mr. Cuthbert and Inspector Young saw our guests safely to their temporary quarters, and came back half drenched. After a little chat, we said 'goodbye' to Inspector Young and retired to bed, knowing that we should be picked up by a train about two in the morning.

1/2/10 Tuesday

(*Amabele Junction, Komgha*)

Awoke early before leaving Amabele Junction, which we had reached in the night. With slippery rails and a heavy load, the train came to a standstill about a mile out of the station, and after repeated desperate tugs, which were disastrous to our crockery, it returned to the starting place and shed itself of one heavy bogie truck. Thus relieved, progress was made in spite of the drizzle, and we reached Komgha about nine, where we uncoupled and had a quiet breakfast in a siding. While I was having a walk along the railway, the R.M. called and arranged for a subsequent meeting in the coach. Then Secretary Campbell and Mr. Swan came, and the new school site and building were fully discussed. In the afternoon, Mr. O'Connell came again and I visited the site with him, and then communicated with the Department. We had a quiet dinner by ourselves, and the evening afterwards was spent in dictating memoranda. Atkinson continues to be interesting; my guess about him being a ship's steward turns out to be true: his posts as such having been posts of honour and his ships the finest of the crack lines! So he affirms.

2/2/10 Wednesday

(*Butterworth*; *visit to Bawa Falls*)

Awoke to find the days of grey mist gone, and the sun streaming in at every chink – a most lovely fresh morning. Campbell called to say 'goodbye' before breakfast, and Inspector Bennie arrived in time for breakfast, Henderson of Lovedale having come with the latter from Amabele. Had a most delightful run down the winding slopes to the Kei River and

---

43   The Gordon family were the Earls of Aberdeen, whose estate was at Cromar, Aberdeenshire.

up the opposite side to Toleni heights. It was Inspector Bennie's first journey over the ground by rail, and he was greatly interested in comparing it with his first journey of all, which took place in an ox-wagon when he was a child. At Ndabakasi, Ross of Toleni called to enquire about the hour of meeting next day, and finding Henderson, carried him off to Cunningham for the night. Henderson came to the coach to shake hands, which he did dutifully and without a smile. Reached Butterworth about 2.30, and found Inspector McLaren, Miss Cogan, and the R.M. (Mr. Warner) awaiting us. Made arrangements for the rest of the day and attended to letters till four, when Inspector McLaren arrived to take me to Bawa Falls. Enjoyed the hour's drive over the rolling hills, the walk to the Falls through the mimosa and wild verbena, the drive back with a fine view of Butterworth, and the good two hours' business conversation with Inspector McLaren. The Falls, which are higher than the Tsitsa, are interesting, the rivulet of water having made only a shallow smooth groove down a vertical rock-face. On returning, there was only time to change, learn who had called – Mr. Gerrie and Miss Cogan, the latter with a bowl-full of fresh roses – and then proceed to Mrs. McLaren's to supper to meet the three Inspectors, Mr. Hobden having arrived in my absence at the Falls. Did my best to make the evening enjoyable to Mrs. McLaren, and to profit by the talk in reference to the morrow's work, the humorous side of affairs not being neglected. Inspectors Bennie and Hobden having walked home with us to the coach, the latter side was further exploited over a night-cap.

3/2/10 *Thursday*
(**Butterworth**)

Had a delightful still night and slept fairly well until 5.30. Morning dull and grey once more. Took a walk on the railway track before breakfast, and read Noyes's 'Enchanted Island'. The comedy of the early morning was Atkinson giving out the week's washing to an old Kafir hag. Regardless of her knowledge of English, he kept up a constant fire of directions and general chatter while he handed out the linen. "You're a beauty, you are; six napkins; six mind you, Jemima; 12 collars. Oh, you smoke, do you? Take my advice, darling, give it up!" and so on for a quarter of an hour on end. Close on 10 o'clock the official shorthand writer arrived, and then the Rev. Lennard. This was the signal to leave for the Town House, and when I got there, all the delegates had arrived except Ross of Cunningham. Arranged preliminaries without delay, and got over two and a half hours of deliberation with smoothness and reasonable dispatch. Agreed to meet at three for a second sederunt. Had Inspector Hobden and Miss Cogan to lunch, which as regards conversation was shoppy but pleasant enough. Hobden and Cuthbert much struck with the unwarlike, not to say cowed, air of the Conference members, and Cuthbert reported that Aldred, the shorthand writer from East London, was proving excellent. At three we resumed work, and kept steadily at it till 5.30, the way being again smooth, but Henderson, Lennard, and Callaway pressing the development of a Kafir literature! Kept them well in hand, however, and thus the first day ended, to the surprise of the Inspectors, with real evidence of growing friendship. After the meeting, Canon Bulwer and Father Callaway called while I was having tea, and then Miss Cogan came to take me for a drive. The daring way she rescued me from the Church claimed my admiration. She had confided to Cuthbert how Inspector McLaren had got in front of her in the matter of the drive to Bawa Falls, but that she would pay him out yet. The route chosen was across the bridge, past the main outspan, and then out on the Kentani Road. The air was beautifully fresh; and though the sunset showed little colour, the views of the rolling green hills as we ascended and of the extensive lowlands as we came back, were most pleasing. Altogether the outing was enjoyable, and I also regretted the Bawa misadventure. On returning met Hobden coming from the coach and was glad to find that Inspector Bennie had been greatly pleased with the outcome of the first day of the Conference. Miss Cogan came to dinner, which was a little more jovial, perhaps because of the said promising outcome. During it, I turned the conversation so as to bring in the story, which I had manufactured, regarding the letter for Miss Cogan given to us by the station master at Beaufort West. The result was all that could be desired, and Cuthbert laughed until his pipe went out. She was asked, with mock seriousness, if she did not see that she had been convicted of keeping up a non-official correspondence with Inspector Anderson, and whether it would not be the best course to make a clean breast of the whole affair. It was also suggested that the proper thing would have been to open the letter in the presence of her official superior, and Cuthbert held out the sacrificial paper-knife. A tactical slip was made by her in referring to Mvenyane, and we thus had a fresh opening, which of course we took full advantage of. She stood the teasing, however, remarkably well, and we had a very happy evening. I was remorseful afterwards, but if she was annoyed she did not show it, and I think was not long in forgiving me. I hope also she enjoyed 'Yoichi Tenko' and 'The Cornflower Millionaire', which I read aloud for her pleasure on the coach stoep.[44]

4/2/10 Friday

(**Butterworth**)

Awoke early and saw the prospect of a hot day. Had breakfast an hour sooner, so as to begin Conference work at nine. The sederunt of three hours turned out to be not so agreeable, because of the attempt of Mr. Henderson to bring in, by astuteness, another dose of the vernacular. Was compelled to give him a few fatherly words. At lunch we had Inspector Hobden with us. At the afternoon Conference, affairs took an unexpected turn, the remaining agenda being got over in double-quick time. It turned out that Henderson had been acutely disappointed at the reception given to his forenoon attempt to edge in the vernacular, and 'retired into his tent'. By five o'clock it was quite clear that a very short meeting [the] next morning, to revise the resolutions, would end the whole affair. After the meeting I took a stroll along the railway track past Lamplough, coming home just as the light failed, to find that our dinner guests had arrived – Inspector Bennie, Hobden and Miss Cogan. Bennie left soon to attend to the minuting of the day's proceedings, promising to smooth Henderson down and come back and report. In the two and a half hours of his absence, the conversation dealt in shop and chaff, even a 'whistling' incident coming in undeservedly. Then Mr. Cuthbert, having seen Miss Cogan home, came and reported progress as to the shorthand clerk's work in the station waiting room, and he and Inspector Hobden 'went up town' and left Mr. Bennie and myself and the Rev. Ross of Toleni to have a quiet talk. Went to bed about 11.30.

5/2/10 Saturday

(**Butterworth**; *visit to Bunga's Industrial School*)

Rose early, having had a disturbed night, and having, as I thought, heard revellers return around 2.30. Morning beautifully fresh after the slight rain. Henderson looked in for a moment at the Conference to leave suggested amendments on yesterday's minutes, and immediately thereafter took the morning train for Lovedale. All our work was over, and agreeably over, by 10. Had then an hour of business in the coach. First came Inspector

---

44 Both are poems by Alfred Noyes (1880–1958): 'The Two Painters' (A Tale of Old Japan); 'The Tramp Transfigured' (An Episode in the Life of a Corn-flower Millionaire). Noyes was the author of 'The Highwayman' and other epic romantic poems.

McLaren and Mr. Carmichael about certain arrear payments of school furniture, and following them, Father Callaway and Canon Bulwer about All Saints ceasing to be classed as a Training School. At eleven the R.M.'s trap came to take me to the Bunga's Industrial School, where beside the R.M., I met Carmichael, Chisnell the instructor and the Kafir house-father. There were only five boys at work, and the place was anything but lively. Had an interesting talk on the attempts to express 'square foot' in Kafir, and branched out in other matters of a similar kind, being very fortunate to be deep in it when Father Callaway and Canon Bulwer arrived, the former of whom is a zealous advocate for the vernacular. At lunch we had the Rev. Lennard with his quasi-ward, Miss Cogan, and had some quiet pleasant conversation. Was very glad to receive a reply telegram from home, and to learn that Rita was staying at Mowbray Hall. Mr. Gerrie of the High School called, and talked local geology and botany. Later Mr. Daly, auctioneer, etc. and formerly a good member of the School Board, came along with Mr. Lyon of Blythswood, and much gossip resulted on Butterworth and Blythswood affairs. To dinner we had Inspector Hobden and Miss Cogan, Inspector Bennie and Mr. Carmichael calling in afterwards; then when Mr. Cuthbert, Mr. Carmichael and Inspector Hobden had again 'gone up town', the three of us remaining had a long chat on Grahamstown Training School, and on Sister Clara and her new fad – Dutch. After I was left alone, it was hard to turn in, the evening being so fine.

6/2/10 Sunday
(Visit to Bunga Model Farm, Teko)

Rose early, and after doing some mixed reading and some writing, went for a short stroll back [along] the railway. Breakfasted alone, and was ready for our visit to the Bunga Model Farm at Teko with the incomparable Mr. Carmichael.[45] When Mr. Cuthbert made his appearance, I learned that some hitch had occurred, and that he and Inspector Hobden would not accompany Mr. Carmichael, the latter having seriously offended one of them or both. At 9.30 the carts arrived, Mr. Carmichael in one with his native boy, Miss Cogan with hers, the third cart (Inspector McLaren's) being awaited. I at once joined Miss Cogan and we started, Mr. Cuthbert saying a quite cordial 'goodbye' to 'the People's Walter' as Miss Cogan styles our fellow-traveller. The morning was cool with a blue sky well covered with fleecy clouds, and the drive was charming. There was, indeed, no especially fine view, merely a rolling grass-green country, which seemed illimitable when we got on the heights; but it had a generally quiet beauty and was restful in the extreme. Once or twice we halted and turned around to discuss the landscape with our fellow-traveller and to make sure that he should have no feeling of being 'left out'. After some inquiry, we at last hit on the entrance to the farm and arrived at it about eleven. The manager was found to be a Kenneth MacKay, who nine years ago had driven me to Mulder's Vlei when he was a student at Elsenburg and who, for another link of connection, was the son of Mrs. MacKay of Mount Frere and of happy remembrance on my last visit to the Territories. With him was his sister, who had been in Edinburgh at that time. They were both painfully quiet at first and shy, but notwithstanding the chilling presence of the 'exquisite Walter', we made way towards a friendly chat on the stoep. Soon, however, the ladies were left to themselves, as it was desired that I should see the farm and its stock. First of all, the Friesland herd was brought up for inspection, then a smaller Cape herd, then a Hereford bull, then a flock of prized sheep – all of which I gravely remarked on as they passed in review. Doubtless my comments were at least as intelligent as those of the lord of the manor, but I am

---

45 The Bunga Model Farm was later known as Teko Agricultural School, Butterworth. Walter Carmichael was stationed at Tsolo Agricultural School, another centre of agricultural training.

certain they wanted air and style, and had only at their back, a glimmering of humour instead of a supernatural assumption of wisdom. Meanwhile the minions of the table were dispatched to a distant hilltop, and before long returned riding studhorses, whose names were supposed to be familiar to me as household words. Sooth to say I enjoyed the sight, one animal in particular being very handsome. Miss Cogan did so also, for in this part of the programme the ladies took a part, the showground being close to the garden gate. It was next discovered by the two visitors that lunch was in the wind, and though surprised, they yielded gracefully. The little host and hostess were nervous kindness itself, Mr. Carmichael talked 'Shakespeare and the musical glasses', and Miss Cogan and I chaffed each other about the drinking of amasi.[46] Then a second surprise occurred, due to our host diffidently but anxiously warning his superior that his cart was inspanned. It then gradually dawned on us that Mr. Carmichael was on his way to Ibeka to catch the post-cart for Idutywa, and that as for us, we were expected to leave when we liked and find our way back to Butterworth. The arrangement, of course, we accepted with all courtesy and helped to speed the parting host. We did not, however, stay much longer, indeed only long enough for Miss Cogan to show a kindly interest in the sister's dairy, while I held a fitful conversation with the brother on the stoep. As we were a little in doubt about the proper turns to take on the way homeward, Mr. MacKay very kindly sent a native boy on horseback with us, and we said a grateful goodbye about 2.30. The drive was still more enjoyable than in the morning, and we didn't hurry: we even made a digression away to the right round the hill near old Chief Veldmann's place, halting at some native huts for the sake of a view and a talk. On reaching the coach, a third surprise awaited us, when we apologized guiltily for being late for lunch, the fact being that we had never been expected; and when we told our story, we got in return an explanation of all the mystery. It seems that after I accepted on Thursday Mr. Carmichael's invitation to visit the farm, he opened negotiations with Mr. Cuthbert about transport, with a view to obtaining it at no cost to himself, and let it be known that he had informed Mr. MacKay about the proposed visit, and had ordered lunch for himself, Dr. Muir, Mr. Cuthbert and Inspector Hobden. On Mr. Cuthbert suggesting Miss Cogan's name, some flimsy objection was raised, and it was then seen that the little visit had been suggested in order that Mr. Carmichael might give me his company for an hour and a half in a cart and talk shop; whereupon Mr. Cuthbert, like a good man and true, promptly declined the invitation for himself and afterwards induced Inspector Hobden to do the same. Hence Mr. Carmichael's visit of the previous evening to the coach, when, as it now turns out, Mr. Cuthbert told him that he "had arranged for Miss Cogan to drive the Chief, and that doubtless the Bunga would see to any other conveyance that might be necessary". The reason for keeping all this quiet until we returned was to spare Miss Cogan and to make sure that she should have the outing, which the schemer would have denied her. The pleasure was still more mine than hers, and as it was during dinner that the whole affair was cleared up, I promptly proposed the toast of 'Confusion to the Bunga', and this was responded to with unflattering ejaculations and weird howls. To crown all, we then also learned that the cart and boy, which conveyed Carmichael, were Father Callaway's, and that it had already returned from Ibeka to carry off its real owner on the morrow. In the afternoon, Mr. Lyon of Blythswood and Mr. Daly had called; then Mr. Alexander of the 'Transkei Gazette', who told me his whole story from the time of his engagement to come from Scotland to be master-printer at Lovedale; and lastly Mr. Gerrie, who was

46 'Shakespeare and the musical glasses': this is a literary reference to a quote from Oliver Wakefield's novel, *The Vicar of Wakefield* (1761): 'They would talk of nothing but high life, and high-lived company; with other fashionable topics, such as pictures, taste, Shakespeare and the musical glasses.' [Chapter 9] Thus, Muir is implying that Carmichael's conversation was 'fashionable' but empty and vapid.

particularly entertained by the history of Mr. Coutts of Horseshoe Farm and the similar history of the Macdonalds of Lady Grey. After dinner we sat in the dark on the coach stoep and smoked and chatted, Inspector Bennie mounted on the rail in front of the rest of us and keeping the talk on delightfully cheery lines. One thing of importance was settled, namely, that on account of Sister Clare's new conversion and Mother Florence's illness and imminent departure, Inspector Bennie's urgent request for a visit to Grahamstown should be agreed to and that a stoppage at Alice for Lovedale could not be made. At last our visitors were escorted as far as Miss Cogan's gate, and we parted with every hope for a good day to travel by on the morrow. Looked in at the shorthand writers at work in the station waiting room, and was delighted to find them report that another ten minutes would conclude the typewriting, and I went to bed with a free mind, and read a crabbed mathematical paper of Spottiswoode's.[47]

7/2/10 Monday

(Komgha; Amabele; Blaney Junction; King William's Town)

Up early and was ready by 8.30 for callers, after doing a considerable deal of writing and other work. On looking back over the meeting and surveying its members, I felt myself fortunate in getting to know Ross and Callaway, men most unlike each other, but both of them good and staunch and true. Of our own people, Miss Cogan came first, then Inspectors Bennie, McLaren and Hobden, the first of these three inspectors going with us to Grahamstown; then came Inspector Davey of the Posts and Telegraphs, then the proprietor of the Bungalow, then the station master Kirk. Inspector McLaren reported that he was still poorly, and might have to put himself in medical hands; I induced him to come on to Ndabakazi and we cheered him by the way. Mr. Cuthbert, who had been professing to follow the 'no-breakfast' rule, we also cheered, but in a different way, having found him at the office table about ten taking a hearty meal. He had been tempted by red herrings, and had fallen. The train had five trucks of Kafirs, 194 men, on their way to the mines, and consequently it moved slowly and was noisy. The heat too was great and the Kafir women at Toleni Bridge drove a roaring trade in supplying a sort of gruel approximating to Kafir beer. At Kei Bridge, where dinner was served, we were simply roasted, the temperature inside the coach being 105°. Here we received a prodigious pile of letters from the Office, and these occupied us to Komgha and further. At Amabele we had to wait for a couple of hours, and I visited the school, the building of which had once stood at Kabusie. Here also, in a passing train, I met the Rev. van Lingen of Cathcart and formerly of Simonstown. A thunderstorm at last came and heavy rain fell, so that by the time we reached Blaney Junction in the dark, the temperature had changed immensely for the better. At Kingwilliamstown, Inspector Bond awaited us on the platform, and after making little arrangements with him for the morrow, we turned in and tried to slake the thirst, which the day's heat had developed.

8/2/10 Tuesday

(King William's Town; Middledrift; Bedford; Cookhouse)

Awoke to find the coach in the old dead-end close to the road. Inspector Bond came to take Mr. Bennie to breakfast with him, and I seized the period of loneness to do some writing. The morning was very dull and drizzly. While sitting on the coach stoep, certain that no one knew of our presence in town, Mr. Varder the vice-chairman of the School

---

47 'crabbed': difficult to decipher.

Board presented himself. And there had to follow a lengthened chat, pleasant enough, on school affairs; he had seen Mr. Cuthbert returning from market. When Mr. Bond came back with Mr. Bennie, a number of points connected with his circuit fell to be dealt with, almost all of them arising out of Sutton's recent visit to Capetown. This work had just been finished when Inspector Christie Smith arrived, and coolly proposed to accompany us to Middledrift to discuss his book, his furlough, etc. Fortunately, Mr. MacKay of the Bank called, and though I could not get a comfortable chat with him, Mr. Smith's affairs received in consequence a little curter treatment. Soon goodbye had to be said, and we left in a wetting rain. At Middledrift, Dr. Roberts joined us as he had intimated, and all the way to Alice he filled me with wonder at his weak flattering talk, a clear indication that he is one thing today and another thing tomorrow. What interested me most was his description of the visit of the Locations Commission, consisting of Stanford, Molteno and Lansdowne, whose whole subject of examination was education! Apparently, he had allowed himself to be guided to speak as his questioners wished, and now he was having his reactionary fit of remorse. The Rev. Lennox, he said, had also been examined, the two having been left in charge by Henderson, who had other fish to fry at Butterworth. Another interesting tale was the double love story of Dr. Kelbe, former chairman of the Alice School Board – a story which fully explained the recent sale of his practice and his hint to me, when he called in Capetown, that he meditated settling in Uganda. What a good fellow he is – and how undeserved his troubles are! Notwithstanding these tit-bits of information, we said goodbye to Roberts without regret. Inspector Bennie, I found after leaving, had also been gathering fresh food for thought, the old housekeeper at Lovedale, Mrs. Geddes, having come to meet him and report that the Lovedale troubles had spread to her department, and that she would be forced to leave the place she had served so well; Mr. Bennie was warmly indignant. The day continued wet and depressing, and by the evening, the temperature was 35 degrees lower than it had been the previous day. At Bedford, Mr. Martin of the School Board and Mr. Ferguson called, and while the train waited in a drenching shower, good business connected with the Poor School was transacted. Had considerable amusement afterwards with Inspector Bennie typing the agreement on a Blickensderfer, Young, the Office clerk, being really worn out with having all my memoranda and letters added to his usual work.[48] Reached Cookhouse late and didn't get to bed till one o'clock, the excitement of the place being Miss Twycross's attempted suicide, consequent on the breaking-off of her most recent engagement at East London. One of her least alarming attempts was made with a combined draught of chlorodyne, tatcho and red ink; doubtless the result would have been more effectual if she had been more cleanly in her instincts, and left some of the ingredients out.[49] She had just been sent off to Grahamstown in charge of an able-bodied nurse. What a commentary the whole affair is on her old accusations against Mr. Cuthbert! Before we turned in, we indulged in a comparison of the case with that of Professor Exham, who recently in similar circumstances selected with care a particular artery and would have bled to death but for the arrival of the ship's doctor. His betrothed had kept him and a rival dangling for a considerable time, until one of them discovered in Capetown that she had been married for five years! This, bad as it is, was no excuse, in our opinion, for poor Exham interfering in any way with the welfare of his own arteries.

48   Blickensderfer: the first truly portable, full-keyboard typewriter; sold at a competitive price compared with the larger typewriters such as the Remington, it became a best seller.

49   Chlorodyne was a patent medicine, containing laudanum, tincture of cannabis and chloroform. Tatcho was a popular proprietary hair restorer. The combination of these two ingredients with the red ink would have produced a lethal brew indeed!

Fig. F: Grahamstown Training College. Photograph of undated postcard (original in colour). Collection: Sigi Howes.

9/2/10 Wednesday
(**Alicedale; Grahamstown**)

Awoke to find the coach well on the way to Alicedale, which we reached at breakfast time, the day being still overclouded and damp and dull. Dr. Smith called and I agreed to take forenoon tea with Mrs. Smith at eleven. Was sorry to find her a little washed out and spirit-less, not at all the cheery little chattering woman of five years ago. Her little daughter Sheila, however, was very engaging, and yarned to me after the fashion of Lady Peggy's brother, but without enough of warm blood to show any of the audacious mischief of Lady Peggy herself. After Dr. Smith and Bennie and Cuthbert had gone, I was treated to a streamlet of innocent gossip, mainly about her old colleagues in the Department and not unmixed with just a little longing for the uncaged days. At one o'clock, Mr. Cruden the schoolmaster called and later the station master, Wayt, and we left five minutes afterwards accompa-nied with milk and fruit and vegetables from three kindly families. A good lunch was then made, and this, aided by the damping mist of Highlands, induced an unrefreshing afternoon nap. At Grahamstown met Mr. Neilson, and talked over his school's affairs for a little. Drove then to the Training College to say goodbye to Mother Florence, who sails on the 14th. Had a long and rather serious talk with the Mother and her substitute, Sister Elizabeth, in reference to the newly-developed '*Schwärmerei*' of Sister Clare.[50] Finding that Sister Elizabeth grasped the situation and would in time take action quietly but firmly, I thought it best not to see the offender, and therefore not to see her new lieutenant, Miss Todd; and I consequently came straight back to the coach, where I dictated memoranda to

50   '*Schwärmerei*' (German): fanaticism.

Young while Mr. Cuthbert and Inspector Bennie paid their own private visits. When the latter returned, and we had started dinner without Mr. Cuthbert, believing that he was staying to dine with Mr. Neilson, I explained to Mr. Bennie what I had said to the Sisters and he undertook to follow it up. Mr. Cuthbert, however, soon after arrived, bringing Miss Todd with him, as well as Mr. Neilson, and during dessert there was a lively conversation about sisterhoods and the taking of the veil, all for Miss Todd's benefit. She quite entered into the fun, but she was clearly not her old self, and it looked as if the glamour of the Sisters would soon wear off. Our three visitors accompanied us to West Hill Station, where cordial goodbyes were said. On comparing notes as we smoked on the coach stoep, I found that Mr. Cuthbert had also been at St. Peter's to see Sister Clare and Miss Todd, and that in the course of a rollicking hour's conversation, they had drawn from him enough to enable them to guess my attitude to Sister Clare's Fenianism.[51] I was greatly chagrined at this, and, after thinking over and discussing the whole thing, I prepared a wire for Inspector Bennie, asking him to see that the Mother Florence should take no action, and Mr. Cuthbert wrote to my dictation a long letter to Inspector Bennie making a clean breast of the whole affair and explaining the telegram. To make sure that the letter would be delivered before breakfast, it was arranged to send it back to the station master by the train returning to Grahamstown during the night. We had both been tired out before our visitors had left and had hoped to go to bed soon: the unfortunate mischance forced on me three additional hours of worry, which I should gladly have done without.

10/2/10 *Thursday*
(Port Elizabeth; Uitenhage; Kleinpoort; Klipplaat)

Awoke to find ourselves in the old siding at Port Elizabeth, with the sea breaking quietly and friendlily against the railway wall. But what a drizzly, dull, depressing morning! About breakfast time Inspector Milne turned up, smiling but worn looking. Talked Conference matters and general education policies with him, but we were unexpectedly interrupted by the arrival of Mr. Mackintosh M.L.A. who began business by chuckling at his success in running me to earth. His errand was really Mrs. Mackintosh's, that ambitious matron having clearly packed the good little man off with a metaphorical threat that, if he came back unsuccessful, there was a broomstick or the divorce court awaiting him. Fortunately I was able to send him away happy, after discussing O.R.C. education, and after learning from him that he and the Rev. Marchand had declined Mr. Merriman's request to sit on the new Educatie Commissie, for which of course he, like a leal man and true, had little respect.[52] Then Mr. Milne and I had a begging call from a quondam friend of Mr. Cuthbert's, a subscription list being presented along with a heart-breaking account of his twenty years' struggle as a farm-school teacher and an inmate of hospitals. As I knew the old reprobate from the office books, and he did not know me, the situation was not free from humour. Work as a teacher, he said, was not now to be got by men like him, Dr. Muir insisting on T.3 certificates and characters and what not. In my voice, however, he recognized, he said, the sympathy of an old teacher, one whom fortune had favoured, but who nevertheless would not forget as Dr. Muir had done, the pit out of which he had been dug. The net result of all of this was that I parted with half a sovereign, ostensibly because of the said sympathy, but really as an inadequate solatium to a good man for having ruined

---

51 'Fenianism': literally, the principles of the organisation that wished to overthrow British rule and establish an independent Irish republic. However, Muir is simply seeking to describe Sister Clare's radicalism.

52 O.R.C.: Orange River Colony (now the Free State); 'leal' (Scots): loyal/faithful.

him. And so the old sweep departed, and Mr. Milne could at last laugh unrestrained. Our next visitor was the redoubtable Mr. More, the general manager of the narrow-gauge railway to Avontuur. Of course, he came as a burning friend of education, the place where he now wanted a school being near Onzer and bearing the enduring name of Joubertina. Equally, of course, the school must be industrial, and so by the imports and exports swell the traffic returns of the great undertaking over which Mr. More presides. I let him talk for half-an-hour until he began to repeat himself, and came away from him the possessor of a fine blue-print map of the railway and district. At 2.10 we left with the Oudtshoorn train, which halted for ten minutes at Uitenhage and gave me the opportunity of a little talk with Mr. Hurndall M.L.A., Mr. McJannett of the Industrial School, and the babbling Mr. Kleinschmidt of the School Board Office.

At our first stop thereafter, we were joined by Mr. De Wet A.R.M. of Uitenhage on his way to hold a periodical course at Kleinpoort. Fortunately I had just got from his friend Mr. Milne the latest part of Harmsworth's 'World's Great Books', and I left the two friends pretty much to themselves.[53] The magazine contained extracts from Wendell Holmes's writings and I read again the 'Schoolmistress's Love Story' with all the old admiration and with even more than the old pleasure; and this led to a resolve that the next time I had somebody's birthday to mark, 'The Autocrat of the Breakfast Table' should be my purchase.[54] At Glenconnor, the neat school building with its flourishing pepper trees was a satisfactory sight; there also I had the gratification of receiving a cheery telegram from Inspector Bennie in reply to our messages of Wednesday night. After a long slow run through the country of red soil and succulent scrub, we reached Kleinpoort after night had fallen, and enjoyed the rare pleasure of a visit from Mr. Grewar. How warmly the fine erect old man shook me by both hands, looking me straight in the face and saying, "Little difference! Little difference! Just thinner and younger." Unfortunately, there was not time to chat, and with a jocular salutation to Cuthbert in the two languages of his boyhood at Uitenhage, "Hoe gaat het? Hoo's a' wi' ye?" he went out into the dark – a man with a clean record and of deserved prosperity – all his children except one daughter being now married and all of them doing well. Klipplaat we were to reach at a late hour, and though we were to find there the General Manager, Mr. Clarke, and other railway officials, I thought better of it and went to bed.

11/2/10 Friday
(*Oudtshoorn*)

Awoke early, notwithstanding the depressing overcast sky, and for a considerable time there was no one stirring but Atkinson and myself. Willowmore was reached before a cup of tea became available, and there the train made a long tiresome halt, surfeiting us with the unprogressive look of the place. Mr. Cuthbert didn't get up until we were entering Tooverwater Poort, a sight which Young greatly enjoyed. The Oudtshoorn valley we saw at its absolute very best, the heavy white clouds being just sufficiently high to show the hill-tops of Enon conglomerate, and to rest on the peaks of the more distant Zwartebergen.[55] After Vlakteplaats, we had lunch or breakfast according as the partaker might name it, and then the clouds lowered and closed in on us, and a drenching rain followed that lasted all the way into Oudtshoorn. Read Rogers's chapter on the geology of the valley, but found

53 *World's Great Books* (1910) by Alfred Harmsworth: a fortnightly literary self-educator.
54 My Last Walk with the Schoolmistress, from *The Autocrat of the Breakfast Table* (1858), by Oliver Wendell Holmes: socio-comical essays.
55 'Enon Conglomerate': the red conglomerate rock formation of the hills near Oudtshoorn.

it too heavy after the busy morning I had had of writing.[56] Had another long halt at the place now called Le Roux where the coach had stabled in the days of 'construction'; where on a Saturday night, Currie the engineer of the line, and an old pupil, had come to a jovial supper with us and told us of his life in China in the time of the Boxer Rebellion;[57] and where on the Sunday Cuthbert and I climbed the red pudding-stone hills and discovered a wonderful echo, which if told to "Come and have a drink," replied "I don't mind if I do". Meanwhile the rain poured and the sluits ran yellowish-red water, and every live thing outside, including the ostriches among the lucerne, looked like 'drookit craws'.[58] Reached Oudtshoorn about four o'clock, and found Inspector Mitchell, Mr. Wallis and Dr. Truter of the Municipal School Board and Mr. Bosman the acting secretary of the Divisional Board, awaiting us. After a little general talk, meetings for the evening and the morrow were arranged for, and when our visitors had gone, we fell upon the piles of correspondence that had accumulated for us at the station. To look at them was depressing. Inspector Mitchell stayed to dinner, and the educational situation in South Africa was again talked over. At eight o'clock, Dr. Truter called with his motor car and conveyed us to the Town Hall, where a long agenda paper was gone through before a full meeting of the Municipal Board. Although a little heat was generated by Mr. Wallis, the result was satisfactory and amicable. On the way back and afterwards, the weather was the only real talk, rain having again come on in torrents, and I was reminded on all hands that it had been the same on the occasion of my last visit. A very slight skim of the English mail papers in bed was sufficient to put me to sleep.

12/2/10 Saturday

(Oudtshoorn)

During the night was often wakened by heavy rains; morning gloomy and outlook far from cheering. After breakfast, Inspector Mitchell arrived with a face that added to our fears. The post-cart from George, he said, had not arrived, and this, almost for certain, meant that the rivers were impassable. Then at ten o'clock Dr. Russell turned up in a powerful Siddeley motor car, his body being about as broad as long, the hair of his face clipped instead of shaven, and his general air that of Tartarin of Tarascon in the boldest of moods.[59] After friendly greetings and jocular references to our last foregathering, his breeziness subsided, and we formed ourselves into a serious committee of four on the weather. It was at last resolved to see for ourselves what the first rivers on both routes were like, and we were soon scudding like a whirlwind in the car towards the Oliphant's River Bridge. For that river one look sufficed; it was running 'from bank to brae'. After crossing we took the turning to the right, and made for the Klip River, meeting ominously enough on the way, two feather carts that had set out for Mossel Bay an hour before. At the drift we found the river swirling heavily and at least eight feet deep; so we looked and turned. Then coming back to the bridge, we took the road to George which skirts the cliffs of red conglomerate, and tooting loudly at the abrupt corners, at last came in sight of the Kamanassie River, rolling as heavily as the others. Thus, our last hope was gone, and

56   Arthur William Rogers (1872–1946), a geologist who charted the remote regions of the Cape.

57   'Boxer Rebellion': this was an officially supported peasant uprising in China in 1900, in which the rebels attempted to drive all foreigners from the country. An international force subdued this rebellion.

58   'drookit craws' (Scots): soaking wet crows.

59   'Tartarin of Tarascon': a character in an eponymous novel by Alphonse Daudet; a prodigious adventurer, despite being both plump and middle-aged.

returning to the station, we wired to Mossel Bay the state of the drifts and asked to know their wishes about the function fixed for Monday. Capetown was also told that we were held up. Still we could not refrain from studying the weather, and hoping against hope. After lunch, a cheery telegram came from 'the three homes', and I learned that Marion had taken Rita's place at Mowbray Hall.[60] At 3.30 I had to drive to town to attend a meeting of the Divisional School Board – a trivial affair which, however, gave me the opportunity of meeting the vice-chairman Mr. Gavin and Mr. Matare; country members were absent because of the swollen rivers. A call was then made on Dr. Russell, with whom we had a potent substitute for afternoon tea, and a long talk on affairs in general. His natty house crowded with 'a fouth o' auld nick-nackets' was as interesting as ever – books, curios, and engineering models in every corner, and yet with no appearance of litter.[61] Still more attractive was his motor-repairing house, where his real ability is centred. There I could gladly have spent hours. Two Siddeleys were standing side-by-side in their beauty, and his original Panhard was spread out on the floor in pieces. Each of the two former, I noticed, bore a small silver plate with a girl-name engraved on it, possibly the only symbol left of an old romance. The one I had admired the day before, and the one I liked best, was 'Alice'; and it was cheering to hear that when the drifts would allow, she would accompany us to Mossel Bay. In this matter of the long journey over the mountains, his goodness has been quite touching. Although having strained relations with the School Board, he would insist upon driving us, declaring that the three days would not be a loss but a gain, as he had need of a change from the deadly dullness of Oudtshoorn. He recalled amusing incidents of our last trip with great gusto, and especially a jovial and superabundant lunch we had had in a river bed. From these reminiscences, at 6.30 we were all startled by the sound of a horn, and the cry at once arose that the post-cart had struggled through. In driving homeward, however, the signs of a change of weather were few and having got the 'Spectator' and 'Punch' from Dr. Russell, I retired soon to my cabin with a resolve to reconcile myself to the inevitable.

13/2/10 Sunday
(Oudtshoorn)

Woke very early having been disturbed by four trucks of ostriches that were to leave by the morning train. The sky had wonderfully changed in the night, and was especially bright in the west, the direction whence all the rain had come. While I read and wrote in bed the improvement continued, and by the time I had dressed, the whole vault was blue. Stealing quietly out of the coach I had a short walk back [along] the railway line, and never felt so exhilarated, the surrounding mountains being so beautiful and the morning air was so fresh. Even Young was ebullient at breakfast, and the station master Crozier made a belated call to say a few polite words. At eleven Inspector Mitchell drove up, and he also beamed. He called to hand me a pile of books, and to suggest a drive. This last I had to decline, but Mr. Cuthbert went, promising to say kind things for me to Mrs. Mitchell and to report on the Grobbelaars River on the other side of which Mr. Mitchell's home in Oudtshoorn lies. When they came back to lunch, all had been arranged for the morrow's journey. At four

---

60 'the three homes': possibly the three places from which news from home emanated: Mowbray Hall (the family home) and the 'Office' (the head office of the Education Department) were two of these places. However, Muir also received books from 'the Rectory', and called there to 'say goodbye' before he left home (*Diary 1* 23/8/09 Monday and *Diary 3* 21/1/11 Saturday). Possibly the Rector of a nearby church was a close friend.

61 'a fouth o' auld nick-nackets' (Scots): a quotation from Robert Burns's poem, 'On the Late Captain Grose's Peregrination', and meaning 'a hoard of old nick-nacks'.

o'clock Dr. Russell called in his motor to take me for a drive. The road chosen was that to the Cango Caves, and nothing could have been more enjoyable. The previous day's rain had put a growing look on everything, and the river between the lofty hills was running like a river. Schoemann's Hoek resembled a garden as far as the untidiness of the people would allow. The fields of tobacco and flowering lucerne were luscious, and the crowded hundreds of ostriches gave a peaceful air of wealth and comfort. I know no corner of South Africa so rich-looking and so beautiful, save possibly in the neighbourhood of Constantia. But how much more beautiful it might be! The school building we passed was ridiculously small for such a thickly populated valley, and architecturally was a disgrace. The journey out of fourteen miles was accomplished in a little over an hour, a speed which gave us a nice breeze in our faces. We landed at Dr. Russell's on the way back, and took 'tea' as yesterday, examining with interest rare copies of Andrew Smith's Zoology, Culpeper's Herbal, etc. which we unearthed from amongst much literary rubbish.[62] On returning to the coach, we found that Mr. Wallis and Mr. Thomas had called. After supper the packing for the morrow began, the cart given us by the Oudtshoorn people for our luggage being arranged to come at six a.m. This done, we looked in on the station master whom I had first met at Colesberg years ago, and who is a walking chronicle of the doings of General French during the war. His wife's sister, Mrs. Reed, who is a deserted daughter of old MacFarlane of Colesberg and teacher at the station school, gave us some good music, and a railway official hailing from Lincoln, where he had been a choir boy, supplied music-hall songs with wasted ability when he could sing 'The Holy City' like a full-grown cherub.[63] Didn't get to bed till after one.

14/2/10 Monday
(**Oudtshoorn**; Mossel Bay)

Up at six when the cart arrived; not a breath of wind stirring and a hot day in view; even the white strip of clouds that yesterday in places rested above the mountains had all gone. Inspector Mitchell came at ten and Dr. Russell at eleven to report the prospects of the drifts. At 12.30 we had lunch, and the big motor car arrived promptly at one. A minute or two afterwards we were flying over the Oliphant's River Bridge, Dr. Russell and myself in front, Mitchell and Cuthbert in the body, lolling back in luxurious ease, and all of us half in hope and half in doubt as to the success of our journey. The Klip River we found considerably fallen, and we ventured in with all the motor's power. Spluttering and splashing and jolting, we struggled through, and out on the opposite bank to have our glee at once damped by finding ourselves stuck in the sloping sand and mud. The omen was disappointing, but Frickie, the assistant chauffeur, soon unstrapped his spade to make a rut in front of the driving wheels, and the rest of us packed the rut with worn pebbles; then with a heave-ho at the back and a tremendous whirr of the engine, our first difficulty over, and we sped on again. From this point the route was all new, and I was greatly interested in the country and views obtained. On reaching Candelaar's River, Dr. Russell looked gloomy, the water being both broad and deep; and after we had all had our examination from the bank and Frickie had waded in, the decision was adverse. Fortunately, a large cart with six mules turned up and almost simultaneously, Inspector Mitchell's cart. In the latter, three of us were taken across in relays, and soon there followed the six mules with the car and

---

62 Andrew Smith, *llustrations of the Zoology of South Africa* (1838–1850), 5 volumes; Nicholas Culpepper, *The Complete Herbal* (1653).

63 'The Holy City': a religious Victorian ballad dating from 1892, with music by Michael Maybrick and lyrics by Frederic Weatherly; it was commercially successful around the beginning of the 20th century.

Dr. Russell, whom we greeted with more or less serious cheers as he was hauled past us up the bank. Our next adventure was of a different character. On descending a slope at great speed, one or two sharp little explosions were heard underneath, and when a halt was made, it was found that two conducting wires had fused. In a jiffy, Frickie had the contents of the tool-wallet spread out, and Dr. Russell was at the perspiring work of making repairs while the others of us looked on and drank beer. The mishap cost us half-an-hour but with the result that the confidence I had already felt in our portly chauffeur *as* a chauffeur was extended to him as an engineer. With this feeling, therefore, and a superadded joviality, we drove onward prepared to meet our next adventure halfway. And sure enough, at Morass River we found it. Notwithstanding the name, the drift does not bear a bad character, the banks for one thing being almost level with the water, and after a little investigation, it was decided to go boldly in with all on board. Good luck attended us until within fifteen feet of the further side, when we came on a hidden bank of sand and with one expiring splutter, the car stopped dead. The first requisite, of course, was to get the passengers ashore, and this was accomplished through a pick-a-back arrangement with Frickie, who enjoyed his work until the R.E.O's turn came, and then it was we who enjoyed it.[64] A good length of rope was next got out, and with the whirring and splashing car at one end of it and four more or less able-bodied haulers at the other, we once more got out of trouble. As the credit was entirely our own, the cheers this time were more hearty. Dr. Russell deplored the fact that through the want of a camera he could not suitably commemorate our prowess, but we modestly reminded him that the Department had already a well-earned reputation for being able to 'pull through'. At the foot of the last and steepest ascent, the heat of the stagnant air was intense, and a halt was called to clear out the sizzling water of the radiator, and to take in a new supply from a trickling mountain stream. The result was altogether satisfactory and we mounted the long slope with delightful ease. Not long after, we reached the half-way house at the top of the pass, and a most extensive view of the hills on hills was our reward. Among these for some considerable time we glided in and out, but always descending. The distant sea was occasionally visible and added to the beauty of the views; and our concluding judgement was that the Robinson Pass had been unduly depreciated. The descent into the populous Brandwacht Valley was especially pleasing, the so-called village being really, like Schoemann's Hoek, a big collection of small farms. Here it was, too, that our greatest event came off – the crossing of the Brandwacht River. Even a distant glance showed that the passage was going to be of interest, for the idle populace had assembled on both banks. On nearing, we were relieved to see on the further side, the cart which had left Oudtshoorn Station at six in the morning with our baggage, and further to find that a cart with four mules, a wagon with fourteen donkeys, and another wagon with six-span of oxen were preparing to cross. The mule-cart was the first to venture; then our baggage cart came over and took me across; then Mr. Cuthbert was transported in the ox-wagon; and finally the motor car, being hitched to the rear of the heavy donkey wagon, was with the help of much yelling and whip-cracking, landed safely beside us. How pluckily the little donkeys strained as they came up the bank! When Mr. Mitchell passed us sitting on the wagon-load of wood with the big silvered lamps of the motor-car in his charge, we were greatly tempted, but the presence of the people, white and coloured, put us on our guard, and therefore like 'the scattered ranks of Tusculum' we forbore to raise a cheer.[65] On the passage of Dr. Russell, the temptation was stronger for he had struck an attitude, and

64 'R.E.O.': a jocular reference to Cuthbert, whose formal role was that of Railway Education Officer, for which this term is the acronym.

65 This is a misquotation from Macaulay's poem 'Horatius':
'And even the ranks of Tuscany
Could scarce forbear to cheer.'

appeared in all the dignity of a veritable 'God in the Car'.[66] After leaving the river we had an amusing race with four ostriches in the road: they ran well but their fear and their stupidity were against them. The next river was the Harenbosch and, unfortunately, when we reached it there were no wagons at the drift. Frickie's examination was satisfactory, save as to one point, where he feared a quicksand, and after an indaba we resolved not to attempt to cross unaided. Some men who were mending a fence on the opposite side were consequently hailed to, but with the noisy rushing river between us and them, negotiation proved difficult. Frickie was accordingly dispatched as an ambassador, and came back with a shameless request for so much money for helping the car over and so much each for the carrying of the passengers. On the first point we preferred to say nothing, and putting the proposal to Dr. Russell, we found that he unwillingly felt constrained to accept; but on the second point we asserted our birthright as freemen. Our blood was up. And our shoes and stockings were soon off. As soon therefore as the clodhoppers had waded across, we took to the water like a string of cranes, and under Frickie's guidance made the passage with credit and satisfaction to ourselves and with more than satisfaction to Dr. Russell. He, good man, soon followed with four real 'shovers' behind the car, and while we got ready again for carriage travelling, we exchanged views as to the appearance each presented to the others while in the waters of the drift. In good spirits we motored on once more, being assured by Mr. Mitchell that we had seen the worst. And so indeed it proved, for though we still had 'one more river to cross', we easily went through it with all on board.[67] As we were nearing Mossel Bay, the evening train met us puffing cheekily on its way to George. The last two or three miles of motoring were delightful, the bay being beautiful and the sea air refreshing. The Standard Hotel was reached at seven o'clock exactly, so that the journey of 68 miles had only occupied us six hours, notwithstanding all our mishaps. Dinner was already on, but we were able to join before the others left the table; and immediately after our meal, Dr. Russell led us down in the dark to the front of the jetty, where we smoked a cigarette or two in the cool of the evening breeze. Here Mr. Vintcent, the chairman of the Municipal School Board, Mr. Moodie, the chairman of the Divisional Board, and Mr. McGaffin, the headmaster of the Boy's School, sought us out, and there and on the way back to the hotel the arrangements for the morrow were made known to us. On the hotel stoep, just before retiring for the night, I was delighted to find my special friend Mrs. Coote, late Miss Hunter, whose welcome was almost an embrace. How she came to be there, when her home is on the other side of Oudtshoorn, she proceeded very frankly to explain, and I was glad to be able to say that in passing Le Roux Station four days previously, I had sent all manner of kindly greetings to her. I brought forward Cuthbert who, with an eye to the commissariat, reminded her of her present of ducks three years ago, and we had a merry meeting. She is more matronly that when I last saw her, but she is bright and clever and downright as of old; and it was pleasant to hear from Inspector Mitchell that her husband was continuing to prosper, being now the possessor of the very farm which seven years ago I visited with Engineer Currie to see how ingeniously a trickle of water had been traced back until a plentiful spring had been reached. There are no children to brighten their household, and Mr. Coote shuts himself up in his farm with a bucolic devotion; but Mr. Mitchell says the pair are good and true to each other, and their home is a pleasant one for a wandering Inspector to come across. Before eleven, Dr. Russell and I turned in for the night, and I lay

66 *God in the Car*: the title of a novel by Anthony Hope, author of the rather better known *The Prisoner of Zenda*; Muir might have been interested by *God in the Car* (published 1894), as it is said that the leading character is based on the empire builder Cecil Rhodes (who appointed him to his office).

67 'one more river to cross': a Negro spiritual.

Fig. G: Opening of Mossel Bay Boys' Public School by Dr. Muir, 15 February 1910.
Collection: Sigi Howes.

down with both windows half-open to catch the revivifying air of the bay. I had only intended to read a page or two of a little book called 'The Golden Age', lent to me by Inspector Mitchell, but the author's dainty style soon caught me, and I had to read on to a finish. Mr. Cuthbert's heavy step was 'airting' to his room when I blew out my candle, and I found myself drowsily resolving in the dark to pass the book on to Mam and Cam and Nellie and any friend else who may be fond of children.[68]

15/2/10 Tuesday

(Mossel Bay; opening of Mossel Bay Boys' High School; George)

Rose at seven to find the bay half obscured by a bank of sea mist. Spent a little time jotting down on an envelope a few hints of matters, to speak at the day's ceremony. At breakfast got a picture postcard from Mrs. Coote, the view on it being a photograph of the great Mossel Bay attraction, which Hely-Hutchinson, with native blarney and unexampled knowledge, described as the second-best bathing-place in the whole world. At eleven o'clock the school processions started from the old building, and at 11.15 Mr. Vintcent called to drive me to the new [building]. Dr. Russell, Cuthbert and Mitchell preceded us in much greater state. On arriving there, we found a large concourse of people, more than had been hoped for considering the state of the drifts. After introductions on the stoep, and the formal opening of the door, the whole gathering passed through to the back quadrangle and assembled for the speech-making. Meanwhile I had examined all the rooms, and found everything satisfactory, not to say beautiful. Mr. Vintcent's remarks were quite nice and not unfluently made, and Mr. Moodie's, though halting, were still more gratifying. My own talk lasted half an hour, and I was fortunate in being able to say one or two things that may sting the people who talk about economy and 'Dr. Muir's expensive palaces'. The Rev. Murray and Mr. McGaffin followed in eulogistic style, and the pleasant gathering broke up. A meeting

---

68   'airting' (Scots): direct one's way.

with the School Board followed and Mr. Vintcent then drove me back to the hotel. At 1.15 there was a very nice lunch served, to which between thirty and forty sat down, and I had again to talk education when the toast of my health was drunk. The last of the three toasts, that of 'The Chairman', was set down for the Rev. Murray; but he kindly gave me permission to take his place, and I thus had the desired opportunity of referring in a sentence to the chairman's father, "the most esteemed friend I had made in Cape Colony". Among those who were introduced after lunch, the most interesting was a hale and vigorous white-haired man called Donald Robertson, 'the grower of the best wool in the district', and the brother of a former well-known member of Parliament. Though born in Capetown, he still viewed himself as Scotch, but carefully separated his family from the descendants of the Rev. Dr. Robertson of the D.R.C, and from the Robertsons of Mowbray, equally Scotch these families might be. At 3.15 Dr. Russell was ready with his 'Alice' and we drove up to the Recreation Ground to put in an appearance at the school sports.

For such a town the gathering seemed wonderfully large, and we spent quite a pleasant half hour watching the races and talking with newly made friends. Miss Reid of the Girls' School was present, and was quite sweetly envious of the Boys' School. At last goodbyes were said, and Dr. Russell, before starting on the return journey, took me for a drive through the highest part of the town whence one saw the bay and surrounding hills in all their beauty. There was only one remaining streak of the morning's mist to temper the sun glare.

From the hotel we started punctually at four, the baggage-cart having left at 3.30. Our object now being to reach George, we struck off our former road at the turning which makes for Great Brak River. On arriving there, it was surprising to see how 'Searledom', as I once called it, had grown.[69] One of the brothers, the M.L.A. for Queenstown, had not been present at the school function, and I stopped the car and called at his mansion, making, however, the unfortunate mistake of taking a ringleted sister of Dr. Kolbe for Mrs. Searle. After crossing the string of low bridges, we pulled up opposite the shoe factory to prepare the motor for the coming climb. We also partook of sandwiches and a drink, the others amusingly contriving that I should take my glass of beer rather conspicuously, to serve as a protest against the rabid teetotalism of the place. All the same, one is bound to say that the hamlet is a model of cleanliness and comfort. The three brothers, I was told, belong to three different Churches, and the firm thus derives all the material benefits appertaining to such a wide spiritual connection: this, however, is probably scandal. The drive up the wooded heights was simply delightful; and, when afterwards on the level, we went with great speed with our eyes turned to the range of hills which on the morrow we had to cross. At Blanco the scenery became again wooded and soft, although the fine grounds of Montague White's residence seemed a little uncared for. By seven o'clock we had entered George and pulled up at Parson's Hotel, so that exactly three hours had sufficed for thirty miles. Strangely enough, I was shown in to my old room on the ground floor, and had thus recalled to me the incident of the thief's visit. Dinner was a function that compared unfavourably with that at Mossel Bay: the bread and butter, however, were good and with a bottle of wine, they were not unsatisfying. We all agreed that the hotel was not the place it had been, and Cuthbert went further and banned it from basement to roof for charging 3/6 for wine, which he could buy at Stellenbosch for a couple of tickeys.[70] After smoking a cigarette on the neglected stoep, I proposed that Mr. Mitchell and I should visit Mrs. Meyer

69 'Searledom': referred to by Muir as such, because the village of Great Brak River had been founded by the Searle family, who emigrated to South Africa from Surrey, England, in 1845. The shoe factory, Bolton Footwear, is still in operation today.
70 'tickey': this term was used for the silver 3d coin.

at the Girls' School and so run the chances of hearing some music. We accordingly struck out into the deep darkness of the George streets, and apparently by mere good luck found ourselves after a little at Mrs. Meyer's door. Disappointment met us at first, but a visit to the Teachers' Common Room secured us a cheery welcome and the sending out of runners, so that we soon were ensconced in the private drawing room with the stately principal and a bevy of assistant teachers around us. First we had to satisfy natural curiosity in regard to our sudden descent upon the place, and then a mere suggestion about music did the rest.

The main performers were Miss Hamilton, recently of Somerset East Girls' School, and Ida van Niekerk, a niece of Mrs. Meyer's. The former I was at first prejudiced against, believing her to be one of the redoubtable trio who originated the Somerset East scandal, but I fortunately remembered her real story in time. Her little limp nervous form was an extraordinary contrast to that of her fellow musician, who though a girl in her early teens is painfully and aggressively stout. Both had real skill, and one of them had real feeling. At first we had pieces for violin and piano, the performers exchanging instruments with delightful ease. Then having had a hint from Mr. Mitchell, I asked the girl Ida for her songs and named one or two of them that I liked to hear. These she sang to me surprisingly well, the climax being reached when, assisted by a violin obligato, she rendered 'Those Dear Eyes' with a yearning feeling not to be expected in a person of twice her years.[71] This set me thinking and I didn't ask for more. I learned afterwards that she is to be sent to Europe to be trained, Mrs. Meyer being still occupied, like the fine strong woman she is, in mothering all her distant kith and kin who stand in need of help. A little after ten we said goodbye to the pleasing household of women, and returned to the company of rougher diamonds. Still, when sitting again with the said diamonds on the stoep, I could not but recall that the similarly childless Dr. Russell had something of Mrs. Meyers' strain in his nature, having lavished goodness on his deserted sister-in-law, Mrs. Dickson, and her children. Before we retired it was resolved that we should not ask for a hotel breakfast next morning, but should picnic on the veld.

16/2/10 Wednesday
(George; **Oudtshoorn**)

Awoke at five, and dressed by candlelight, the morning being deeply overcast. By six we had all assembled round the motor car at the front door, and a minute afterwards we were coasting down the slope to the little bridge at the entrance to the village. Although there was little sparkle in the company, I think we are all feeling virtuous, and we certainly enjoyed the air of the grey dewy morning. On the way to Blanco, we passed other early travellers, an energetic bicyclist and a ragged sundowner.[72] We also came across the two outspanned wagons, the owners in the one case making a fire for morning coffee, and in the other, crawling out from under the wagon to begin the same duty. At the entrance to the pass, the light had become a little less grey, and the cloudy pall had risen high above the mountain tops: a finer morning for travelling there could not be. The abrupt turns, somewhat obscured by the trees, and the steep gradients required careful driving, but Dr. Russell was fit for any emergency. When halfway up at the waterfall, we drew up in close to the mountain's side, and halted in order to replenish our radiator with water, and there a big wagon had to be steered gingerly past us, the mother and children in its upper

71 There is no trace of a song entitled 'Those Dear Eyes'. It is possibly a reference to the well-known Russian romance song 'Dark Eyes'.

72 'sundowner' (Australian): a tramp; one who seeks food and lodging at sundown when it is too late to work.

story having just begun to stir for the day. At the top, which we reached a little after seven, there was the slightest possible drizzle of rain, but the view nevertheless was grand. North Station, which on our last visit we had stopped at in the rain hoping to find Dr. Truter's car, we now whizzed past at lightning speed; then came the stretch which I had formerly done on foot while our four horses rested at an outspan; and the further we went the more the coming rivers bulked in our minds. At last Doorn River came in view; and at its first drift we were lucky, for a Jew feather-buyer turned up in a cart with a fine pair of grey horses, just as Frickie in the water and I on the bank were seeking for an appropriate route across. The passengers were soon transported behind the two greys, and the car followed with more ado but with equal success. At the second drift, there was neither Jew nor Gentile to help, and all hands were piped to the task.[73] In the first place, Frickie had discovered a dangerous hole close to the side, and, while we were freeing ourselves of shoes and stockings, he was already busy splashing boulders into it. The lower boundary of the drift had originally been a row of heavy stepping stones, but there were now three gaps in it, and Mr. Mitchell and I had consequently no easy task in seeking out by its means a safe route for the car. Fortunately, we found that Frickie's hole was the only one, and time could willingly be spent on attending to its needs. When all was ready, with two of us on the further bank and Mr. Cuthbert and Frickie to give the car a start, there came the usual whirr and splutter, and Dr. Russell was battling in the drift. To our delight all went well, and as soon as he came to a stop beside us, we made for the breakfast basket. Meanwhile, Frickie and the R.E.O. had taken to the stepping stones and, with outstretched arms, were balancing themselves as best they could on the submerged boulders. The sight made the rest of us merry as grigs. R.E.O. had forgotten the boyhood's dodge of tying the two shoelaces together and suspending the shoes like panniers round the neck: he was thus unnecessarily hampered.[74] Further he had on a long black limp overcoat, and therefore had to hold up his skirts. We derisively shouted to him to hurry up for breakfast, but he gingerly made sure of every step, and made the passage without mishap. As for Frickie, he was as often off the stones as on them and didn't seem to mind. The breakfast of sandwiches and beer was enjoyed to the full, and then we set off on our last lap. No other drift troubled us, and we were soon at the red cliffs skirting the Kamanassie with Oudtshoorn in full view. The railway station was reached at 10.30, the journey of forty miles having been accomplished in four and a half hours. Piles of letters and papers were awaiting us, and I had to set to at once and spend a worrying forenoon on them. Atkinson had not expected us so soon and was in the middle of a spring cleaning, which he ought to have done the day before, and I didn't bless him. After lunch I scanned my English papers, and then tackled some more work, stopping it for a little to talk to Mrs. Mitchell and her two little girls. A hired cart came at five and I made duty calls on Dr. Truter, Mr. Wallis, Mr. Thomas and Dr. Russell. The last named came to dinner with us and when he praised the menu, I remarked that I had as much confidence in Mr. Cuthbert's catering as in his (Dr. Russell's) motor-driving and forthwith we drank his health with all the honours. The evening otherwise was sedate, the talk being mainly on improved motor machinery and automatic railway couplings. We said goodbye and retired early.

73 'piped to the task': the bosun's call on a naval ship, commanding all hands on deck.

74 'merry as grigs' (Middle English): merry as a cricket or grasshopper; 'panniers': a borrowing of the Old French 'panier' meaning a bread basket; applied to a basket carried in pairs slung over the back of a beast of burden (but in this case borne by a person).

17/2/10 Thursday

(Klipplaat)

Spent a lazy morning among my books and papers, and was hardly ready for breakfast at 8.30. Noticed that the swallows, whom I observed building their nest in a railway truck, had finished their work in our absence, and that the truck had been marshalled for dispatch with ostriches: a domestic tragedy was therefore at hand. At 9.40 we quietly started on our homeward journey, after wiring to Mowbray Hall and the Office that Sunday would probably see us under the shadow of Table Mountain. I at once settled down to a long day of reading and work, scarcely ever looking up at the surrounding country as it sizzled in the blue. At lunch, as at breakfast, we revelled in Mossel Bay soles. After leaving Willowmore, we had dinner, with soles again, and Fullarton Station found us out on the stoep for the evening with the books laid away. At the highest point of the railway (Antonie's Siding, 3,050 feet), there was a nice evening breeze, the pleasure of which was tempered by a band of howling Kafirs in a distant hut. Klipplaat we reached a little after ten, and I had to stumble away through the darkness to visit a grumbling teacher about the ventilation of her school. Found her to be a lone well-nourished widow, Madam Blanc by name, though 'Mrs. White' would have done as well, and her school to be a neat little wooden building bounteously equipped. True, it had a low wooden ceiling, but the space between the ceiling and the roof being thoroughly ventilated by wide louvres, a score of connecting auger holes was all that was necessary for comfort. Having said this, I left the two to discuss other detailed grievances; but discussion it could scarcely be called, for the lady's tongue never lay, a fact which doubtless was sufficient explanation for the loneless, aforesaid. The station was badly lighted, and the connecting trains were late, but we got away at last, and I turned in for the night.

18/2/10 Friday

(Graaff-Reinet; Middelburg; Rosmead; Naauwpoort; De Aar; Deelfontein)

Was wakened at five by an awful racket at Graaff-Reinet Station, and soon thereafter got up. After breakfast I sat out on the coach stoep to enjoy the ascent of the Sneeuwberg. Near Blaauwater Station, where the road and rail are within a quarter of a mile of each other, we were delighted with the beautiful horsemanship of a lady-rider who kept pace with the train. She sat so well that, for the sake of artistic completeness, I felt myself nourishing the hope that she might also be pretty; but, as Cuthbert said she had been one of the seven Miss Colletts, I gave it up. At the highest point of the railway (Loosberg, 5,727 feet) and the highest point of any of the Cape Railways, a good wind was blowing, and it increased as we began the descent, the sail-cloth shelter of the coach stoep being made to crack like a teamster's whip. Middleburg was reached about one o'clock, and a long enough stay was made to fill up the coach with camp dust. Similarly, at Rosmead the wind-and-dust fiend raged, and I at last shut myself in my cabin, reasonable cleanliness being impossible otherwise. Our one wish was to get home with all speed. Such days, however, help on work; and I wrote and copied like a galley slave. At 5.30 we came to Naauwpoort and, sure as eggs is eggs, the coach drew up again alongside the dining saloon with the old gramophone in full blast. Unfortunately, Dr. Baird and Mr. Duncan called, and I could neither converse with him nor listen to the music; one soprano song full of bravura passages was very fetching. The train being late, our stay was short. Just as we started, Inspector Morrison joined the coach, and full of his work as usual, he fastened on me like a leech. I think I dree'd my weird without wincing, but I nonetheless suffered from internal combustion.[75] On the way

---

75 'dree one's weird' (Scots): submit to one's fate.

to De Aar the wind fell, and we had a fine evening with a lovely Karroo sunset. At De Aar, Mr. Cuthbert managed excellently, and I shall consequently reach home on a Saturday evening instead of Sunday. The wires were set amoving at once. A number of people were waiting to meet me, the hour being half past ten and at the end of a tiring day! Still I had to yield. Our own people, Mr. Lamont and Inspector Grant, were of course very welcome and did their business with dispatch. With the school committee squabblers, Mr. Bishop and Dr. Symington, the case was different, and I let them see that I thought so. Miss Botma, one of the best of our T.3 teachers, came out of gratitude for recent practical recognition of her work, and having shaken hands over it we wasted no words. And then the whistle sounded. While I had been thus engaged, Mr. Cuthbert had gathered up the news of the neighbourhood, including the story of Dr. Symington's unauthorized support of Abbey the temperance lecturer, and the committee's action consequent thereon. The discomfiture of his enemy tickled R.E.O. so much that he at once drank the avenger's health in a night-cap. A little after eleven I went to bed, but at Deelfontein there came a tremendous post, and sleep being banished, I read on till all hours. Cuthbert apparently did the same, for now and again he would open my door an inch or two and shove in a tit-bit on the Molteno case.

19/2/10 Saturday

(Laingsburg; Touws River; Hex River; Wellington; Salt River; Rosebank)

Rose unrefreshed, and feeling filthy with dust caused by the efforts of an already fast train trying to make up two hours of leeway. Fortunately, no one was stirring, and I performed my ablutions thoroughly and with leisure. Laingsburg was reached at ten; and, notwithstanding all the push and racket, we had not gained a minute since leaving De Aar. At Touws River things were not much better. The descent of the Hex River slopes was done in broad sunlight and I would have enjoyed it, had I not been headachy and out of sorts. At Wellington we were an hour and a half late, and there Mr. Cuthbert had to leave us, otherwise he would not have reached Stellenbosch until [the] next day. Another half hour was saved from Wellington to Salt River; and as the Wynberg train from town was purposely held back at Salt River, I got on to Rosebank by eight o'clock – glad to be home.

Fig. H: Rosebank Station Cape Town. DRISA PB3180_001. Transnet Heritage Library Photo Collection.

DIARY 3

Diary of S.G.E.'s tour to Prieska and Barkly West

21/1/11 to 2/2/11

21/1/11 Saturday

(*Salt River*)

After calling at the Rectory to say goodbye, reached home to find that it was time to go to the station. Sam accompanied me to Salt River by the 4:28 train, by which also Mr. Millard travelled; and after a little delay, the 'Perishable Goods' rolled in and I joined the old coach No. 362, which I was glad to find had not been dismantled. Found there George (a messenger boy from the office), Young (Mr. Cuthbert's clerk), Ben (the new 'chef') and Cuthbert himself. George, I learned, was to wait at table and make himself generally useful: this addition was meant to be an aid to our comfort. We shall wait and see. When dinner came, we gathered further that Ben was a grey-haired, robust West-Indian hailing from Barbados, and that he spoke English well, although with a curious high-pitched intonation. I retired early to bed as the cold in my head was beginning to be troublesome.

22/1/11 Sunday

(*Matjiesfontein*)

Rose early after a rather tiresome night, having been awakened often. Found the last portion of the Hex River ascent beautiful in the morning light. Spent forenoon reading Ross's book on 'The Prevention of Malaria' and was greatly interested.[76] By the time we reached Matjiesfontein, the morning air and light were perfectly lovely. The place at first seemed very deserted, but in a while a few people were seen moving, and it turned out that they were returning from morning service. Along the silent platform came Mrs. and Miss Logan and a second young lady that I did not at first recognize. Logan himself, I learned, was in Capetown much to his wife's regret.[77] The stranger lady soon absorbed the conversation, reminding me, with a demure smile, that she knew me although I had forgotten her; that when I last met her I had read a poem or two to her, and that if I was disposed to discredit her, she would venture to repeat a verse there and then. I replied that I should be glad if she would carry out her threat, discredit or no discredit; but here Mrs. Logan spoiled the fun, by leaving Cuthbert and bearing down on me with the remark that I had apparently begun with Miss Grant where I had left off. It then flashed on me who Miss Grant was, and then I looked at her anew; she was pretending to throw a sideways glance of reproach at Mrs. Logan but her whole face was smiles. Poor girl, I remembered having first seen her when she was in deep sorrow because of the death of her father who was killed on the railway at Touws River. The Logans had in consequence befriended her, and it was at their house that I afterwards found her one evening when returning from the North or from the Eastern Province. Since then she had been to England to school and had developed into a quietly charming young lady with a lot of latent fun. As the day advanced, the heat increased and a plague of flies broke out, this last being due, according to Cuthbert, to the coach having been housed for some time recently near the railway stables. Did a little mathematical work in the afternoon, notwithstanding the wretched attack of catarrh, and in the evening, which was lovely, rested and smoked on the stoep.

---

76 *The Prevention of Malaria* (1911) by Ronald Ross: the author was a natural mathematician, who in 1897 had proved the hypothesis that malaria was transmitted by mosquitoes.

77 James Douglas Logan (the so-called 'Laird of Matjiesfontein') was superintendent of the stretch of railway at Matjiesfontein. He first opened a refreshment station there for passing trains. Subsequently Logan built the Lord Milner Hotel during the Anglo-Boer War.

23/1/11 Monday

(*De Aar; Britstown; Prieska*)

Woke to find the Karroo air still perfect. Reached De Aar a little after 11 and was welcomed by Inspector Grant who, I was glad to find, wished to travel to Prieska with us. Next Dr. Symington arrived, bringing with him Cronwright-Schreiner, to grumble about Cuthbert and the Railway School.[78] I heard them patiently, making quite clear that I was trying to be patient. They left me with a bad taste in my mouth; their ways are so crooked and their feelings so mean and petty. Next came Mr. Mitchell, the teacher who is leaving De Aar because of poor health, and who had been heartlessly treated by the two worthies just mentioned. Along with him was his young Scotch wife, who must acutely feel her husband's trials but who seemed to have a good deal of quiet grit. They were proceeding to the Peninsula. The train was late in leaving, but nobody seemed concerned. At Britstown Mr. Cilliers of the Provincial Council called to shake hands. Soon thereafter we came to Houw Water, near which are the farms and irrigation works of the Smartt Syndicate – all having a look of promise. Beyond this there was little of interest in the country, and it was a little tiresome to toil slowly through it. At dinner we consequently chatted to Mr. Grant about his circuit, and made him pertinaciously argumentative. After the sun went down, we returned to the stoep to smoke, and continued the banter about the origins of his gout and his loss of faith in whisky. It was pitch dark when we reached our own destination, Prieska, even the station buildings scarcely visible. Out of the mirk, however, emerged two forms, whom Grant introduced as the Rev. Venter and Mayor Laurence, both young and both ready talkers.[79] Ultimately I was relieved of the mayor by Cuthbert who remembered him as a boy at Grahamstown; but the relief was unreal, for Mr. Venter had been thoughtlessly given a long cigar and he had many educational theories to expound. In the end I got to bed about midnight, the temperature being more like that of midday.

24/1/11 Tuesday

(*Prieska*)

Shortly after breakfast the Rev. Venter arrived refreshed. Talk and smoke resumed on campstools in the shade of the coach; then the four of us went to see the two old buildings in which the school was held, and on the way saw anything else worth seeing. We next directed our steps towards the Orange River, of which, big as it was, we had not yet seen a glimpse. The Gibbon's Park was then traversed, a 'park' of the usual riverbank type, but nevertheless a memorial of a worthy man's energy.[80] Among the thorn trees the heat was very trying, even although the wide river was rolling brown at our feet. We rested for a little while on a bench in the shade, and then dragged our way back to town. When opposite Grant's hotel, he seriously asked me if I would go in to glance at certain statistics which he had promised me, and as I agreed to do so, Grant said goodbye to the parson who was understood not to be interested in the figures. The parson then left for home, and we three were delighted to enter on a stoep shaded with ferns and creepers, and still more pleased to enter there from a cool and tidy smoking room, where ice-cold beer appeared as if called up by a magician's wand. We saw no statistics, and we have since been in the

---

78 Samuel Cronwright-Schreiner (1863–1936), husband of the author Olive Schreiner, lived in De Aar at the time of this diary. From 1902–1910 he had been a member of the Cape Legislative Assembly. He and his wife had been supporters of the Boer cause during the Anglo-Boer War.

79 'mirk': old-fashioned spelling of 'murk', gloom.

80 Gibbons: Dr. John Stephen Gibbons, district surgeon of Prieska, 1883–1906.

habit of asking for 'figures' when something less dry was really meant. On returning to the coach for lunch, we found the temperature inside to be 100°: a siesta afterwards in pyjamas was then excusable. By 3 o'clock the thermometer had risen to 104°, and sleep became impossible. I consequently got up and went into the writing room, and, in order to divert my attention from the heat, doggedly sat down to copy out the mathematical article on which I had been spending odd moments since leaving home. By 6 o'clock the task was finished, a properly sized envelope made to hold it, and the address written. I question whether Metcalfe and Co. of Cambridge have had many manuscripts copied under such circumstances.[81] Just as I rose to seek a concluding drink, a rap came to the door, and I proceeded to entertain the caller in my pyjamas. He proved to be Veale, the C.C. and R.M. late of Humansdorp, a grave discontented man but most polite and kindly. We talked until almost sunset. Cuthbert returned at 7.15 having, of course, been scouring the town for acquaintances and having been fairly successful. In the evening we dined with Grant at his hotel, and though the talk was slow, the dinner was ample and good. Tables were out under the creepers on the stoep, and there were overhead gas-lights among the leaves.

It was difficult to believe that we were hundreds of miles from anywhere; one of two of the ladies made even a fair approach to gayness of evening toilette. When dinner was over, the diners remained on the stoep, simply rearranging themselves, and engaging more promiscuously in conversation. Inspector Grant was a little shocked to find one of his lady teachers there, when she ought to have been at his school on a distant farm. She and her cavalier, the A.R.M., had chosen to dine inside, and I had only a glimpse of her through a partly open window. She was a fresh and pretty girl with any amount of animation. Our party was joined as the evening went on by the youthful Mayor and one or two others, but the talk never got above the commonplace. A Colonel Ayliff of Grahamstown chatted placidly, although we had little in common; I must have known his people, but Grahamstown was not spoken of. We retired to our hot bunks about midnight.

25/1/11 Wednesday
(**Prieska**; opening of Prieska Public School)

On awaking found wind changed and temperature a little lower. After breakfast Inspector Grant called with Deecker of the 'Northwestern Press', who struck me as something of a reprobate, an old rolling-stone that had gathered little but evil in his journalistic career. Mrs. Deecker, who helps him to run the paper, was often referred to by them as one of the Harts of the Eastern Province. The story of the two since the time when they started the first paper in Pretoria would, I am certain, be queer reading. Our next callers were the gay Lawrence, who brought with him a Mr. Spyker, the son of my old accountant and a prosperous surveyor in these parts: both of them were in fine white clothes. From the Mayor I obtained the programme of the afternoon's function. Inspector Grant came back again with a Cape cart and a beautiful pair of horses, and we set off to visit the mission schools, both of which (the D.R.C. Coloured and the Wesl. Ch. native) were far from pleasing, and on such a hot day smelt strong. We then drove out towards Prieska Poort to try to catch a cooling breeze, but the effort was vain. After lunch we were allowed to rest. At five the Mayor and a Mr. Todd arrived to escort us to the new building, which during the day had been gradually adding to its strings of flags. There was a large crowd of people, who patiently sat or stood and were roasted, like the speakers, in the open Prieska sun. But is not the whole story told in the columns of the 'Northwestern Press'? After the function there came a few introductions and a meeting or two with committees, and I was especially glad to

---

81   W. Metcalfe and Son, publishers of *The Messenger of Mathematics*.

Fig. I: Prieska Public School 1912. Collection: Sigi Howes.

meet the Rev. Hofmeyr of Kakamas and a Mr. Louw, a fine progressive farmer who has had his present schoolteacher (Miss Pearson) for ten years. The Mr. Todd, above-mentioned, turned out to be a member of McIvor's firm, the forwarding agents of De Aar, and he claimed having met me there years ago. He is a pushing Scots-Irishman of real public spirit, and is trying to have interest maintained in Mr. Gibbon's good works – the Park, the Public Library, etc. His own house and garden are proofs of his industry and ability. In showing me over the garden, he specifically drew attention to a little petrol motor which he set working and which immediately brought up a surprising volume of water for irrigation purposes. The dinner in the evening was considered a great success, and was wonderfully well managed for such a far-outlying town. The mayor was chairman, the speakers were Mr. Grove, the guest, Mr. Mantle, and Mr. Van …, Mr. Davy and Mr. Heywood; and the languages were English and Dutch alternately. Mr. Mantle, the proposer of 'Our Land', was most successful, his style being that of a humorous Wesleyan lay-preacher. Mr. Grove was strikingly friendly and his statement that I should find a hearty welcome in every Dutch household in the district was loudly cheered. The 'Northwestern Press' cannot a second time be referred to for details, as the worthy editor was not invited.

Learned in the course of the evening that the young lady teacher who had been enjoying herself with the A.R.M. the preceding evening had definitely decided not to proceed to her post. The farmer, her employer, had duly arrived to convey her to her work, but was 'left lamenting';[82] the story was that she meant to return to Capetown, and that possibly the impressionable A.R.M. knew the reason why.

Put myself to sleep with the concluding chapters of Hall Griffin's 'Life of Robert Browning' and thus exhausted all the literature I had brought with me.[83]

82 'left lamenting': a quote from 'Lord Ullin's Daughter' by Thomas Campbell.
83 *Life of Robert Browning* (1910) by William Hall Griffin.

26/1/11 *Thursday*

(*Prieska, Britstown, De Aar*)

Rose early and was glad to find my cold beginning to disappear. Visit from Deecker, who wanted me to read a manuscript in Maskew Miller's hands on the Jameson Raid; the book, he said, was written by Mrs. Deecker and was sure to create a sensation. I left him with the unpleasant feeling that he and his literary spouse might quite well turn out to be little else than blackmailers. This was confirmed later by Cuthbert and Laurence, who described Mrs. Deecker as a stately and ingratiating old damsel in a black moustache. As a set-off, we had a delightful visit from the station master Wilson and all his pretty family, the desire of the little folks being to see the wonders of the coach. Along with them also came the little son of the postmaster, who twice a day had been sent with a present of milk for 'Dr. Muir's coffee'. He now introduced his small sister 'Maggie', who with her fine black eyes was a striking contrast to the station children. It was a pretty sight to see the six little ones piloted through our quarters. The train was to start at 9.15 and by 9 there were quite a number of townsfolk gathered to say goodbye. Mrs. Duncker, the wife of a member of the School Board and an adherent of the D.R. Church, came to plead for the admission of her two girls, as boarders and pupil-teachers, to St Hilda's (E.C.) School in Capetown, and with inward wonder at the inconsistencies of bilingualism, I undertook to help. At last we were off. Mayor Laurence, who was on his way to Capetown, joined us in the coach and stayed to lunch. At Britstown, the R.M., Mr. Borcherds, called with an invitation to alight and visit the Smartt farms, but of course I had to decline; our last meeting at Indwe was pleasantly recalled. The run thence into De Aar was marked by a wordy wrangle between Mr. Cuthbert and Grant, the former having raised his spirit-level to 'talkativeness'. On reaching De Aar, I could have wished that he would remain in the coach, and I said so to Mr. Grant. As a matter of fact, however, he disappeared when I was engaged and did not return till 11.15, his haunt being doubtless Mrs. Cowling's and his business, the unsavoury gossip of the place. The Eastern Province train from Capetown came in about ten, and I was accosted by Judge Kotze, from whom I was glad to learn the news of Rhodes College as we strolled the platform. Mr. Kauthack also came up, and on learning that he had Mrs. Kauthack with him, who was taking her boy to St. Andrew's College, Grahamstown, I asked to be introduced and found her to be spectacled and nice. Before turning in for the night I read some portions of 'Jane Eyre', the only readable book I could find on the coach.[84]

27/1/11 *Friday*

(*Modder River*)

Left after breakfast for Modder River, Mr. Grant calling to say goodbye. The goods train to which we were attached proceeded most slowly, and we gladly utilized the time in attending to accumulated correspondence. At Orange River we crossed a south-going passenger train containing numerous school children and learned that a boy had overbalanced himself, when the train lurched at the station points, and was killed. Heard Mr. Aucamp's voice on the train, he being evidently a passenger to Capetown to resume his parliamentary duties. It was interesting to see again the country which we had visited in war times, and still more so to find ourselves quietly shunted back into the old siding familiar to Cam when she once accompanied me.[85] The clay-built swallow's nests were as large as ever, and their occupants

84 *Jane Eyre* (1847) by Charlotte Brontë.

85 A reference to a much earlier journey on which he had been accompanied by his younger daughter, Cam.

Fig. J: De Aar Station Building 1895. DRISA P0427. Transnet Heritage Library Photo Collection.

as noisy. In the dark of the evening I strolled around the school buildings and thought of Westerman and the old troubles: their glory had departed.[86]

28/1/11 Saturday

(**Modder River**)

A quiet day of work and reading. Head-cold better. Shocked by a telegram from Inspector Satchel in reference to a girl teacher who had misconducted herself in the Zambesi Express and is summoned to appear before the Kimberley Court on the 4th proximo.

Set the wires amoving in the hopes of arresting trouble [see below]. Discussed with him Ida Wesner's case and told him that I thought the Railway people had behaved discreditably on the train and had exaggerated the story afterwards.

29/1/11 Sunday

(**Modder River; Kimberley**)

Cold much less troublesome, and probably got to its last stage. Heat as before. Read in the morning portions of 'Guy Mannering', the only other book in the coach. Mr. de Vries called before eleven with his Cape cart, and took us for a drive. We visited first the turbine-driven dynamo on the Modder River below the village of Ritchie (formerly Rosmead); then the main pumping station, which I had seen years before; then Long's gardens, watered in this way from the river. Was distressed to learn that Long, after all his pioneer efforts, had recently had to sell his property at about a third of cost price, the buyers being a young Wolhuter from Kimberley and a De Villiers. The orchard of the latter, we visited under his guidance and saw immense quantities of peaches, pears, etc. We were told by De Vries that this orchard, which had been purchased for £500, would bring in this year about £400 for fruit. All the same, the methods employed seemed primitive and wasteful. Our last call was at De Vries' own house, where we had tea, and were loaded up with fruit and vegetables,

86   The battle of Magersfontein, an Anglo-Boer War battle, was a tactical victory for the Boers, although a contingent of Scandinavians, fighting for the Boer cause, was virtually destroyed. Those who fell in action were reburied on the battlefield by Mr. W. Westerman of Modder River Station.

preparatory to returning to the coach. (While reading on the stoep in the afternoon I was surprised to find Inspector Satchel approaching, he having come by a Kimberley train. We kept him to dinner, and he returned to Kimberley in the evening.) Took note, on the way back, of the school site and erven given free by Mr. Ritchie of Rosmead.[87] In the evening, left by the second portion of the passenger train, and were soon in Kimberley. On the platform to meet us were Inspector Satchell, Mr. and Mrs. Haarhoff and Dr. MacKenzie and Mr. Henderson. I agreed to go to supper with the Haarhoffs, but declined to spend the night with them as I had to leave at 8 the following morning for Barkly.[88] Mrs. Haarhoff and I then drove off in her motor, which she silently left me to admire but which I am sure she wished me to look upon as a dream of comfort and elegance. It was delightful to meet her again, and we were soon engaged in wordy contests. There came to supper Dr. Mackenzie, Satchel and the Manager of De Beers and a quite jolly little gathering it was. During the after-supper smoke, a wondrous gramophone was turned on, and we listened with delight and amazement to Caruso, Melba, Clara Butt, Tetrazinni and others. I could not but feel that I shall yet be compelled to buy one of the originally hated instruments. We then examined Haarhoff's 'Old Masters' and other Italian curios; and it was midnight before we even thought of retiring. Alf Williams had gone sooner, doubtless because the gramophone was just about as superb and costly as his own: he has one or two traits like his father, to whom I asked to be remembered.[89] When I finally rose to go, I was told that the motor was ready to take me to the station, and that it would again be there in the morning at 9 to convey me to Barkly. I thus went to bed with a quite free mind. All the four people of the coach were sound asleep when I let myself in.

30/1/11 Monday
(**Kimberley**; Barkly West)

Up first about 5.30, and set all stirring preparatory for the day's expedition. Everything ready by 8 o'clock and Mr. Haarhoff's luxurious motor arrived at 8.15 so that we (Mr. Cuthbert and I) were soon spinning in the direction of Barkly West. Notwithstanding heat and dust, we were most comfortable, much more than on my former visit. The country, however, was not more attractive than of old, the bends of the Vaal River being alone of any interest. Arrived at the struggling town shortly after nine and found old members of the 'deputa', including the leader Captain Tuckey, hanging about the street in front of the hotel. After formal introductions in Tuckey's best style, we retired for a drink of cool beer whilst arrangements were being made about obtaining a meeting room in the Public Library. On arriving at the library, we were surprised to find business well begun, the redoubtable Tuckey being in full blast with the delegates in a horseshoe in front of him, some stray individuals on a wall bench near the door, and a reporter ensconced in a corner. After I had taken a seat on the chairman's right and got Mr. Cuthbert beside me, the interrupted harangue was resumed, the subject being on the items of a so-called 'agenda' paper. I bore with the rigmarole for a little longer than I ought, and then brought the speaker up with a round turn and a broad hint that I had come to do business. Thenceforward I conducted affairs myself taking the various schools and their delegates in turn

87 'erven' (Afrikaans): plots of land, marked off for building purposes.
88 At the time of the 1894 election, Haarhoff had been a member of the Afrikaner Bond, but was known to be well-disposed to Rhodes and the De Beers company in Kimberley; therefore it is not unexpected that Haarhoff's other guest at the dinner was Alf Williams of De Beers.
89 Alpheus Fuller Williams (1874–1953), a mining engineer, had succeeded his father, Gardner Williams, as De Beers general manager.

– but keeping Sydney (i.e. Tuckey's school) to the last. Progress was made in surprisingly smooth fashion, and the way being clear, it was not difficult to put the redoubtable in his proper place and to wind up the meeting in decent form. The R.M. (Mr. Lloyd) joined the meeting shortly after business had begun, and was on occasion very helpful, his contributions being of the nature of pointed interjections when incorrect statements were being made to me. I regretted afterwards that I had not seen Mr. Lloyd before the meeting, and learned something of Tuckey's ways. Unfortunately, too, individual delegates occupied my time after the meeting and I had to leave in haste without again having an opportunity. I declined drinks with civility, but was inwardly sorry to do so; so we consequently halted at the first house of refreshment on the way home and had Ohlsson's beer brought out to us.[90] About the half-way house, the motor burst a tube, but a Stepney tire was promptly put in place and we reached the Kimberley Station almost within the hour.[91] A cold lunch was soon on the table and was more enjoyed by me than Chef Ben's usual elaborate menus. The heat, which had gradually been increasing, became almost intolerable in the afternoon, and there was nothing for it but to lie in one's bunk and perspire. Callers however became urgent about 4. The first batch consisted of the Rev. Pescod, Dr. Mackenzie and Inspector Satchel, their business being the new building schemes, and their conversation lengthened and occasionally heated. Then came Inspector Myles of the Railway Detective Department, who before he left undertook to do his utmost to have the scandal case against Ida Wesner withdrawn. Next came Henderson of Stockdale Street School, who, however, offered to wait while I drove to the Haarhoff's to say goodbye. Found them on the balcony looking at the retreating rain clouds that had tantalized us all with a few big drops. Drank a large whisky and soda with Haarhoff and discussed with Mrs. Haarhoff her brother's, the magistrate's, affairs at Molteno. With a little sparring we agreed, as we always do, and she related with gusto how the R.M. one day recently, when Pelz the D.R.C. missionary became offensive, transformed himself from Magistrate to Man and pitched the reverend brother out of the office. She fears trouble, of course, from Hertzog, but feels that a little prompt justice like this is worth standing a wigging for. We parted with warm wishes that we might all meet next on April 12th on board the 'Walmer Castle' bound for England. On returning to the coach, I chatted a little with Henderson, then dined, and then returned to the stoep in case anyone else should call. Our most esteemed visitor was Mrs. Bennie, the six-months' widow of 'Wee' Bennie, who used to be the heaviest man in [the] Cape Colony. I learned from her with surprise that the Haarhoff's present fine house used to be hers until her husband died, and that during the siege, a shell went through it from roof to basement without harming in the least any one of the thirteen inmates. Her other reminiscences of wartime were most interesting; as also her stories of early days in Kimberley, her father and her husband being among the first pioneers. When she left the coach with Henderson, she disclaimed any need to be piloted, as every foot in the goods yard was known to her. An unexpected arrival was Weldon, who had driven me through the Transkei; he was in Kimberley on a visit and seeing from the papers that I was also there, he called to 'pay his respects'. He looked back with pleasure to our Transkei tour, although he had been in bed for a fortnight after it from an injury received from one of his horses. As soon as the train began to move we went to bed, being glad to get into our pyjamas and be reasonably cool.

90 Ohlssons Cape Breweries, operating from the Foresters Arms, was a leading Cape Town brewery; it was in fierce competition with Castle Breweries, established in 1895.

91 'stepney tire': at that time motor cars were not supplied with a spare tire. The 'stepney tire' was a circular metal rim without spokes that could be clamped onto the rim of the wheel that had the flat.

31/1/11 Tuesday

(*De Aar*)

Awoke early, but was late in rising through a belief on George's part that I, like Mr. Cuthbert, was still asleep. The result was that for the first time I breakfasted in pyjamas. Young, who had been up at six, had of course a healthier appetite and enjoyed especially the peaches handed in by De Vries after midnight at Modder River. Air considerably cooler, and bathroom tank again in working order so that one enjoyed being made 'clean'. Reached De Aar about 11, and found that through lack of engine, however, we should have to wait until 8 in the evening. Passing passenger trains were all double-headed and crowded. C. away most of the day at the school or elsewhere, and I wrote from morning to night. Station master Pennington called to shake hands; his wife's death has cut him up dreadfully. He has resolved to board his two girls at Grahamstown and his boy at King-williamstown and to live alone. I was very sorry for him: he and his wife were above the common. Just as we were preparing [to] leave at night, the Rev. Venter of Prieska called, having come to De Aar to meet his wife who is returning from the coach. He told me that the temperature at Prieska the day after I left had been 112°, the highest ever reached in the place. After dinner, working was impossible because of the vibration, and I sat on the stoep and smoked and enjoyed the stars and the coolish breeze in silence. Went to bed about 10.

1/2/11 Wednesday

(*Fraserburg Road; Laingsburg; Touws River*)

Wakened after midnight by Ben who had been roused by the night-foreman at Hutchinson and handed a telegram for me. I groped for Ben's hand in the dark and struck a match after he had gone; the message being that the case against Ida Wesner must go on but will be withheld from the newspapers. Did not readily get to sleep again. At 6.30 in the morning, the coach was found to be at rest in Fraserburg Road Station, and the air fairly cool. When dressing, an immense bundle of correspondence was handed in to me, and all hopes for a quiet day utterly dissipated. The trains we passed continued to be full of children's fresh faces on their way to school. After lunch the temperature began to rise rapidly again, and for a good part of the afternoon stood at 100°. Read 'Nature' and the 'London Weekly

Fig. K: Fraserburg Road Station 1895. DRISA P0359. E.H. Short. Transnet Heritage Library Photo Collection.

Times' and sweltered until 3.45, when I was forced to sponge myself and get normally dressed to meet a deputation at Laingsburg. Found them all in readiness: Mr. Hugo (the secretary) the Rev. Cilliers and three others. Visited with them the three proposed sites and as they had good horses, this was done in a few minutes without delaying the train. Received a beautiful present of peaches from Mr. Hugo as we said goodbye. Journey therefrom to Touws River, which we reached at 9.15, was rather tiresome. Fortunately, however, the temperature had fallen to 80°. After a lot of tedious shunting in the dark, we were settled for the night at the far end of the camp in 'Plantation' siding.

2/2/11 Thursday
(Touws River)

Rose unrefreshed, having suffered yesterday from the heat and the ice-cold drinks, which Cuthbert was constantly proffering. Touws River does not improve as years go on. At breakfast, which Young and I dawdled over, we seemed to see nothing but the lowest type of Coloured people; engine drivers and a shunter or two might be white, but all else were degraded-looking hybrids. They seemed also more numerous than they needed to be: when the coach had to have its water-tanks filled from the hose, it took four of them to superintend the operation. The fast passenger train, which was to take us up, did not arrive on time, and on inquiry we found that it was more than an hour late. I consequently went to the bookstall for a novel but could get nothing better than 'The Scarlet Pimpernel'.[92] Cuthbert was invisible all morning among his railway friends. When the train did arrive, it certainly did not dawdle; and we soon felt that the driver meant to make up time. At Mulder's Vlei, Cuthbert joined the Stellenbosch train. Salt River was reached about 6.30, and a very short wait sufficed to bring a train for Rosebank.

---

92   *The Scarlet Pimpernel* (1905) by Baroness Orczy.

DIARY 4

Diary of S.G.E.'s tour to Fraserburg, Graaff-Reinet, etc.

1/3/11 to 18/3/11

1/3/11 Wednesday

(**Cape Town**)

Quite fagged out and worried about the Select Committee on Bilingualism when I came home, consequently didn't enjoy my dinner and was forgetful about papers and things to be taken with me. While we were having coffee on the stoep, Marion arrived to stay with Mam and, in shaking hands absentmindedly, offered to add a kiss but recovered herself quite unnecessarily. Lift with Sam about 8 o'clock for Capetown, where we found to our surprise, the old Coach (No. 362) tagged on at the end of the second portion of the evening train for the north. Was pleased to be on board once more, although the glory had somewhat departed, the pictures having been removed and the office dismantled. The absence of George, the messenger-worker, and Young the coach clerk was a relief – to me at any rate. The coolness of the evening air and my tiredness made us retire early.

2/3/11 Thursday

(**Fraserburg Road**; *visits to Tamboersfontein and Beckplaats*)

Awoke to find the morning dull and almost cold, and that for a first night I had slept astonishingly well. Reached Fraserburg Road about 12, and found Cuthbert on the platform, he having joined the first portion of the train when we had overtaken it at breakfast time. His escapade had not helped on preparations, notwithstanding his assertions to the contrary, his real reason being a desire for suitable company and for a train with a kitchen and bar. The coach being shunted into a siding, we lunched on cold salmon and bread and beer while the cart from Fraserburg was being got ready and the four horses inspanned. Before starting, Fagg the architect of the new school building called and reported that he was on the same journey, travelling by another private cart; a Mr. Schalkwyk of the Fraserburg School Board also called, his conveyance being the post-cart. At 1.10 we set out, our driver proving at once that he was skilful and reliable; we soon found out, indeed, that he knew every inch of the road, having driven the mail for years. At 20 miles out, we halted and had a drink, Fagg's teetotalism encouraging us to open another bottle. Supper we had at Tamboersfontein, the first farm we came across, our own table being a little pile of bricks in the lee of the garden wall. Here the post-cart with Schalkwyk overtook and passed us, pushing on to get to Fraserburg next morning. Our next two hours took us into the mountains in the dark, and we lost sight of the twin hills, appropriately named Tafelberg and Spitzkop, which, apparently, we had been aiming for all day. Beckplaats, which we at length drew up at, we could see nothing of. To please its owner, we took a cup of his coffee in the parlour, and agreed to sleep in his spare room. The post-cart left before we turned in, giving us an opportunity of another farewell to Schalkwyk. Fagg took possession of a garden seat on the stoep outside our open window, and the three of us slept in our clothes. I lay down with the feeling of being in a strange land, in spite of Mr. Bibijee's (Viviers') kind intentions.[93]

3/3/11 Friday

(*Visits to Oudekloof Farm and Ratelfontein; Fraserburg*)

Woke finally at 4 after a most disturbed night. First the wind got up and flapped the window curtains like sails, then a lost soul moaned on the other side of a locked door, then

---

93 It is not apparent why Muir chose to give Viviers the nickname of 'Mr. Bibijee' (apparently Punjabi). In Punjabi 'bibi' is a term of respect for a noble woman, and '-ji' is a gender-neutral suffix, also a term of respect. Thus the nickname could be nothing more than a sarcastic gesture of respect on Muir's part.

Cuthbert snored, and worst of all, a large mouse or a small cat climbed up the trailing bed-cover and ran past my head. Roused Cuthbert, who rose promptly though only half-awake, and stumbled out of doors striking matches as he went. Soon I heard him shouting for the driver, and then waking Fagg to help him shout. As almost our only dressing was to put on a heavy great coat, we had to tramp the stone stoep in the starlight for a considerable time, exchanging queries with 'Bibijee' and trying to enjoy his well-meant cup of coffee. At length we started into the darkness, and how we kept the road I know not. Apparently, we were following up a dry river bed and getting further into the hills. When the first rays of morning struck the rocky krantzes ahead of us, we found the country more interesting than the previous day's, which had been nothing but sand and stones. The river valley after a little closed in, and as we ascended, we crossed and recrossed the bed more than a score of times. Meanwhile we had also been developing a serious hunger, and all were glad when the head of the valley became visible in the distance, and an untidy little farmhouse and orchard stood in our way. The two carts were soon being outspanned, and breakfast baskets dumped out alongside the orchard wall. The farmer, a thin ascetic, appeared and manifested what we gathered was for him a lively interest, his visitors being known and expected. By invitation, we took possession of his entrance-parlour, and ate our meal with the help of a cup of coffee apiece, Fagg consuming two cups so as to enable me to substitute beer – an obligement which seemed a little like a breach of teetotal principles.[94] The coffee was brought in by the farmer's daughter, a healthy buxom quiet-mannered girl with whom I afterwards opened a little conversation. She had learned English from her sister, she said, when there was a little Private Farm School on the Plaats. The sister had advantages having been sent to the Cape Modern Athens to attend the Bloemhof; then the mother died, and the remaining sister had had to take the mother's place.[95] Their name was Sieberhagen and their place was Oudekloof. There was no appearance of prosperity to be seen about and yet the orchard was full of fruit and was well-watered from a dam in the river bed and from a spring surrounded by trees. It contained, in particular, a large mulberry tree with luscious berries going to waste in canfuls. These I tasted but the old man's kindness warmed up the longer we stayed, and he seemed disappointed that I did not taste also of all the unripe fruit he had in view. The drivers, however, were inspanning after a heavy meal of burnt mutton and woodashes, and we could urge the plea that Fraserburg waited us and that we must not arrive late.[96] We left therefore at 9, appeased as to our hunger and satisfied otherwise, merely warning Miss Sieberhagen that I should want one of her pretty half-Persian cats on my return. The road led sleepily upwards, winding round the amphitheatre which had Oudekloof at its base, and when we got to the top, the view backwards was quite picturesque. Henceforward the country was flat, and though dry and sandy was clearly more valuable than that on the other side of the mountains. After a two hours' 'scoff', we outspanned again, the farm being called Ratelfontein. It had apparently just changed owners, and the house was unfurnished, being inhabited only by a young man Johnston from Oudtshoorn. A splendid spring had been tapped by an open rock-cutting, and the value of the farm had gone up 300 per cent. It was quite refreshing to look down on the huge dam, which the running stream kept filled after passing through the orchard. Young Johnston acted as our

---

94 'obligement' (Scots): a kindness or favour.

95 The Girls' Public School, Stellenbosch, became known as the Bloemhof Seminary because this was the school at which the 'bloeme' (flowers) of the nation were cultivated, according to the chair of the School Board, Ds. J.H. Neethling. Muir refers to the school as the 'Cape Modern Athens', a tongue-in-cheek allusion to Raphael's fresco in the Vatican, 'School of Athens', representing all the greatest figures of antiquity gathered together, sharing ideas.

96 Perhaps this was a traditional slow roast of Karroo mutton, cooked on wood ash for low heat over a prolonged cooking period.

guide to the 'sights' and then we returned to the stoep to do a little beer-drinking, being joined in this by an Oudtshoorn farmer called Becker, who had come into Fraserburg to take up land for ostriches. Becker reminded me that he had once driven me to Kruis Rivier and I immediately gathered from him that he was a brother-in-law of the ostrich kings, the Potgieters.[97] Even here ostriches were the constant and only subject of talk, and I recalled that the slow and sober-faced Sieberhagen of Oudekloof had shown us three broods of chicks in different stages of advancement. Our next 'scoff' took us to Fraserburg, and we went at once to the hotel, avoiding both parsonage and school board office. Cuthbert promptly ordered up a couple of pails of water and while I bathed, he entertained downstairs the people who had come out to meet us at 1 o'clock and were disappointed, viz, the R.M. (Rowan), the parson (Daneel), the Mayor (Dyson), the District Surgeon (Henderson) and the School Board secretary (Strobos). After a moderately refreshing cup of tea, the new school building, which had been pleasantly visible from the verandah, was visited in the company of Fagg the architect and the Rev. Daneel.[98] This led on to a visit to the parsonage garden, where fruit galore was pressed on us, but where also the ostrich had found a home and was breeding. Daneel explained that his wife was a daughter of the Rev. Geo. Murray of Oudtshoorn, and that the birds and their chicks were to remind her of her childhood's district, and we professed to understand the feeling. In the evening there was a crowded *conversazione* in the town hall, the entertainment consisting of piano solos, songs and glees, the last managed by Mr. and Mrs. Rowan, who both took part.[99] There were also speeches by Rowan, Daneel, the guest, and Louw the former School Board secretary of Oudtshoorn, but now the manager of a syndicate's farm on the Sack River. Between whiles the kindly R.M. led us off the platform through a passage to his office, where smokes and drinks were provided liberally. Here Cuthbert and the Irish doctor (Henderson) did well, and added to the joviality of the occasion. Midnight came before we retired, the R.M. and the pastor seeing us home. We learned later that on our departure the young folks took to dancing, and that they had secured a good deal of enjoyment before the parson could be brought on to the scene to intervene. When I inquired who had been the parson's base informant, the blame was divided between the sweet and gentle Mrs. Rowan, who is a sister and speaking likeness of Miss Joubert of Bloemhof, and the hard and rather virile Mrs. Daneel, who had 'Calvinist' written on her countenance.[100] One lady, the Mayor's plump and rosy-cheeked young wife from Hamburg, was generally held innocent.

4/3/11 Saturday

(*Fraserburg; opening of Fraserburg Public School*)

Up early, Cuthbert calling in his pyjamas to wake me when I was dressed. Morning occupied with the Irish doctor and other callers. Meeting of School Board in room of new

97 Kobus Potgieter still farms ostriches at Rietfontein today. His great-grandfather started shooting ostriches for their feathers in 1846, and by 1910, three Potgieter brothers (the ostrich kings) had accumulated 6,000 birds, the largest ostrich operation in the world: *South Magazine, 2011.*

98 William George Fagg (1867–1938) was a partner in the Cape Town firm of architects, Black & Fagg. He trained in England, practised for a time in Tasmania, and subsequently in the Cape. He was also responsible for the design of Worcester Girls' High School and Victoria West High School during Muir's era: *ArteFacts SA: Fagg, William George.*

99 'conversazione' (Italian): a private soiree of people connected with the arts.
  'glee': an English part song, usually for unaccompanied men's voices.

100 'speaking likeness': an obscure reference to a little-known children's book by Christina Rossetti, *Speaking Likenesses* (1874): in the book the three characters encounter their strangely disfigured doppelgangers. Thus, Muir implies that the sisters are each other's doubles, but with a disfiguring twist (we know not what).

Fig. L: Fraserburg Public School 1911, now Hoërskool Fraserburg. Collection: Sigi Howes.

school building at 11.30 was formal and full and lengthy, but went well, all the members, including even the militant Mr. Louw of Oudtshoorn, being well pleased with the result. Took a nap after lunch but was wakened by a violent storm of wind and dust and rain, which threatened to interfere with the afternoon ceremony. It soon calmed a little, however, and when Dr. Henderson came at 5 to escort me to the new building, there was sufficient lull to enable us to proceed on foot. As we neared the site, a long procession was seen approaching from the direction of the old school building. When all had been assembled outside the main door, and I had begun to speak, the rain returned, and I used the fact to get my will as regards speaking inside. The crowding, of course, was a little unpleasant and Daneel's translation of my speech was a trifle unnecessary, but the general result was satisfactory. Strangest of all, the anti-Englander, Louw, led with three cheers at the close. The early evening was full of forebodings, the rain having become more serious, suggestive of heavy roads and impassable drifts on the Kukumas.[101] The complimentary dinner fixed for 9 was a great success, there being about 40 present, even the parson turning up to his people's surprise. Mayor Dyson presided; Rowan proposed my health; Old Townshend in Dutch toasted the architects, and Fagg replied with an eye on future business. The speeches were pleasantly separated by musical items – piano solos by the brothers Strobos and songs by Rowan and Keller the landlord. Keller's song was 'Mrs. Enery 'Awkins' in Dutch and the audience joined heartily in the chorus: "Mrs. Dompietje is a bei mooi naam".[102] The rousing event of the evening, however, was the performance on the bagpipes by the agent of the Standard Bank, who quietly left the table and shortly after entered again with his

101 It is not clear which river is the Kukumas. Perhaps it has changed its name.
102 'Mrs. Enery 'awkins' was an 1892 cockney song of comic music hall singer, Albert Chevalier. Muir's Afrikaans is incorrect and he must mean: 'Mev. Dompietje is 'n baie mooi naam': 'Mrs. D is a very beautiful name'.

pipes in full blast. After playing once round the dining room, he took to the stoep and played a brave and stirring march, which made Cuthbert start from his seat and follow the pipes with a martial strut that set the company into shouts every time the two performers passed the open door. The break-up took place at 12 and the goodbyes were most friendly. I then learned that only *five* of the forty guests were from 'the old country', and that besides the doctor, there was another Irishman, the postmaster. Cuthbert did not, of course, go upstairs with me but remained with the bagpipes, Dyson, Henderson and other roisterers, till at least I had fallen asleep; indeed, he wakened me on his way up at about 1.30.

5/3/11 *Sunday*

(*Visits to Ratelfontein, Oudekloof, Beckplaats and Tamboersfontein;* **Fraserburg Road**)

Slept badly, being concerned about the early start. At last determined to get up, and after the greatest difficulty got Cuthbert out of bed and found the time to be 3.35, with just half-an-hour to get ready for the start. A great scurry followed, but we had time to note that the sky was clear and the stars bright; there was no danger, therefore, of a late arrival at Graaff-Reinet because of swollen rivers. After all we were too early for Japie and the cart, which, because of a rebellious horse, did not turn up till 4.30, and which did not finally start till 4.35. As we drove off leaving our candle burning on a stoep seat, the street and town were quiet as the grave. Until daylight came we were very listless, and sometimes slept. It was 7 o'clock before we arrived at Ratelfontein and had hopes of breakfast. Even Johnston had now deserted the place, and when we took possession, we found everything very squalid. A table, a chair, and a settle-bed were all the furniture.[103] From the table, Cuthbert first removed a month-old tablecloth, the bare deal being much more cleanly; and then he opened the two baskets, which our Fraserburg friends had handed us on parting. One contained 13 Namaqua 'partridges' and a chunk of bread; the other contained two small bottles of champagne. A better breakfast I have seldom had.[104] At 8 we resumed the journey, feeling warmer, and being cheered by the breaking through of the sun. The previous night's ongoings were recalled over a cigarette, but talk soon languished and drowsiness took possession of us until we began to drop down on Oudekloof. When we arrived, a more than Sunday calm possessed the place; and when old Sieberhagen at last appeared, his mien was subdued and severe. True, he invited us to come 'binnen', but not with his former cheery hospitality, and I thought it best to say that I should stretch my legs and look in later.[105] Shortly after he had left us, we heard family worship in progress, and Cuthbert looked at me with a thankful air. As the time approached for inspanning and all was quiet, we went towards the door to pay our call, but abruptly stopped on the lowest step when a hoarse voice struck up another psalm tune. After a second-long wait, which I devoted to the friendly half-Persians, we observed a lanky youth proceed from the house, leaving the door open, and make for the stables. We now felt safe enough and with a reconnoitring once, we entered.[106] A very kindly reception was given us, and I renewed my acquaintance with the daughter while Cuthbert made friends with the old man. We were also introduced to a visitor, an old-looking lady (aged 83) who had come from Caledon all the way. As I gathered a little of her history, Cuthbert wiled the father out-of-doors and treated him to a 'dram', the treat being much appreciated as I was afterwards told. The drive down the Kukumas River was very tiresome, and ultimately almost overpowering

---

103 'settle-bed': a sofa-bed that could be converted into a bench when not in use.

104 The Namaqua partridge is, in fact, a sandgrouse.

105 'binnen' (Dutch): inside.

106 The half-Persians were the cats Muir had admired on the earlier visit to Oudekloof.

with heat. At Beckplaats all was deadly still, and without disturbing anyone, we drew up in the shade of the house and lunched and fed the hens and puppies. Viviers turned up after a while and chid us for not entering uninvited. He very kindly also offered us coffee in his parlour, but we failed again to see his young wife, who was said to weigh something enormous. After an outspan of 1½ hours, we sped on again in the heat, and endured the tiresomeness as best we might. About six we reached the long expected Tamboersfontein, and there we supped by the same pile of bricks as on the outward journey, the creature comforts being bread and polony and champagne. As in the morning, Cuthbert confined himself to beer, and possibly had the best of it. He also pressed on me an excellent cigar which he had got from Mayor Dyson, and this I lingered over with pleasure. As before, Tamboersfontein had an air of life: the post-cart arrived, and young people lounged about, seeing and being seen. At 7 o'clock we started, and very soon found ourselves plodding wearily onwards in the dark. After many false hopes had been raised, the lights of Fraserburg Road distant signal were identified and by 11.30 the coach was reached. Frank the Barbadian was glad to see us emerging out of the night, and having picked up his bed from the coach stoep, carried in our belongings and gave us a drink.

6/3/11 *Monday*

(*De Aar; Naauwpoort*)

Was wakened in the night by the coach moving at great pace when I had expected to remain at Fraserburg Road until after breakfast. Learned in the morning that Cuthbert had got us hitched onto the Johannesburg train about 2 o'clock, and that we should consequently be in De Aar about midday. Being tired in the morning, I was easily persuaded to breakfast in pyjamas. After dressing, however, the tired feeling went, and I took to work at my index of mathematical papers. The stay at De Aar was short, and we thus reached Naauwpoort in the afternoon. Dr. Baird and Mr. Smith called, and with them I inspected the School Boarding House for railway children. After supper I tackled the index again, and succeeded in finishing it in slip form. Telegrams were also attended to and a letter to Mrs. McIntosh of Port Elizabeth about Lord Meath's visit.[107] Cuthbert went to visit his cronies and while he was away, there came a very heavy storm of thunder and rain, the lightning being alarming but grand. Went to bed before the train started and before Cuthbert returned.

7/3/11 *Tuesday*

(*Graaff-Reinet*; *opening of a new building at the Girls' High School*; *Aberdeen Road*)

Awoke shortly after 5 to find ourselves passing Middelburg, the few hours of stay at Rosmead having passed unnoticed. The morning was chilly, and the country shrouded in a thick wetting mist as we proceeded over the heights toward Graaff-Reinet. Inspector Craib joined us about breakfast time at a small roadside station, having come over from Rosmead in an adjoining coach. Had a lengthened talk with him about Graaff-Reinet School matters without reproaching him too much, and then had scarcely time to observe the great improvements at Colonies Plaats and in the valley of the Sunday's River.[108] Reached the town at 1 o'clock and was met by the Revs. Albertyn and Louw, and the Mayor Liebenberg to arrange [the] programme. At 1.45 Rev. Louw returned, and in his company I drove

107 Reginald Brabazon, Lord Meath (1841–1929), was known for his philanthropy. He was an ardent imperialist and introduced Empire Day in England.

108 The owner of Colonies Plaats, later Koloniesplaas, was Chris J. Watermeyer, who was a keen hydrologist as well as a farmer. He made close observations of rainfall and river flow. Perhaps his interest in water might explain the improvements in the valley.

Fig. M: Graaff-Reinet, Train in Station, 1896. DRISA P0129. Transnet Heritage Library Photo Collection.

to the three elementary schools, the two industrial schools and the spinning school. At the latter, Mr. van Gass was waiting and we discussed the economics of such schools in bantering fashion. The next, and chief visit, was to the new Girls' School building where the hour 3 to 4 was spent with its principal, Miss Murray. Then came tea at the house of the Rev. Albertyn, who turns out, notwithstanding his swagger, to be the minister of the *second* charge, and whose equally handsome wife is a daughter of the Rev. Morgan who used to be in Robben Island.[109] This was followed by a great procession and by the formal opening of the building. The speech-making in the quadrangle was departed from, the meeting taking place in the Grand School Hall, which for all its size was quite unfit to contain all the visitors. The speakers were Mayor Liebenberg, the Rev. Albertyn, the Rev. Louw (in Dutch) and the guest. The passage with which I concluded from Miss Gilliland pleased me more than ever when I read it.[110] Afternoon tea was served in the garden of the old seminary, and I was glad to meet there the old Rev. Mr. van Niekerk formerly of Middelburg, old Mr. Te Water, Mellor the new principal of the Boys' High School and others. Then came a notable meeting with the School Board – the main object of my visit – when there was plain speaking about finance and their general business methods. Work was finished just in time for the train. Inspector Morrison called at the station, and he and Inspector Grant travelled with us during the evening. Before we left there came a present of grapes from Mrs. Cloete as a sign that she had now forgiven me for having, as she said, got the better of her in bargaining for the new seminary site. It was late before we

109 'minister of the second charge': the church and congregation in Graaff-Reinet clearly supported two ministers, and Albertyn was the subordinate minister.

110 Mary Gilliland wrote an abridged version of Bunyan's 'Pilgrim's Progress'. She also wrote on ethics and philosophy. We can speculate as to the passage from Gilliland with which Muir would have chosen to conclude his speech. However, under her married name, Gilliland had very recently written an article 'Women as Citizens', the theme of which was that 'woman was the center and central power of civilization'; as such it was right that women should assert their right to full citizenship. It is suitably moderate, and yet stirring, for a girls' school audience, that Muir may well have chosen to quote from this mildly feminist article: *Gilliland Husband 1909*, p. 473.

Fig. N: Girls' High School, Graaff-Reinet c. 1911, now the Laer Volkskool. Collection: Sigi Howes.

reached Aberdeen Road and got stabled in the 'triangle' for the night but, nevertheless, we sat discussing affairs with Craib until his return train arrived about 2.

8/3/11 Wednesday
(Aberdeen Road)

Awoke early after a good sleep in the quietness of the 'triangle'. Worked hard in the forenoon and afternoon at telegrams and general office work. In the evening did a little mathematics, thus pleasantly closing a satisfactory day.

9/3/11 Thursday
(Aberdeen)

Up early and had breakfast by 8 in expectation of the promised motor car from Aberdeen. We had not long to wait, and were soon spinning along in comfort. The driver was the owner, a Port Elizabeth man named Seaman, who as a speculation had purchased three American cars of the Ford type, and had proceeded to exploit the Aberdeen people who had to travel by rail. All success for him for four hours in a cart over a flat uninteresting country is too much to endure for the pleasure even of getting out of Aberdeen. Our journey occupied only an hour and a half, and we could easily have done it in less. The town we found lay in a slight hollow by the side of a dried-up stream, its most conspicuous object being the D.R. Church building, which in colour and design is an offence to the eye.[111] To welcome us, there assembled Bradshaw the C.C., Stile the Wesleyan parson, the Irish School Board secretary, Milne the headmaster, and Messrs. Steinhobel and Van der

---

111 The church had been completed in 1907 in the Cape Gothic tradition. It is remarkable for its spire, a little over 50 m tall and somewhat disproportionate to the rest of the building. The church dominates the central square of Aberdeen.

Berg, members of the Board. Cilliers the D.R.C. parson arrived later and was found to be wily and sanctimonious and heartily tyrannical as ever.[112] His motor was a soap-box on wheels, but being his, it had to be spoken of in tones of admiration. Every time I entered it during out tour of inspection, he would comment on its smoothness or other imaginary quality; and I bore it all like a saint on the point of having a fit. Notwithstanding the superb character of the conveyance, however, it took some time to visit all the school classrooms because every school was cruelly broken up and scattered. The new site was also visited and was well discussed in view of local differences of opinion as to where the building should be placed. Lunch followed, the place of Cilliers being taken by the Mayor (Logie). It was a quite jolly gathering, and as all present were rebels against the toryism of Cilliers, there was much fun at his expense.[113] The story of 'the ticket of six' which was run in Cilliers' interest, and run with fatal success, was a never-failing source of fun.[114] It ousted Logie and his lot to Cilliers' great glee, but at the first meeting of the Board, the two best members of the 'ticket' – Steinhobel and Van der Berg – deserted and progress became the hateful watchword. After coffee and liqueurs on the stoep, the C.C. took me to the Exhibition Hall and introduced me to the chief ladies, including his stately wife. The place was crowded with exhibits and visitors, and there was every evidence that my visit was welcome. At the close of the address, Milne's choir of schoolgirls pleased and tickled the people with their rendition of 'Will ye no' come back again?'[115] Walked or rather squeezed through the hall with Mrs. Bradshaw to view the handiwork, and then escaped to the hotel stoep. The escape, however, was not final, for at four I was due to drink tea with thirty ladies on the balcony of Chitty's tearooms. What looked at first like an ordeal turned out to be quite a pleasant 'diversion', the three ladies to whom I was particularly allotted being intelligent and agreeable. It was striking to find that everyone with any pretensions to good looks were English – Mrs. Bradshaw, Mrs. Le Roux from Sea Point, a young school teacher in spectacles, and the widow Boltze, with whitey-grey hair and bright black eyes and a Gains-borough hat. Mrs. Le Roux, indeed, had real beauty of the plump pink-and-white type; I was sorry to hear that her husband had been boycotted in his business as an attorney for marrying an English girl. An oldish Mrs. de Villiers at my table was also very nice; but though she spoke English well, I did not learn her nationality. From tea we changed to a parting whisky-and-soda in the hotel parlour, an interesting Dutch farmer contributing now to the amusement, and raising three cheers as our motor car moved off. The run back in the dark was a little tiresome, and not without its annoyances, for Cuthbert had imbibed much too freely and fell asleep in the most ungraceful and dangerous positions. I took occasion by silence to show him that I viewed him as a pig.

10/3/11 Friday

(Uitenhage; Port Elizabeth)

Awoke in Uitenhage Station with the rain pouring heavily. During breakfast, the School Board secretary was seen hanging about on the outlook, and Inspector Milne, who joined the coach on arrival, arranged with him for the desired meeting. This took place later at the School Board office, the prominent members being Dr. MacPherson, the Rev. Angus,

---

112 Muir spelt the Huguenot name of the parson 'Celliers' but the foundation stone of the church dated 29 July 1906 identifies him as Ds. D.H. Cilliers. Accordingly, the spelling of the parson's name has been duly corrected.

113 'toryism': traditionalism and conservatism.

114 There is no clue as what the 'ticket of six' entailed; it is assumed it was a game of chance.

115 Will ye no' come back again?': a Scots poem by Lady Nairne, set to a traditional folk tune; passed off as a Jacobite song (and known as 'Bonnie Charlie'), it was in fact written well after the 1745 rising.

Fig.O. Port Elizabeth Train Entrance 1895. E.H. Short. DRISA P0079. Transnet Heritage Library Photo Collection.

and Messrs. Lundie, Luyt and Mackie. Considerable business was transacted, and with fair rapidity. On returning to the coach I found McJanner of the Industrial School, and listened as patiently as I could to his subdued grumbling. In the afternoon, Port Elizabeth was reached, and without warning Mr. Kayser was upon us. Of course I had to visit the Girls' High School with him; but having yielded I was glad to see it and to give some pleasure to Miss Anderson. It was also gratifying to learn how she and Mr. Way had carried out my wishes in regard to Lord Meath's visit, which had been entirely successful. In the evening we dined with Inspector Milne at the Grand Hotel, and I enjoyed to the full a real bottle of Château Lafite.[116] Met the Meaths and found them very grateful for assistance given them. Had a word or two also with Mrs. Bunten, the proprietress, to revive the old times. The Watts of the Bank of Africa introduced themselves on the ground of knowing Cam and Maud Mullins, and we exchanged commonplaces. Our train left at 9 and we carried off Inspector Milne with us.

11/3/11 Saturday
(Grahamstown; Alicedale)

Awoke in Grahamstown Station after having been several times disturbed in the night by rain. Inspector Bennie called before breakfast, then Inspector Gie and later Inspector Farmington. Arranged programme for the day with Inspector Bennie, and then attacked business with him and the others. At 11 o'clock drove to the High School and thence to the Training College, the result being a joint scheme for the reception of Lord Meath on Tuesday. Met Mother Florence, who had just returned from and had travelled from Cape-town with the Meaths, Sister Elizabeth, and later Sister Clare, and discussed proposed Training College developments, taking care to damp their intrigues about a School of Music. Hurried next to Town Hall to meet the School of Art Committee and then to be bored at considerable length by Dr Becker. Spent the afternoon in a drive round the

---

116 This is an example of Muir's characteristic misspellings; he spelt the name of the wine 'Lafitte' and there is a Château Lafitte in the Jurançon. However, his spelling has been corrected, as it is more than likely he was referring to the rather better-known Lafite Rothschild.

mountain, finding endless schoolgirls out enjoying themselves in the woods. Arranged for Bennie's furlough in order to facilitate his marriage arrangements, Inspector Gie being a most willing substitute. Left by the 9 train, Inspector Bennie and Mr. Neilson accompanying us as far as West Hill, and Inspector Milne and Gie as far as Alicedale.

12/3/11 Sunday
(Cookhouse; Alice)

Awoke in Cookhouse Station. Learned at breakfast that Dr. and Mrs. Smith of Alicedale had called at the coach at midnight but that Cuthbert did not disturb me because I had just fallen asleep. Morning beautiful after rain, and journey delightful. Bedford, Adelaide, Fort Beaufort and surrounding country looking better than I had ever seen it. Fort Beaufort was left about 2, and though the atmosphere had become somewhat sultry, we enjoyed the subsequent ascent and the backward view of the town. At Alice, which was reached about 3, and while Cuthbert's siesta was in progress, seemed to have prospered since our last visit. A large red-roofed hotel had sprung up, seemingly out of all proportion to the wants of the place; an additional cottage or two had been built about the railway and Dr. Kelbe's trees had grown luxuriantly. Mr. Henderson of Lovedale promptly called to make arrangements for my next day's visit, and we gave him tea to encourage talk. Mr. Liefeldt also called in a friendly way, and Mzimba being readily led up to, I learned of Lovedale's recent overtures towards recovering its hold on Mzimba's churches and schools.[117] On my suggestion, Liefeldt offered to send a messenger to ask Mzimba to call next day about 12 with the relevant papers. After a little, the team from Kingwilliamstown arrived bringing Inspector Bond, with whom I had a little hurried preparatory talk. Then Dr. Roberts came, and we got exciting news about the U.F.C. Commission's visit to Lovedale.[118] We also learned the meaning of Inspector Morrison's telegram of the preceding day, which read 'I.S. dead' and which we took to mean 'John Steven dead', but which really stood for 'Interstate Native College Scheme found wanting by Commission'. The first reading was considered most probable as the shipbuilder, John Steven, was a member of the Commission and a confirmed invalid. Headmaster Rankin also called, and Dr. Roberts then left, promising to return in the evening. Bond came to dinner and when Roberts fulfilled his promise, 'the fun of the fair' began. With glee we threw cold water on his statements about the Commission, and he repeated them with heat and exaggeration. Instead of water, we later threw whisky, with, of course, more serious consequences; and ultimately at midnight, when I saw him to the gate of the Goods Yard, he denounced his enemy as 'the biggest liar in South Africa'.

13/3/11 Monday
(Alicedale; visit to Lovedale; **King William's Town; Blaney Junction**)

Up early in anticipation of an interesting day. From Liefeldt came fruit and a message about Mzimba. At 9 Henderson arrived with his 'spider' and work began.[119] First the Public School and Poor School were visited and then we went Lovedale-wards. Shaw and his experimental plots seemed really interesting, but I was evidently expected merely to admire and pass on. The soybean, however, I managed to fasten on, and had the pods

---

117 Rev. Pambani Jeremiah Mzimba (1850s–1911) was the first South African-trained black Presbyterian Church minister. He taught at Lovedale Institution and subsequently formed his own independent church (the True Free Church). After his death, his son took over as head of the Mzimbatite Church.

118 'U.F.C.': United Free Church of Scotland.

119 'Spider' can only be a derogatory reference to Henderson's subordinate, Dr. Roberts.

of one, or bush rather, counted, the results being over 250 – close I think on 300. From Shaw we went to Hunter and a small tree nursery. Then came a long series of classrooms in anything but sensible order: the Training School (Roberts), the A.I. School (Haughton), the Girls' Industrial (Miss Wood), the Elementary School, etc. being all mixed up, both as to situation and superintendence. At 11 we had tea at Dr. Roberts's – a friendly enough gathering, but not marked by ease and freedom. Thereafter the workshops were visited, and what was more interesting, the hospital with its guardian, Dr. McVicar. By 12.15 the inspection was over, and by 12.30 I was back at the coach to meet Mzimba, and found him the same poxy old rebel. After lunch Roberts and Cowan called, hoping to have a pronouncement on my visit and were disappointed. At 3 the train carried us off east-ward, and we had our last few words with Inspector Bond. Atkinson of Keiskama Hoek and son-in-law of Bishop Key joined us at Middle Drift as Bond left, travelling with us to Debe Nek. There I was delighted to see on the platform ex-Inspector Ely, but it was sad on coming closer to find him aged-looking and frail. At K.W.T. all was quiet: no visitors. Stay at Blaney and journey southward were rather tiring, so that a long business talk with Inspector Young, who joined us at Southern Wood, was not soothing. It was a set-off to observe the English scented names of the suburban stations: Summer Pride, etc.

14/3/11 Tuesday
(East London; Blaney Junction; Dohne)
The morning's work opened with the Training School schemes of Father Kelly, a tiresome grumbler. Then came Inspector Morrison with Lovedale news gleaned from his former pastor Dr. Howie, one of the Commission, who having come to bless, had soon probed deep enough into Inter-State Native College affairs to make him 'decline to have anything to do with a project founded on deceit'. Morrison was maliciously happy, but I had greater cause for satisfaction in never having interfered to represent my view of the affair to the Commission, leaving the four worthies to the entire freedom of their own wills. They were represented as resenting the very mention of Emgwali, so often had it been held up as a model to them. Two of them, however, did actually visit it, under pressure as it were. They were now at Blythswood, where other humiliations awaited them. By the time Morrison was delivered of all of this, the chairman and secretary of the Board were waiting. With them I then visited the Girls' School, paying particular attention to the rooms that were overcrowded, and being struck with the excellent order and nice manners everywhere visible. Next came the Boys' School, where similar overcrowding prevailed, and where a class of between 40 and 50 small boys gave me a pleasant surprise by offering to sing 'My Ain Folk'. Their teacher being the well-known 'Lieut. Col.' Williams, a real musician, I accepted; and was greatly charmed. They sang the verses in unison, each verse being followed by the refrain sung by a sweet-voiced cherub of a boy in the first instance, and then by the choir in two-part harmony. From the High School we went first to the College Street School to discuss its renovation, and then to the new Poor School in process of erection. After lunch the great business of the visit was undertaken – the meeting with the School Board. The members were clearly on the warpath, and Mr. Rees opened with a set speech, breathing fire and fury about the neglect of East London by the government. Fortunately, they gave me opportunities for repartee, and before long they were all in good humour, even the redoubtable young Malcomess.[120] We parted on terms of friendship as of old. At the close, Mr. Kennedy Humphreys pled the case of the children of the Chinaman and his English wife; after which the German Consul and Parson Gutsche sought to have

120 Carl Malcomess, son of the East London entrepreneur, Hermann Malcomess.

the German School inspected. As the train left at 5, there was just time to say goodbye and embark. We were most thankful to be off, and eat our dinner in peace. At Blaney there was considerable delay, but we were fortunate to have a call there from our old acquaintance, Hughes of the Bunga's farm at Tsolo, and from Sorbie of the 'East London Dispatch'. The latter travelled with us to Dohne, and talked all the way, quite interestingly too, as his subject was the Gaika's Loop railway accident in which he was involved.[121]

15/3/11 Wednesday

(Sterkstroom; Molteno; Stormberg Junction; Cradock)

Was wakened at Sterkstroom by Dr. Robertson at six o'clock, shouting to Cuthbert in the adjoining cabin. The disturbance was fortunate as I had to be dressed and finished with breakfast before our arrival at 7.30 at Molteno in order to meet Mr. Deary, who had promised to travel to Stormberg Junction with me and discuss Rev. Pepler and Molteno School affairs. Along with Mr. Deary came Inspector Spurway, and the arrangement worked admirably. At Stormberg we had to suffer a long delay, and Mrs. Crewe, on her way to East London, who was also waiting called to shake hands. The journey to Rosmead was rather tiresome, but there Inspector Anderson joined us, and we had a cheery lunch together. While waiting for the south-going train, I met on the platform D.M. White of Port Elizabeth; also an Inspector of the Public Works Department from whom I got a deal of useful information about the condition of school buildings. Inspector Spurway got away before us on his backward journey, and I killed the time in glancing through a 'Book of Scottish Verse' ('The Edinburgh') lent me by Inspector Anderson.[122] It consisted of about 1,000 pages in India paper, not very well edited by Prof. Dixon of Glasgow, but full of delightful old favourites. After hearing Inspector Anderson's report on Mossel Bay, I decided to divert him to Wellington so as to secure the appointment of Davis of Mossel Bay as first assistant, and possibly successor, to Mr. Harvie of the Training College, meanwhile taking him on to Cradock to discuss Lovedale. Reached Cradock in the evening, but sat up till after midnight reading ballads and talking of them and a book of epigrams, which Anderson had with him. Cuthbert and he were greatly entertained by my reading of Outram's 'Annuity', Lockhart's 'Captain Paton', and Walter C. Smith's description of a Scottish lady of the old school, these gems being formerly unknown to them.[123] During the reading and talk there was a distant accompaniment provided by the band of a circus, which had been attracted by the local show.

16/3/11 Thursday

(Cradock)

Awoke with a feeling of insufficient and unrefreshing sleep. Saw Inspector Anderson away a little after 9 on his backward journey. The chairman (Mr. Metcalfe) and the secretary (Mr. van Niekerk) called with a cab about 10 and I spend an hour or so visiting the three schools and examining into the need for additional accommodation. Met for the first time Miss Collingwood, the principal of the Girls' School, and Miss Paterson, the notorious friend of Grant of Aliwal North. The School Board meeting proved troublesome, but the

---

121 23 people were killed, and a large number injured, in a railway accident at Gaika's Loop near Cathcart on 5 January 1911, after six coaches of the train derailed around a sharp bend.

122 *The Edinburgh Book of Scottish Verse* 1300–1900 (1910) edited by William Dixon.

123 The first is a satirical poem by George Outram immortalising the annuity; the second, entitled 'Captain Paton's Lament', is a serio-comic lament; the third poem is unidentifiable but by Walter C. Smith, chiefly remembered for his hymn 'Immortal, Invisible, God Only Wise'.

outcome was not unsatisfactory, and it ended with a friendly lunch in the hotel. In the afternoon, Father Fitzhenry called and neutralised Father Kelly of East London; also Mr. Russell, the head of the Boys' School. A goods train carried us off about six, the evening being marked by lurid clouds all round. Went early to bed after reading and rereading ballads, etc. to Cuthbert.

17/3/11 Friday

(Naauwpoort; De Aar)

Had a good sleep, although the engine at our back, going up the Carlton Bank, was sufficiently disturbing. Awoke early in Naauwpoort, where we were delayed and where the whole morning was devoted to the Cradock memoranda – a long list. Took a short walk up the hill behind the workmen's cottages, and was lucky enough to discover a curious larva that encloses itself in a collection of spikes like a hedgehog. This I managed to convey to the coach in a paper bag, where we fed it with a bit of potato and caged it in a matchbox.[124] About 4 o'clock Miss Cogan arrived from Colesberg, and went on with us to De Aar, much to our enjoyment. Lovedale, Blythswood, etc. engaged our conversation and much relevant and irrelevant gossip was exchanged. We recalled the Blythswood of 1908 and I had read her 'The name had silken ties of mem'ry' and Professor Blackie's poem from the 'Edinburgh Book of Verse'. Said a hurried goodbye to her at De Aar and left her to the tender mercies of Mrs. Cowling.

18/3/11 Saturday

(Wellington; Salt River)

A tiring day of office work, and when just congratulating myself on being free, a telegram came from the Office saying that Mr. Murray would join us at Wellington and travel back to town, getting instructions on a pile of papers![125] And thus the two last hours of the tour were spent, and I arrived at Salt River a tired man.

---

124 This is not a totally fanciful experiment: apparently an insect in larval stage may consume food to fuel its transition.

125 It is believed this is a reference to Charles Murray, a long-serving official within the Cape Education Department. Murray was the secretary of the Department when Muir arrived in 1892 (*Borman 1989*, p. 126) and may well have continued to hold this office until the date of this diary entry in 1911 (which would be consistent with him receiving from Muir 'instructions on a pile of papers'). Murray was also secretary of the Council of the University of the Cape of Good Hope, then the examining university.

DIARY 5

The S.G.E.'s Diary of a tour to Butterworth, etc., in the East, and Kenhardt, etc., in the North-West

3/10/11 to 23/10/11

3/10/11 Tuesday

(**Cape Town**)

Said goodbye to Mam and Rita on the stoep at a quarter to eight, feeling glad that Rita was there. At Capetown found Inspector Craib, Duffett and Freeman waiting, and was introduced to the substitute for our old coach 362. It looked well, but having been got only at the last moment was not very shipshape, and was exceedingly poorly lit. It turned out not to be the property of the Railway Department but to belong to Pauling's firm, and not having been recently used, the electric gear was all out of order, while no alternative for electric light was provided. Just as we were starting, candles were secured, without candlesticks, and a lamp was impounded. It thus took some time to shake down, and I had an uneasy feeling on steaming out of the station that something or other had been forgotten.[126] Fortunately I had pencilled a number of directions to Freeman in the train from Rosebank to Capetown, including an order to look after Mam's birthday and a present for Rita by taking out to them himself six Waterman pens to choose from. Our first supper on board was a marked success, save for the light. The cook turned out to be a young Portuguese obtained from the Railway Catering Department – quite superior-looking to all his predecessors. My bedroom was roomy and comfortable, furnished among other things with a writing-table and a pigeon-holed desk. The common room was large and well seated; the bathroom was as good as that of the old coach, and as for the stoep, it was a perfect treat, being broad enough not to be encumbered by a nice Madeira chair in which one could lounge at ease. On the whole, things looked promising. It would be strange if Cuthbert did not commandeer a lamp or two before another evening came. In this mood I went early to bed.

4/10/11 Wednesday

(**Fraserburg Road; De Aar**)

Not up until eight o'clock, having passed Matjiesfontein some time before. Breakfast was even a greater success than the previous evening's dinner. Most of the day was spent in the stoep wicker-chair, where reading could be done with perfect comfort and with a nice current of fresh air playing around one. I consequently made great progress with my mathematical work, Schellbach's paper of 1836 and Ligowski's of 1861.[127] The flowers in some parts of the Karroo were abundant – for example, for many miles on both sides of Prince Albert Road; when we got to Fraserburg Road there were none to speak of. In the evening I read two sketches from 'Mad Shepherds', which greatly tickled Cuthbert. In the evening, too, the temperature had fallen a little, and one could look forward to a fair night's rest after getting away from De Aar.

5/10/11 Thursday

(**Steynsburg; Stormberg Junction; Sterkstroom**)

Awake at Steynsburg with the cries of hotel touts sounding strangely in my ears. Reached Stormberg Junction about breakfast-time, and settled down to work. Prepared article on the abolition of Poor Schools for the 'Gazette', and copied it out for myself in time to catch

---

126 'shake down': on the bottom of the firebox of a steam locomotive, there are grates to hold the fire, and an ashpan underneath. The grates are shaken either manually or (in a larger locomotive) by a powered grate shaker. This is known as the process of shaking down.

127 Two German mathematicians, Karl Heinrich Schellbach (1805–1892) and Wilhelm Ligowski (1821–1893).

the Capetown train. Leaving about five o'clock, we reached Sterkstroom in the dark. Dr. Robertson joined us on the stoep, where we smoked and talked gossip about Queenstown affairs, educational and medical. It was eleven o'clock before we got away.

6/10/11 Friday

(**Dordrecht Station**; *Dordrecht*; **Sterkstroom; Queenstown**)

Awoke at Dordrecht Station with Dordrecht three miles away. After breakfast came a tele-phone message stating that a cart was arranged for, and that the School Board would meet shortly after my arrival. In due course the cart came, accompanied by the Rev. Marais, for many years minister of Molteno. The drive to the town was very interesting in comparison with what I remembered of my first visit nineteen years ago. After some delay, a meeting of the Board was brought about, the members turning up being Hogsett, the influential storekeeper; Fish the ditto draper; Dr. Rowland, Mr. Klee, and the sea lawyer Vermooten, with the Rev. Marais in the chair. The great list of agenda was less lengthily discussed than they had anticipated and, on the whole, an amicable understanding was reached. The A1 School was next visited (headmaster, Chisholm) and the poor utilization of the splendid site duly noted. Then I lunched with Mrs. and the Rev. Marais, who were very friendly and sent me off with a parcel of home-grown rhubarb. The parson drove us to the station, and he and Dr. Rowland chatted with me until the train arrived.

On reaching Sterkstroom, there was again a longish wait, but we at last got off on the tail-end of the 'Kafir mail'. Reached Queenstown in due course, and went promptly off to bed, from which I heard the voice of Dr. Logie making inquiries in vain.

7/10/11 Saturday

(**Queenstown; Amabele**)

Kirkby, the School Board secretary, arrived at about nine o'clock to make arrangements; then came Dr. and Mrs. Logie with their baby boy and a bouquet of roses; next Captain Whindus, the chairman of the Board, who talked business until his fellow members arrived. Of these, the most interesting was Shearer the ex-chairman, son of the U.P. Minister of

Fig. P: Queenstown 1895. E.H. Short. DRISA PB0242. Transnet Heritage Library Photo Collection.

Larkhall in Lanarkshire! Visited with them the new site of the Girls' School, the present Girls' School (Miss Webb) with its tumble-down Kindergarten room, the Boys' School (Mr. Wilkinson) with its scarcity of accommodation, and then returned to the coach. Meanwhile it had been discovered that Miss Cogan was in town examining the mission schools and Dr. Logie had gone for her and brought her to the station. Had tea with her on the stoep of the coach while the others waited, and gossiped of Lovedale, merely broaching the subject of Miss Dunsmore's marriage. There was, I think, mutual regret at having to depart without more gossip. Left at one o'clock. Would have liked to sit on the carriage stoep and survey the pleasing landscape with its green fields and its wattle trees in blossom, but there was a tendency to rain and the temperature was uncomfortably low. At Tylden saw in the distance 'the blighted begonia', now known to Mr. Cuthbert as 'Mother Cameron', and her assistant Miss Cluver, daughter of Dr. (!) Cluver of Stellenbosch. Reached Amabele in the evening. Before turning in had a short walk in the varying moonlight along the line. Cuthbert having found a crony in Robinson, the chief engineer of construction, was not in any haste to go to bed.

8/10/11 Sunday

(*Amabele*)

Cold during the night, but lovely by dressing-time. The sights of the country were full of interest. First there passed on the road a hundred yards away two horsemen of brave mien with long fishing-rods held like spears. Then a little later in the opposite direction came two young fellows and a girl on horseback – the horses good, the men's clothes rough and ready, and the girl's habit a common print dress. Lastly, from the grassy hillside, a railway clerk or other official strode along with a basin of newly gathered mushrooms. I was surprised to find, therefore, that at breakfast a basin of mushrooms was served, Cuthbert having followed the example of his brother official. My morning walk was along the railway in the Butterworth direction, being continued until Amabele was on the opposite side of the valley, its dozen red-roofed houses looking out from the young trees of the camp. Further away, somewhat past the shoulder of the knoll, was Kei Road Station. When I returned at eleven o'clock, Engineer Robinson, whom I had met at George three years ago, called and we had a drink together and an interesting talk about Venezuela, Caracas, etc., which he had come to know in the pursuit of his profession. About one o'clock Inspector Bond arrived by train, having walked eight miles from Kingwilliamstown to catch it. Lunch followed, and it was quite jovial, for Bond had brought a bottle of Niersteiner,[128] which put Santhagen[129] into the shade. A cinder in my eye, which had been causing me considerable pain, was poked and dabbed at by Cuthbert and Bond with no good effect. Took a walk in the afternoon with Bond to the top of the plateau to see the valley with the Kei Road Station on the opposite side. Bond left at seven, and the evening train at nine brought in several coaches of noisy Kafirs, who were not aids to sleep. Went to bed early to nurse my sore eye.

9/10/11 Monday

(*Butterworth*; *opening of Butterworth Public School*)

Awoke early. After much yelling and miscellaneous noise among the Kafir passengers, the train began to move, at about six o'clock. The morning was bright and cold. By breakfast time we had reached Komgha, and just when we were about to leave the station, two

128 Nierstein is a wine-growing region in Rheinhessen, Germany.

129 A wine made by the French origin distiller, René Santhagens, principally known for having introduced the Cognac method of distillation into the Cape.

Fig. Q: Butterworth Public School, viewed from the north side, photographed a couple of years after Muir opened the new building in October 1911. Collection: Mark Finnigan via William Martinson.

advocates came to call, one of them being the younger Currey, whom I had known in Capetown and lost sight of for years, and the other a younger Upington, who was new to me. The descent down the Kei Bridge proved more enjoyable than ever, the easy chair on the broad stoep of the coach helping to make it so. During a longish halt at the station on the other side of the Kei, another advocate called who appeared to know me well; then came another who was introduced as Gardiner and a Rhodes scholar. Just as the train was about to start, I asked them to stay and sent a message to Currey and Upington to join us at eleven o'clock tea. As a consequence, we had a very pleasant all-round chat while ascending to Toleni Bridge. The unknown advocate remembered my reading 'Gunga Din' to Sir David Gill in the drawing room at Mowbray Hall many years ago, and I then guessed him to be a Stapleton, which was right. This made me read to them 'How I tried to act the Good Samaritan' from 'Mad Shepherds', and they were greatly pleased.[130] Another acquaintance met in the train was Liefeldt of Alice, who it seems acts as Kafir interpreter on circuit, and I learned of the death of Mzimba. At Ndabakazi, Inspector McLaren met me and remained to lunch with us and to talk over local affairs. On reaching Butterworth I was met at the station by Warner (R.M.), Blanck (Mayor), Gerrie (headmaster), etc., and arranged as to the opening ceremony. Found a letter awaiting from Judge Graham – the Judge on Circuit – with an invitation to dinner, his registrar (McKerran) having also arrived with a verbal message. In accepting, I had a word or two with the latter, and found him to be a Scot from Edinburgh with a lot of youthful bubble. When left alone I made a few notes as heads of my proposed speech, and soon the R.M. and the others again arrived to escort me to the school. The function was quite successful, including the distribution of sports prizes and the trial of being photographed. Had afternoon tea at the coach, and was interviewed first by the Rev. Baker (Wesleyan) of [the] Lamplough Institution, and then by the Rev. Callaway (English Church), the latter being new and interesting, with a self-denying scheme for educating the Pondoland trader's children of mixed race. In the dusk I walked away back along the railway, as I did at my last visit. Cuthbert accompanied me to

130 *Mad Shepherds, and Other Human Studies* (1910) by L.P. Jacks.

Judge Graham's to dinner at 7.30, but left early along with McKerran, so that I had a long and cheery conversation on the subject of Hertzog, politics, etc. At 10.30 I was called for to take a look in at the Mayor's ball, where I found about forty couples enjoying themselves to the music of the slowest and dreariest of waltz tunes. Spoke to the Mayoress (Mrs. Blanck, a massive German), to the ex-Mayor (Taylor), to the advocates Currey and Upington, etc. and then had a final whisky and soda with the Mayor. Reached the coach with McLaren and Cuthbert at one o'clock, and talked on the stoep until a quarter to two.

10/10/11 Tuesday

(**Komgha**; opening of Komgha Public School)

Awoke early, there being nobody moving save Kafirs passing on the way to work. The morning being warm, I sat on my bed and copied out the last page or so of my account of Hankel's paper on orthosymmetric determinants.[131] Before Robert came with tea, I had finished, which means that all the mathematical work taken with me had been done. Mr. Gerrie and Mr. Alexander of the 'Transkei Gazette' called to say goodbye, and Inspector McLaren joined us to travel as far as Toleni Bridge. Thereafter I had a pleasant afternoon dictating and writing notes for the 'Education Gazette'. In the bed of the Kei River, the heat was excessive, our stay of forty minutes on the east side to allow a goods train being a little of a torture. Most of the passengers had walked across and sheltered themselves in the so-called hotel until the train came across. All the way up the winding ascent, I sat on the stoep and enjoyed the view, while Cuthbert slept. At last the heat proved overpowering, and I had to lie down, only to be suddenly awakened at Komgha to receive official visitors – Mr. Swan (chairman of the School Board), Mr. Campbell (secretary of the Board), Dr. Shanks (chairman of the School Committee), Dr. Seale, Mr. Snyman and Mr. de Kock. Conversation formal save for the contribution of old Campbell and of Dr. Seale, who had once practised in Wishaw and knew the Scotts of Garrion. After them, to my surprise, came the Rev. Stroebel of Griquatown, who it seems had just been inducted at Komgha. In the afternoon I paid a visit to the new building, being conducted over it by the chairman of the School Board and Mr. Williamson, the headmaster. Saw at once that fencing and one or two other things were necessary but did not commit myself. On returning to the coach, I spent two mortal hours on the Komgha building papers. The two large volumes and the six years of correspondence were very annoying. Cuthbert did not return until 7.30, his time having been spent in allaying his thirst and in hearing the grievances of the place. The abstention of the R.M. (Mr. Garstin) from educational affairs, it appeared, was due to the neglect which he had experienced at Tarkastad; and the A.R.M. (Van Aardt) attempted to justify the abstention. The station master (Phillips, late of Matjiesfontein) called with his hand-lamp to guide us to the hotel. We found the dining room and dinner exactly as they appeared four years ago. The absence of O'Connell, however, was greatly felt. Swan, the chairman, had little social skill, and the guests were not forward in making advances. My right-hand neighbour was the kindly young Irish doctor, Seale, he having on his right Kidd of the post office. I ascertained that Mrs. Seale was Dr. Shanks' sister and that both doctors had come out from Ireland during the war. Dinner dragged along until my reply speech, when the ice thawed. The songs were not enlivening. Stroebel spoke well and wisely. Finally, an opportunity came, and I asked leave to propose the chairman's health. Campbell's health I adroitly linked on, thereby succeeding in working in some fun about the auditors and in ensuring two replies. Campbell's speech of thanks and reminiscences was uproariously amusing – his school life at Greenock, his examination by

---

131 Hermann Hankel (1839–1873), German mathematician known for introducing the Hankel matrix and the Hankel transform.

Fig. R: Blaney Junction, Station Buildings and Platforms, 1895. DRISA P0291. E.H. Short. Transnet Heritage Library Photo Collection.

Dr. McCulloch (author of the famous 'Course of Reading'), his dislike of Grammar.[132] By the time it was over, we were a roomful of brothers. 'God save the King' was sung heartily, and 'Auld Lang Syne' with clasped hands!

11/10/11 Wednesday
(*Komgha; Amabele; Blaney Junction*)

Rose late (8.45). Morning misty and very dull. Swan and Campbell called about 10.30 to escort me to the building. There was a nice little gathering. The magistrate (Garstin) turned up, and was quite friendly. He knew Kenhardt and we talked of the journey thither. Mrs. Seale I met and found quite charming, her accent being sweetly marked with a surface ripple from Dublin. Another lady who looked capable was Miss Weir, the Kindergarten teacher. The whole went off quite nicely, and after partaking of tea and cake I left. In my speech, I omitted reference to the gift of so beautiful a site, but I wrote at once to Dr. Shanks to make up. Took an hour's quiet walk along the railway as on a former occasion, and on returning to lunch, found that a goods train going in our direction had unexpectedly turned up. The station master was hurriedly interviewed, and as a consequence, we were hooked on and wafted off, leaving apologies to the Rev. Stroebel and any others that might call. Reached Amabele in due course, where we had to wait two hours. Took a long and lonely walk on the railway, in the opposite direction this time – that is to say, towards Kei Road – and came across a *Solanum* new to me, with a flower and red fruit. On returning we joined another goods train bound for Blaney. The night was dark and the wind cold. Shortly after reaching the station at nine o'clock, I found that it was bedtime.

12/10/11 Thursday
(*Blaney Junction; King William's Town; Alice; Cookhouse*)

A good night. Awoke early, and on looking out, found myself at Blaney in full view of a field of railway 'sleepers'. Morning grey and damp, but not cold. Took a walk of an hour and a

132 *Course of Elementary Reading in Science and Literature* (1849) by J.M. McCulloch.

half along the Kingwilliamstown railway and mooned and meditated. Our train started at about eleven o'clock, and we were soon in King, where our first caller was Inspector Bond, with a letter from Mrs. Bond and an addition to our commissariat. The only other person on the platform was Archdeacon Holmes, who was taken by surprise when he saw me passing out of the station and made a boyish spasm of salute. Cuthbert had sent a message to Dr. Roberts of Lovedale, suggesting that he should meet me at Redhill, and another to Henderson telling him of my passing Alice, where anything urgent or important might be discussed. The two worthies reversed their roles, and Henderson had a good first innings, hanging on at Alice till almost the starting of the train, although he knew of Roberts and Cowan. The two latter, when the way was clear, of course came with a rush, and were excited in their efforts to counteract the supposed Henderson effect. "Houghton was a broken man," Roberts said, and "Henderson was chastened." The visit of the Free Church Commission from Scotland was too big a subject to enter on in any fulness, but the remarks if few were not wanting in strength. Of course I could not but poke fun at Roberts about Emgwali, but that matter had to be kept within bounds. The journey thenceforward was only memorable by reason of a thunderstorm – one of the worst I ever saw. At first the lightening played all round us at a considerable distance, but finally we went into the disturbed area, and then the flashes and thunder and rain became terrific. Although it was grand and impressive and interesting, we were quite glad to leave it in the rear. Cookhouse was reached at about eleven o'clock. Cuthbert disappeared as usual on school business, and did not return until one. Meanwhile the rain poured heavily, and thunder again came and wakened me at twelve. The consequence was that I had two hours' enforced reading of 'Nature'.

13/10/11 Friday

(**Cradock**; *opening of new hall at Cradock Girls' High School*)

Awoke when starting from Cookhouse; reached Cradock a little after nine; bad thunder-shower. Met by Mr. du Plessis and Mr. van Niekerk (secretary). Found ceremony was to be made an opportunity for requests or demands and cut off the forenoon's programme.

Fig. S: Cookhouse, Train in Station, 1895. DRISA P0071. E.H. Short. Transnet Heritage Library Photo Collection.

Inspectors Russell and Craib turned up unexpectedly, and we had arranged for Inspector Spurway, who joined us with his baggage. Pleasant chat until lunch. After lunch the Rev. Reinecke called. At 2.15 the two Board deputies came again and carried me off to see the Boys' High School and the Poor School in regard to additional accommodation. Then came the Board meeting, with Butler the irritating in the chair. Attended to what was needed, and firmly resisted his monomania about further boarding accommodation. Drove next to the Girls' High School, and suggested tea to Miss Collingwood – which was scarcely fair when her place was dismantled to provide tea for us at the Hockly Hall. Formal opening with the Rev. White in charge, and cadets as guard of honour.[133] White very kind in his speech on handing key; own speech exceedingly well received. Reinecke made a very flattering speech, and Butler was in bad taste as usual. Pleasant tea afterwards, where I met the new C.C.[134] (Bellairs from Caledon) and his wife, and the C.C. from Stellenbosch (Hewett) and his wife. Miss Murray from Sea Point was attractive looking in her white hair. Miss Collingwood bore herself well all through. Back to [the] coach, where we had another tea on [the] stoep with Inspectors Russell and Craib. Mr. Reinecke called again to say a warm word of goodbye. Left at six, and had a jolly dinner with Inspector Spurway for guest. Told the story of Inspector Hagen and his masonic rig-out, ending in his being asked for a medical certificate; we all laughed until sore. Went soon to bed. Post having brought a volume of Sylvester from the Public Library, I read a little, but soon fell asleep.

14/10/11 Saturday

(***Norval's Pont***; *visit to Harmsworth's farm; Venterstad; Biscuitfontein;* ***Norval's Pont***)

Wakened at Norval's Pont early to find air sharp and clear. Soon in bustle of preparation for journey. Left by cart at 7.15, feeling cheerful and fit. The first farm we passed turned out to be Harmsworth's, of old Colesberg fame. Reached Venterstad about eleven and set to work at once. Young Bergh, of Schweizer and Bergh, got hold of and meeting of factions arranged for, six and six.[135] Adjournment to site near kopjes. Is the story not written and sent to Duffett? Some English farmers in town, e.g., Harold Anderson (originally of Capetown), Harris, etc. Saw the notorious young Van der Heever, husband of a Crosbie of Capetown; Irish Dr. Coates, who married a Van de Heever who took drugs, etc.; Schierhout, the giggling and talkative magistrate, etc. Bergh the best of all. Hurried up and was ready to start on return journey by one o'clock. Reached Biscuitfontein about two and outspanned at the spruit for lunch. Having borrowed a gridiron from the innkeeper, we lit a fire and old John cooked the lamb chops, while we were having our first course of polony and cold bacon. Meal thoroughly enjoyed, as we had breakfasted at 6.45. Journey tiresome, with a blazing sun in our faces and with anxiety about the train. Reached Norval's Pont about 5.40, while coach was being put on to the end of the goods. Bathed our burned faces in dop,[136] dined sparsely, and then I dictated [a] memorandum until bedtime. Went to bed quite tired out.

---

133 The opening ceremony was to open the new hall of the Cradock High School, the Hockly Hall (a memorial to a Miss Hockly, who had been a teacher at the school). Muir's speech at the ceremony was, fittingly, a tribute to Miss Hockly, as he notes that he reproduced the tribute a couple of days later on 15/10/11 Sunday (presumably for publication).

134 Civil Commissioner.

135 This is a terse sentence: there were two opposing factions of six persons, with whom separate meetings were held.

136 'dop' (South African slang): alcohol.

15/10/11 Sunday
(*Naauwpoort; De Aar*)

Awoke in Naauwpoort to find morning air sharp and bright. After breakfast walked back along the railway towards Norval's Pont. Watched dung-rolling beetles at work. In one case, the spouse was crunched on the ball and was being trundled along by the vigorous head of the household. She received many bad bumps, but never budged. If a more than common accident happened, the worker hurried up to her to ascertain if all were right, and then took to work again with renewed vigour. In another case, there were two fighting for the crown. At the close of the second round, the defeated beetle first thought of trying a third, but changing his mind, took to the air with a revengeful hum, trying to make believe that he would live to fight another day. Back to coach by about 11.30. Sought the shade and reproduced as well as I could my tribute to Miss Hockly. Mr. Sorrie, the successor to Mr. Smith who died a week or two after I left for England, called and I had a talk with him about Free State education and especially about his experiences at Brandfort, where he had been headmaster. English teachers in the Free State, he said, had fallen in number from about 200 to 70. Hertzog's law, pure and simple, he stated, was not in force anywhere, and neither Dutch nor English was as well taught as before. During Hertzog's period of legislation, the feeling between the two races, which had been quietly improving, grew more bitter than during the war. After lunch I worked again at paragraphs for the 'Gazette', knowing that the acting editor would be pressed. About four o'clock a goods train came in, and after saying goodbye to Dr. Baird and Mr. Sorrie, we (not Cuthbert) left for the north, Cuthbert to overtake us at Dwaal by the passenger train, which was to start later. Read Sylvester, Vol. II., in the shade on the stoep. Sure enough, at Dwaal the dashing passenger came past and deposited Cuthbert from the dining saloon. Saw someone waving to me from the last saloon, and was delighted to find that it was Dr. Smartt. I just managed to shake hands across the six-foot way. Returned to quiet mathematical work, shaded from the western sun; then when dusk came on, we dined, and finally got into De Aar close on the heels of the passenger. Dr. Smartt sent word across to the siding that he would call after his dinner. Cuthbert disappeared willingly, and the consequence was a talk that lasted from eight to ten-thirty. The light died down, and we sat and discussed Hertzog and Botha appropriately in the gloom. Then we had a whisky and soda and still talked, agreeing to continue tomorrow on the way to Britstown.[137]

16/10/11 Monday
(*Britstown; Prieska*)

Disturbed during the night, and on getting up about 1.30, found bright light issuing from Cuthbert's room, the cause being that he had fallen asleep after plastering his face with lanoline and had forgotten his table lamp. A shunt might have caused an upset and fired the coach. Rose early and read some Sylvester. Morning bright, and De Aar looking more attractive than usual. After breakfast we shunted into [the] end of Prieska branch platform, where I sat on the stoep and worked till the through passenger trains came in. One of the passengers in a full train from Capetown was the fat boy from Pickwick, but so improved in status as to be able to travel first class. To emphasise his enormous bulk, he led about a tiny terrier with a rug about the size of the boards of a shilling novel. The other members of his family were normal and were cheery and fresh-coloured like himself. The crowded

---

137 It is not surprising to find Smartt heading for Britstown by train. Smartt had been a physician in that town and farmed near there as well. Despite being an active parliamentarian in Cape Town, he maintained good relationships with farmers.

train implied emigration. Did not get away until 11.45. Dr. Smartt joined us at Brand, the first station, and left us at Britstown, having had a long talk and joined us at lunch. (Picture in 'Argus' of the concert at Bloemfontein, the singers being Dutch, Afrikaans, Taal, Very High Dutch, and the child at their feet with his leesboek.)[138] Long wait at Britstown; Dr. Smartt off in his motor before we started. He said the parson of Kenhardt was in the train. Spent a couple of hours going over the papers connected with the Kenhardt school building; and felt full of wrath at the misconduct of business and at the P.W.D. in particular. Reached some wayside station at 5.20, where we had a halt of half-an-hour, during which Cuthbert interviewed the Rev. Volsteedt. Wired in consequence to the C.C. of Prieska that, leaving on Tuesday morning, we must be back on Friday night to catch Saturday's train to Capetown. After dinner sat out on the stoep and studied the stars; Santhagen of Stellenbosch having provided us with a better claret in quarts than in pints and this being our first quart, we were quite without care – or rather I was, for Cuthbert and Robert had to pack for tomorrow's early start. The commissariat for four days on the veld was no small matter – two fowls, half a cold ham, lamb chops, etc., and a dozen bottles of beer. And yet we must travel light, because of the speed to be insisted on. Reached Prieska at 8.20, only fifteen minutes after time. The first to board the coach were ex-mayor Lawrence and the A.R.M., Van Alphen, son of the old teacher of that name. Lawrence was Jewish as of old; Van Alphen wished eagerly to help with [the] journey; the contractor Messler, on hearing of the hurried back journey, talked of £25! and of impossibilities. Had him in and in the presence of the others, talked to him in business fashion; when he left, he was subdued and moderate. Next came Todd of MacIvor's forwarding agency, and he repaid his enemy Lawrence. Hubbard the station master came to hand in letters, etc. Amusing memorandum of guidance from Inspector Grant, who was kept by the flood on the other side of the Orange River at Upington. Mad platelayer called to have his faulty arm attended to by the 'Doctor'. Policeman Gash also called, and contributed to the discussion about the difficulties of our journey. He is the brother of Miss Gash, formerly of Qumbu and part-heroine of Cuthbert's kitchen adventures there. Packing began at ten: a great undertaking which occupied an hour and a half. Went to bed impressed with the fact that the great effort of our lives was going to be made. To be called at four o'clock and to start at five.

17/10/11 Tuesday

(**Prieska;** via Klipfontein; Marydale; visit to Brakboschpoort)

Wakened at one o'clock by movements outside and had some difficulty in falling asleep again. Lit lamp twice to see that all was right. At 3.45 the call of the veld alarm-clock came, and I refused to budge until four. Dressed by 4.30, and found an excellent cup of coffee and a slice of buttered toast on my table on returning from the bathroom. Cart arrived about the same time, Messler himself coming to see us off. Morning fresh and clear with a sickle moon. Started at 4.45, finding need before we had gone far to put our coats over our knees. Daylight began to break soon after, and before an hour or so, the rays were on our backs and the shadows of the horses were right ahead of them on the road. Vegetation by the wayside poor in the extreme, the only tree a stunted thorn. By 6.15 the farmhouse of Mr. Coetzee, M.P.C., came in sight in the hollow, with a flock of goats on the slope behind it. Mr. Coetzee had been on the outlook and met us at his gate. To my surprise he was comparatively young and slim and spoke English with ease and well. We dismounted and took coffee on the stoep, with the tiny square of garden in front bright with petunias and other modest flowers. Mrs. Coetzee, who brought the coffee, was prematurely aged

138 'leesboek' (Afrikaans): reading book.

and worn, but had a kindly smile among her wrinkles and spoke English naturally. The School Board of Kenhardt was freely criticized and the special wants of the North-West were discussed; and then we sped on our way, Mr. Coetzee smilingly doubting our ability to reach Prieska in time for Saturday's train. By 7.30 we had reached Klipfontein, where we stopped to breakfast by the wayside. A fire of twigs gave us excellent chops, and these with bread and beer made us happy, sitting in the shade of the cart, I on Cuthbert's tin box and Cuthbert on a cart cushion. By the time we had inspanned, the sun was telling us what to expect later. The hour of leaving was 8.45, and we started refreshed. Cuthbert soon dozed, and after an hour we took a whiff to encourage conversation.[139] The landscape never varied, the road being hard on the limestone outcrops and sandy in the red bottoms. The vegetation also never altered; the everlasting witgatbosch (?)[140] and 'aarddoorn'[141] reigned alone, and were shrivelled and stunted at that. By 11.15 we approached the second outspan, marked only by a more-than-usually gnarled thorn tree. Shade was hard to get, because the leaves were the size of tea-leaves; but the tin box and a cushion were requisitioned, and we had a drink of beer with a couple of 'Marie' biscuits that were sweet enough for a thee-partij.[142] No house had been seen since the previous outspan, and there was none yet in sight. The road was visible for a great distance, making straight for a low range of hills, behind which, we were told, Marydale was situated. Our driver, a little wizened youth who spoke English well, showed us the direction in which Draghoender lay, a road going off to the right, about three miles back, being the one which led to it. Just as we were about to start, a cart was seen coming over the rise behind us, and we at once thought of the Kenhardt parson (Volsteedt) and his ouderling.[143] Sure enough it was, and when they had outspanned we hobnobbed. Liebenberg, as the ouderling was called, knew no English, but we learned from him how he had been delayed leaving Prieska till 6.30, and we could see for ourselves what good horses he had. Our next scoff[144] was only six miles, namely, to Stuurman, where we found a beautiful pond of water raised by air-pumps, and where we lunched. Just as we had finished, the farmer (Mr. Snyman) came along to let his cows out of the kraal, and we got into conversation. He proved very intelligent and spoke good English and was evidently a pushing progressive man. Our boy John put a shoe on one of the horses while conversation lasted, and to our chagrin, the parson's team overtook us again and passed us. The next hour and a half was hot and tiresome, and Cuthbert and I both wobbled and slept. Marydale, we were at last told, was behind the rise, and we bestirred ourselves. It turned out to be a few scattered houses in a fertile flat. The hotel, store, etc., we found to be in the hands of a young Scotsman named Bayne, who was running them for Stephen Fraser and Co. of Port Elizabeth, they having taken them over for the debts of the previous owner. Bayne was evidently good stuff and was already hoping to find a purchaser at a price which would repay the owners, who of course have no wish to do retail business. The approaching Sunday was to be nachtmaal, and great preparations were afoot – the store replenished in all its departments, temporary beds placed in every corner, loads of

---

139 'whiff': he must mean 'a breath of fresh air', in the sense of a brisk walk.

140 The witgat tree (*Boscia oleioides*), Shepherd's tree in English, named because of its conspicuous white trunk.

141 Possibly a reference to the Karroo thorn tree (*Vachellia karroo*), a species of acacia.

142 Muir's own invention of Dutch/Afrikaans, a 'tea party'.

143 'ouderling' (Afrikaans): church elder (in the Dutch Reformed Church).

144 'scoff' (South African slang): 'food'. It came to be used during the Anglo-Boer War, because the rations from England were consigned to the Senior Commissioned Officer, S.C.OFF, and hence associated with food by the troops.

food got in readiness, and even the bar-shelves stocked with all varieties of liquor.[145] Was introduced to two Jeppes, who told me all their Capetown connections – the Jeppes, their grandfather Landsberg, their sisters Mrs. Lithmann; Mrs. d'Astre, I was sorry to hear, was dead. They freely talked of all the school inspectors they had had, Theron (though an Afrikander) being the only unpopular one. Marydale is the property of Gert Snyman (member of the defunct School Board which I am to resurrect), and was named after his wife (Maria); it is hoped soon to be a municipality, when a church will be built. The beery-looking Jeppe told me of the sale of old Landsberg's pictures at ruinous prices, and how he had bought a life-sized Adam and Eve for fifty shillings: he seemed to think that if the figures had been clothed, he would have got the pictures for less. A policeman called who had yesterday crossed the Orange River with Inspector Grant, and we gathered that Grant might meet us at Marydale on our return. Franz Snyman called and the teacher Venter, the former a brother of Gert Snyman and given to local preaching, the latter a raw-boned recruit from Robertson. Bayne brought in his wife, a cheery young matron from Dundee: her husband has been ten years and she nine in South Africa. Last of all, we were shown Bayne's pretty pair of horses, which answered to the word of command like soldiers, and yet not through fear. We began our last lap about 5.15, having about nine miles to go to Brakboschpoort. On arrival, old Jeppe gave a most kindly welcome, and led us into his homely building. There he slowly dribbled on in talk, the subject being his 21 years of experience at his present place, his 18 years of experience of schoolteachers, his disappointment with his neighbours as to education, etc. etc. When we proposed a move, we learned we had to share the same bed, much after the fashion of our Fraserburg tour. The question of supper was apparently in no haste of solution, and I left Cuthbert to hurry up matters. In view of our early start, we should have been in bed by eight. Mrs. Jeppe was a contrast, being vigorous both in speech and action: her opinions on lady teachers were quite refreshing. We got off to bed at 8.30, Cuthbert sleeping on a stretcher beside the cart, where his bed was made by Mrs. Jeppe, while Miss Robey the teacher held the candle. For some time, I lay awake, listening to Mr. Jeppe, Mrs. Jeppe and Cuthbert talking in the kitchen.

18/10/11 Wednesday

(Via Rooiputs; Kenhardt)

Wakened at 3.15, and on lighting my candle, heard Cuthbert and John talking in the direction of the cart. Cuthbert came over and finding me up, proposed starting at once. Dressing took about ten minutes, the most lengthy part of it consisting in rubbing my lips and cheeks with lanoline. Cuthbert packed up while I stumbled out in the dark to see how John was getting on. The rugs had been rolled up, and now the kit-bag, etc., were roped on; and John had gone for the horse when old Mr. Jeppe appeared, mumbling in his usual undertone, his hair tousled, his braces in loops by his side. He was concerned that we were starting without coffee, and we professed to be coffee-haters. He still kept mumbling in explanation of his being late, and when he suggested milk and whisky, I agreed cheerily, and away he went shuffling in the darkness. On the stoep by the light of a spluttering candle we measured our whisky-tots and filled the glasses half up with boiled milk, and tossed the mixture off having little taste of what we had swallowed. Then came a kindly assistance at the inspanning, a low rumble of talk reaching me from among the horses – now English to Cuthbert, now Dutch to John, while the candle stood neglected on

---

145 'nachtmaal' (Dutch): the Eucharistic sacrament in the Dutch Reformed Church ('nagmaal' in Afrikaans). In rural areas, the nagmaal gathering was an important get-together amongst the rural folk from outlying farms, who otherwise saw their neighbours rarely.

the ground. At last all was ready and we took our seats while Jeppe explained to John at the leaders' heads how the main road was to be reached. Good old man, he felt John might still have trouble, and we started, leaving Cuthbert's stretcher a white patch in the darkness; he stumbling ahead to show the way. Sitting in the cart we had no idea where we were going, and only occasionally did we get a glimpse of the guide's shirt or grey head, and still rarer did we hear his explanatory undertone. At length he thought we might be trusted to our own devices, and he let the horses pass him; his goodness was most touching, and we called out a kindly goodbye and thanked him, receiving his good wishes in return. The last glimpse of his rugged head and looped-up braces remained with us for some distance, and would have remained longer, had we not lost the spoor in the darkness. How we ever recovered it I cannot tell, but we were quite thankful when we reached the main road. At this point the sickle moon rose on the horizon behind us, but was of no use by reason of the clouds. Meanwhile the outside temperature was not rising and ours was falling. When the starting hour of the previous day was reached, we were not nearly so comfortable. The wind caught us in front, and a heavy cloud rose in the west. At six we outspanned for forty minutes, but so cold was it that we kept our seats while we dispatched two hard-boiled eggs and a glass of beer. Our next two hours were spent on a most tiresome perfectly straight road; Cuthbert slept and I nodded; and both were heartily thankful when we spied Rooiputs in the hollow. Here we properly breakfasted, making a fire and cooking chops in the approved fashion. The place did not turn out as Grant painted: the mad schoolmaster was gone, and indeed the school was found to be closed. Although there were several shanties round about, as well as the farmer's house, we had little intercourse with the people. Cuthbert inspected a bakkies pump,[146] which brought the water up from about 30 feet. The sun broke through while we outspanned, and we returned to the cart much warmer than when we dismounted. Our next scoff was to be longer and we set out at 9.45. It was wearisome in the extreme, and took us three hours. We outspanned this time quite close to the air-pump and cement tank, and though the water was good, we remained true to beer. Just as we were inspanning, Parson Volsteedt drove up, much to our surprise after his boasting promises of the previous day. His excuse was that he had been unable to leave till 8.30 because his horses were on the veld and had to be sent for. He was equally surprised to see us, having no idea that we would rise at 3.15 and leave before 4. He was in charge of a fresh ouderling, whose name sounded like Christie, and who had an excellent pair of horses. We left first, but after half-an-hour or so we were overtaken, and before long we were left well in the rear. Owing however to the comparative coolness of the day, we made an excellent run, arriving at Kenhardt at 3.15. The whole buildings of the place seemed poor, except the Church and Pastorie, the former being ornate and pretentious and having cost £4,000. The hotel, kept by a Jew, was inexcusably primitive in its bedrooms, but there was an outside bathroom with a geyser, which gave us hot water in a few minutes, and a good bath was secured although the door refused to go nearer than two inches to closing. What a pleasure it was to feel shaved and clean after two days! The School Board secretary (Sachs) called and recalled after I had dressed, and, in his company, I visited the present school building and the deserted boarding-house, bought at a cost of £600 and now a home for stray goats. We picked up Mr. P. Connan on the way (see Grant's letter) and I had a good talk with him about the present trouble. To my surprise he knew Uncle Steven of Glasgow, but was unaware of his death and the death of Aunt Maggie. It is really true that he owns a quarter of a million acres. After returning to the hotel I received a visit from Duhring

---

146 'bakkiespomp' (Afrikaans): this was a water lift that dipped buckets on a chain into a deep well. A donkey was attached to the water lift by a beam, and by walking in circles, the donkey worked the pump/lift.

the magistrate, Dr. Sinton, Connan and Sachs with a view to fixing the Board meeting for eight. We talked on things in general on the stoep, and then they left in order to have their own preliminary meeting, and we arranged to have supper at seven. Till then I strolled in the grey of the gloaming, up and down in front of the hotel. The magistrate duly came for me, and a plain-spoken meeting ensued. All the members were present except Loxton, who was in Capetown, and a distant country member. The time occupied was 2½ hours and the conclusion arrived at was what I sought, viz., resume office and trust to me to do what I had originally intended. How much better the outcome would have been had they not listened to the excitable Irishman! and the said man almost owned as much. After our return to the hotel, MacGregor, a traveller of Mosenthal's[147] of Port Elizabeth, came to offer a bottle of whisky for the road. This I accepted on account of his well-known character, and we learned that Sinton was at the bottom of all the school trouble, as by this time indeed I knew. MacGregor had humour and considerable insight, and it was difficult to get to bed. We turned in about eleven, however, after receiving much gossip. Cuthbert's concern about the enforced change of railway coach had by this time all disappeared on having found a crony; my only trouble to go to bed with was in connection with the proposed conferences at Bloemfontein and Pretoria.

19/10/11 Thursday
(Via Rooiputs and Brakboschpoort; Marydale)

Woke about 3.15, and as I was afraid I might fall asleep again, I wakened Cuthbert at 3.20, who after a little marched across the street with a candle and succeeded in getting hold of John and – more difficult still – in awakening him. In time the manager, who the night before promised tea, was got at and the bill was paid; but it was rather a weary cold wait for me until we started. Took two hours to reach the farm with the windmills and dipping-tank, where Mr. Volsteedt had overtaken us the day before. Passed without stopping for twenty minutes longer to a place on the veld where the horses could have a little grass, and here we had Pyott's crackers and Dutch cheese and beer. It was so cold that I determined to walk to get some heat before taking a seat in the cart again. I accordingly set off when John started for the horses and I managed a mile before I was overtaken and felt quite comfortable all through the next long stage. The sun also broke out now and again, and the air grew warmer. Rooiputs we reached about 10.10, having thus done thirty miles in six hours. Breakfast was not of the usual high quality. The bread we had taken from the coach had become dry and hard as brick, and the bread bought at Kenhardt to replace it was like porous limestone. We were living in the stone age. Chops there were none, the cold chicken was like woody fibre, and the cold ham tasted only of salt. Our sole resource was polony and biscuit: this, however, washed down with beer was not to be despised. Another trouble was the illness of one of our team, to whom laudanum had been administered followed by starch.[148] His name was Tom, and two of the others being named Noble and Why Not, it sounded reproachful when the driver touched them in succession with the whip and called out, "Tom, Why Not, Noble." While we breakfasted, old Visser the farmer leant his arms on the railing of his stoep and at a hundred yards steadily surveyed us, only altering his position now and again to direct his wife or other handy person to 'shoo' the goats off the retaining wall of the dam. This is the man whose susceptibilities Grant had urged us not to offend by referring to his teacher who had died by the roadside! We left

147 Mosenthal's was a leading Cape Colony merchant, whose business was founded on wool, hides and skins.
148 It was one of the 'team' of horses that was ill.

his place at 11.30 and started on the new straight road to Marydale. Certainly it was tiresome in the extreme; we almost seemed to see three miles of it ahead. There was now the additional trouble that the wind blowing from behind us had the same speed as ourselves, and consequently kept us enveloped in dust. After 2½ hours we reached our old outspan, the first from Brakboschpoort on the way out. Strictly speaking we should have had lunch here, but nobody felt fit. We confined ourselves therefore to a drink of beer while the horses roamed about and enjoyed the sweet grass. Our hope that the fresh horses would come as far as this from Brakboschpoort to meet us was disappointed: there was nothing for it but to proceed on towards Brakboschpoort slowly so as to spare the team that had served us so well, and especially the one that was sick. (When we repassed the dead horse we had seen yesterday, we found that it had been skinned, and John explained that this had been done to make reims.[149] To use cowhide for this purpose would have been extravagance, because ox-hide fetches £2 or £3 at the produce-buyer's, whereas a horse's skin is not saleable.) The heat was quite pleasant, the sun being usually hidden behind clouds. We started at about 2.50. It was very interesting to note on nearing Jeppe's, the road which we had the previous morning travelled in the dark, and especially the portion of it which we took under the old man's guidance. After all there was nothing to have been afraid of unless the losing of our way. The stony ridge was as bad in the light as in the dark. Old Jeppe was delighted to see us, and was generally in a brighter and cheerier frame of mind. Unfortunately, he had to tell us that the fresh horses had not arrived. During the afternoon tea he discussed the situation with his sons, and it was desired to supply a horse for our sick one to take us on to Marydale. On coming out to the stoep, the missing cart and four fresh horses were seen approaching. Our next disappointment was that Messler had sent orders to John to hand us over to the new driver and come on himself the next day. To this I yielded with reluctance, although the newcomer was in appearance of a better stamp. The change of horses being made, we said a series of goodbyes, the Jeppes having with them five sons and a daughter-in-law, and parted with Brakboschpoort with kindly feelings. The journey to Marydale, 8½ miles, was done under the hour, the horses being good and fresh and the new Jehu[150] very capable in all his requirements except English. Mr. and Mrs. Bayne were glad to see us; we had a wash, read out telegrams and prepared replies for tomorrow; supped comfortably with Mr. Bayne, Mr. Pybus (the postmaster) and three young men; and finally prepared for bed, intending to leave at 6.30.

20/10/11 Friday

(*Via Stuurman, Klipfontein and Glen Allen;* **Prieska**)

Awoke about four o'clock, but dozed until six, and found morning bright and bracing. New driver, Kruger, most punctual, and Mr. Bayne most attentive; we consequently were ready to start at the appointed minute, 6:30. Horses in prime condition, and we reached Stuurman (Mr. F. Snyman) in a minute or two over the hour.[151] Called as we had promised,

149 'reims' (origin Dutch, appears specifically to have been a word used in Africa): strips of raw-hide used as a rope or bridle.

150 Muir's biblical reference (Kings 2: 9) is obscure and not particularly apposite. Jehu was the revolutionary general who killed Joram, King of Israel; before he did so, a first, and then a second, horseman rode out to ask him if he was coming in peace. Hence Muir has applied this name to the second horseman of the trip.

151 The farm was Stuurman's Put. The name of the farm is recorded in materials relating to the fieldwork photographer, Dorothea Bleek, who visited the farm in 1911, recording the help she received from the farmer's wife, Mrs. Snyman. Muir spelt the name of the farming couple 'Snijman' but this has been corrected.

and Mrs. Snyman, a nice little body, received us, apparently because the husband was shaving.[152] She talked excellent English, too good not to awaken a suspicion that she herself was English, and we had a very pleasant chat. Snyman himself was wholesome-looking and breezy, and was evidently pleased that we had called. We stayed only ten minutes, being anxious to reach our breakfast outspan about six miles further on. On the way we recalled that Mrs. F. Snyman was a Jeppe, and all was clear. We enjoyed both the ride and the breakfast, having no tendency to sleep as we had yesterday. Our last bottle of beer was drunk, and Mrs. Bayne having given us half a loaf of decent bread and six hard-boiled eggs, we did not fare badly. We next posted on to Klipfontein, in order that the horses might have water. This we reached a few minutes before twelve, and we agreed that it would be a little shameless to have another meal; so, beer being done, we contented ourselves with broaching our solitary bottle of Santhagen's claret and having a cooling drink mixed with Van Riebeeck. Our oprechte Afrikaner had in the meantime developed a little English, and we consequently asked him to join, which he heartily did, although expressing fears as to his magen.[153] To pass the time I had before reaching Klipfontein, read to Cuthbert the story from 'Mad Shepherds' called 'Mr. Perryman's Tall Hat', and Kruger was found to be listening as attentively as if it had been a Bijbel storietje.[154] He could not resist laughing at the humour of it, or supposing he could not understand English, Cuthbert's convulsive laughter had proved contagious. The sky continued overcast, so that the heat did not annoy us; it would certainly have been scorching if the sun had come out, for there was not a breath of wind in the hollows. The farm at Klipfontein was very poor-looking and the surroundings were depressing, so we were glad to inspan again and move on. About an hour brought us to Mr. Coetzee's, which was all in the stillness of the afternoon nap. He was greatly surprised to see us, believing that if we came at all, it would be late at night. On his stoep we drank coffee twice and discussed the educational affairs of the North-West and much else. He confirmed the story we had heard about his upbringing, to the effect that he had been adopted by two old Scotsmen of the name of Stewart, been educated by them, and finally been left heir to the farm where he now lived. This accounted for the name of his farm (Glen Allen), for the good English of his household, for the books and reading material lying about, and in particular for the presence on a stoep chair of a copy of a Fifeshire newspaper! Just as we were preparing to go, a cart arrived from Prieska with the Rev. Venter on his way to Marydale for nachtmaal, and we then learned that Mr. Coetzee had got express orders to arrange for a meeting. Prieska school affairs had thus to be all gone over again and in less pleasant fashion, for the parson liked to hear the sound of his own voice, even when delivering platitudes. At length we parted in very friendly fashion, and Kruger's horses, having fed well and rested long, carried us Prieska-ward in spirited style. Again our arrival took everyone by surprise, and most of all Robert, our Portuguese cook, who had not been told of our successful pressure on Messler and did not expect us to arrive for at least another day. The coach No. 169 turned out not at all bad, and we were soon busy on our ablutions, or at any rate I was, for Cuthbert had first to think of the provisions for our remaining journey, and went to the village to forage. All the shops were shut, but he hit on Mr. Todd, who took him to his garden and gave him what vegetables he wanted, together with a fowl contribution from Mrs. Todd. Supper was soon in readiness, and we enjoyed it to the full. Shortly afterwards the Capetown train arrived, and a pile of letters with it, including Tuesday's English mail. Sorry to hear by telegram

152 'body' (Scots): a person (Muir is not making a personal comment on her looks!).

153 'oprechte' (Dutch): sincere or honest; 'maag' (Afrikaans): stomach.

154 'Bijbel storietje' (Dutch): Bible story.

that Mam's trouble had come back on her, and that she was in bed; however, I shall now be home in three days. Good news from Macmillan and Co. about the 'Rural Reader', also from Newcastle-on-Tyne Public Library.[155] The magistrate (Mr. van Noorden) called and was very kind and attentive, also ex-mayor Lawrence; and Todd and Cuthbert set off at the earliest after supper, ostensibly to call at the Post Office, which of course he could not do. I read for a little time, and then went to bed (9.30). Finished 'Nature' and the weekly London 'Times', getting up every now and then to slaughter flies with a bath towel. Although the enemy was exterminated, I could not sleep, and I next tackled my letters and telegrams, pencilling on them all the proper replies. Cuthbert returned at midnight with guarded step.

21/10/11 Saturday
(Prieska; Houwwater; Britstown; De Aar)

Rose a little unrested, and found whole sky overcast and rain drizzling. Hurried up breakfast, and visited school building, meeting Duhring, the architect, the School Board secretary, etc. The one question of importance was the proposed school wall and railing. Old Decker, the editor, turned up and was persistent, but I got off unharmed, I hope. Mr. Spijker, the surveyor, was at the station with the others to shake hands; also Messler, the cart-hirer, proud of having seen us through. In the saloon a young lady, I was told, was waiting for me, and she turned out to be the station master's tiny daughter with a pretty handful of sweet peas and ferns. Lawrence the ex-mayor handed in at the last moment a 'Sunday Post' poem on Botha, headed 'Mij Zelf en God'. After starting, I took immediately to dictating, and hadn't got half through on reaching Omdraaisvlei Station at 12.30. Up to and during lunch we worked on, but even at Houwwater Station (two o'clock) we were still struggling, the real difficulty being that the Dordrecht notes, which should have been done at the time, were set aside for a more convenient season. We were especially anxious to be finished by the time of reaching Houwwater, because we expected Dr. Smartt to join us there. As however he didn't, we were not prevented from plodding on. After finishing, we tackled the question of office accommodation, and were still at it when Britstown was reached. Here it was found that Dr. Smartt had booked his seat, but was not on the platform. I consequently had time to make a copy of the poem on Botha, which I had found clever. However, at the last moment Dr. Smartt turned up, and I met for the first time his manager, Mr. Muggleston. Thenceforward to De Aar, we had quite an interesting time together. Dr. Smartt knowing most of the people I had been dealing with, at least as far as Prieska. He knew in particular Grove, the chairman of the Prieska School Committee, Coetzee of Glen Allen, the Snymans and the Jeppes; and it was pleasing to find how well he and I agreed in our judgements, because his knowledge was much more extensive than mine. The headings of our lists might have been restricted to S (straight) and S' (scoundrel). But we sometimes prefixed a big D and sometimes wanted another σ for <u>sanctimonious</u>.[156] D, σ and S' could not be said to err on the side of obscurity or vagueness. The bilingual ballad 'Mij Zelf en God' pleased him immensely, and led to racy anecdotes told in Dr.

155 'Rural Reader': This is most probably a reference to the *Farm and Garden Rule Book: A Manual of Ready Rules and Reference* (1911) by Liberty Hyde Bailey (an American botanist considered to be the father of modern horticulture). It was published by The Macmillan Company in 1911. However, it had been first published in 1889 by the Rural Publishing Company, and therefore it is natural that Muir might have referred to it as the 'Rural Reader'. It is just the sort of seminal horticultural book that would have interested Muir.

156 The Greek letter of the alphabet Sigma is written as 'σ' other than at the end of a word. It is not clear, but perhaps his classification of a person as a 'D σ S' may signify someone to be a 'damned sanctimonious scoundrel'.

Smartt's warmly dramatic style. From these we passed to 'How I tried to act the Good Samaritan' and 'Macbeth and Banquo', with the result that we were in De Aar before we had begun to think of it. There we had more than an hour and a half to stay and I spent the time in writing, which I had more pleasure in doing because of a cheerier telegram from home. Before the train had started, our electric lights shone up, and we had less concern about accidents from lamps while shunting. It was 7.30 before we started, and at the last moment I learned that Inspector Anderson was in the train. As he had already dined, he whiled away the time in Cuthbert's room until our dinner was over and the table cleared. The after evening's talk turned out to be very enjoyable. Dr. Smartt told some of his best stories about Barry Sullivan, and I read 'Farmer Perryman's Tall Hat'.[157] Anderson's sound taste for really good literature became again manifest, and he kept in the background his assumed love for anything – good, bad or indifferent – that bore a Greek or Latin dress. The two visitors left at Deelfontein, and after attending to the papers at De Aar, I gladly went to bed.

22/10/11 Sunday

(Beaufort West)

A cold night and scanty bed-clothes. What extremes of temperature we have had! Found the coach at rest at Beaufort West and a sharp wind whistling through it. Dr. Smartt had gone to Capetown of course, but Anderson was somewhere in the town, being on his usual tour of examination of pupil-teachers. After breakfast I took 'Nature' and my note-book, and slowly ascended the hill alongside the railway camp, thereafter following the ridge from one tumbledown fort to another. On coming back, the temperature had improved, and Inspector Anderson was awaiting 'on business'. I laughed away his latest differences with Mr. Rodger about the P.T.3 Syllabus, chaffed him about his newborn belief in Sister Clare, and generally put him in good humour. Read the 'Times' literary supplement after lunch and rested, while the windows got spotted with drops from the tail-end of a distant thunderstorm. By teatime the storm got nearer, and we had a heavy shower. After it ceased Inspector Freeman called, having come into town at one o'clock without knowing we were in the neighbourhood. Old Mr. Cohen, School Board secretary, also called, a young daughter of his bringing a pretty posy of roses. Another shower of rain compelled a long interview, and I was interested to find that he came to the Colony, originally from Munich, over thirty years ago and had never revisited the fatherland. He gave me a sketch of next day's business and undertook to come with a conveyance in the morning at nine and arrange hours with Cuthbert. It was seven o'clock before Cuthbert returned from the village, and dinner was at once served, there being little conversation because of the self-forced talkativeness of the late-comer. After coffee, Inspectors Anderson and Freeman came to spend the evening, and a very interesting time we had. At first the incidents of trek formed the subject for exchange of stories; then there was a great set to on classics, in which Anderson found himself in a minority of one, but in which he held on as doggedly as ever to his infatuation for Greek epigrams and similar idols. At times the coach was a little noisy, and the air of it was a little noisome with the fumes of tobacco and whisky. A soberer mood was brought about by two sketches from 'Mad Shepherds', which again gave general pleasure. Before the gathering broke up, the rain had exhausted itself and, as Cuthbert let the visitors out of the kitchen door, it was found that the time was 12.30.

---

157 This is probably a reference to the Irish-origin stage actor, Barry Sullivan (1821–1891). Smartt studied medicine at the University of Dublin and graduated in 1880. This was a time during which Sullivan was playing, mainly in the north of England and in Cork and Dublin, where he was popular. Smartt must have known Sullivan in Dublin.

23/10/11 Monday

(*Beaufort West*)

Morning still thundery and inclined to be wet. My first visitor was the Rev. Hofmeyr of Kakamas, with whom a meeting was arranged for noon. The Civil Commissioner (Mrs. Broers, late of Capetown) and the chairman of the School Board (Mr. Truter) called at 9.15, and with the latter I visited the new 'Poor School' building on the eve of being finished, and met Forsyth the architect and with him the builder, who was the second tenderer for the Kenhardt School. Drove then to the Girls' School and refreshed my memory with the imperfections of the building; also saw Miss Kiddell and her various teachers and pupil-teachers, the latter being under examination by Inspectors Anderson and Freeman. At 10.30 met the School Board, which proved very amenable, the chairman, Mr. Truter, standing all the time so as effectually to dominate the other members. Broers the C.C. was a little struck with the ease and promptitude with which Truter was handled and the business expedited; all the same, much was due to the fact that Truter is not at all a bad fellow. After the meeting, the Rev. Hofmeyr (brother of the Kakamas parson) of Central Africa Mission and now Acting Minister of Beaufort West went with me to the Residency to eleven o'clock tea.[158] Some beautiful standard roses in the front garden were shown to me, and I found Mrs. Broers good-looking and handsome, and Miss Broers slim and sweet and pretty. Returned to the Council Chamber at twelve and spent some time with the Rev. Hofmeyr over a paper of twelve heads. Drove back to the coach, and Mr. Truter called to accompany me to the Boys' School and to talk confidentially over Miss Kiddell. After lunch there was little time for anything, as we had to leave at 12.45 or so. The Inspectors and Mr. Truter called for a last word. On the way homewards it rained steadily, and I spent the whole afternoon in dictating memoranda – some dozen of them – and had to return to it after dinner. Cuthbert and Robert saw to the necessary packing, and everything was in readiness by ten o'clock.

158 'Central Africa Mission': The Universities' Mission to Central Africa, a Church of England mission initiated in Oxford, Cambridge, Dublin and Durham.

DIARY 6

The S.G.E.'s Diary of a tour as far north as Mafeking

5/3/12 to 16/3/12

5/3/12 Tuesday

(**Worcester**)

Went to Office as usual, but travelling luggage taken with me and at Capetown transferred to coach '174'. Hard pressed in getting things in order before leaving and, as bad luck would have it, had to see [the] Administrator about [the] definition of 'Higher Education', and was kept till almost last moment. Got off at last, Freeman and Duffett being both helpful. Coach '174' was found to be a one-man coach, that is to say, there was no second sleeping cabin, but otherwise it promised to be most comfortable, the most notable new feature in it being a speed recorder of American construction. The shaking-down process was slow as the attendant (Somerby) was new to the job. Cuthbert reported extreme difficulty in getting any one, and anticipated that he himself would have to assist at the cooking. This, however, I knew would be no hardship as it is one of the things he has a real interest in. Our goods train seemed as fast as the old passenger trains, and soon after lunch we found ourselves at Wellington. The English mail had brought proofs from Edinburgh Royal Society, as well as other reading matter, and these occupied the time till Worcester was reached. On the platform waiting for us were old Meiring and his Airedale terrier, Gie the R.M., the Rev. de Villiers, and Inspector Robertson. Soon found that C. had blundered, as a carriage was at hand to drive me to Mr. Gie's house, where I was expected to have my quarters for two days. Explanations ensued and a compromise effected by accepting an invitation to dinner. I then asked to see the new school building, and found the inspection most cheering. In outward appearance it looked surprisingly well, and the workmanship was excellent – certainly a most handsome school. Strange to say, the contractor turned

Fig. T: Worcester, Railwaymen and Children, 1895. DRISA P0176. E.H. Short. Transnet Heritage Library Photo Collection.

out to be one of the two who had built Montagu School and whom I had met there 18 or 19 years ago. Roberto the talkative one had only been moderately prosperous, and after a longish stay in Montagu had 'gone to the north', while Townsend had settled in Worcester where he was justly held in high esteem. The evening dinner at the 'residency' was not exhilarating, the strangers, beside ourselves, being Inspector and Mrs. Robertson. Our hosts, I was sorry to find, were a little disappointed that I had preferred my quarters in the coach, and both of them told me that they had had the pleasure recently "of putting up my son-in-law" (Athel). After coffee a chance visitor came in, the very last man I had expected to see in Worcester, Dr. Young of Steynsburg, and the conversation brightened. It appeared that he was acting for Dr. Hugo for a few weeks, and we consequently were not long in hearing Worcester gossip and Steynsburg stories, and Glasgow reminiscences. I saw also that he was burning to recall to the Gies a jovial night we had spent in his house at Steynsburg, when his wife (a sister of Judge Hopley's) and I had sung 'O wert thou in the cauld blast' with great applause and much whisky-drinking.[159] We left soon after, an altogether proper evening. Gie, I had learned, was of Huguenot extraction, his name in the original being 'De la Haye', as witness the family tree on the wall of his study. Mrs. Gie's people did not come to the front, but it was evident that she also aspired to be somebody. The two were very good specimens of a Cape 'magistraat' and his wife.

6/3/12 Wednesday
(**Worcester**; *opening of Worcester Girls' High School;* **Hex River**)
Woke early after a night of shunting to find that the heat had gone and that there was promise of a delightful day. Malan the secretary of the School Board was early in evidence, papers in breast pocket and conscious seriousness in his eye –

'A child might understand

the deil had business on his hand.'[160]

Mr. Meiring, too, with the boyishness of an octogenarian was not behind hand. And all the while I was feeling that I ought to be thinking of my opening speech. To crown all, the Predikant drove up just as C. had wiled the others aside, and there was nothing for it but to try to be gracious in submission to fate. At 10.30 the way was taken to the old school, where underneath the trees there were gay dresses and tea and cake. Also to add interest, there was Parson Sprengel wearing the badge of the Order of the Red Eagle – or other improperly coloured bird – to show the Kaiser's appreciation of him as a promoter of *Deutschthum* among the barbarians.[161] When 11 o'clock struck, a procession was formed, headed by the Predikant De Villiers and the S.G.E. – *arcades ambo*[162] – and uncoiled itself in the direction of the new building. There we found the adult public of the town already assembled, and they and we were rewarded for braving the open sun by seeing the schoolgirls approach in two bands from different directions and take up their prearranged positions with just enough military precision to enhance the charm of their white dresses and bright faces. Their numbers were surprising for a town of the size, and it was indeed a charming sight. When all was in place, the Predikant 'took speech in hand' – Dutch speech followed by English; his processional partner formally declared the building open and the large crowd rolled in. But is the story not all in print? And did not the editor of the 'Worcester Standard' spread himself out 'on the subject of the S.G.E.'s speech'?

159 A poem by Robert Burns, and a duet by Mendelssohn.

160 'Tam O'Shanter' by Robert Burns.

161 '*Deutschtum*' (German): German cultural identity.

162 '*arcades ambo*' (Latin), Virgil: both Arcadians/two people of like occupations.

After the function came a lengthened meeting with the School Board and School Committee and, among other things, the burning question of the pensioning of the lady-principal (Miss Cilliers) was amicably settled. On the way to lunch at Inspector Robertson's, I called in on Dr. Hugo who, I had heard, was laid up with a rheumatic attack, and who recalled his School Committee feuds while I sat on his bed and thought of the pleasure which the day's doings would have given to his father. At lunch the 'gardening Auntie', a sister of Mrs. Robertson's, was instructed by C. in the way to sulphur vines by stuffing an auger hole in the stem near the soil. I fear that in the Auntie's hands, the results will not be encouraging. At 2 we drove off (Inspector R and I) to visit the site of the proposed Boys' High School building, and were met by Mr. [...] of the Town Council, who promised to support an application for an additional gift of land to round off the property.[163] Next we drove with the Rev. De Villiers to the old Residency, a place of extraordinary dimensions, to see the new Industrial School housed in part of it. Visited in the grounds the grave of the original founder of the town. This and the large tamarisk trees in the courtyard were, apart from the 'poor-white' carpenters and cobblers and tailors, the most interesting sights. Had tea with the pompous superintendent and his wife and then returned by agreement to have another tea with Mrs. Robertson. In the end the coach was reached, and with a hand shake from Inspector Robertson, who would gladly have accompanied us to the north, from cock-sparrow Malan, and from duck-white Mr. Beck, we steamed away about 4.30. In the evening a little work was done, but only a little, as after all the day had been tiring. The Hex River ascent was broken by a longish wait for a down-coming train, and I took to Salmon-Fiedler and Trudi to kill time.[164] An early bed, however, was better.

7/3/12 Thursday

(*Travelling northward from Worcester to De Aar*)

Pleasant travelling northward: a little office work, a little mathematics, and a cigarette now and again served to fill the day. How one's appetite improves when one gets up to the altitude of Jandeboers! First, the breakfast is bigger to the extent of a chop and onions; next the '11 o'clock' is a tumbler of wine and a biscuit in place of Mrs. Freeman's Mazawattee;[165] third, the lunch is a dinner with wine in proportion; and fourth, comes the dinner proper as if lunch had never been heard of. C. must have fried onions at every meal and, sooth to say, Somerby's frying is a work of art, the surface colour being the merest suspicion of brown and yet not a vestige of rawness on the taste. As for drinks, we agree to differ; my tipple is 'Santhagens red', two small bottles daily; and C's is a 'House of Commons' and soda.[166] When a visitor calls, however, I have no difficulty in sacrificing myself on the altar of convention.

163 The name of the Town Councillor is illegible.

164 Otto Wilhelm Fiedler (1832–1912), a German mathematician, who edited the textbooks of George Salmon, hence known at Salmon-Fiedler; Nicola Trudi (1811–1884), an Italian mathematician.

165 'Mazawattee': the Densham family, who traded as wholesalers, gave this brand name to tea supplied in packets to retailers; the name was based on a combination of the Hindi word 'maza' (pleasure) and the Sinhalese word 'wattee' (a garden). They founded the Mazawattee Tea Company in 1887.

166 Buchanan Blend whisky was supplied to the House of Commons from 1896 onwards, and the whisky house gained good advertising by promoting the product on the label: 'as supplied to the House of Commons'. In particular, their Black+White blend of 1905 was advertised in this way, and they were only required to remove this from their advertising in 1915. Thus, in 1912 it was simply referred to familiarly as 'House of Commons' whisky.

8/3/12 Friday
(*De Aar; Orange River*)

Breakfasted while halting in De Aar. Also finished proofs and posted them for England. Read and collated first two editions of Baltzer on the way to [the] Orange River Station, which we reached after lunch.[167] Found Lomnitz, the vice-chairman of the School Board, waiting with a good pair of horses to take us to Hopetown. The journey occupied an hour, and Lomnitz was well plied with questions. The chairman of the Board turned out to be Watney of the Standard Bank, who years ago had been my partner at a game of golf in Burghersdorp. Visited first the disappointing school building, which had been erected when Du Toit the chairman of the Afrikander Bond was at the height of his power, and thereafter the two hired buildings necessary for the overflow. Next walked up to the edge of the plateau which overlooks the town hollow, and accepted the fine new site. Taken lastly to tea with Mrs. Lomnitz, a most lively little lady full of the gossip of the 'peninsula'. Was glad to find the teacher as progressive as his father, Rosenouw of Riversdale. The railway was reached again by 6 o'clock, and we halted for the evening. An engineer called in a friendly way, introducing himself as Hallack, as knowing the Spilhauses and Bowdens and having been married in Mowbray Hall.[168] Although some of these things might be to his credit, we were not impressed. The evening was starry and still, and a smoke on the coach stoep with some appearance of work before us was not without its charm.

9/3/12 Saturday
(*Modder River; Kimberley*)

Awoke to find ourselves in the old stance at Modder River, the morning being lovely. Read in bed with head and book close to the open window, and afterwards on the stoep in short sleeves. Dreadfully chagrined to get news of Amundsen at the S. Pole.[169] Same newspaper reported the great strike in England and the small conference of Administrators in Cape-town. Had a call from old Laing of the newspaper stall, and found him less crazy than usual. Left in time to reach Kimberley about 7 in the evening. Had a prompt call from Inspector Satchel, who to my surprise had the air of an intending suicide. He reported himself as being disappointed and depressed beyond measure because of the changes in his circuit. I was forced soon to pull him up, and even to remind him of the depth of woe in which I had first found him after the war. Then I lectured him and then I asked him to stay to supper, much to C.'s discomfort. Meanwhile Henderson of Stockdale Street School had called, and after supper C. went off with Henderson and his wife. As C. had been 'best-man' to the two at the new year, the three had doubtless much to talk of and C. did not return till after 1 o'clock, Satchel having left at 12. Henderson, I was glad to observe, had been pulled together and improved, and it was clear that 'Wee Bennie's' widow had simply taken him in charge for his good. When he called about 10 to report the due posting of a letter and to bring a box of cigarettes which C. had purchased for me, he was in spotless white and all else in keeping. After spending an hour in making an abstract of a chapter of Trudi, I became tired of waiting and turned in.

167 Richard Baltzer (1818–1887), a German mathematician.

168 He is claiming to know both the families of Nellie Spilhaus and Cam Cornish-Bowden, Muir's two daughters.

169 Amundsen had arrived at the South Pole in mid-December 1911 (and therefore beaten Scott's party in accomplishing this). However, he was only able to break the news of his triumph to the press when he arrived in Hobart, Tasmania, on 7 March 1912. Hence Muir received this news at this point in time.

Fig. U: Vryburg. Tiger Kloof Educational Institution, established by London Missionary Society. DRISA N11587. Transnet Heritage Library Photo Collection.

10/3/12 Sunday

(*Tiger Kloof; Vryburg*)

A cold night, or at least a night made chilly with wind. Left Kimberley before breakfast, which indeed we finished at Windsorton Road. Much struck as of old with the veldt, a magnificent cattle country. Reached Warrenton about 11, and Tigerkloof a little after 3.[170] The pile of buildings created by the London Missionary Society during the last seven years was an agreeable surprise. Built on the edge of the kloof, of a dark-blue stone, and roofed in red, they combined with the trees which had been planted to make a pleasing picture from the railway. In the siding, the Rev. Reed was waiting in cap and gown and the train halted long enough to allow of our learning from him what his programme was for the following day. Vryburg Station, which we reached about 4, seemed somewhat more extensive than of old, and the progress of farming was indicated by a creamery close at hand in which an oil-engine was intermittently blurting. A letter from Rosenblatt, the chairman of the School Board, promised that he would call for us on the morrow, and thus we felt free. After writing memoranda up to close of Inspector Satchel's visit, we therefore set off for a walk, taking a northward direction along the railway and passing on the way, the 774th mile-post from Capetown. Impressed at every step with the tremendous extent of country. Observed also that the railway strip was broad in proportion viz. 100 yards. The new flowers though few were interesting, and still more the chimney-like structures of the white ants. After dinner had a spell of hard work till 12, arranging the Cape School Boards in the order (1) of the number of pupils, and (2) of the number of schools. The mosquitoes that at dinner seemed

---

170 Muir refers to the institution throughout as 'Tigerkloof' but it is generally written as two words, Tiger Kloof.

to be in millions slackened off with the approaching coolth of the evening. Nevertheless C., knowing an infallible cure, was determined on action. He accordingly made for the light of the booking-office, and attained from the station master a tin of the specific Keating's insect powder.[171] With this he besprinkled my pillow, bed-cover and anything else that came in his way. Finished up with a flourish of his tin as if he had already slain thousands. When I went to bed, I couldn't help feeling uncleanly, but then I also hoped for the martyr's crown. By one o'clock I had lost any vestige of faith I had ever possessed. Keating's powder may ordinarily be effective, but the Vryburg station master's tin was a failure. Or feasibly, like whisky, the powder may affect different individuals in different ways, stupefying some and in others raising the very devil. The latter was the case with those mosquitoes that spent the night with me, or by nature they must have been 'desperately wicked'.

11/3/12 Monday

(**Vryburg; Tiger Kloof;** *opening of the new industrial building at Tiger Kloof Educational Institution*)

In the morning the sky was overcast and the air chilly, and a stroll about the camp after breakfast seemed quite bracing. At 9:30 Rosenblatt arrived with the School Board secretary, Winter, and soon after we were at work in Vryburg. The Public School and its two overflows were visited and condemned; the new site was visited and approved. At 11 the Municipal Board meeting took place, Crosbie, ex-M.L.A., being present and the redoubtable Predikant Perold, each with his followers. Butler, with whom Inspector Milne lodged at Cradock, would also have been present, had I not discovered that he was editor of the 'Northern News'. The result was satisfactory to all. At 12.15 the Divisional Board met, the Rev. Perold now being chairman and Vorster, secretary, and the only other members Rosenblatt and Roberts the R.M. This occupied us till after one when we were due at the main hotel of the town for lunch. Both parties of the town were represented, the two leaders, Rosenblatt and Perold, being face to face at opposite ends of the table. The proceedings were quiet and pleasant and by the time that we had smoked a cigarette, it was time to go to the station. The Welsh graduate from Aberystwyth, whom Prof. Jones had written about, accompanied us thither with one or two others, and we discussed his future. On approaching Tigerkloof, we saw all the students and their teachers drawn up in front of the railway shelter and when the coach was left behind in the siding, three parsons advanced towards it. These turned out to be the Rev. Reed, the Rev. Cullen, and the more or less reverend McGee. With them we walked back toward the halt and were introduced to the various white teachers and trade-instructors severally, and to the native teachers collectively. Then the students having given a military salute and been marched off to their quarters, we and the other Europeans walked leisurely towards the Institution. During the walk we were met by a small European child with white hair, who introduced herself to me as 'Nellie McGee'. And taking my hand, [she] toddled along and chattered as if I had known her from her birth. We first went to the principal's quarters, where apparently Mrs. McGee was in charge, a quiet good-looking little Scotch lady hailing from Tillicoultry. There having left 'Nellie', we formed into two parties to stroll around the place and so get an idea of what it was composed. In this way Mr. Reed showed me from the outside his office, the school proper, the dining hall, the workshop, the teachers' quarters, the row of Bible-readers' houses, the garden, the quarries, the rock water-tanks, to finally bringing

171 Keating's Powder was an insecticide containing pyrethrum, found in the chrysanthemum flower. The advertisements of the powder advised that it be sprinkled on the pillow before bedtime and, therefore, Cuthbert was enthusiastically applying this product as advertised.

me out of the grounds not far from the coach. C. was less expeditious with his conductors, having found in McGee a brother spirit; but when he returned, we titivated a little and soon after set off again for supper with the missionaries. Of the three, I found Cullen the most interesting, a sturdy old Scotsman in black clothes and hearty ploughman's boots, but with a fine face and beautiful eyes. Reed pled guiltily to being half Scotch, and as his middle name is Cullen, it is probable that the two are related. He (Reed) knew Edinburgh well and had begun life as a civil engineer; his accent, however, was purely English. The talk was continued after supper on the stoep, there being sufficient light from within and from the stars; and finally, the three convoyed us home to the coach.

12/3/12 Tuesday

(*Tiger Kloof*)

Awoke early and read for a little in bed by the open window. A little before 7, there came from the direction of the Institution, the sound of hymn-singing, and we were reminded of our own surroundings. The train from the north passed while we were at breakfast, and C. hobnobbed with More, the railway divisional superintendent, first met with when he was in charge of the narrow-gauge line from Port Elizabeth to Avontuur. Set off at 10.30 to see all the Institution's classes at work with their teachers, Gordon the carpenter, Harvey of the training school, Ballantyne the builder, Foster the gardener, Harrison the bookkeeper, etc. Waited by special invitation to have lunch with students and staff – a quite interesting function. In the body of the large hall, the students were arranged across the breadth as if at [a] church service, while on a raised platform at the end was a table for Europeans. The meal was evidently a light one for the students as it did not last as long as ours. Our waiters were the native teachers in training, the office being considered an honour. There must, I think, have been about sixteen of us, the Rev. Reed at one end, McGee at the other, and Rev. Cullen at the middle of one side. My vis-à-vis on Mr. Reed's left was Mrs. McGee, and opposite her and on my left, there was deposited on the platform between two cushions the four-months baby, with 'Nellie McGee' ostensibly in charge, but with the mother visibly in charge of both. The conversation was not sparkling but was kindly. The little lady on my right was English, her vis-à-vis was a perfervid Edinburgh man, and this mixture of nationalities led me to ask for details on the subject. According to the principal the English and Scotch were equal in numbers; of Welsh there were none and of Irish there were none: and as for himself he was half-and-half. I observed that after lunch baby McGee was much in demand, the men taking her little hand or chin, and the women borrowing her to hold. The explanation given of this was that she was the first and only child born in the Institution. Possibly also, however, the existence of childless parents was of some account in the matter. C., notwithstanding the absence of proper liquid nourishment, was in his element during lunch and after. He gossiped and joked with the women, and laid down the law to the men; when I left to return to the coach he had just got his pipe lit and was simply warming to his subject. The signal for returning to the Institution was to be the arrival of the train from Vryburg, as visitors were expected thence to grace the function. When therefore the train passed the coach to draw up at the halt, I followed it part of the way and made for the principal's office. A bugle soon sounded to show that all was ready, and the chosen there assembled marched in pairs to seats opposite the main entrance of the school, having in their front the students, 160 in number, in uniform; on their right and left the teachers and friends of the Institution; and, more trying than all, at their backs the burning sun. A hymn was first sung, with the bugle to lead. The principal then welcomed the S.G.E and spoke of the history of the place. The S.G.E on being thus introduced gave the history from his point of view, and thereafter improved the occasion, and finally declared the building open. The close was marked by the bugle leading off with 'God Save the King', which was robustly sung. The tea which followed in the Hall was more animated than the lunch, my fate being the dogmatic Butler from Vryburg, his wife and the Rev. Wookey. Next came a business meeting at the principal's, after which we sought the coach as for a quiet and kindly haven. We had been expected to stay to dinner, but I legged off – a change which perturbed Somerby, for he had also been attending the function and had found attractive friends. With C.'s assistance, however, a good plain Bohemian dinner was in the end forthcoming, and this there was the great pleasure of washing down with a bottle of wine, as became a Christian. The change to this last from lukewarm rainwater was so marked that the fountains of humour were opened, and great was our enjoyment. Somerby, when he came in with the cheese, thought that the 'Groot Baas' was doubled up with a fit.[172] After 9, when re-subdued, we walked over to the kloof to smoke a last pipe. On the way we met a little band of teachers and their wives taking a moonlight stroll towards the coach to say goodbye. With these C. returned to show them our quarters and after joining me to take a few official notes, he apparently hankered for more congenial society. By 11 we were all ready for bed, and C. and I were convoyed as before.

As we were to be picked up by a train in the early morning, we took the precaution of tying a handlamp to face the south and turning on its red light. All the same we went to bed anxious.

13/3/12 Wednesday

(*Mafeking*)

Two mosquitoes occasionally woke me and I wasn't altogether sorry. At last I heard a train coming northwards and was all ears. It rattled down the slope towards the halt, and staggered up the slope towards us, but any slowing it made was evidently involuntary. Not a brake creaked, not a whistle blew: and soon it was all past the points and the sound of it lessening in the distance. Up I got and stumbled in the dark to alarm C., who was snoring heavily. When he succeeded in grasping my facts, he was more put out than I, and in fumbling for his match-box knocked it over and increased the excitement. At last a light was struck and the time found to be 3.20. This was a second mystery, for no Cape train is ever ahead of time, and our time for being picked up was 3.32. The working time-table was then got hold of, and it was discovered that a Friday train scheduled to pass Tigerkloof at 3.13 might run on other days if the pressure of traffic demanded. Herein was a spark of hope, and we went out on the stoep to examine our lamp and to discuss the chances. We had not stood for the space of two minutes when I thought I heard the well-known engine bark away to the south. Both listened eagerly and again it came, and C. heard and agreed. We waited, therefore, with increasing confidence, and sure enough it was not long until it was heard again and heard nearer: and then certainty came when the engine headlight appeared over the rise near gauger's cottage at the south end of Tigerkloof.[173] On reaching the hollow near the halt, the driver whistled for our red light, and in reply we gave him the green. The steam of his vacuum brake then snored, and on reaching the coach, he was going dead slow so as not to pass the points too far that led into the siding. Our troubles were thus over,

---

172 'Groot Baas' means literally the 'big master': 'baas' was a term applied by a servant to his master, but in Muir's case, this also coincided with the fact that he was known as the 'Chief' within his Department.

173 The job of a 'gauger' on the railways was to operate the oil storage tanks and test the quality of the oil for use.

and though we heard the guard swearing at our coach link that refused to couple, we took his wrath philosophically and returned to our beds.

Our next awakening was final for the day, but as it was still early, I took to reading. Found that we were passing through a grassy country with dwarf thorn trees. By breakfast time we had reached Maritzani, and we had a more than ordinary good appetite. Somerby had overslept himself, the porridge was a little raw, the chop and bacon and onions were in too close partnership, but we didn't grumble.

Mafeking was reached a little after 9 and on the platform we found awaiting us the R.M. (Welsh, brother of Dr. Welsh of Umtata and of the girl Welshes of K.W.T.), John Proctor (the teacher formerly of the S.A. College House), the Rev. Rolland (Wesleyan minister) and Hall (the secretary of the School Board). With them we visited the school, the overflow school, and the proposed new site. Then having discussed business, we were conducted to Proctor's for 11 o'clock tea. From there, with Mr. Rolland and Proctor as guides, we drove to the native Stad. On the way we found that the parson was the son of

Fig.V: Colonel Robert Baden-Powell, Mafeking, 1899. Collection: National Army Museum, London.

the old magistrate Rolland, and he became more interesting. Found the native school in two separate buildings, both very poor. The principal teacher was Samson, not unknown to fame, and the assistant was a Tyamzashe of Lovedale.[174] Examined with interest the church school, which had near the base of an outside wall a memorial stone recalling Sir Chas. Warren's stay in 1885. Was also shown the hollow up which Eloff, President Kruger's grandson, came with his men on the occasion of the last attempt to capture Mafeking. Then, too, there was pointed out the B.S.A. police station, which Eloff had rushed after setting fire to the huts of the Stad, and where before many hours had passed, he had to surrender to his own captive. The Stad, though inhabited by 3,000 Barolong, and though still controlled by its own chief, had no appearance of its former importance.[175] The number of children in school was a mere fraction of the whole, and the Rev. Rolland was not by any means hopeful. We left him there with his little daughter, and drove back to the station. Wallis, the railway engineer whom we hoped to meet, as being the brother of the late chairman of the Oudtshoorn Municipal School Board, we found to be out of town: but the station

174 Unusually Muir grasps the name of a black member of the staff, and spells it properly! Benjamin Tyamzashe (1890–1978) had been educated at Lovedale, and he subsequently taught at Tiger Kloof. He was a talented Xhosa choral composer, and it may be that Muir focused on him more than usual because of his interest in music.

175 Barolong is a tribe of Tswana people who live in this area.

master Barker took his place as host. An electric trolley of Wallis' department, Barker said, was just about to leave for Ottoshoop in the Transvaal, the present end of the line being constructed to connect Mafeking with Zeerust, and that if we cared to go with it, we might find the trip enjoyable. Having finished our work we accepted with alacrity, hurried to the coach, called urgently for bread and cheese and beer, and were soon ready for the road. The trolley had two cross-seats for three men each, and one seat beside the driver. Its business for the present was to convey three men to replace the three who were working the ballast engine and train at the head of construction. These accepted the back seat, with their blue enamelled tea-cans and food-boxes at their feet; C. and I were in the seat immediately behind the driver. A start was made about 12, and the country being quite level, the speed soon grew exhilarating. When we came to the Transvaal border – Buurman's Drift – a gate stood across the line, and we had to stop and have it opened. At intervals gangs of natives were passed, some ballasting, some digging ballast, and some putting finishing touches to the track. When we came within a mile or so of Ottoshoop, we were brought to a standstill by the ballast train whose relieving staff our electric motor was bringing to their posts. The accompanying gang of native navvies numbered about a hundred, there being a sub-gang of twelve or fourteen to every truck. When the truck became filled up, the sub-gang clambered and squatted on the gravel like so many penguins. The last filled truck had of course to be waited for, and while we waited we examined with much interest the weathered dolerite just showing up in places above the flat surface of the veld. At length all was ready, and we followed the train on to Ottoshoop Station, where the ballast was to be dumped to form the station yard. Here the sectional engineer (Quigley) joined us, and as he had to return to his quarters at Buurman's Drift, we had the pleasure of his company, and our queries about his work and the country were as clearly answered as the speed of the trolley would allow. His Irish brogue suggested the homeland, but he hastened to explain that he was colonial born, his father being like himself an engineer; and we recalled an engineer of that name once resident at Queenstown. His irregular featured face and his frank excitable Irish way made him an interesting companion, and we regretted he wasn't going all the way with us. We reached Mafeking again about 3, and had only time to get the coach shunted and turned when Proctor and the magistrate arrived with two carts to take us to places of interest in the siege. They brought with them a townsman who had been all through the trying time, a Mr. Algie, now Town Clerk, and though he had like the old wife's teapot a poor delivery, we profited much by his disjointed talk. The main points of interest outside the town were Cannon Kopje and the Game Tree Fort; but the Town Hall was equally attractive. The red sandstone memorial in front of the latter, we thought quite beautiful: the guns encircling the memorial had each of them something to arrest attention, and the collection of missiles inside the Hall raised lots of questions. And all the time I kept thinking of Baden-Powell, Lord Edward Cecil, Hanbury Tracy and others, who had been fellow-passengers with me from England in 1899 on their way to Mafeking to be ready for contingencies.[176] To close the afternoon's outing, our entertainers proposed a visit to the club, and there we had a whisky-and-soda, which stimulated conversation if it did not cement our friendship. The resulting impression upon us was that there was an air of Englishry about the whole town. All the children in school were of English extraction, except eight; the talk in regard to the siege was always of the so-called English virtues shown in the defence; and the good points of the town were due to English ideas of civic government. Even had some of these been English weaknesses, we should have found them attractive, but we didn't say so. At last train-time was announced by the barman, and we hurried to the station, where our first piece of information was that the train was running half-an-hour late. On the platform

176 In the original diary entry, Muir simply refers to Baden-Powell as 'B.P.', as if this was how the latter was known by his personal acquaintances.

many people were assembled, most of them probably merely to receive a fillip of excitement from the evening train's arrival. While we strolled on the outskirts, the magistrate spoke confidentially about Proctor's failings, and I guessed that some of them had only become evident after a private tiff between the two. The talk was not finished before Mrs. Proctor arrived with an earthenware jar of native manufacture as a present for Mrs. Muir, and she was followed by Proctor with a book of photographs of the siege. Later came the three lady teachers in white to say goodbye, and then Krefft the assistant-master in equally spotless attire. The most interesting caller of all, however, was the tall Inspector of Locations, a fine type of Englishman, whose two daughters I had met at Hermanus as boarders at Morton's school and with whom I had conversed at Bot River Railway Station.[177] In time all was over in the way of leave-taking, and the train in motion, and we could settle down comfortably to dinner. Retired early.

14/3/12 Thursday

(Kimberley; Orange River)

Finished breakfast just outside Kimberley but were delayed there half-an-hour. At the station the Rev. Pescod soon arrived with one or two other members of the School Board, and I was prevailed on to have a meeting at the Board Office. There was a longish list of agenda but we got through them satisfactorily. Dr. Mackenzie, Burke and a Mr. McBeath were speakers, but all of them were inclined to be reasonable; and the chairman, though persistent, did his duty with credit. Mr. Oats of De Beers sent his motor round and we then visited the overcrowded schools, meeting everyone there with a kind reception. This occupied us quite up to 1 o'clock, when we returned to the coach for lunch. We then learned through a wire from Capetown that only two days before, at the annual meeting of the Kimberley Board, Mr. Pescod had made an inflammatory speech on the subject of the very things which had been satisfactorily dealt with that morning. There was nothing for it but to ring up the School Board office and indicate a not very mild surprise. In a little while, this had the effect of bringing Mr. Pescod to the coach, and in C.'s presence I spoke with marked plainness to him. His explanations, however, brought out the fact (1) that at the time of his annual speech I had not settled to meet the Board, (2) that at the meeting in the morning he was under the impression that I had seen the said speech, and (3) that he and the Board had been goaded into rebellion by the Administrator's action in sending Dr. Thornton to hamper them by an exaggerated report on the unsanitariness of their buildings. He thus received partial absolution, and we left soon after for the south. In the afternoon and evening C. toiled with his pencil, writing to my dictation – an overworked man! He had however an agreeable respite at Orange River Station. There on arrival he hurried off "to get hold of De Aar on the 'phone'" and there we had a long wait in the dark with the coach drawn up opposite a room in which a prayer meeting was being loudly conducted. After a time, to escape the preacher's voice, I took a stroll along the opposite platform and I soon became aware of another meeting of a less serious character. Across the way in the S.M's office, blazingly lit up, was C. in the centre of a group of congenial railway spirits, all smoking like bad chimneys, and having a right good time at capping one another's stories. To have returned after that to serious official duties would have been trying, and consequently I retired early and read Salmon-Fiedler in bed.

---

177 *Scholtz 2018*: Christina and Walter Morton built the 'Bay View' in Hermanus in 1897, first as a private dwelling and subsequently used the building as a girls' boarding school. Thus 'Morton's school' was the school known as Roskeen Boarding School, located at the Bay View, which subsequently became the Bay View Hotel.

15/3/12 Friday

(De Aar; Naauwpoort)

Awoke in De Aar in the siding nearly opposite the school. C. off telegraphing before breakfast; one feels that if he were completely debarred from 'wiring' he would pine and die. For a moment he looked in again to say that there was no wire from Miss Cogan, and then he was off again to regions unknown. By accident, however, I saw him confabbing with Mrs. Cowling over the garden gate; and he had to be called thence to breakfast. Soon after we left for Naauwpoort, and he then had his punishment, for I dictated memoranda almost every inch of the way. The only respite he had was for a 'drink' about 11; and once when he said that he thought he could manage to draft one of them himself, I told him that this raised him in my estimation as a secretary, which was something better than a cross between a Cook's conductor and a boy-typist.[178] After lunch he disappeared on most important school business, but really for a good gossip with any old acquaintances that chance might throw in his way. One consequence of this was that I had peace to read and write: and as the day was warm but overcast, I occupied a campstool on the stoep in my shirt sleeves and enjoyed Nina H. Kennard's 'Life of Lafcadio Hearn'.[179] Mr. Sorrie the principal of the school called; and though he had nothing but good to report, I saw that he was worrying himself about defects in his school, which he found himself unable to do away with. About 4 o'clock the train from the Eastern Section came in and brought Miss Cogan. It also, however, brought the Rev. S.P. Malherbe, formerly of Philadelphia. As Miss Cogan was there by engagement, I couldn't pass her over in favour of a merely chance visitor. I consequently didn't ask him in but talked to him from the stoep until the train started for De Aar, and asked C. to explain. On the way Miss Cogan told me all her troubles, and finally had supper with us just before the Junction was reached. There was no dallying, and we were soon speeding southwards in solitary state with our friends 'left lamenting' on the platform. The day had been very tiring and I soon went off to bed.

16/3/12 Saturday

(Wellington; Salt River)

Woke shortly after midnight, and couldn't get to sleep again. Coach in an alarming state of shake, and the heat great. Read 'Life of Lafcadio Hearn' for about 2½ hours without any soporific effect. At last rose and slipped quietly with my towel and sponge to the bathroom and had a refreshing scrub, after which I slept until about 7. After breakfast dictation work began, and continued without intermission till lunch, and after lunch for about an hour more. In the end practically everything outstanding was cleared off, and I felt at ease. At Wellington the temperature was very high, and there C. left us after seeing all my baggage packed. I then lay down on the shady side of my cabin, and read Huntington's 'Palestine' and tried in vain to doze.[180] When we reached Salt River, the 5.57 for Wynberg was just moving off, but there was another train at 6.13; and though the crowd on the 'perron'[181] was great, there was no south-easter, and waiting was therefore bearable.

---

178 'Cook's conductor': Thomas Cook & Son, the travel agency, was the innovator of the conducted tour. Thus, Muir is teasing Cuthbert by suggesting that his skills were those of the tour guide.

179 Kennard, Nina (1911). *Life of Lafcadio Hearn*: Hearn was a writer of Japanese legends and ghost stories.

180 Huntingdon, Ellsworth (1911). *Palestine and its Transformation*.

181 'perron' (French): platform.